Preliminary Edition

INTRODUCTION TO
PHILOSOPHY

The Ultimate Questions

Peter Lupu

Kendall Hunt
publishing company

Cover image © Shutterstock, Inc.

Kendall Hunt
publishing company

www.kendallhunt.com
Send all inquiries to:
4050 Westmark Drive
Dubuque, IA 52004-1840

Copyright © 2014 by Peter Lupu

ISBN 978-1-4652-4783-4

Printed in the United States of America

Contents

Book Introduction

Philosophy is a way of life enlightened by the highest form of self-reflection about the most fundamental and ultimate question of human existence. This is at least my own view of what Philosophy is all about. Throughout the forthcoming chapters and pages I will try to illustrate to you this conception in the best possible way I can: that is, by inviting you to explore with me some of the most exciting examples of fundamental philosophical questions.

Our life journey inevitably takes us through the landscape of philosophical questions. It is up to each and every one of us to enrich ourselves by pondering the questions we encounter or remain oblivious to their enriching potential. The primary purpose of this book is to encourage students to listen to this call and thereby enrich themselves with its fruits. What you learn throughout this journey is yours for the rest of your life; no one and nothing can ever take it away from you.

However, before we embark on this journey I wish to share with you a couple of important observations about philosophy. The first observation, which I wish to dispel at the outset, pertains to two misconceptions about philosophy that are broadly held outside the halls of academic philosophy. There are those who think that Philosophy is an esoteric and abstract field that is completely isolated from the course of everyday life and, hence, it is for the most part irrelevant to their own life. Others, who have not had the opportunity to participate in the journey upon which you are about to embark, think that philosophy begins and ends with a "philosophy of life". Since most people feel that they already have a "philosophy of life", they conclude that it is useless to immerse themselves in a systematic study of philosophy.

Both of these views have a kernel of truth from which the wrong conclusion is drawn. Philosophy indeed begins with reflection on our everyday activities, beliefs, customs, traditions, practices and the world in which we are situated. Reflection, as it typically does, leads one to wonder, which in turn leads to questions (a child does this best!). Once the questions are raised, inquiry begins, and the process leads to conceptual analysis, explication, clarification, theory building, synthesis, and more. The next, and very important step, is application: the analysis and theories built on them must be applied back to the world and our practices. The measure of their success is the extent to which they organize, explain, explicate, our overall practice best. The process repeats itself if (and *when*, since there is always a 'when' in philosophy) there is a misalignment between philosophical theory and practice. I call this the "Philosophy Cycle". I invite you to participate in it. How?

Well, you undoubtedly come to this course (or any course in philosophy) with a "philosophy of life" and with some fairly entrenched views about most of the subjects we will cover. I invite you to study this material by taking a step back from your own views. Explore the nature of the questions (philosophical inquiry always begins with a question!). Understand the proposals and philosophical positions presented by various authors. Try to discern the underlying motivation for these views: almost always there is some deep and important aspect that motivates views, even if ultimately they are not as successful as one hoped. Identify the strengths and weaknesses of each view. Only after you did your best to understand the view, criticize it from your own point of view. Remember this motto:

"Understanding comes first; there is always time for judgment!"

Let us now turn to the second observation. You might wonder at this point what kind of discipline is philosophy. What does it involve? How does one engage in the learning of philosophy? Or perhaps you would put these questions in this form: What is the definition of the subject matter of philosophy?

I cannot supply you with a definition of philosophy that commands universal agreement (even among professional philosophers) and that captures all that has been considered as part of the philosophical discipline. No one can! However, I can answer your inquiries with something that comes as close as possible to answering them. Philosophy includes three essential elements: First, and foremost, philosophy is characterized by a set of *ultimate questions* which philosophers asked and did their best to answer. Second, philosophy is a *rational* form of inquiry. And, third, philosophy is the accumulative product of the wisdom of many generations of philosophers in their attempt to answer these questions. In other words, it includes the set of solutions or answers that were accumulated throughout the long history of the subject matter of philosophy. To sum this up in one sentence:

> Philosophy is a set of **ultimate questions** which philosophers examined by the use of a **rational method** combined with the most **insightful answers** collected throughout its history.

You might wonder about the point behind the emphasis in philosophy with a *rational* method. This is a good (philosophical) question and it is not that easy to answer it. Nonetheless, let me try to do my best.

It all begins with the questions. Philosophical question are inspired by our unquenching thirst *to know the truth* about the deepest dimensions of our existence, nature, and purpose. However, we do not wish to merely *stumble* upon the truth by sheer accident or luck. We want, and deeply believe that we deserve, better. We feel that only those answers that are well thought out; solid, and well-supported, merit our self-reflective consideration. And this requirement means that we expect philosophical answers to the ultimate questions to be at the least supported by rational arguments. It is, of course, up to us whether we end up endorsing the conclusions of such arguments. But, as self-reflective persons, we demand from proposed answers to be supported by well thought out arguments. The questions deserve this much and so do we.

Chapter 1 General Introduction

Philosophy of Religion has evolved into an extremely rich, extensive, and ever growing sub-discipline of Philosophy. It encompasses a diverse variety of questions that aim to address central aspects of religious language, belief, faith, practice, as well as a myriad of other dimensions of religious life. While these questions delineate the natural scope of the subject matter, they simultaneously reach beyond into neighboring branches of Philosophy such as Metaphysics, Epistemology, Moral Theory or Ethics, Philosophy of Language and Mind, Logic, etc. And in some cases, an in-depth treatment of some topics in Philosophy of Religion requires reaching even beyond philosophy itself into fairly technical scientific domains.

The subject matter of Philosophy of Religion is, of course, *religion*. But this observation inevitably raises the question: *What is religion*? Have you ever asked yourself this question? Perhaps this is a worthwhile opportunity to take some time and reflect on this question. And it is worth emphasizing that exploring this question is valuable whether or not you grew up in a religious environment, whether you see yourself currently as a religious person, or whether you see yourself as a skeptic about religious matters.

Of course, as you know, there are a wide variety of different religions that have been practiced during human history and many that are still practiced. So when we ask the question "What is religion?" we are looking for some common element(s) that *all practices* we are intuitively willing to see as a religion exhibit *and only* these practices exhibit. In other words, we are looking for a set of features, characteristics, or conditions each of which is **necessary** for a practice to be viewed as a religion and, moreover, they are jointly **sufficient**.

necessary, sufficient

It is not obvious that there exists a common set of characteristics which all practices we are willing to deem as religion exhibit and only such practices exhibit. In other words, it is not obvious that the *concept of religion* can be given a *definition* in terms of such a common set of characteristics (i.e., a set of necessary and sufficient conditions; [see Definition-Box]).

Project: *Before we go on, how about you attempt right now to come up with such a common set of characteristics. I advise that you start by making a list of religions with which you are familiar. You may consult various Internet sources to complete the list. Then try to see whether you can find as many features as you can that they all share. Next examine your list to insure that only religions share features on the list: i.e., that phenomena or practices that are not normally thought of as religions do not also feature items from your list. For if some practices other than religions share some characteristics on your list, then those characteristics are not unique to religion. Hence, your list contains some characteristics that are not necessary in order for something to be a religion, for practices other than religions also feature these characteristics.*

As it turns out, most people who ponder this question professionally (e.g., philosophers, theologicians, anthropologists, etc.,) doubt that such a common set of characteristics exists. If so, then a definition of *religion* in terms of a common set of characteristics that are necessary and jointly sufficient for a practice to be a religion cannot be given. So where do we go from here?

Luckily, we do not need to explore any further a *general definition* of religion, for in this book we will concentrate our attention only on a certain class of religions, the so-called *Abrahamic religions*, which include Judaism, Christianity, and Islam. Moreover, we will focus primarily upon certain common features shared by all three Abrahamic religions. The set of these common features, or the intersection between all three Abrahamic religions, is called **Monotheism** or **Theism** in short.

What is Theism? Theism happens to have an extremely rich intellectual history and a fascinating worldview. I will introduce you to this worldview in stages. In the first stage I will describe three central themes that are essential to a theistic worldview:

While the three Abrahamic religions differ markedly in many ways, they share in some form or another all the elements included within Monotheism or Theism.

Transcendent Reality

i.   A central tenet of theism is the idea that beyond the physical and tangible world there exist a non-physical and non-tangible world. This world beyond the physical is called **Transcendent Reality**.

ii. This **Transcendent Reality** contains one and only one (i.e., unique) **Divine and Person-like Being** that features a set of special divine attributes, properties and perfections. We refer to this unique being by the name of a '**Theistic God**' or 'God' for short. (Of course, this being has different names in different languages.) Transcendental Reality may also contain other entities such as souls, for instance.

iii. God is the creator of the physical universe as well as the creator of all life including human beings. Human beings, however, enjoy an exclusive relationship with God. This special relationship is **uniquely moral** in character. Therefore, we shall call this unique relationship the **Moral Bond** between God and humans. As we shall see shortly, this moral bond between God and humans includes more than merely God's moral demands upon us.

To sum up: Theism is a worldview which recognizes the existence of a transcendent reality which contains a unique Divine and Person-like being who has a moral bond exclusively with humans.

I am sure that at this point several questions arise in your mind. You might wonder, for instance: How do we *know* that a transcendental reality even exists, since it is not tangible? Or how do we *know* that this transcendental reality contains a God as described by theistic beliefs? Or how do we *know* that human beings enjoy a special moral bond with this theistic God? These are all good and legitimate questions which we will address below (although we may not produce a decisive answer to them). If you wondered about these questions or have others in mind, please write them down in your notebook so that you can revisit them as we proceed. For now we will focus on the second stage of introduce you to the theistic worldview. Our focus will be on the following question:

> *What are the divine attributes, special properties, or perfections which God, and only God, is thought to have?*

Below I will list the most common divine attributes associated with the Theistic God. I recommend that you review them carefully and remember them for they will play a pivotal role as we proceed further.

God's Divine Attributes

1. **Omniscience**: *omniscience* means all-knowing. In what sense is God *all-knowing*? Well, the traditional view is that God is all-knowing or omniscient in the sense that God knows everything that **can** be known.

Notice the central role the word 'can' plays in the last sentence. The word 'can' in the last sentence restricts the scope of God's knowledge to that which "can be known". What is the purpose of this restriction?

Consider the following very thorny question: Does God know the future? For instance, does God know today what you will choose to eat for breakfast tomorrow morning? It is important to distinguish here *knowledge* from both *reliable prediction* as well as *lucky guess*. As we shall see in the chapter on the Theory of Knowledge (Epistemology) these distinctions are crucial. One thing we can say presently: if God knows a proposition, say P, then P is true. This is how we define the concept 'to know'. But if God knows right now what you will choose to eat for breakfast tomorrow morning, then the proposition which states what you will eat for breakfast tomorrow morning is already true today. But then how could you choose tomorrow what to eat for breakfast if that is already pre-determined today. So this is one problem that one may think about regarding God's omniscience.

2. **Omnipotence**: *omnipotence* means all-powerful. In what sense is God *all-powerful*? The traditional view says that God is omnipotent or all-powerful in the sense that God can do everything that is **logically possible**.

Once again we face a restriction on the scope of God's potential actions, except this time the restriction is expressed by the words 'logically-possible'. What kind restriction is expressed by the words 'logically-possible'? In a nutshell, *logically-possible* means everything that is not in violation of the laws of logic (i.e., is consistent with the laws of logic), particularly the law of non-contradiction. The basic idea is that even God cannot violate the laws of logic (particularly the law of non-contradiction). It is useful to note that some very influential philosophers maintained that God can violate the laws of logic (notably Rene Descartes held this view). However, we shall ignore such views and accept the restriction in question.

But now consider this question: Can God change the past? We may rephrase this question in the following way. Bring in front of your mind any past event which you really would have liked not to have happened. Now ask yourself this question: Could God today arrange matters so that the undesirable past event simply vanishes like it never happened (i.e., it *really* never happened!)? Is it logically-possible for God to perform such a feat? Well, it is not very clear that even God could reverse the past in this way. But if even God cannot perform such a feat, is it because doing so would violate any laws of logic? Or is such a feat impossible because of the nature of time? While we may not be able to pursue this very intriguing (yet extremely difficult philosophical) question, I recommend that you spend a bit of time thinking about it.

3. **Omni-benevolence**: *omni-benevolence* means maximally caring and loving. Thus, God is omni-benevolent in the sense that God loves and cares for us human being to the maximum possible.

Two points to note about omni-benevolence. First, omni-benevolence implies that God is Person-like and, therefore, like us has feelings and emotions such as love and caring. Second, the definition of omni-benevolence implies that loving and caring are the sort of attitudes that can have an upper limit.

4. **Morally-Perfect**: *moral-perfection* means that (i) Whatever God does *ought* to be done and whatever *ought* to be done God does; and (ii) God knows all moral principles either because God is *omniscient* or because God is the *source* of all moral principles.

Both clauses in our definition of God's *moral-perfection* raise extremely complicated problems and questions. For instance, many skeptics wonder how can a morally perfect being do, and command others to do, some of the most horrendous things narrated in the Old Testament? Similarly, many wonder how can a morally perfect being such as God allow the terrible suffering that occurs in abundance throughout the world to the most innocent of humans (children, for instance)? We shall deal with these questions when we explore the Problem of Evil. However, you may begin thinking about these questions as we journey along.

5. **Necessary Existent**: If God exists at all, then God *must* exist or *necessarily* exists. The words 'must' 'necessary' mean here that God's existence is not a mere accident or a contingent matter, so that if things in the world would have been somewhat different, then God would not have existed at all. To see how this works, consider the table in front of you. Surely, the table actually exists; no one denies that. But, now, you certainly can imagine a different way the world could be, a different path as it were, so that just seconds before this very table was produced something prevented it from being made. And so it was never made. Clearly, that is possible. Well, then the table in front of you would never have existed. The table, unlike God, is a *contingent* existent.

6. **Incorporeality** and **Immutable**: (i) *Incorporeality* means that the theistic God is thought not to be in material or physical form and, therefore, God is not embodied; (ii) *Immutability* means that God *cannot* be subject to any change of any kind.

A few comments are in order regarding the twin doctrines of Incorporeality and Immutability. First, it is worth noting that while Christianity accepts both of these divine attributes, exemption of some kind must be made regarding the Catholic doctrine of Incarnation whereby The Son (i.e., the second member of the trinity) took the form of the body of Jesus Christ. Second, there is a tight relationship between incorporeality and immutability. Since the Theistic God is thought not to be a material entity, God is not composed of any parts or elements and is not to be conceived as made up of any mixture, combination, grouping, blending, or fusion of any elements, items, or substances. (In Theology this doctrine is called God's Divine Simplicity). Therefore, God is not subject to any change of any kind, including but not only, changes caused by decay of parts; movement of parts; addition/subtraction of elements, etc. While these consequences of God's incorporeality and immutability have far reaching consequences, and have been the subject of extensive discussion in Theology and Philosophy of Religion, we will not be able to pursue these issues any further.

7. **Creator and Sustainer**: God *created the physical universe* including everything that is required in order for this universe to evolve and be sustained including the *laws* that govern it and everything that is implied by the creation of such laws. God created human beings. God sustains the existence of the physical universe and, when necessary by God's light, God intervenes through *Divine Action*, which we call 'miracles'.

While the doctrine that God created the universe, including us human beings, is familiar and well known, it raises very intricate questions, particularly in connection with a competing scientific account of the beginning of the physical universe and its nature. We will have the opportunity to discuss some of these issues in a later chapter.

The above seven divine attributes should suffice for our purposes. It is worth noting that some other divine attributes and perfections are discussed in the literature, but we do not need to explore them here (e.g., omnipresence). It is time now to state the most important doctrine of Theism; namely Monotheism:

> **Monotheism**: *There is one, and only one, being that satisfies all of the above divine attributes and perfections.*

The doctrine of monotheism is the most important and fundamental tenet of theism. It is the principal doctrine that distinguishes theism from non-theistic religions and, thus, sets apart all three Abrahamic religions from all others. In short, from the point of view of theism, the oneness of God cannot be given up under any circumstances; from a theistic point of view, then, monotheism is non-negotiable. As we shall see, this fact looms large in some of the issues we will encounter below. Throughout Part I of this book by *Theistic God* or *God* we shall mean a divine being that satisfies the Monotheistic doctrine.

In Part I of this book on Philosophy of Religion we will focus primarily upon three central themes within theism: (i) Faith & Reason; (ii) Proofs for the Existence of God; and (iii) The Problem of Evil. There are a variety of other fascinating topics within the Philosophy of Theism and Theology that we will regrettably not have the opportunity to focus on in the present book. Some of these topics include the topic of *miracles*; the nature of *prayer* and its variety of purposes; the nature of *worship* and *devotion* to God; *religious symbols* and their meaning; etc. Those of you who are interested in exploring these topics should be able to find suitable literature (a good resource, as always, is Stanford Encyclopedia of Philosophy (SEP) and Internet Encyclopedia of Philosophy (IEP)).

Before we proceed to the next chapter, however, there is one more preliminary issue I would like to discuss with you. The topic of religion has become, quite regrettably, a very sensitive topic and in many circles almost a taboo topic to open and frank discussion. There are many underlying and deep reasons for this unfortunate sociological fact, but there it is and we need to deal with it. It is worth acknowledging this fact right at the start so that we can overcome these obstacles and learn something from our journey. I wish to remind you of one of the things I have emphasized in the Introduction to this book: *understanding comes first; there is always time for judgment*. In order to facilitate an opening of the minds to the topics we are about to discuss in Philosophy of Religion, I would like to invite you to think of the phenomenon of theistic religion along three layers. As you will see shortly, a lot of misunderstanding about religion stems from confusing these three layers.

The three layers I have in mind are: **Religious Institutions**; **Religious Life**; and **Religious Canons**. Now each of these layers belongs to a broader category. Thus, Religious Institutions are a sub-category of *Institutions*; Religious life, I suggest, belongs to the wider category of *Spiritual-Life*; and, finally, the sub-category of Religious Canons belongs to the more inclusive category of *Propositions*.

Each of these broader categories features its own *standards of evaluation*. Thus, we evaluate the integrity of any Institution (e.g., Government, Schools, Enforcement Agencies, Hospitals, and Religious Establishments) based upon *the degree to which the overall behavior of the Institution conforms to its expressed mission*. An institution which for the most part acts in conformity with its expressed mission receives high marks with respect to integrity compared to an institution which acts in a manner that promotes ends that are either in violation of its expressed mission or do not directly contribute to it. Institutions that fall into the second class we deem *corrupt*, precisely because such institutions fail to pursue their expressed mission. Since Religious Institutions are a subcategory of Institutions, the same standard of evaluation applies to them as well. If a religious institution acts in a manner that shows a clear preference for ends that are in conflict with its expressed mission or that are unrelated to this mission, then to that extent such an institution is corrupt. For instance, if an educational institution declares as its expressed mission to educate, yet acts in a manner that clearly places profitability above education, then to that extent such an institution is corrupt.

Let us now examine the standards we use to evaluate *propositions* (the third layer). It is worth noting that we are presently concerned only with *declarative* propositions (statements or sentences) rather than with questions, commands, promises, etc. The most important feature of a meaningful proposition is that it is **true** or **false** (or as they say in philosophy: **truth-value**). The second concern that we immediately have when it comes to propositions is the extent to which there is any **support**, **evidence**, or **corroboration** for its truth or falsity. Thus, we evaluate propositions in general and, therefore, religious propositions in particular in terms of their *truth-value* (are they true or false?) and the extent to which there is *evidence* for their truth or falsity.

Finally, let us now address the trickiest of all three layers, the layer of *Spiritual Life*. The whole subject of a spiritual life is extremely difficult and controversial. Even formulating clearly what is spiritual life turns out to be complicated and controversial. Some think that the whole concept of spirituality is based upon antiquated superstitions, whereas others insist that they know exactly what is spiritual life, although it is ineffable (i.e., cannot be conveyed in a language). In light of such a controversy I must admit that what I am about to propose is my own take on the matter of spirituality. It is up to you whether or not you accept my proposal.

I suggest that a person's life is *spiritual* to the extent **that they dedicate a significant portion of their time, energy, and mental resources to pursuing activities devoted to the truth, the good, and the beautiful and for the sake of these values and not for the sake of material gain**. In this sense, a person dedicated to the discovery of truths in whatever area of knowledge; or dedicated to the production and/or understanding of art; or dedicated to the pursuit of moral understanding and moral conduct, to that extent such a person's life is a spiritual life.

Now, the proposed standard for evaluating spiritual life has profound consequences for evaluating religious life. A person who is dedicated to the pursuit of a better understanding of the transcendental reality and, in particular, of God's nature for its own sake and not for any personal gain either through cognitive pursuits or by means of suitable activities enjoys a religious life. By contrast, a person who is involved in religious activities on a regular basis, but does so only for the purpose of material or personal gain and is indifferent to gaining a better understanding of the divine fails to enjoy a religious life.

Now that we have articulated the three layers together with the standards of evaluating each of the layers we can put this information to use. It is important to guard against the following fallacy: **it is a mistake to employ the standards of evaluating one layer for the purpose of assessing another**.

Thus, there are those who deem religious propositions (e.g., A theistic God exists) promoted by certain religious institutions as *false* merely on the grounds that they consider such institutions to be *corrupt*. Even if mistrust of the religious institutions in question is warranted, it does not follow that the *propositions* promoted by such institutions must be *false*. And conversely, even if one completely trusts the integrity of their favorite religious institution, it does not follow that the propositions promoted by such an institution are *true*. Similarly, merely because one thinks that certain religious *propositions* (e.g., A theistic God exists) are true and thinks that they possess credible support for the truth of such propositions, it does not follow that a religious institution that promotes the truth of the same proposition is beyond suspicion with respect to their integrity.

To sum up: the assessment of the truth-value of religious propositions is a matter of evidence that is pertinent to their truth and falsity, whereas the assessment of the integrity of religious institution pertains to the extent to which their conduct conforms to their expressed mission. One should never confuse these two layers and the relevant standard of their evaluation.

I hope you will remember these warnings as we proceed further and deeper into the landscape of Philosophy of Religion.

Chapter 2 Faith & Reason

Let us call the proposition "A Theistic God exists" the 'theistic proposition'. We may ask whether the theistic proposition is *true* or *false* and also what *support* we may marshal for either. We will deal with these questions in chapters 3 and 4 of Part I. But we may also ask a different question: *What is the **appropriate attitude** to take regarding the theistic proposition?* This later inquiry addresses the question of whether *faith alone* suffices as a justified basis for the belief in the theistic proposition or is *reason* required in order to justify religious faith.

I will now define the concepts of *faith* and *reason* so as to put in a sharper focus the complex relationship between the two with respect to religious faith. First, however, I wish to emphasize that, just like 'religion', the concepts of *faith* as well as that of *reason* are very complicated concepts and, thus, may have a multitude of meanings in different contexts. Therefore, the proposed definitions do not claim exclusivity; the definitions aim to capture one important sense of each of the concepts of *faith* and *reason*. These are, what I call, *working definitions:*

> **Faith** = df. *The belief in the theistic proposition in the absence of reason and without requiring any supporting evidence or proof.*

> **Reason** = df. *A method that requires supporting evidence or proof for holding any belief or making any claim.*

I hope you can see from the above definitions why faith and reason may appear to conflict. Since the theistic propositions (i.e., A Theistic God exists) is a claim, faith prescribes to believe in this proposition without any supporting evidence, whereas reason prescribes to seek such supporting evidence. Is it possible to reconcile these two apparently opposing attitudes toward the theistic proposition? This is the central question of the present chapter.

The history of the debate about the proper ground for accepting the theistic proposition goes back to the very beginning of the emergence of theistic religions (and most likely in one form or another predates it). This history is turbulent. Sometimes faith and reason are in an adversarial relationship, whereas other times they appear to complement each other. There are essentially three positions one may take regarding the relationship of faith and reason with respect to the theistic proposition:

a. Faith and only faith is the appropriate grounds for accepting the theistic proposition.
b. Reason and only reason is the appropriate grounds for accepting the theistic proposition.
c. Both faith and reason complement each other and both are required in order to properly accept the theistic proposition.

The proponents of positions (a) and (b) tend to describe the debate in the form of "Faith *versus* Reason". Position (a) is often called in the literature 'fideism'. Some adherents of fideism even view reason as a rival to, and therefore an adversary of, faith. On the other hand, proponents of position (b), that reason alone is the appropriate grounds for theistic belief are often called 'rationalists'. *Rationalists demand that reason must be the basis of any belief, including the belief in the theistic proposition.* Therefore, according to rationalists, fideism is an *irrational* attitude towards religious belief and, therefore, must be rejected even in matters of religious belief. Position (c); i.e., the position which maintains that faith and reason can be reconciled, is often called 'Natural Theology'. Notice that natural theology presupposes that one already has religious faith in the truth of the theistic proposition. Given such faith, natural theology maintains that it is possible to utilize our rational faculties (i.e., reason) in order to discover truths about God's nature and some of God's intentions.

The selection of original articles below covers to some degree each of these positions. For instance, Pascal represents the view that faith and reason can be reconciled and, hence, to some degree he is a proponent of natural theology. By contrast, Clifford's article demands that the method of reason (see definition) alone should be the basis or ground for any belief, including religious belief. Keirkegaard is a proponent of *fideism* and maintains that reason has no role to play in matters of religious belief. William James' article is a bit more difficult to peg. While James holds that there is nothing irrational about *adopting* certain belief without prior evidence, and hence based on faith alone, there is nothing inherently wrong about seeking evidence for such belief *subsequent* to adopted them. I hope you will find the selected articles below intriguing and enjoy reading them.

According to fideism, the appropriate attitude one must take with respect to the theistic proposition is that of faith and faith alone.

Natural Theology means that God's nature and God's intentions behind the creation can be revealed by means of a rational inquiry

Faith is a Logical Bet (Known as Pascal's Wager)

Blaise Pascal

INFINITE—NOTHING. — Our soul is cast into a body, where it finds number, time, dimension. Thereupon it reasons, and calls this nature, necessity, and can believe nothing else.

Unity joined to infinity adds nothing to it, no more than one foot to an infinite measure. The finite is annihilated in the presence of the infinite, and becomes a pure nothing. So our spirit before God, so our justice before divine justice. There is not so great disproportion between our justice and that of God, as between unity and infinity.

The justice of God must be vast like His compassion. Now, justice to the outcast is less vast, and ought less to offend our feelings than mercy towards the elect.

We know that there is an infinite, and are ignorant of its nature. As we know it to be false that numbers are finite, it is therefore true that there is an infinity in number. But we do not know what it is. It is false that it is even, it is false that it is odd; for the addition of a unit can make no change in its nature. Yet it is a number, and every number is odd or even (this is certainly true of every finite number). So we may well know that there is a God without knowing what He is. Is there not one substantial truth, seeing there are so many things which are not the truth itself?

We know then the existence and nature of the finite, because we also are finite and have extension. We know the existence of the infinite, and are ignorant of its nature, because it has extension like us, but not limits like us. But we know neither the existence nor the nature of God, because He has neither extension nor limits.

But by faith we know His existence; in glory we shall know His nature. Now, I have already shown that we may well know the existence of a thing, without knowing its nature.

Let us now speak according to natural lights.

If there is a God, He is infinitely incomprehensible, since, having neither parts nor limits, He has no affinity to us. We are then incapable of knowing either what He is or if He is. This being so, who will dare to undertake the decision of the question? Not we, who have no affinity to Him.

Who then will blame Christians for not being able to give a reason for their belief, since they profess a religion for which they cannot give a reason? They declare, in expounding it to the world, that it is a foolishness, *stultitiam;* and then you complain that they do not prove it! If they proved it, they would not keep their words; it is in lacking proofs, that they are not lacking in sense. "Yes, but although this excuses those who offer it as such, and takes away from them the blame of putting it forward without reason, it does not excuse those who receive it." Let us then examine this point, and say, "God is, or He is not." But to which side shall we incline? Reason can decide nothing here. There is an infinite chaos which separates us. A game is being played at the extremity of this infinite distance where heads or tails will turn up. What will you wager?

Reprinted from Blaise Pascal, Thoughts, translated by W. F. Trotter (New York: Collier & Son, 1910).

According to reason, you can do neither the one thing nor the other; according to reason, you can defend neither of the propositions.

Do not then reprove for error those who have made a choice; for you know nothing about it. "No, but I blame them for having made, not this choice, but a choice; for again both he who chooses heads and he who chooses tails are equally at fault, they are both in the wrong. The true course is not to wager at all."

—Yes; but you must wager. It is not optional. You are embarked. Which will you choose then; Let us see. Since you must choose, let us see which interests you least. You have two things to lose, the true and the good; and two things to stake, your reason and your will, your knowledge and your happiness; and your nature has two things to shun, error and misery. Your reason is no more shocked in choosing one rather than the other, since you must of necessity choose. This is one point settled. But your happiness? Let us weigh the gain and the loss in wagering that God is. Let us estimate these two chances. If you gain, you gain all; if you lose, you lose nothing. Wager then without hesitation that He is.—"That is very fine. Yes, I must wager, but I may perhaps wager too much."—Let us see. Since there is an equal risk of gain and of loss, if you had only to gain two lives, instead of one, you might still wager if there were three lives to gain, you would have to play (since you are under the necessity playing), and you would be imprudent, when you are forced to play, not to chance your life to gain three at a game where there is an equal risk of loss and gain. But there is an eternity of life and happiness. And this being so, if there were an infinity of chances, of which one only would be for you, you would still be right in wagering one to win two, and you would act stupidly, being obliged to play, by refusing to stake one life against three at a game in which you had an infinity of an infinitely happy life to gain. But there is here an infinity of an infinitely happy life to gain, a chance of gain against a finite number of chances of loss, and what you stake is finite. It is all divided; wherever the infinite is and there is not an infinity of chances of loss against that of gain, there is no time to hesitate, you must give all. And thus, when one is forced to play, he must renounce reason to preserve his life, rather than risk it for infinite gain, as likely to happen as the loss of nothingness.

For it is no use to say it is uncertain if we will gain, and it is certain that we risk, and that the infinite distance between the *certainty* of what is staked and the *uncertainty* of what will be gained, equals the finite good which is certainly staked against the uncertain infinite. It is not so, as every player stakes a certainty to gain an uncertainty, and yet he stakes a finite certainty to gain a finite uncertainty, without transgressing against reason. There is not an infinite distance between the certainty staked and the uncertainty of the gain; that is untrue. In truth, there is an infinity between the certainty of gain and the certainty of loss. But the uncertainty of the gain is proportioned to the certainty of the stake according to the proportion of the chances of gain and loss. Hence it comes that, if there are as many risks on one side as on the other, the course is to play even, and then the certainty of the stake is equal to the uncertainty of the gain, so far is it from the fact that there is an infinite distance between them. And so our proposition is of infinite force, when there is the finite to stake in a game where there are equal risks of gain and of loss, and the infinite to gain. This is demonstrable, and if men are capable of any truths, this is one.

"I confess it, I admit it, But still is there no means of seeing the faces of the cards?"— Yes, Scripture and the rest, &c. — "Yes, but I have my hands tied and my mouth closed; I am forced to wager, and am not free. I am not released, and am so made that I cannot believe. What then would you have me do?"

True. But at least learn your inability to believe, since reason brings you to this, and yet you cannot believe. Endeavour then to convince yourself, not by increase of proofs of God, but by the abatement of your passions. You would like to attain faith, and do not know the way; you would like to cure yourself of unbelief, and ask the remedy for it. Learn of those who have been bound like you, and who now stake all their possessions.

These are people who know the way which you would follow, and who are cured of an ill of which you would be cured. Follow the way by which they began; by acting as if they believe, taking the holy water, having masses said, &c. Even this will naturally make you believe, and deaden your acuteness. — "But this is what I am afraid of." —And why? What have you to lose?

But to show you that this leads you there, it is this which will lessen the passions, which are your stumbling-blocks.

The end of this discourse.—Now what harm will befall you in taking this side? You will be faithful, honest, humble, grateful, generous, a sincere friend, truthful. Certainly you will not have those poisonous pleasures, glory and luxury, but will you not have others? I will tell you that you will thereby gain in this life, and that, at each step you take on this road, you will see so great certainty of gain, so much nothingness in what you risk, that you will at last recognize that you have wagered for something certain and infinite, for which you have given nothing.

"Ah! This discourse transports me, charms me," &c.

If this discourse pleases you and seems impressive, know that it is made by a man who has knelt, both before and after it, in prayer to that Being, infinite and without parts, before whom he lays all he has, for you also to lay before Him all you have for your own good and for His glory, so that strength may be given to lowliness.

The Will to Believe

William James

When we look at others, it seems as if they could do nothing when the intellect had once said its say. Let us take the latter facts up first.

Does it not seem preposterous on the very face of it to talk of our opinions being modifiable at will? Can our will either help or hinder our intellect in its perceptions of truth? Can we, by just willing it, believe that Abraham Lincoln's existence is a myth, {5} and that the portraits of him in McClure's Magazine are all of some one else? Can we, by any effort of our will, or by any strength of wish that it were true, believe ourselves well and about when we are roaring with rheumatism in bed, or feel certain that the sum of the two one-dollar bills in our pocket must be a hundred dollars? We can say any of these things, but we are absolutely impotent to believe them; and of just such things is the whole fabric of the truths that we do believe in made up,—matters of fact, immediate or remote, as Hume said, and relations between ideas, which are either there or not there for us if we see them so, and which if not there cannot be put there by any action of our own.

In Pascal's Thoughts there is a celebrated passage known in literature as Pascal's wager. In it he tries to force us into Christianity by reasoning as if our concern with truth resembled our concern with the stakes in a game of chance. Translated freely his words are these: You must either believe or not believe that God is—which will you do? Your human reason cannot say. A game is going on between you and the nature of things which at the day of judgment will bring out either heads or tails. Weigh what your gains and your losses would be if you should stake all you have on heads, or God's existence: if you win in such case, you gain eternal beatitude; if you lose, you lose nothing at all. If there were an infinity of chances, and only one for God in this wager, still you ought to stake your all on God; for though you surely risk a finite loss by this procedure, any finite loss is reasonable, even a certain one is reasonable, if there is but the possibility of {6} infinite gain. Go, then, and take holy water, and have masses said; belief will come and stupefy your scruples,—*Cela vous fera croire et vous abêtira.* Why should you not? At bottom, what have you to lose?

You probably feel that when religious faith expresses itself thus, in the language of the gaming-table, it is put to its last trumps. Surely Pascal's own personal belief in masses and holy water had far other springs; and this celebrated page of his is but an argument for others, a last desperate snatch at a weapon against the hardness of the unbelieving heart. We feel that a faith in masses and holy water adopted wilfully after such a mechanical calculation would lack the inner soul of faith's reality; and if we were ourselves in the place of the Deity, we should probably take particular pleasure in cutting off believers of this pattern from their infinite reward. It is evident that unless there be some pre-existing tendency to believe in masses and holy water, the option offered to the will by Pascal is not a living option. Certainly no Turk ever took to masses and holy water on its account; and even to us Protestants these means of salvation seem such foregone impossibilities that Pascal's logic, invoked for them specifically, leaves us unmoved. As well might the

Mahdi write to us, saying, "I am the Expected One whom God has created in his effulgence. You shall be infinitely happy if you confess me; otherwise you shall be cut off from the light of the sun. Weigh, then, your infinite gain if I am genuine against your finite sacrifice if I am not!" His logic would be that of Pascal; but he would vainly use it on us, for the hypothesis he offers us is dead. No tendency to act on it exists in us to any degree.

{7}

The talk of believing by our volition seems, then, from one point of view, simply silly. From another point of view it is worse than silly, it is vile. When one turns to the magnificent edifice of the physical sciences, and sees how it was reared; what thousands of disinterested moral lives of men lie buried in its mere foundations; what patience and postponement, what choking down of preference, what submission to the icy laws of outer fact are wrought into its very stones and mortar; how absolutely impersonal it stands in its vast augustness,—then how besotted and contemptible seems every little sentimentalist who comes blowing his voluntary smoke-wreaths, and pretending to decide things from out of his private dream! Can we wonder if those bred in the rugged and manly school of science should feel like spewing such subjectivism out of their mouths? The whole system of loyalties which grow up in the schools of science go dead against its toleration; so that it is only natural that those who have caught the scientific fever should pass over to the opposite extreme, and write sometimes as if the incorruptibly truthful intellect ought positively to prefer bitterness and unacceptableness to the heart in its cup.

> It fortifies my soul to know
> That, though I perish, Truth is so—

sings Clough, while Huxley exclaims: "My only consolation lies in the reflection that, however bad our posterity may become, so far as they hold by the plain rule of not pretending to believe what they have no reason to believe, because it may be to their advantage so to pretend [the word 'pretend' is surely here redundant], they will not have reached the {8} lowest depth of immorality." And that delicious *enfant terrible* Clifford writes; "Belief is desecrated when given to unproved and unquestioned statements for the solace and private pleasure of the believer,.... Whoso would deserve well of his fellows in this matter will guard the purity of his belief with a very fanaticism of jealous care, lest at any time it should rest on an unworthy object, and catch a stain which can never be wiped away.... If [a] belief has been accepted on insufficient evidence [even though the belief be true, as Clifford on the same page explains] the pleasure is a stolen one.... It is sinful because it is stolen in defiance of our duty to mankind. That duty is to guard ourselves from such beliefs as from a pestilence which may shortly master our own body and then spread to the rest of the town.... It is wrong always, everywhere, and for every one, to believe anything upon insufficient evidence."

III

All this strikes one as healthy, even when expressed, as by Clifford, with somewhat too much of robustious pathos in the voice. Free-will and simple wishing do seem, in the matter of our credences, to be only fifth wheels to the coach. Yet if any one should thereupon assume that intellectual insight is what remains after wish and will and sentimental preference have taken wing, or that pure reason is what then settles our opinions, he would fly quite as directly in the teeth of the facts.

It is only our already dead hypotheses that our willing nature is unable to bring to life again But what has made them dead for us is for the most part {9} a previous action of our willing nature of an antagonistic kind. When I say 'willing nature,' I do not mean only such deliberate volitions as may have set up habits of belief that we cannot now escape from,—I mean all such factors of belief as fear and hope, prejudice and passion, imitation and partisanship, the circumpressure of our caste and set. As a matter of fact we find ourselves believing, we hardly know how or why. Mr. Balfour gives the name of 'authority' to all those influences, born of the intellectual climate, that make hypotheses possible or impossible for us, alive or dead. Here in this room, we all of us believe in molecules and the conservation of energy, in democracy and necessary progress, in Protestant Christianity and the duty of fighting for 'the doctrine of the immortal Monroe,' all for no reasons worthy of the name. We see into these matters with no more inner clearness, and probably with much less, than any disbeliever in them might possess. His unconventionality would probably have some grounds to show for its conclusions; but for us, not insight, but the *prestige* of the opinions, is what makes the spark shoot from them and light up our sleeping magazines of faith. Our reason is quite satisfied, in nine hundred and ninety-nine cases out of every thousand of us, if it can find a few arguments that will do to recite in case our credulity is criticised by some one else. Our faith is faith in some one else's faith, and in the greatest matters this is most the case. Our belief in truth itself, for instance, that there is a truth, and that our minds and it are made for each other,—what is it but a passionate affirmation of desire, in which our social system backs us up? We want to have a truth; we want to believe that our {10} experiments and studies and discussions must put us in a continually better and better position towards it; and on this line we agree to fight out our thinking lives. But if a pyrrhonistic sceptic asks us *how we know* all this, can our logic find a reply? No! certainly it cannot. It is just one volition against another,—we willing to go in for life upon a trust or assumption which he, for his part, does not care to make. [2]

As a rule we disbelieve all facts and theories for which we have no use. Clifford's cosmic emotions find no use for Christian feelings. Huxley belabors the bishops because there is no use for sacerdotalism in his scheme of life. Newman, on the contrary, goes over to Romanism, and finds all sorts of reasons good for staying there, because a priestly system is for him an organic need and delight. Why do so few 'scientists' even look at the evidence for telepathy, so called? Because they think, as a leading biologist, now dead, once said to me, that even if such a thing were true, scientists ought to band together to keep it suppressed and concealed. It would undo the uniformity of Nature and all sorts of other things without which scientists cannot carry on their pursuits. But if this very man had been shown something which as a scientist he might *do* with telepathy, he might not only have examined the evidence, but even have found it good enough. This very law which the logicians would impose upon us—if I may give the name of logicians to those who would rule out our willing nature here—is based on nothing but their own natural wish to exclude all elements for {11} which they, in their professional quality of logicians, can find no use.

Evidently, then, our non-intellectual nature does influence our convictions. There are passional tendencies and volitions which run before and others which come after belief, and it is only the latter that are too late for the fair; and they are not too late when the previous passional work has been already in their own direction. Pascal's argument, instead of being powerless, then seems a regular clincher, and is the last stroke needed to make our faith in masses and holy water complete. The state of things is evidently far from simple; and pure insight and logic, whatever they might do ideally, are not the only things that really do produce our creeds.

IV

Our next duty, having recognized this mixed-up state of affairs, is to ask whether it be simply reprehensible and pathological, or whether, on the contrary, we must treat it as a normal element in making up our minds. The thesis I defend is, briefly stated, this: *Our passional nature not only lawfully may, but must, decide an option between propositions, whenever it is a genuine option that cannot by its nature be decided on intellectual grounds; for to say, under such circumstances, "Do not decide, but leave the question open," is itself a passional decision,—just like deciding yes or no,—and is attended with the same risk of losing the truth.* The thesis thus abstractly expressed will, I trust, soon become quite clear. But I must first indulge in a bit more of preliminary work.

{12}

V

It will be observed that for the purposes of this discussion we are on 'dogmatic' ground,—ground, I mean, which leaves systematic philosophical scepticism altogether out of account. The postulate that there is truth, and that it is the destiny of our minds to attain it, we are deliberately resolving to make, though the sceptic will not make it. We part company with him, therefore, absolutely, at this point. But the faith that truth exists, and that our minds can find it, may be held in two ways. We may talk of the *empiricist* way and of the *absolutist* way of believing in truth. The absolutists in this matter say that we not only can attain to knowing truth, but we can *know when* we have attained to knowing it; while the empiricists think that although we may attain it, we cannot infallibly know when. To *know* is one thing, and to know for certain *that* we know is another. One may hold to the first being possible without the second; hence the empiricists and the absolutists, although neither of them is a sceptic in the usual philosophic sense of the term, show very different degrees of dogmatism in their lives.

If we look at the history of opinions, we see that the empiricist tendency has largely prevailed in science, while in philosophy the absolutist tendency has had everything its own way. The characteristic sort of happiness, indeed, which philosophies yield has mainly consisted in the conviction felt by each successive school or system that by it bottom-certitude had been attained. "Other philosophies are collections of opinions, mostly false; *my* philosophy {13} gives standing-ground forever,"—who does not recognize in this the key-note of every system worthy of the name? A system, to be a system at all, must come as a *closed* system, reversible in this or that detail, perchance, but in its essential features never!

Scholastic orthodoxy, to which one must always go when one wishes to find perfectly clear statement, has beautifully elaborated this absolutist conviction in a doctrine which it calls that of 'objective evidence.' If, for example, I am unable to doubt that I now exist before you, that two is less than three, or that if all men are mortal then I am mortal too, it is because these things illumine my intellect irresistibly. The final ground of this objective evidence possessed by certain propositions is the *adaequatio intellectûs nostri cum rê.* The certitude it brings involves an *aptitudinem ad extorquendum certum assensum* on the part of the truth envisaged, and on the side of the subject a *quietem in cognitione,* when once the object is mentally received, that leaves no possibility of doubt behind; and in the whole transaction nothing operates but the *entitas ipsa* of the object and the *entitas ipsa* of the mind. We slouchy modern thinkers dislike to talk in Latin,—indeed, we dislike to talk in set terms at all; but at bottom our own state of mind is very much like this whenever we uncritically abandon ourselves: You believe in objective evidence, and I do. Of some things we feel that we are certain: we know, and we know that we do know. There is something that gives a click inside of us, a bell that strikes twelve, when the hands of our mental clock have swept the dial and meet over the meridian hour. The greatest empiricists among us are only empiricists on reflection: when {14} left to their instincts, they dogmatize like infallible popes. When the Cliffords tell us how sinful it is to be Christians on such 'insufficient evidence,' insufficiency is really the last thing they have in mind. For them the evidence is absolutely sufficient, only it makes the other way. They believe so completely in an anti-christian order of the universe that there is no living option: Christianity is a dead hypothesis from the start.

VI

But now, since we are all such absolutists by instinct, what in our quality of students of philosophy ought we to do about the fact? Shall we espouse and indorse it? Or shall we treat it as a weakness of our nature from which we must free ourselves, if we can?

I sincerely believe that the latter course is the only one we can follow as reflective men. Objective evidence and certitude are doubtless very fine ideals to play with, but where on this moonlit and dream-visited planet are they found? I am, therefore, myself a complete empiricist so far as my theory of human knowledge goes. I live, to be sure, by the practical faith that we must go on experiencing and thinking over our experience, for only thus can our opinions grow more true; but to hold any one of them—I absolutely do not care which—as if it never could be reinterpretable or corrigible, I believe to be a tremendously mistaken attitude, and I think that the whole history of philosophy will bear me out. There is but one indefectibly certain truth, and that is the truth that pyrrhonistic scepticism itself leaves {15} standing,—the truth that the present phenomenon of consciousness exists. That, however, is the bare starting-point of knowledge, the mere admission of a stuff to be philosophized about. The various philosophies are but so many attempts at expressing what this stuff really is. And if we repair to our libraries what disagreement do we discover! Where is a certainly true answer found? Apart from abstract propositions of comparison (such as two and two are the same as four), propositions which tell us nothing by themselves about concrete reality, we find no proposition ever regarded by any one as evidently certain that has not either been called a falsehood, or at least had its truth sincerely questioned by some one else. The transcending of the axioms of geometry, not in play but in earnest, by certain of our contemporaries (as Zöllner and Charles H. Hinton), and the rejection of the whole Aristotelian logic by the Hegelians, are striking instances in point.

No concrete test of what is really true has ever been agreed upon. Some make the criterion external to the moment of perception, putting it either in revelation, the *consensus gentium,* the instincts of the heart, or the systematized experience of the race. Others make the perceptive moment its own test,—Descartes, for instance, with his clear and distinct ideas guaranteed by the veracity of God; Reid with his 'common-sense;' and Kant with his forms of synthetic judgment *a priori.* The inconceivability of the opposite; the capacity to be verified by sense; the possession of complete organic unity or self-relation, realized when a thing is its own other,—are standards which, in turn, have been used. The much {16} lauded objective evidence is never triumphantly there, it is a mere aspiration or *Grenzbegriff,* marking the infinitely remote ideal of our thinking life. To claim that certain truths now possess it, is simply to say that when you think them true and they *are* true, then their evidence is objective, otherwise it is not. But practically one's conviction that the evidence one goes by is of the real objective brand, is only one more subjective opinion added to the lot. For what a contradictory array of opinions have objective evidence and absolute certitude been claimed! The world is rational through and through,—its existence is an ultimate brute fact; there is a personal God,— a personal God is inconceivable; there is an extra-mental physical world immediately known,—the mind can only know its own ideas; a moral imperative exists,—obligation is only the resultant of desires; a permanent spiritual principle is in every one,—there are only shifting states of mind; there is an endless chain of causes,—there is an absolute first cause; an eternal necessity,—a freedom; a purpose,—no purpose; a primal One,—a primal Many; a universal continuity,—an essential discontinuity in things; an infinity,—no infinity. There is this,—there is that; there is indeed nothing which some one has not thought absolutely true, while his neighbor deemed it absolutely false; and not an absolutist among them seems ever to have considered that the trouble may all the time be essential, and that the intellect, even with truth directly in its grasp, may have no infallible signal for knowing whether it be truth or no. When, indeed, one remembers that the most striking practical application to life of the doctrine of objective certitude has been {17} the conscientious labors of the Holy Office of the Inquisition, one feels less tempted than ever to lend the doctrine a respectful ear.

But please observe, now, that when as empiricists we give up the doctrine of objective certitude, we do not thereby give up the quest or hope of truth itself. We still pin our faith on its existence, and still believe that we gain an ever better position towards it by systematically continuing to roll up experiences and think. Our great difference from the scholastic lies in the way we face. The strength of his system lies in the principles, the origin, the *terminus a quo* of his thought; for us the strength is in the outcome, the upshot, the *terminus ad quem*. Not where it comes from but what it leads to is to decide. It matters not to an empiricist from what quarter an hypothesis may come to him: he may have acquired it by fair means or by foul; passion may have whispered or accident suggested it; but if the total drift of thinking continues to confirm it, that is what he means by its being true.

VII

One more point, small but important, and our preliminaries are done. There are two ways of looking at our duty in the matter of opinion,—ways entirely different, and yet ways about whose difference the theory of knowledge seems hitherto to have shown very little concern, *We must know the truth;* and *we must avoid error,*—these are our first and great commandments as would-be knowers; but they are not two ways of stating an identical commandment, they are two separable laws. Although it may indeed happen that when we believe the truth *A,* we escape {18} as an incidental consequence from believing the falsehood *B,* it hardly ever happens that by merely disbelieving *B* we necessarily believe *A.* We may in escaping *B* fall into believing other falsehoods, *C* or *D,* just as bad as *B*; or we may escape *B* by not believing anything at all, not even *A.*

Believe truth! Shun error!—these, we see, are two materially different laws; and by choosing between them we may end by coloring differently our whole intellectual life. We may regard the chase for truth as paramount, and the avoidance of error as secondary; or we may, on the other hand, treat the avoidance of error as more imperative, and let truth take its chance. Clifford, in the instructive passage which I have quoted, exhorts us to the latter course. Believe nothing, he tells us, keep your mind in suspense forever, rather than by closing it on insufficient evidence incur the awful risk of believing lies. You, on the other hand, may think that the risk of being in error is a very small matter when compared with the blessings of real knowledge, and be ready to be duped many times in your investigation rather than postpone indefinitely the chance of guessing true. I myself find it impossible to go with Clifford. We must remember that these feelings of our duty about either truth or error are in any case only expressions of our passional life. Biologically considered, our minds are as ready to grind out falsehood as veracity, and he who says, "Better go without belief forever than believe a lie!" merely shows his own preponderant private horror of becoming a dupe. He may be critical of many of his desires and fears, but this fear he slavishly obeys. He cannot imagine any one questioning its binding force. For my own part, I {19} have also a horror of being duped; but I can believe that worse things than being duped may happen to a man in this world: so Clifford's exhortation has to my ears a thoroughly fantastic sound. It is like a general informing his soldiers that it is better to keep out of battle forever than to risk a single wound. Not so are victories either over enemies or over nature gained. Our errors are surely not such awfully solemn things. In a world where we are so certain to incur them in spite of all our caution, a certain lightness of heart seems healthier than this excessive nervousness on their behalf. At any rate, it seems the fittest thing for the empiricist philosopher.

VIII

And now, after all this introduction, let us go straight at our question. I have said, and now repeat it, that not only as a matter of fact do we find our passional nature influencing us in our opinions, but that there are some options between opinions in which this influence must be regarded both as an inevitable and as a lawful determinant of our choice.

I fear here that some of you my hearers will begin to scent danger, and lend an inhospitable ear. Two first steps of passion you have indeed had to admit as necessary,—we must think so as to avoid dupery, and we must think so as to gain truth; but the surest path to those ideal consummations, you will probably consider, is from now onwards to take no further passional step.

Well, of course, I agree as far as the facts will allow. Wherever the option between losing truth and gaining it is not momentous, we can throw the {20} chance of *gaining truth* away, and at any rate save ourselves from any chance of *believing falsehood,* by not making up our minds at all till objective evidence has come. In scientific questions, this is almost always the case; and even in human affairs in general, the need of acting is seldom so urgent that a false belief to act on is better than no belief at all. Law courts, indeed, have to decide on the best evidence attainable for the moment, because a judge's duty is to make law as well as to ascertain it, and (as a learned judge once said to me) few cases are worth spending much time over: the great thing is to have them decided on *any* acceptable principle, and got out of the way. But in our dealings with objective nature we obviously are recorders, not makers, of the truth; and decisions for the mere sake of deciding promptly and getting on to the next business would be wholly out of place. Throughout the breadth of physical nature facts are what they are quite independently of us, and seldom is there any such hurry about them that the risks of being duped by believing a premature theory need be faced. The questions here are always trivial options, the hypotheses are hardly living (at any rate not living for us spectators), the choice between believing truth or falsehood is seldom forced. The attitude of sceptical balance is therefore the absolutely wise one if we would escape mistakes. What difference, indeed, does it make to most of us whether we have or have not a theory of the Röntgen rays, whether we believe or not in mind-stuff, or have a conviction about the causality of conscious states? It makes no difference. Such options are not forced on us. On every account it is better not to make them, but still keep weighing reasons *pro et contra* with an indifferent hand.

{21}

I speak, of course, here of the purely judging mind. For purposes of discovery such indifference is to be less highly recommended, and science would be far less advanced than she is if the passionate desires of individuals to get their own faiths confirmed had been kept out of the game. See for example the sagacity which Spencer and Weismann now display. On the other hand, if you want an absolute duffer in an investigation, you must, after all, take the man who has no interest whatever in its results: he is the warranted incapable, the positive fool. The most useful investigator, because the most sensitive observer, is always he whose eager interest in one side of the question is balanced by an equally keen nervousness lest he become deceived. [3] Science has organized this nervousness into a regular *technique,* her so-called method of verification; and she has fallen so deeply in love with the method that one may even say she has ceased to care for truth by itself at all. It is only truth as technically verified that interests her. The truth of truths might come in merely affirmative form, and she would decline to touch it. Such truth as that, she might repeat with Clifford, would be stolen in defiance of her duty to mankind. Human passions, however, are stronger than technical rules. "Le coeur a ses raisons," as Pascal says, "que la raison ne connaît pas;" and however indifferent to all but the bare rules of the game the umpire, the abstract intellect, may be, the concrete players who furnish him the materials to judge of are usually, each one of them, in love with some pet 'live hypothesis' of his own. Let us agree, however, that wherever there is no forced option, the {22} dispassionately judicial intellect with no pet hypothesis, saving us, as it does, from dupery at any rate, ought to be our ideal.

The question next arises: Are there not somewhere forced options in our speculative questions, and can we (as men who may be interested at least as much in positively gaining truth as in merely escaping dupery) always wait with impunity till the coercive evidence shall have arrived? It seems *a priori* improbable that the truth should be so nicely adjusted to our needs and powers as that. In the great boarding-house of nature, the cakes and the butter and the syrup seldom come out so even and leave the plates so clean. Indeed, we should view them with scientific suspicion if they did.

IX

Moral questions immediately present themselves as questions whose solution cannot wait for sensible proof. A moral question is a question not of what sensibly exists, but of what is good, or would be good if it did exist. Science can tell us what exists; but to compare the *worths,* both of what exists and of what does not exist, we must consult not science, but what Pascal calls our heart. Science herself consults her heart when she lays it down that the infinite ascertainment of fact and correction of false belief are the supreme goods for man. Challenge the statement, and science can only repeat it oracularly, or else prove it by showing that such ascertainment and correction bring man all sorts of other goods which man's heart in turn declares. The question of having moral beliefs at all or not having them is decided by {23} our will. Are our moral preferences true or false, or are they only odd biological phenomena, making things good or bad for *us,* but in themselves indifferent? How can your pure intellect decide? If your heart does not *want* a world of moral reality, your head will assuredly never make you believe in one. Mephistophelian scepticism, indeed, will satisfy the head's play-instincts much better than any rigorous idealism can. Some men (even at the student age) are so naturally cool-hearted that the moralistic hypothesis never has for them any pungent life, and in their supercilious presence the hot young moralist always feels strangely ill at ease. The appearance of knowingness is on their side, of naïveté and gullibility on his. Yet, in the inarticulate heart of him, he clings to it that he is not a dupe, and that there is a realm in which (as Emerson says) all their wit and intellectual superiority is no better than the cunning of a fox. Moral scepticism can no more be refuted or proved by logic than intellectual scepticism can. When we stick to it that there *is* truth (be it of either kind), we do so with our whole nature, and resolve to stand or fall by the results. The sceptic with his whole nature adopts the doubting attitude; but which of us is the wiser, Omniscience only knows.

Turn now from these wide questions of good to a certain class of questions of fact, questions concerning personal relations, states of mind between one man and another. *Do you like me or not?*—for example. Whether you do or not depends, in countless instances, on whether I meet you half-way, am willing to assume that you must like me, and show you trust and expectation. The previous faith on my part in your liking's existence is in such cases what makes {24} your liking come. But if I stand aloof, and refuse to budge an inch until I have objective evidence, until you shall have done something apt, as the absolutists say, *ad extorquendum assensum meum,* ten to one your liking never comes. How many women's hearts are vanquished by the mere sanguine insistence of some man that they *must* love him! he will not consent to the hypothesis that they cannot. The desire for a certain kind of truth here brings about that special truth's existence; and so it is in innumerable cases of other sorts. Who gains promotions, boons, appointments, but the man in whose life they are seen to play the part of live hypotheses, who discounts them, sacrifices other things for their sake before they have come, and takes risks for them in advance? His faith acts on the powers above him as a claim, and creates its own verification.

A social organism of any sort whatever, large or small, is what it is because each member proceeds to his own duty with a trust that the other members will simultaneously do theirs. Wherever a desired result is achieved by the co-operation of many independent persons, its existence as a fact is a pure consequence of the precursive faith in one another of those immediately concerned. A government, an army, a commercial system, a ship, a college, an athletic team, all exist on this condition, without which not only is nothing achieved, but nothing is even attempted. A whole train of passengers (individually brave enough) will be looted by a few highwaymen, simply because the latter can count on one another, while each passenger fears that if he makes a movement of resistance, he will be shot before any one else backs him up. If we believed that the whole carfull would rise {25} at once with us, we should each severally rise, and train-robbing would never even be attempted. There are, then, cases where a fact cannot come at all unless a preliminary faith exists in its coming. *And where faith in a fact can help create the fact,* that would be an insane logic which should say that faith running ahead of scientific evidence is the 'lowest kind of immorality' into which a thinking being can fall. Yet such is the logic by which our scientific absolutists pretend to regulate our lives!

X

In truths dependent on our personal action, then, faith based on desire is certainly a lawful and possibly an indispensable thing.

But now, it will be said, these are all childish human cases, and have nothing to do with great cosmical matters, like the question of religious faith. Let us then pass on to that. Religions differ so much in their accidents that in discussing the religious question we must make it very generic and broad. What then do we now mean by the religious hypothesis? Science says things are; morality says some things are better than other things; and religion says essentially two things.

First, she says that the best things are the more eternal things, the overlapping things, the things in the universe that throw the last stone, so to speak, and say the final word. "Perfection is eternal,"—this phrase of Charles Secrétan seems a good way of putting this first affirmation of religion, an affirmation which obviously cannot yet be verified scientifically at all.

{26}

The second affirmation of religion is that we are better off even now if we believe her first affirmation to be true.

Now, let us consider what the logical elements of this situation are *in case the religious hypothesis in both its branches be really true.* (Of course, we must admit that possibility at the outset. If we are to discuss the question at all, it must involve a living option. If for any of you religion be a hypothesis that cannot, by any living possibility be true, then you need go no farther. I speak to the 'saving remnant' alone.) So proceeding, we see, first, that religion offers itself as a *momentous* option. We are supposed to gain, even now, by our belief, and to lose by our non-belief, a certain vital good. Secondly, religion is a *forced* option, so far as that good goes. We cannot escape the issue by remaining sceptical and waiting for more light, because, although we do avoid error in that way *if religion be untrue,* we lose the good, *if it be true,* just as certainly as if we positively chose to disbelieve. It is as if a man should hesitate indefinitely to ask a certain woman to marry him because he was not perfectly sure that she would prove an angel after he brought her home. Would he not cut himself off from that particular angel-possibility as decisively as if he went and married some one else? Scepticism, then, is not avoidance of option; it is option of a certain particular kind of risk. *Better risk loss of truth than chance of error,*— that is your faith-vetoer's exact position. He is actively playing his stake as much as the believer is; he is backing the field against the religious hypothesis, just as the believer is backing the religious hypothesis against the field. To preach scepticism to us as a duty until {27} 'sufficient evidence' for religion be found, is tantamount therefore to telling us, when in presence of the religious hypothesis, that to yield to our fear of its being error is wiser and better than to yield to our hope that it may be true, It is not intellect against all passions, then; it is only intellect with one passion laying down its law. And by what, forsooth, is the supreme wisdom of this passion warranted? Dupery for dupery, what proof is there that dupery through hope is so much worse than dupery through fear? I, for one, can see no proof; and I simply refuse obedience to the scientist's command to imitate his kind of option, in a case where my own stake is important enough to give me the right to choose my own form of risk. If religion be true and the evidence for it be still insufficient, I do not wish, by putting your extinguisher upon my nature (which feels to me as if it had after all some business in this matter), to forfeit my sole chance in life of getting upon the winning side,—that chance depending, of course, on my willingness to run the risk of acting as if my passional need of taking the world religiously might be prophetic and right.

All this is on the supposition that it really may be prophetic and right, and that, even to us who are discussing the matter, religion is a live hypothesis which may be true. Now, to most of us religion comes in a still further way that makes a veto on our active faith even more illogical, The more perfect and more eternal aspect of the universe is represented in our religions as having personal form. The universe is no longer a mere *It* to us, but a *Thou,* if we are religious; and any relation that may be possible from person to person might be possible {28} here. For instance, although in one sense we are passive portions of the universe, in another we show a curious autonomy, as if we were small active centres on our own account, We feel, too, as if the appeal of religion to us were made to our own active good-will, as if evidence might be forever withheld from us unless we met the hypothesis half-way. To take a trivial illustration: just as a man who in a company of gentlemen made no advances, asked a warrant for every concession, and believed no one's word without proof, would cut himself off by such churlishness from all the social rewards that a more trusting spirit would earn,—so here, one who should shut himself up in snarling logicality and try to make the gods extort his recognition willy-nilly, or not get it at all, might cut himself off forever from his only opportunity of making the gods' acquaintance. This feeling, forced on us we know not whence, that by obstinately believing that there are gods (although not to do so would be so easy both for our logic and our life) we are doing the universe the deepest service we can, seems part of the living essence of the religious hypothesis. If the hypothesis *were* true in all its parts, including this one, then pure intellectualism, with its veto on our making willing advances, would be an absurdity; and some participation of our sympathetic nature would be logically required. I, therefore, for one cannot see my way to accepting the agnostic rules for truth-seeking, or wilfully agree to keep my willing nature out of the game. I cannot do so for this plain reason, that *a rule of thinking which would absolutely prevent me from acknowledging certain kinds of truth if those kinds of truth were really there, would be an irrational rule.* That for me {29} is the long and short of the formal logic of the situation, no matter what the kinds of truth might materially be.

I confess I do not see how this logic can be escaped. But sad experience makes me fear that some of you may still shrink from radically saying with me, *in abstracto,* that we have the right to believe at our own risk any hypothesis that is live enough to tempt our will. I suspect, however, that if this is so, it is because you have got away from the abstract logical point of view altogether, and are thinking (perhaps without realizing it) of some particular religious hypothesis which for you is dead. The freedom to 'believe what we will' you apply to the case of some patent superstition; and the faith you think of is the faith defined by the schoolboy when he said, "Faith is when you believe something that you know ain't true." I can only repeat that this is misapprehension. *In concreto,* the freedom to believe can only cover living options which the intellect of the individual cannot by itself resolve; and living options never seem absurdities to him who has them to consider. When I look at the religious question as it really puts itself to concrete men, and when I think of all the possibilities which both practically and theoretically it involves, then this command that we shall put a stopper on our heart, instincts, and courage, and wait—acting of course meanwhile more or less as if religion were *not* true[4]—till {30} doomsday, or till such time as our intellect and senses working together may have raked in evidence enough,—this command, I say, seems to me the queerest idol ever manufactured in the philosophic cave. Were we scholastic absolutists, there might be more excuse. If we had an infallible intellect with its objective certitudes, we might feel ourselves disloyal to such a perfect organ of knowledge in not trusting to it exclusively, in not waiting for its releasing word. But if we are empiricists, if we believe that no bell in us tolls to let us know for certain when truth is in our grasp, then it seems a piece of idle fantasticality to preach so solemnly our duty of waiting for the bell. Indeed we *may* wait if we will,—I hope you do not think that I am denying that,—but if we do so, we do so at our peril as much as if we believed. In either case we *act,* taking our life in our hands. No one of us ought to issue vetoes to the other, nor should we bandy words of abuse. We ought, on the contrary, delicately and profoundly to respect one another's mental freedom: then only shall we bring about the intellectual republic; then only shall we have that spirit of inner tolerance without which all our outer tolerance is soulless, and which is empiricism's glory; then only shall we live and let live, in speculative as well as in practical things.

I began by a reference to Fitz James Stephen; let me end by a quotation from him. "What do you think {31} of yourself? What do you think of the world?... These are questions with which all must deal as it seems good to them. They are riddles of the Sphinx, and in some way or other we must deal with them.... In all important transactions of life we have to take a leap in the dark.... If we decide to leave the riddles unanswered, that is a choice; if we waver in our answer, that, too, is a choice: but whatever choice we make, we make it at our peril. If a man chooses to turn his back altogether on God and the future, no one can prevent him; no one can show beyond reasonable doubt that he is mistaken. If a man thinks otherwise and acts as he thinks, I do not see that any one can prove that *he* is mistaken. Each must act as he thinks best; and if he is wrong, so much the worse for him. We stand on a mountain pass in the midst of whirling snow and blinding mist, through which we get glimpses now and then of paths which may be deceptive. If we stand still we shall be frozen to death. If we take the wrong road we shall be dashed to pieces. We do not certainly know whether there is any right one. What must we do? 'Be strong and of a good courage.' Act for the best, hope for the best, and take what comes.... If death ends all, we cannot meet death better."[5]

Notes

1. An Address to the Philosophical Clubs of Yale and Brown Universities. Published in the New World, June, 1896.
2. Compare the admirable page 310 in S. H. Hodgson's "Time and Space," London, 1865.
3. Compare Wilfrid Ward's Essay, "The Wish to Believe," in his *Witnesses to the Unseen,* Macmillan & Co., 1893.
4. Since belief is measured by action, he who forbids us to believe religion to be true, necessarily also forbids us to act as we should if we did believe it to be true. The whole defence of religious faith hinges upon action. If the action required or inspired by the religious hypothesis is in no way different from that dictated by the naturalistic hypothesis, then religious faith is a pure superfluity, better pruned away, and controversy about its legitimacy is a piece of idle trifling, unworthy of serious minds. I myself believe, of course, that the religious hypothesis gives to the world an expression which specifically determines our reactions, and makes them in a large part unlike what they might be on a purely naturalistic scheme of belief.
5. Liberty, Equality, Fraternity, p. 353, 2d edition. London, 1874.

The Subjective Truth, Inwardness; Truth is Subjectivity

Soren Kierkeguard

WHETHER truth is defined more empirically, as the conformity of thought and being, or more idealistically, as the conformity of being with thought, it is, in either case, important carefully to note what is meant by being. And in formulating the answer to this question it is likewise important to take heed lest the knowing spirit be tricked into losing itself in the indeterminate, so that in fantastically becomes a something that no existing human being ever was or can be, a sort of phantom with which the individual occupies himself upon occasion, but without making it clear to himself in terms of dialectical intermediaries how he happens to get into this fantastic realm, what significance being there has for him, and whether the entire activity that goes on out there does not resolve itself into a tautology within a recklessly fantastic venture of thought.

If being, in the two indicated definitions, is understood as empirical being, truth is at once transformed into a *desideratum,* and everything must be understood in terms of becoming; for the empirical object is unfinished and the existing cognitive spirit is itself in process of becoming. Thus the truth becomes an approximation whose beginning cannot be posited absolutely, precisely because the conclusion is lacking, the effect of which is retroactive. Whenever a beginning is *made,* on the other hand, unless through being unaware of this the procedure stamps itself as arbitrary, such a beginning is not the consequence of an imminent movement of thought, but is effected through a resolution of the will, essentially in the strength of faith. That the knowing spirit is an existing individual spirit, and that every human being is such an entity existing for himself, is a truth I cannot too often repeat; for the fantastic neglect of this is responsible for much confusion. Let no one misunderstand me. I happen to be a poor existing spirit like all other men; but if there is any lawful and honest manner in which I could be helped into becoming something extraordinary, like the pure I-am-I1 for example, I always stand ready gratefully to accept the gift and the benefaction. But if it can only be done in the manner indicated, by saying *ein zwei drei kokolorum,* or by tying a string around the little finger, and then when the moon is full, hiding it in some secret place—in that case I prefer to remain what I am, a poor existing human being.

The term "being," as used in the above definitions, must therefore be understood (from the systematic standpoint) much more abstractly, presumably as the abstract reflection of, or the abstract prototype for, what being is as concrete empirical being. When so understood there is nothing to prevent us from abstractly determining the truth as abstractly finished and complete; for the correspondence between thought and being is, from the abstract point of view, always finished. Only with the concrete does becoming enter in, and it is from the concrete that abstract thought abstracts.

But if being is understood in this manner, the formula becomes a tautology. Thought and being mean one and the same thing, and the correspondence spoken of is merely an abstract self-identity. Neither formula says anything more than that the truth is, so understood as to accentuate the copula: the truth *is,* i.e. the truth is a reduplication. Truth is the subject of the assertion, but the assertion that it is, is the same as the subject;

for this being that the truth is said to have is never its own abstract form. In this manner we give expression to the fact that truth is not something simple, but is in a wholly abstract sense a reduplication, a reduplication which is nevertheless instantly revoked.

Abstract thought may continue as long as it likes to rewrite this thought in varying phraseology, it will never get any farther. As soon as the being which corresponds to the truth comes to be empirically concrete, the truth is put in process of becoming, and is again by way of anticipation the conformity of thought with being. This conformity is actually realized for God, but it is not realized for any existing spirit, who is himself existentially in process of becoming.

For an existing spirit *qua* existing spirit, the question of the truth will again exist. The abstract answer has significance only for the abstraction into which an existing spirit is transformed when he abstracts from himself *qua* existing individual. This can be done only momentarily, and even in such moments of abstraction the abstract thinker pays his debt to existence by existing in spite of all abstraction. It is therefore an existing spirit who is now conceived as raising the question of truth, presumably in order that he may exist in it; but in any case the question is raised by someone who is conscious of being a particular existing human being. In this way I believe I can render myself intelligible to every Greek, as well as to every reasonable human being. If a German philosopher wishes to indulge a passion for making himself over, and, just as alchemists and macromancers were wont to garb themselves fantastically, first makes himself over into a superrational something for the purpose of answering this question of the truth in an extremely-satisfactory manner, the affair is no concern of mine; nor is his extremely satisfactory answer, which is no doubt very satisfactory indeed—when you are fantastically transformed. On the other hand, whether it is or is not the case that a German professor behaves in this manner, can be readily determined by anyone who will concentrate enthusiastically upon seeking guidance at the hands of such a sage, without criticism but seeking merely to assimilate the wisdom in a docile spirit by proposing to shape his own life in accordance with it. Precisely when thus enthusiastically attempting to learn from such a German professor, one would realize the most apt of epigrams upon him. For such a speculative philosopher could hardly be more embarrassed than by the sincere and enthusiastic zeal of a learner who proposes to express and to realize his wisdom by appropriating it existentially. For this wisdom is something that the Herr Professor has merely imagined, and written books about, but never himself tried. Aye, it has never even occurred to him that this should be done. Like the custom clerk who writes what he could not himself read, satisfied that his responsibilities ended with the writing, so there are speculative philosophers who write what, when it is to be read in the light of action shows itself to be nonsense, unless it is, perhaps, intended only for fantastic beings.

In that the question of truth is thus raised by an existing spirit *qua* existing the above abstract reduplication that is involved in it again confronts him. But existence itself, namely, existence as it is in the individual who raises the question and himself exists, keeps the two moments of thought and being apart, so that reflection presents him with two alternatives. For an objective reflection the truth becomes an object, something objective, and thought must be pointed away from the subject. For a subjective reflection the truth becomes a matter of appropriation, of inwardness, of subjectivity, and thought must probe more and more deeply into the subject and his subjectivity.

But then what? Shall we be compelled to remain in this disjunction, or may we not here accept the offer of benevolent assistance from the principle of mediation, so that the truth becomes an identity of subject and object?[2] Well, why not? But can the principle of mediation also help the existing individual while still remaining in existence himself to become the mediating principle, which is *sub specie aeterni,* whereas the poor existing individual is confined to the strait-jacket of existence? Surely it cannot do any good to mock a man, luring him on by dangling before his eyes the identity of subject and object, when his situation prevents him from making use of this identity, since he is in process of becoming in consequence of being an existing individual. How can it help to explain to a man how the eternal truth is to be understood eternally, when the supposed user of the explanation is prevented from so understanding it through being an existing individual, and merely becomes fantastic when he imagines himself to be *sub specie aeterni?* What such a man needs instead is precisely an explanation of how the eternal truth is to be understood in determinations of time by one who as existing is himself in time, which even the worshipful Herr Professor concedes, if not always, at least once a quarter when he draws his salary.

The identity of subject and object posited through an application of the principle of mediation merely carries us back to where we were before, to the abstract definition of the truth as an identity of thought and being; for to determine the truth as an identity of thought and object is precisely the same thing as saying that the truth *is,* i.e. that the truth is a reduplication. The lofty wisdom has thus again merely been absent-minded enough to forget that it was an existing spirit who asked about the truth. Or is the existing spirit himself the identity of subject and object, the subject-object? In that case I must press the question of where such an existing human being is, when he is thus at the same time also a subject-object? Or shall we perhaps here again first transform the existing spirit into something in general, and thereupon explain everything except the question asked, namely, how an existing subject is related to the truth *in concreto*; explain everything except the question that must in the next instance be asked, namely, how a particular existing spirit is related to this something in general, which seems to have not a little in common with a paper kite, or with the lump of sugar which the Dutch used to hang up under the loft for all to lick at.

So we return to the two ways of reflection; and we have not forgotten that it is an existing spirit who asks the question, a wholly individual human being. Nor can we forget that the fact that he exists is precisely what will make it impossible for him to proceed along both ways at once, while his earnest concern will prevent him from volously and fantastically becoming subject-object. Which of these two ways is now the way of truth for an existing spirit? For only the fantastic I-am-I is at once finished with both ways, or proceeds methodically along both ways simultaneously, a mode of ambulation which for an existing human is so inhuman that I dare not recommend it.

Since the inquirer stresses precisely the fact that he is an existing individual, then one of the above two ways which especially accentuates existence would seem to be especially worthy of commendation.

The way of objective reflection makes the subject accidental, and thereby transforms existence into something indifferent, something vanishing. Away from the subject the objective way of reflection leads to the objective truth, and while the subject and his subjectivity became indifferent, the truth also becomes indifferent, and this indifferent is precisely its objective validity; for all interest, like all decisiveness is rooted in subjectivity. The way of objective reflection leads to abstract thought, to mathematics, to historical knowledge of different kinds; and always it leads away from the subject, whose existence or non-existence, and from the objective point of view quite rightly, becomes infinitely indifferent. Quite rightly, since as Hamlet says,[3] existence and non-existence have only subjective significance. At its maximum this way will arrive at a contradiction, and in so far as the subject does not become wholly indifferent to himself, this merely constitutes a sign that his objective striving is not objective enough. At its maximum this way will lead to the contradiction that only the objective has come into being, while the subjective has gone out; that subject the existing subjectivity has vanished, in that it has made an attempt to become what in the abstract sense is called subjectivity, the mere abstract form of an abstract objectivity. And yet, the objectivity which has thus come into being is, from the subjective point of view at the most, either an hypothesis or an approximation, because all eternal decisiveness is rooted in subjectivity.

However, the objective way deems itself to have a security which the subjective way does not have (and, of course, existence and existing subjectivity be thought in combination with objective security); it thinks to escape a danger which threatens the subjective way, and this danger is at its maximum: madness. In a merely subjective determination of the truth, madness and truth become in the last analysis indistinguishable, since they may both have inwardness.* Nevertheless, perhaps I may here venture to offer a little remark, one which would seem to be not wholly superfluous in an objective age. The absence of inwardness is also madness. The objective truth as such, is by no means adequate to determine that whoever utters it is sane; on the contrary, it may even betray the fact that he is mad, although what he says may be entirely true, and especially objectively true, I shall here permit myself to tell a story, which without any sort of adaptation on my part comes direct from an asylum. A patient in such an institution seeks to escape, and actually succeeds in effecting his purpose by leaping out of a window, and prepares to start on the road to freedom, when the thought strikes him (shall I say sanely enough or madly enough?): "When you come to town you will be recognized, and you will at once be brought back here again; hence you need to prepare yourself fully to convince everyone by the objective truth of what you say, that all is in order as far as your sanity is concerned." As he walks along and thinks about this, he sees a ball lying on the ground, picks it up, and puts it into the tail pocket of his coat. Every step he takes the ball strikes him, politely speaking, on his hinder parts, and every time it thus strikes him he says: "Bang, the earth is round." He comes to the city, and at once calls on one of his friends; he wants to convince him that he is not crazy, and therefore walks back and forth, saying continually: "Bang, the earth is round!" But is not the earth round? Does the asylum still crave yet another sacrifice for this opinion, as in the time when all men believed it to be flat as a pancake? Or is a man who hopes to prove that he is sane, by uttering a generally accepted and generally respected objective truth, insane? And yet it was clear to the physician that the patient was not yet cured; though it is not to be thought that the cure would consist in getting him to accept the opinion that the earth is flat. But all men are not physicians, and what the age demands seems to have a considerable influence upon the question of what madness is. Aye, one could almost be tempted sometimes to believe that the modern age, which has modernized Christianity, has also modernized the question of Pontius Pilate, and that its urge to find something in which it can rest proclaims itself in the question: What is madness?* When a *Privatdocent*, every time his scholastic gown reminds him that he ought to say something, says de omnibus *dubitan-diem ets*, and at the same time writes away at a system which offers abundant internal evidence in every other sentence that the man has never doubted anything at all: he is not regarded as mad.

Don Quixote is the prototype for a subjective madness, in which the passion of inwardness embraces a particular finite fixed idea. But the absence of inwardness gives us on the other hand the prating madness which is quite as comical; and it might be a very desirable thing if an experimental psychologist would delineate it by taking a handful of such philosophers and bringing them together. In the type of madness which manifests itself as an aberrant inwardness, the tragic and the comic is that the something which is of such infinite concern as the unfortunate individual is a particular fixation which does not really concern anybody. In the type of madness which consists in the absence of inwardness, the comic is that though the something which the happy individual knows really is the truth, the truth which concerns all men, it does not in the slightest degree concern the much respected prater. This type of madness is more inhuman than the

---

* Even this is not really true, however, for madness never has the specific inwardness of the infinite. Its fixed idea is precisely some sort of objectivity, and the contradiction of madness consists in embracing this with passion. The critical point in such madness is thus again not the subjective, but the little finitude which has become a fixed idea, which is something that can never happen to the infinite.

other. One shrinks from looking into the eyes of a madman of the former type lest one be compelled to plumb there the depths of his delirium; but one are dares not look at a madman of the latter type at all, from fear of discovering that he has eyes of glass and hair made from carpet-rags that he is, in short, an artificial product. If you meet someone who suffers from such a derangement of feeling, the derangement consisting in his not having any, you listen to what he says in a cold and awful dread, scarcely knowing whether it is a human being who speaks, on a cunningly contrived walking stick in which a talking machine has been concealed. It is always unpleasant for a proud man to find himself unwittingly drinking a toast of brotherhood with the public hangman;[4] but to find oneself engaged in rational and philosophical conversation with a walking stick is almost enough to make a man lose his mind.

The subjective reflection turns its attention inwardly to the subject, and desires in this intensification of inwardness to realize the truth. And it proceeds in such fashion that, just as in the preceding objective reflection, when the objectivity had come into being, the subjectivity had vanished, so here the subjectivity of the subject becomes the final stage, and objectivity a vanishing factor. Not for a single moment is it forgotten that the subject is an existing individual, and that existence is a process of becoming, and that therefore the notion of the truth as identity of thought and being is a chimera of abstraction, in its truth only an expectation of the creature; not because the truth is not such an identity, but because the knower is an existing individual for whom the truth cannot be such an identity as long as he lives in time. Unless we hold fast to this, speculative philosophy will immediately transport us into the fantastic realism of the I-am-I, which modern speculative thought has not hesitated to use without explaining how a particular individual is related to it; and God knows, no human being is more than such a particular individual.

If an existing individual were really able to transcend himself, the truth would be for him something final and complete; but where is the point at which he is outside himself? The I-am-I is a mathematical point which does not exist, and in so far there is nothing to prevent everyone from occupying this standpoint; the one will not be in the way of the other. It is only momentarily that the particular individual is able to realize existentially a unity of the infinite and the finite which transcends existence. This unity is realized in the moment of passion. Modern philosophy has tried anything and everything in the effort to help the individual to transcend himself objectively, which is a wholly impossible feat; existence exercises its restraining influence, and if philosophers nowadays had not become mere scribblers in the service of a fantastic thinking and its preoccupation, they would long ago have perceived that suicide was the only tolerable practical interpretation of its striving. But the scribbling modern philosophy holds passion in contempt; and yet passion is the culmination of existence for an existing individual—and we are all of us existing individuals. In passion the existing subject is rendered infinite in the eternity of the imaginative representation, and yet he is at the same time most definitely himself, The fantastic I-am-I is not an identity of the infinite and the finite, since neither the one nor the other is real; it is a fantastic rendezvous in the clouds,[5] an unfruitful embrace, and the relationship of the individual self to this mirage is never indicated.

All essential knowledge relates to existence, or only such knowledge as has an essential relationship to existence is essential knowledge, All knowledge which does not inwardly relate itself to existence, in the reflection of inwardness, is, essentially viewed, accidental knowledge; in degree and scope is essentially indifferent. That essential knowledge is essentially related to existence does not mean the above-mentioned identity which abstract thought postulates between thought and being; not does it signify, objectively, that knowledge corresponds to something existent as its object. But it means that knowledge has a relationship to the knower, who is essentially an existing individual, and that for this reason all essential knowledge is essentially related to existence. Only ethical and ethico-religious knowledge has an essential relationship to the existence of the knower.

Mediation is a mirage, like the I-am-I. From the abstract point of view everything is and nothing comes into being. Mediation can therefore have no place in abstract thought, because it presupposes *movement*. Objective knowledge may indeed have the existent for its object but since the knowing subject is an existing individual, and through the fact of his existence in process of becoming, philosophy must first explain how a particular existing subject is related to a knowledge of mediation. It must explain what he is in such a moment, if not nearly *distrait*; where he is, if not in the moon? There is constant talk of mediation and mediation; is mediation then a man, as Peter[6] believes that *Imprimatur* is a man? How does a human being manage to become something of this kind? Is this dignity, this great philo*sophicum*, the fruit of study, or does the magistrate give it away like the office of deacon or grave-digger? Try merely to enter into these and other such plain questions of a plain man, who would gladly become mediation if it could be done in some lawful and honest manner, and not either by saying *ein zwei drei kokolorum*, or by forgetting that he is himself an existing human being, for whom existence is therefore something essential, and an ethico-religious existence a suitable *quantum satis*. A speculative philosopher may perhaps find it in bad taste to ask such questions. But it is important not to direct the polemic to the wrong point, and hence not to begin in a fantastic objective manner to discuss *pro* and *contra* whether there is a mediation or not, but to hold fast what it means to be a human being.

In an attempt to make clear the difference of way that exists between an objective and a subjective reflection, I shall now proceed to show how a subjective reflection makes its way inwardly in inwardness. Inwardness in an existing subject culminates in passion; corresponding to passion in the subject the truth becomes a paradox; and the fact that the truth becomes a paradox is rooted precisely in its having a relationship to an existing subject. Thus the one corresponds to the other. By forgetting that one is an existing subject, passion goes by the board and the truth is no longer a paradox; the knowing subject becomes a fantastic entity rather than a human being, and the truth becomes a fantastic object for the knowledge of this fantastic entity.

When the question of truth is raised in an objective manner, reflection is directed objectively to the truth, as an object to which the knower is related. Reflection is not focussed upon the relationship, however, but upon the question of whether it is the truth to which the knower is related. If only the object to which he is related is the truth, the subject is accounted to be in the truth. When the question of the truth is raised subjectively, reflection is directed subjectively to the nature of the individual's relationship; if only the mode of this relationship is in the truth, the individual is in the truth even if he should happen to be thus related to what is not true.* Let us take as an example the knowledge of God. Objectively, reflection is directed to the problem of whether this object is the true God; subjectively, reflection is directed to the question whether the individual is related to a something *in such a manner* that his relationship is in truth a God-relationship. On which side is the truth now to be found? Ah, may we not here resort to a mediation, and say: It is on neither side, but in the mediation of both? Excellently well said, provided we might have it explained how an existing individual manages to be in a state of mediation. For to be in a state of mediation is to be finished, while to exist is to become. Nor can an existing individual be in two places at the same time—he cannot be an identity of subject and object. When he is nearest to being in two places at the same time he is in passion; but passion is momentary, and passion is also the highest expression of subjectivity.

The existing individual who chooses to pursue the objective way enters upon the entire approximation-process by which it is proposed to bring God to light objectively,

---

* The reader will observe that the question here is about essential truth, or about the truth which is essentially related to existence, and that it is precisely for the sake of clarifying it as inwardness or as subjectivity that this contrast is drawn.

But this is in all eternity impossible, because God is a subject, and therefore exists only for subjectivity in inwardness. The existing individual who chooses the subjective way apprehends instantly the entire dialectical difficulty involved in having to use some time, perhaps a long time, in finding God objectively; and he feels this dialectical difficulty in all its painfulness, because every moment is wasted in which he does not have God.* That very instant he has God, not by virtue of any objective deliberation, but by virtue of the infinite passion of inwardness. The objective inquirer, on the other hand, is not embarrassed by such dialectical difficulties as are involved in devoting an entire period of investigation to finding God since it is possible that the inquirer may die tomorrow; and if he lives he can scarcely regard God as something to be taken along if convenient since God is precisely that which one takes a *tout prix*, which in the understanding of passion constitutes the true inward relationship to God.

It is at this point, so difficult dialectically, that the way swings off for everyone who knows what it means to think, and to think existentially which is something very different from sitting at a desk and writing about what one has never done, something very different from writing de *omnibus dubitandum* and at the same time being as credulous existentially as the most sensuous of men. Here is where the way swings off, and the change is marked by the fact that while objective knowledge rambles comfortably on by way of the long road of approximation without being impelled by the urge of passion, subjective knowledge counts every delay a deadly peril, and the decision so infinitely important and so instantly pressing that it is as if the opportunity had already passed.

Now when the problem is to reckon up on which side there is most truth, whether on the side of one who seeks the true God objectively, and pursues the approximate truth of the God-idea; or on the side of one who, driven by the infinite passion of his need of God, feels an infinite concern for his own relationship to God in truth (and to be at one and the same time on both sides equally, is as we have noted not possible for an existing individual, but is merely the happy delusion of an imaginary I-am-I): the answer cannot be in doubt for anyone who has not been demoralized with the aid of science. If one who lives in the midst of Christendom goes up to the house of God, the house of the true God, with the true conception of God in his knowledge, and prays, but prays in a false spirit; and one who lives in an idolatrous community prays with the entire passion of the infinite, although his eyes rest upon the image of an idol: where is there most truth? The one prays in truth to God though he worships an idol; the other prays falsely to the true God, and hence worships in fact an idol.

When one man investigates objectively the problem of immortality, and another embraces an uncertainty with the passion of the infinite: where is there most truth, and who has the greater certainty? The one has entered upon a never-ending approximation, for the certainty of immortality lies precisely in the subjectivity of the individual; the other is immortal, and fights for his immortality by struggling with the uncertainty. Let us consider Socrates.[7] Nowadays everyone dabbles in a few proofs; some have several such proofs, others fewer. But Socrates! He puts the question objectively in a problematic manner: *if* there is an immortality. He must therefore be accounted a doubter in comparison with one of our modern thinkers with the three proofs? By no means. On this "if" he risks his entire life, he has the courage to meet death, and he has with the

---

* In this manner God certainly becomes a postulate, but not in the otiose manner in which the word is commonly understood. It becomes clear rather that the only way in which an existing individual comes into relation with God, is when the dialectical contradiction brings the relationship to the point of despair, and helps him to embrace God with the "category of his faith). Then the postulate is so far from being arbitrary that it is precisely a life decision. It is then not so much that God is a postulate, as that the existing individual's view of God is a necessity.

passion of the infinite so determined the pattern of his life that it must be found acceptable—*if* there is an immortality. Is any better proof capable of being given for the immortality of the soul? But those who have the three proofs do not at all determine their lives in conformity therewith; if there is an immortality it must feel disgust over their manner of life: can any better refutation be given of the three proofs? The bit of uncertainty that Socrates had, helped him because he himself contributed the passion of the infinite; the three proofs that the others have do not profit them at all, because they are dead to spirit and enthusiasm, and their three proofs, in lieu of proving anything else, prove just this. A young girl may enjoy all the sweetness of love on the basis of what is merely a weak hope that she is beloved, because she rests everything on this weak hope; but many a wedded matron more than once subjected to the strongest expressions of love, has in so far indeed had proofs, but strangely enough has not enjoyed *quod erat demonstrandum.* The Socratic ignorance, which Socrates held fast with the entire passion of his inwardness, was thus an expression for the principle that the eternal truth is related to an existing individual, and that this truth must therefore be a paradox for him as long as he exists; and yet it is possible that there was more truth in the Socratic ignorance as it was in him, than in the entire objective truth of the System, which flirts with what the times demand and accommodates itself to *Privatdocents.*

The *objective accent falls on WHAT is said, the subjective accent* and *HOW it is said.* This distinction holds even in the aesthetic realm, and receives definite expression in the principle that what is in itself true may in the mouth of such and such a person become untrue. In these times this distinction is particularly worthy of notice, for if we wish to express in a single sentence the difference between ancient times and our own, we should doubtless have to say: "In ancient times only an individual here and there knew the truth; now all know it, except that the inwardness of its appropriation stands in an inverse relationship to the extent of its dissemination.* Aesthetically the contradiction on that truth becomes untruth in this or that person's mouth, is best construed comically: In the ethico-religious sphere, accent is again on the "how." But this is not to be understood as referring to demeanor, expression, or the like; rather it refers to the relationship sustained by the existing individual, in his own existence, to the content of his utterance. Objectively the interest is focused merely on the thought-content, subjectively on the inwardness. At its maximum this inward "how" is the passion of the infinite, and the passion of the infinite is the truth. But the passion of the infinite is precisely subjectivity and thus subjectivity becomes the truth. Objectively there is no infinite decisiveness, and hence it is objectively in order to annul the difference between good and evil; together with the principle of contradiction, and therewith also the infinite difference between the true and the false. Only in subjectivity is there decisiveness, to seek subjectivity is to be in error. It is the passion of the infinite that is the decisive factor and not its content, for its content is precisely itself. In this manner subjectivity and the subjective "how" constitute the truth.

---

* Stages on *Life's Way,* Though ordinarily not wishing an expression of opinion the part of reviewers, I might at this point almost desire it, provided such opinions, although flattering me, amounted to an assertion of the daring truth that what I say is somewhat knows, even every child, and that the cultured know infinitely much better. The fact that everyone knows it, my standpoint is in order, and I shall doubtlessly manage with the unity of the comic and the tragic. If there were anyone who did deny eight perhaps be in danger of being dislodged from my position of equilibrium by happenstance. I might be in a position to communicate to someone the needful preliminary facts, just this which engages my interest so much, this that the cultured are accustomed to that everyone knows what the highest is. This was not the case in paganism, nor in the seventeen centuries of Christianity. Hail to the nineteenth century! What progress has been made since the time when only a few knew it. To know this, perhaps, we must assume that no one nowadays does it.

But the "how" which is thus subjectively accentuated precisely because the subject is an existing individual, is also subject to a dialectic with respect to time, In the passionate moment of decision, where the road swings away from objective knowledge, it seems as if the infinite decision were thereby realized. But in the same moment the existing individual finds himself in the temporal order, and the subjective "how" is transformed into a striving, a striving which receives indeed its impulse and a repeated renewal from the decisive passion of the infinite, but is nevertheless a striving.

When subjectivity is the truth, the conceptual determination of the truth must include an expression for the antithesis to objectivity, a memento of the fork in the road where the way swings off; this expression will at the same time serve as an indication of the tension of the subjective inwardness. Here is such a definition of truth: *An objective uncertainty held fast in an appropriation-process of the most passionate inwardness is the truth,* the highest truth attainable for an *existing* individual. At the point where the way swings off (and where this is cannot be specified objectively, since it is a matter of subjectivity), there objective knowledge is placed in abeyance. Thus the subject merely has, objectively, the uncertainty; but it is this which precisely increases the tension of that infinite passion which constitutes his inwardness. The truth is precisely the venture which chooses an objective uncertainty with the passion of the infinite. I contemplate the order of nature in the hope of finding God, and I see omnipotence and wisdom; but I also see much else that disturbs my mind and excites anxiety. The sum of all this is an objective uncertainty. But it is for this very reason that the inwardness becomes as intense as it is, for it embraces this objective uncertainty with the entire passion of the infinite. In the case of a mathematical proposition the objectivity is given, but for this reason the truth of such a proposition is also an indifferent truth.

But the above definition of truth is an equivalent expression for faith. Without risk there is no faith. Faith is precisely the contradiction between the infinite passion of the individual's inwardness and the objective uncertainty. If I am capable of grasping God objectively, I do not believe, but precisely because I cannot do this I must believe. If I wish to preserve myself in faith I must constantly be intent upon holding fast the objective uncertainty, so as to remain out upon the deep, over seventy thousand fathoms of water, still preserving my faith.

In the principle that subjectivity, inwardness, is the truth, there is comprehended the Socratic wisdom, whose everlasting merit it was to have become aware of the essential significance of existence, of the fact that the knower is an existing individual. For this reason Socrates was in the truth by virtue of his ignorance, in the highest sense in which this was possible within paganism. To attain to an understanding of this, to comprehend that the misfortune of speculative philosophy is again and again to have forgotten that the knower is an existing individual is in our objective age difficult enough. "But to have made an advance upon Socrates without even having understood what, he understood is at any rate not "Socratic." Compare the "Moral" of the Fragments.[8]

Let us now start from this point, and as was attempted in the Fragments, seek a determination of thought which will really carry us further. I have nothing here to do with the question of whether this proposed thought-determination is true or not, since I am merely experimenting; but it must at any rate be clearly manifest that the Socratic thought is understood within the new proposal, so that at least do not come out behind Socrates.

When subjectivity, inwardness, is the truth, the truth becomes objectively a paradox; and the fact that the truth is objectively a paradox shows in its turn that subjectivity is the truth. For the objective situation is repellent; and the expression for the objective repulsion constitutes the tension and the measure of the corresponding inwardness. The paradoxical character of the truth is its objective uncertainty this uncertainty is an expression for the passionate inwardness and this passion is precisely the truth. So far the Socratic principle. The eternal and essential truth, the truth which has an essential relationship to an existing individual because it pertains essentially to existence (all other knowledge being from the Socratic point of view accidental, its scope and degree a matter of indifference), is a paradox. But the eternal essential truth is by no means in itself a paradox; but it becomes paradoxical by virtue of its relationship to an existing individual. The Socratic ignorance gives expression to the objective uncertainty attaching to the truth, while his inwardness in existing is the truth. To anticipate here what will be developed later, let me make the following remark. The Socratic ignorance is an analogue to the category of the absurd, only that there is still less of objective certainty in the absurd, and in the repellent effect that the absurd exercises.

It is certain only that it is absurd, and precisely on that account it incites to an infinitely greater tension in the corresponding inwardness, The Socratic inwardness in existing is an analogue to faith; only that the inwardness of faith, corresponding as it does, not to the repulsion of the Socratic ignorance, but to the repulsion exerted by the absurd, is infinitely more profound.

Socratically the eternal essential truth is by no means in its own nature paradoxical, but only in its relationship to an existing individual. This finds expression in another Socratic proposition, namely, that all knowledge is recollection. This proposition is not for Socrates a cue to the speculative enterprise, and hence he does not follow it up; essentially it becomes a Platonic principle. Here the way swings off; Socrates concentrates essentially upon accentuating existence, while Plato forgets this and loses himself in speculation. Socrates' infinite merit is to have been an *existing* thinker, not a speculative philosopher who forgets what it means to exist. For Socrates therefore the principle that all knowledge is recollection has at the moment of his leave-taking and as the constantly rejected possibility of engaging in speculation, the following two-fold significance: (1) that the knower is essentially *integer,* and that with respect to the knowledge of the eternal truth he is confronted with no other difficulty than the circumstance that he exists; which difficulty, however, is so essential and decisive for him that it means that existing, the process of transformation to inwardness in and by existing, is the truth; (2) that existence in time does not have any decisive significance, because the possibility of taking oneself back into eternity through recollection is always there, though this possibility is constantly nullified by utilizing the time, not for speculation, but for the transformation to inwardness in existing.*

---

* This will perhaps be the proper place to offer an explanation with respect to a difficulty in the plan of the *Fragments,* which had its ground in the fact that I did not wish at once to make the case as difficult dialectically as it is, because in our age terminologies and the like are turned so topsy-turvy that it is almost impossible to secure oneself against confusion. In order if possible clearly to exhibit the difference between the Socratic position (which was supposed to be the philosophical, the pagan-philosophical position) and the experimentally evoked thought-determination which really makes an advance beyond the Socratic, I carried the Socratic back to the principle that all knowledge is recollection.[9] This is, in a way, commonly assumed, and only one who with a specialized interest concerns himself with the Socratic, returning again and again to the sources, only for him would it be of importance on this point to distinguish between Socrates and Plato. The proposition does indeed belong to both, only that Socrates is always departing from it, in order to exist. By holding Socrates down to the proposition that all knowledge is recollection, he becomes a speculative philosopher instead of an existential thinker, for whom existence is the essential thing. The recollection-principle belongs to speculative philosophy, and recollection is immanence, and speculatively and eternally there is no paradox. But the difficulty In that no human being is speculative philosophy; the speculative philosopher himself is an existing individual, subject to the claims that existence makes upon him. There is no merit in forgetting this, but a great merit in holding it fast, and this is precisely what Socrates did. To disagree, which also involves the qualification of inwardness, is the Socratic position; also on the other hand, is to pursue the lure of recollection and immanence. He is fundamentally in advance of speculative philosophy; he does not have a fantasy in which the speculative philosopher first disguises himself, and then goes on forgetting the most important thing of all, which is to exist. But precisely it is this in advance of speculation, he presents, when properly delineated, a certain resemblance to that which the experiment described as in truth going beyond the existence as paradox in the Socratic sense becomes analogous to the paradox sensu

The infinite merit of the Socratic position was precisely to accentuate the fact that the knower is an existing individual, and that the task of existing is his essential task. Making an advance upon Socrates by failing to understand this, is quite a mediocre achievement. This Socratic principle we must therefore bear in mind, and then inquire whether the formula may not be so altered as really to make an advance beyond the Socratic position.

Subjectivity, inwardness, has been posited as the truth; can any expression for the truth be found which has a still higher degree of inwardness? Aye, there is such an expression, provided the principle that subjectivity or inwardness is the truth begins by positing the opposite principle: that subjectivity is untruth. Let us not at this point succomb to such haste as to fail in making the necessary distinctions. Speculative philosophy also says that subjectivity is untruth, but says it in order to stimulate a movement in precisely the opposite direction, namely, to the direction of the principle that objectivity is the truth. Speculative philosophy determines subjectivity negatively as tending toward objectivity. This second determination of ours, however, places a hindrance in its own way while proposing to begin, which has the effect making the inwardness far more intensive. Socratically speaking, subjectivity is untruth if it refuses to understand that subjectivity in truth, but, for example, desires to become objective. Here, on the subject of subjectivity in beginning upon the task of becoming the truth through a subjectifying process, is in the difficulty that it is already untruth. Thus, the labor of the task is thrust backward, backward, that is, in inwardness. So far is it from being the case that the way tends in the direction of objectivity, that the beginning merely lies still deeper in subjectivity.

But the subject cannot be untruth eternally, or eternally be presupposed as having been untruth; it must have been brought to this condition in time, or here become untruth in time. The Socratic paradox consisted in the fact that the eternal was related to an existing individual, but now existence has stamped itself upon the existing individual a second time. There has taken place so essential an alteration in him that he cannot now possibly take himself back into the eternal by way of recollection. To do this is to speculate; to be able to do this, but to reject the possibility by apprehending the task of life as a realization of inwardness in existing, is the Socratic position. But now the difficulty is that what followed Socrates on his way as a rejected possibility, has become an impossibility. If engaging in speculation was a dubious merit even from the point of view of the Socratic, it is now neither more nor less than confusion.

The paradox emerges when the eternal truth and existence are placed in juxtaposition with one another; each time the stamp of existence is brought to bear, the paradox becomes more clearly evident. Viewed Socratically the knower was simply an existing individual, but now the existing individual bears the stamp of having been essentially altered by existence.

Let us now call the untruth of the individual *Sin*. Viewed eternally he cannot be sin, nor can he be eternally presupposed as having been in sin. By coming into existence therefore (for the beginning was that subjectivity is untruth), he becomes a sinner. He is not born as a sinner in the sense that he is presupposed as being a sinner before he is born, but he is born in sin and as a sinner. This we might call *Original Sin*. But if existence

---

eminentiori the passion of inwardness in existing becomes an analogue to faith *sensu eminentiori*. It is none the less infinite, that the characterization which the *Fragments* made that the truth goes beyond the Socratic remains unchanged, it will be easy to show; but maintains apparently the same determinations, or at any rate the same words, about these things, I feared to cause a misunderstanding. Now I think there can be no objection or doubt of the paradoxical and of faith in reference to Socrates, since it is quite correct to do so and is understood. Besides, the old Greeks also used the word deiknymi, though deiknymi in the sense of the experiment; and they used it in such a manner that, especially to a work of Aristotle[10] where the term is employed, it would be possible and very enlightening considerations bearing upon its difference from faith *sensu eminentiori*.

has in this manner acquired a power over him, he is prevented from taking himself back into the eternal by way of recollection. If it was paradoxical to posit the eternal truth in relationship to an existing individual, it is now absolutely paradoxical to posit it in relationship to such an individual as we have here defined, But the more difficult it is made for him to take himself out of existence by way of recollection, the more profound is the inwardness that his existence may have in existence; and when it is made impossible for him, when he is held so fast in existence that the back door of recollection is forever closed to him, then his inwardness will be the most profound possible. But let us never forget that the Socratic merit was to stress the fact that the knower is an existing individual; for the more difficult the matter becomes, the greater the temptation to hasten along the easy road of speculation, away from fearful dangers and crucial decisions, to the winning of renown and honors and property, and so forth. If even Socrates understood the dubiety of taking himself speculatively out of existence back into the eternal, although no other difficulty confronted the existing individual except that he existed, and that existing was his essential task, now it is impossible. Forward he must, backward he cannot go.

Subjectivity is the truth. By virtue of the relationship subsisting between the eternal truth and the existing individual, the paradox came into being. Let us now go further, let us suppose that the eternal essential truth is itself a paradox. How does the paradox come into being? By putting the eternal essential truth into juxtaposition with existence. Hence when we posit such a conjunction within the truth itself the truth becomes a paradox. The eternal truth has come into being in time: this is the paradox. If in accordance with the determination just posited, the subject is prevented by sin from taking himself back into the eternal, now he need not trouble himself about this; for now the eternal essential truth is not behind him but in front of him, through its being in existence or having existed, so that if the individual does not existentially and in existence lay hold of the truth, he will never lay hold of it.

Existence can never be more sharply accentuated than by means of these determinations. The evasion by which speculative philosophy attempts to recollect itself out of existence has been made impossible. With reference to this, there is nothing for speculation to do except to arrive at an understanding of this impossibility; every speculative attempt which insists on being speculative shows *eo ipso* that it has not understood it. The individual may thrust all this away from him, and take refuge in speculation; but it is impossible first to accept it, and then to revoke it by means of speculation, since it is definitely calculated to prevent speculation.

When the eternal truth is related to an existing individual it becomes a paradox. The paradox repels in the inwardness of the existing individual, through the objective uncertainty and the corresponding Socratic ignorance. But since the paradox is not in the first instance itself paradoxical (but only in its relationship to the existing individual), it does not repel with a sufficient intensive inwardness. For without risk there is no faith, and the greater the risk the greater the faith; the more objective security the less inwardness (for inwardness is precisely subjectivity), and the less objective security the more profound the possible inwardness. When the paradox is paradoxical in itself, it repels the individual by virtue of its absurdity, and the corresponding passion of inwardness is faith. But subjectivity, inwardness, is the truth; for otherwise we have forgotten what the merit of the Socratic position is. But there can be no stronger expression for inwardness than when the retreat out of existence into the eternal by way of recollection is impossible; and when, with truth confronting the individual as a paradox, gripped in the anguish and pain of sin, facing the tremendous risk of the objective insecurity, the individual believes. But without risk no faith, not even the Socratic form of faith, much less the form of which we here speak.

When Socrates believed that there was a God, he held fast to the objective uncertainty with the whole passion of his inwardness, and it is precisely in this contradiction and in this risk, that faith is rooted. Now it is otherwise. Instead of the objective uncertainty, there is here a certainty, namely, that objectively it is absurd; and this absurdity, held fast in the passion of inwardness, is faith. The Socratic ignorance is as a witty jest in comparison with the earnestness of facing the absurd; and the Socratic existential inwardness is as Greek light-mindedness in comparison with the grave strenuosity of faith.

What now is the absurd? The absurd is—that the eternal truth has come into being in time, that God has come into being, has been born, has grown up, and so forth, precisely like any other individual human being, quite indistinguishable from other individuals. For every assumption of immediate recognizability is pre-Socratic paganism, and from the Jewish point of view, idolatry; and every determination of what really makes an advance beyond the Socratic must essentially bear the stamp of having a relationship to God's having come into being; for faith *sensu strictissimo,* as was developed in the *Fragments,* 11 refers to becoming, When Socrates believed that there was a God, he saw very well that where the way swings off there is also an objective way of approximation, for example by the contemplation of nature and human history, and so forth. His merit was precisely to shun this way where the quantitative siren song enchants the mind and deceives the existing individual.

The Ethics of Belief
W. K. Clifford

The Duty of Inquiry

A shipowner was about to send to sea an emigrant-ship. He knew that she was old, and not over-well built at the first; that she had seen many seas and climes, and often had needed repairs. Doubts had been suggested to him that possibly she was not seaworthy. These doubts preyed upon his mind and made him unhappy; he thought that perhaps he ought to have her thoroughly overhauled and refitted, even though this should put him to great expense. Before the ship sailed, however, he succeeded in overcoming these melancholy reflections. He said to himself that she had gone safely through so many voyages and weathered so many storms that it was idle to suppose she would not come safely home from this trip also. He would put his trust in Providence, which could hardly fail to protect all these unhappy families that were leaving their father-land to seek for better times elsewhere. He would dismiss from his mind all ungenerous suspicions about the honesty of builders and contractors. In such ways he acquired a sincere and comfortable conviction that his vessel was thoroughly safe and seaworthy; he watched her departure with a light heart, and benevolent wishes for the success of the exiles in their strange new home that was to be; and he got his insurance-money when she went down in mid-ocean and told no tales.

What shall we say of him? Surely this, that he was verily guilty of the death of those men. It is admitted that he did sincerely believe in the soundness of his ship; but the sincerity of his conviction can in no wise help him, because *he had no right to believe on suck evidence as was before him.* He had acquired his belief not by honestly earning it in patient investigation, but by stifling his doubts. And although in the end he may have felt so sure about it that he could not think otherwise, yet inasmuch as he had knowingly and willingly worked himself into that frame of mind, he must be held responsible for it.

Let us alter the case a little, and suppose that the ship was not unsound after all; that she made her voyage safely, and many others after it, Will that diminish the guilt of her owner? Not one jot. When an action is once done, it is right or wrong for ever; no accidental failure of its good or evil fruits can possibly alter that. The man would not have been innocent, he would only have been not found out. The question of right or wrong has to do with the origin of his belief, not the matter of it; not what it was, but how he got it; not whether it turned out to be true or false, but whether he had a right to believe on such evidence as was before him.

There was once an island in which some of the inhabitants professed a religion teaching neither the doctrine of original sin nor that of eternal punishment. A suspicion got abroad that the professors of this religion had made use of unfair means to get their doctrines taught to children. They were accused of wresting the laws of their country in such a way as to remove children from the care of their natural and legal guardians; and

---

[1] *Contemporary Review,* January 1877.

even of stealing them away and keeping them concealed from their friends and relations. A certain number of men formed themselves into a society for the purpose of agitating the public about this matter. They published grave accusations against individual citizens of the highest position and character, and did all in their power to injure these citizens in the exercise of their professions. So great was the noise they made, that a Commission was appointed to investigate the facts; but after the Commission had carefully inquired into all the evidence that could be got, it appeared that the accused were innocent. Not only had they been accused on insufficient evidence, but the evidence of their innocence was such as the agitators might easily have obtained, if they had attempted a fair inquiry. After these disclosures the inhabitants of that country looked upon the members of the agitating society, not only as persons whose judgment was to be distrusted, but also as no longer to be counted honourable men. For although they had sincerely and conscientiously believed in the charges they had made, *yet they had no right to believe on such evidence as was before them.* Their sincere convictions, instead of being honestly earned by patient inquiring, were stolen by listening to the voice of prejudice and passion.

Let us vary this case also, and suppose, other things remaining as before, that a still more accurate investigation proved the accused to have been really guilty. Would this make any difference in the guilt of the accusers? Clearly not; the question is not whether their belief was true or false, but whether they entertained it on wrong grounds. They would no doubt say, "Now you see that we were right after all; next time perhaps you will believe us." And they might be believed, but they would not thereby become honourable men. They would not be innocent, they would only be not found out. Every one of them, if he chose to examine himself *in foro conscientiæ,* would know that he had acquired and nourished a belief, when he had no right to believe on such evidence as was before him; and therein he would know that he had done a wrong thing.

It may be said, however, that in both of these supposed cases it is not the belief which is judged to be wrong, but the action following upon it. The shipowner might say, "I am perfectly certain that my ship is sound, but still I feel it my duty to have her examined, before trusting the lives of so many people to her." And it might be said to the agitator, "However convinced you were of the justice of your cause and the truth of your convictions, you ought not to have made a public attack upon any man's character until you had examined the evidence on both sides with the utmost patience and care."

In the first place, let us admit that, so far as it goes, this view of the case is right and necessary; right, because even when a man's belief is so fixed that he cannot think otherwise, he still has a choice in regard to the action suggested by it, and so cannot escape the duty of investigating on the ground of the strength of his convictions; and necessary, because those who are not yet capable of controlling their feelings and thoughts must have a plain rule dealing with overt acts.

But this being premised as necessary, it becomes clear that it is not sufficient, and that our previous judgment is required to supplement it. For it is not possible so to sever the belief from the action it suggests as to condemn the one without condemning the other, No man holding a strong belief on one side of a question, or even wishing to hold a belief on one side, can investigate it with such fairness and completeness as if he were really in doubt and unblassed; so that the existence of a belief not founded on fair inquiry unfits a man for the performance of this necessary duty.

Nor is that truly a belief at all which has not some influence upon the actions of him who holds it. He who truly believes that which prompts him to an action has looked upon the action to lust after it, he has committed it already in his heart. If a belief is not realised immediately in open deeds, it is stored up for the guidance of the future. It goes to make a part of that aggregate of beliefs which is the link between sensation and action at every moment of all our lives, and which is so organised and compacted together that no part of it can be isolated from the rest, but every new addition, modifies the structure of the whole. No real belief, however trifling and fragmentary it may seem, is ever truly insignificant; it prepares us to receive more of its like, confirms those which resembled it before, and weakens others; and so gradually it lays a stealthy train in our inmost thoughts, which may some day explode into overt action, and leave its stamp upon our character for ever.

And no one man's belief is in any case a private matter which concerns himself alone. Our lives are guided by that general conception of the course of things which has been created by society for social purposes. Our words, our phrases, our forms and processes and modes of thought, are common property, fashioned and perfected from age to age; an heirloom which every succeeding generation inherits as a precious deposit and a sacred trust to be handed on to the next one, not unchanged but enlarged and puri-fied, with some clear marks of its proper handiwork. Into this, for good or ill, is woven every belief of every man who has speech of his fellows. An awful privilege, and an awful responsibility, that we should help to create the world in which posterity will live.

In the two supposed cases which have been considered, it has been judged wrong to believe on insufficient evidence, or to nourish belief by suppressing doubts and avoiding investigation. The reason of this judgment is not far to seek: it is that in both these cases the belief held by one man was of great importance to other men. But forasmuch as no belief held by one man, however seemingly trivial the belief, and however obscure the believer, is ever actually insignificant or without its effect on the fate of mankind, we have no choice but to extend our judgment to all cases of belief whatever. Belief, that sacred faculty which prompts the decisions of our will, and knits into harmonious work-ing all the compacted energies of our being, is ours not for ourselves, but for humanity. It is rightly used on truths which have been established by long experience and waiting toil, and which have stood in the fierce light of free and fearless questioning. Then it helps to bind men together, and to strengthen and direct their common action. It is desecrated when given to unproved and unquestioned statements, for the solace and private plea-sure of the believer; to add a tinsel splendour to the plain straight road of our life and display a bright mirage beyond it; or even to drown the common sorrows of our kind by a self-deception which allows them not only to cast down, but also to degrade us. Whoso would deserve well of his fellows in this matter will guard the purity of his belief with a very fanaticism of jealous care, lest at any time it should rest on an unworthy object, and catch a stain which can never be wiped away.

It is not only the leader of men, statesman, philosopher, or poet, that owes this bounden duty to mankind. Every rustic who delivers in the village alehouse his slow, infrequent sentences, may help to kill or keep alive the fatal superstitions which clog his race, Every hard-worked wife of an artisan may transmit to her children beliefs which shall knit society together, or rend it in pieces. No simplicity of mind, no obscurity of station, can escape the universal duty of questioning all that we believe.

It is true that this duty is a hard one, and the doubt which comes out of it is often a very bitter thing. It leaves us bare and powerless where we thought that we were safe and strong. To know all about anything is to know how to deal with it under all circum-stances. We feel much happier and more secure when we think we know precisely what to do, no matter what happens, than when we have lost our way and do not know where to turn. And if we have supposed ourselves to know all about anything, and to be capable of doing what is fit in regard to it, we naturally do not like to find that we are really igno-rant and powerless, that we have to begin again at the beginning, and try to learn what the thing is and how it is to be dealt with—if indeed anything can be learnt about it. It is the sense of power attached to a sense of knowledge that makes men desirous of believ-ing, and afraid of doubting.

This sense of power is the highest and best of pleasures when the belief on which it is founded is a true belief, and has been fairly earned by investigation. For then we may justly feel that it is common property, and holds good for others as well as for ourselves. Then we may be glad, not that *I* have learned secrets by which I am safer and stronger, but that *we men* have got mastery over more of the world; and we shall be strong, not for ourselves, but in the name of Man and in his strength. But if the belief has been accepted on insufficient evidence, the pleasure is a stolen one. Not only does it deceive ourselves by giving us a sense of power which we do not really possess, but it is sinful, because it is stolen in defiance of our duty to mankind. That duty is to guard ourselves from such beliefs as from a pestilence, which may shortly master our own body and then spread to the rest of the town. What would be thought of one who, for the sake of a sweet fruit, should deliberately run the risk of bringing a plague upon his family and his neighbours?

And, as in other such cases, it is not the risk only which has to be considered; for a bad action is always bad at the time when it is done, no matter what happens afterwards. Every time we let ourselves believe for unworthy reasons, we weaken our powers of self-control, of doubting, of judicially and fairly weighing evidence. We all suffer severely enough from the maintenance and support of false beliefs and the fatally wrong actions which they lead to, and the evil born when one such belief is entertained is great and wide. But a greater and wider evil arises when the credulous character is maintained and supported, when a habit of believing for unworthy reasons is fostered and made permanent. If I steal money from any person, there may be no harm done by the mere transfer of possession; he may not feel the loss, or it may prevent him from using the money badly. But I cannot help doing this great wrong towards Man, that I make myself dishonest. What hurts society is not that it should lose its property, but that it should become a den of thieves; for then it must cease to be society. This is why we ought not to do evil that good may come; for at any rate this great evil has come, that we have done evil and are made wicked thereby. In like manner, if I let myself believe anything on insufficient evidence, there may be no great harm done by the mere belief; it may be true after all, or I may never have occasion to exhibit it in outward acts. But I cannot help doing this great wrong towards Man, that I make myself credulous. The danger to society is not merely that it should believe wrong things, though that is great enough; but that it should become credulous, and lose the habit of testing things and inquiring into them; for then it must sink back into savagery.

The harm which is done by credulity in a man is not confined to the fostering of a credulous character in others, and consequent support of false beliefs. Habitual want of care about what I believe leads to habitual want of care in others about the truth of what is told to me. Men speak the truth to one another when each reveres the truth in his own mind and in the other's mind; but how shall my friend revere the truth in my mind when I myself am careless about it, when I believe things because I want to believe them, and because they are comforting and pleasant? Will he not learn to cry, "Peace," to me, when there is no peace? By such a course I shall surround myself with a thick atmosphere of falsehood and fraud, and in that I must live. It may matter little to me, in my cloud-castle of sweet illusions and darling lies; but it matters much to Man that I have made my neighbours ready to deceive. The credulous man is father to the liar and the cheat; he lives in the bosom of this his family, and it is no marvel if he should become even as they are. So closely are our duties knit together, that whoso shall keep the whole law, and yet offend in one point, he is guilty of all.

To sum up: it is wrong always, everywhere, and for any one, to believe anything upon insufficient evidence.

If a man, holding a belief which he was taught in childhood or persuaded of afterwards, keeps down and pushes away any doubts which arise about it in his mind, purposely avoids the reading of books and the company of men that call in question or discuss it, and regards as impious those questions which cannot easily be asked without disturbing it—the life of that man is one long sin against mankind.

If this judgment seems harsh when applied to those simple souls who have never known better, who have been brought up from the cradle with a horror of doubt, and taught that their eternal welfare depends on *what* they believe, then it leads to the very serious question, *Who hath made Israel to sin?*

It may be permitted me to fortify this judgment with the sentence of Milton[1]—

"A man may be a heretic in the truth; and if he believe things only because his pastor says so, or the assembly so determine, without knowing other reason, though his belief be true, yet the very truth he holds becomes his heresy."

And with this famous aphorism of Coleridge[2]—

"He who begins by loving Christianity better than Truth, will proceed by loving his own sect or Church better than Christianity, and end in loving himself better than all."

Inquiry into the evidence of a doctrine is not to be made once for all, and then taken as finally settled. It is never lawful to stifle a doubt; for either it can be honestly answered by means of the inquiry already made, or else it proves that the inquiry was not complete.

"But," say's one, "I am a busy man; I have no time for the long course of study which would be necessary to make me in any degree a competent judge of certain questions, or even able to understand the nature of the arguments." Then he should have no time to believe.

The Weight of Authority

Are we then to become universal sceptics, doubting everything, afraid always to put one foot before the other until we have personally tested the firmness of the road? Are we to deprive ourselves of the help and guidance of that vast body of knowledge which is daily growing upon the world, because neither we nor any other one person can possibly test a hundredth part of it by immediate experiment or observation, and because it would not be completely proved if we did? Shall we steal and tell lies because we have had no personal experience wide enough to justify the belief that it is wrong to do so?

There is no practical danger that such consequences will ever follow from scrupulous care and self-control in the matter of belief. Those men who have most nearly done their duty in this respect have found that certain great principles, and these most fitted for the guidance of life, have stood out more and more clearly in proportion to the care and honesty with which they were tested, and have acquired in this way a practical certainty. The beliefs about right and wrong which guide our actions in dealing with men in society, and the beliefs about physical nature which guide our actions in dealing with animate and inanimate bodies, these never suffer from investigation; they can take care of themselves, without being propped up by "acts of faith," the clamour of paid advocates, or the suppression of contrary evidence. Moreover there are many cases in which it is our duty to act upon probabilities, although the evidence is not such as to justify present belief; because it is precisely by such action, and by observation of its fruits, that evidence is got which may justify future belief. So that we have no reason to fear lest a habit of conscientious inquiry should paralyse the actions of our daily life.

But because it is not enough to say, "It is wrong to believe on unworthy evidence," without saying also what evidence is worthy, we shall now go on to inquire under what circumstances it is lawful to believe on the testimony of others; and then, further, we shall inquire more generally when and why we may believe that which goes beyond our own experience, or even beyond the experience of mankind.

In what cases, then, let us ask in the first place, is the testimony of a man unworthy of belief? He may say that which is untrue either knowingly or unknowingly. In the first case he is lying, and his moral character is to blame; in the second case he is ignorant or

---

[1] *Areopagitica,*
[2] *Aids to Reflection.*

mistaken, and it is only his knowledge or his judgment which is in fault. In order that we may have the right to accept his testimony as ground for believing what he says, we must have reasonable grounds for trusting his *veracity,* that he is really trying to speak the truth so far as he knows it; his *knowledge,* that he has had opportunities of knowing the truth about this matter; and his *judgment,* that he has made proper use of those opportunities in coming to the conclusion which he affirms.

However plain and obvious these reasons may be, so that no man of ordinary intelligence, reflecting upon the matter, could fail to arrive at them, it is nevertheless true that a great many persons do habitually disregard them in weighing testimony. Of the two questions, equally important to the trustworthiness of a witness, "Is he dishonest?" and "May he be mistaken?" the majority of mankind are perfectly satisfied if *one* can, with some show of probability, be answered in the negative. The excellent moral character of a man is alleged as ground for accepting his statements about things which he cannot possibly have known. A Mohammedan, for example, will tell us that the character of his Prophet was so noble and majestic that it commands the reverence even of those who do not believe in his mission. So admirable was his moral teaching, so wisely put together the great social machine which he created, that his precepts have not only been accepted by a great portion of mankind, but have actually been obeyed. His institutions have on the one hand rescued the negro from savagery, and on the other hand have taught civilisation to the advancing West; and although the races which held the highest forms of his faith, and most fully embodied his mind and thought, have all been conquered and swept away by barbaric tribes, yet the history of their marvellous attainments remains as an imperishable glory to Islam. Are we to doubt the word of a man so great and so good? Can we suppose that this magnificent genius, this splendid moral hero, has lied to us about the most solemn and sacred matters? The testimony of Mohammed is clear, that there is but one God, and that he, Mohammed, is his Prophet; that if we believe in him we shall enjoy everlasting felicity, but that if we do not we shall be damned. This testimony rests on the most awful of foundations, the revelation of heaven itself; for was he not visited by the angel Gabriel, as he fasted and prayed in his desert cave, and allowed to enter into the blessed fields of Paradise? Surely God is God and Mohammed is the Prophet of God.

What should we answer to this Mussulman? First, no doubt, we should be tempted to take exception against his view of the character of the Prophet and the uniformly beneficial influence of Islam: before we could go with him altogether in these matters it might seem that we should have to forget many terrible things of which we have heard or read. But if we chose to grant him all these assumptions, for the sake of argument, and because it is difficult both for the faithful and for infidels to discuss them fairly and without passion, still we should have something to say which takes away the ground of his belief, and therefore shows that it is wrong to entertain it. Namely this: the character of Mohammed is excellent evidence that he was honest and spoke the truth so far as he knew it; but it is no evidence at all that he knew what the truth was. What means could he have of knowing that the form which appeared to him to be the angel Gabriel was not a hallucination, and that his apparent visit to Paradise was not a dream? Grant that he himself was fully persuaded and honestly believed that he had the guidance of heaven, and was the vehicle of a supernatural revelation, how could he know that this strong conviction was not a mistake? Let us put ourselves in his place; we shall find that the more completely we endeavour to realise what passed through his mind, the more clearly we shall perceive that the Prophet could have had no adequate ground for the belief in his own inspiration. It is most probable that he himself never doubted of the matter, or thought of asking the question; but we are in the position of those to whom the question has been asked, and who are bound to answer it. It is known to medical observers that solitude and want of food are powerful means of producing delusion and of fostering a tendency to mental disease. Let us suppose, then, that I, like Mohammed, go into desert places to fast and pray; what things can happen to me which will give me the right to believe that I am divinely inspired? Suppose that I get information, apparently from a celestial visitor, which upon being tested is found to be correct. I cannot be sure, in the first place, that the celestial visitor is not a figment of my own mind, and that the information did not come to me, unknown at the time to my consciousness, through some subtle channel of sense. But if my visitor were a real visitor, and for a long time gave me information which was found to be trustworthy, this would indeed be good ground for trusting him in the future as to such matters as fall within human powers of verification; but it would not be ground for trusting his testimony as to any other matters. For although his tested character would justify me in believing that he spoke the truth so far as he knew, yet the same question would present itself—what ground is there for supposing that he knows?

Even if my supposed visitor had given me such information, subsequently verified by me, as proved him to have means of knowledge about verifiable matters far exceeding my own; this would not justify me in believing what he said about matters that are not at present capable of verification by man. It would be ground for interesting conjecture, and for the hope that, as the fruit of our patient inquiry, we might by and by attain to such a means of verification as should rightly turn conjecture into belief. For belief belongs to man, and to the guidance of human affairs: no belief is real unless it guide our actions, and those very actions supply a test of its truth.

But, it may be replied, the acceptance of Islam as a system is just that action which is prompted by belief in the mission of the Prophet, and which will serve for a test of its truth. Is it possible to believe that a system which has succeeded so well is really founded upon a delusion? Not only have individual saints found joy and peace in believing, and verified those spiritual experiences which are promised to the faithful, but nations also have been raised from savagery or barbarism to a higher social state. Surely we are at liberty to say that the belief has been acted upon, and that it has been verified.

It requires, however, but little consideration to show that what has really been verified is not at all the supernal character of the Prophet's mission, or the trustworthiness of his authority in matters which we ourselves cannot test, but only his practical wisdom in certain very mundane things. The fact that believers have found joy and peace in believing gives us the right to say that the doctrine is a comfortable doctrine, and pleasant to the soul; but it does not give us the right to say that it is true. And the question which our conscience is always asking about that which we are tempted to believe is not, "Is it comfortable and pleasant?" but, "Is it true?" That the Prophet preached certain doctrines, and predicted that spiritual comfort would be found in them, proves only his sympathy with human nature and his knowledge of it; but it does not prove his superhuman knowledge of theology.

And if we admit for the sake of argument (for it seems that we cannot do more) that the progress made by Moslem nations in certain cases was really due to the system formed and sent forth into the world by Mohammed, we are not at liberty to conclude from this that he was inspired to declare the truth about things which we cannot verify. We are only at liberty to infer the excellence of his moral precepts, or of the means which he devised for so working upon men so as to get them obeyed, or of the social and political machinery which he set up. And it would require a great amount of careful examination into the history of those nations to determine which of these things had the greater share in the result. So that here again it is the Prophet's knowledge of human nature, and his sympathy with it, that are verified; not his divine inspiration or his knowledge of theology.

If there were only one Prophet, indeed, it might well seem a difficult and even an ungracious task to decide upon what points we would trust him, and on what we would doubt his authority; seeing what help and furtherance all men have gained in all ages from those who saw more clearly, who felt more strongly, and who sought the truth with more single heart than their weaker brethren. But there is not only one Prophet; and while the consent of many upon that which, as men, they had real means of knowing and did know, has endured to the end, and been honourably built into the great fabric of human knowledge, the diverse witness of some about that which they did not and could not know remains as a warning to us that to exaggerate the prophetic authority is to misuse it, and to dishonour those who have sought only to help and further us after their power. It is hardly in human nature that a man should quite accurately gauge the limits of his own insight; but it is the duty of those who profit by his work to consider carefully where he may have been carried beyond it. If we must needs embalm his possible errors along with his solid achievements, and use his authority as an excuse for believing what he cannot have known, we make of his goodness an occasion to sin.

To consider only one other such witness: the followers of the Buddha have at least as much right to appeal to individual and social experience in support of the authority of the Eastern saviour. The special mark of his religion, it is said, that in which it has never been surpassed, is the comfort and consolation which it gives to the sick and sorrowful, the tender sympathy with which it soothes and assuages all the natural griefs of men. And surely no triumph of social morality can be greater or nobler than that which has kept nearly half the human race from persecuting in the name of religion. If we are to trust the accounts of his early followers, he believed himself to have come upon earth with a divine and cosmic mission to set rolling the wheel of the law. Being a prince, he divested himself of his kingdom, and of his free will became acquainted with misery, that he might learn how to meet and subdue it. Could such a man speak falsely about solemn things? And as for his knowledge, was he not a man miraculous with powers more than man's? He was born of woman without the help of man; he rose into the air and was transfigured before his kinsmen; at last he went up bodily into heaven from the top of Adam's Peak. Is not his word to be believed in when he testifies of heavenly things?

If there were only he, and no other, with such claims! But there is Mohammed with his testimony; we cannot choose but listen to them both. The Prophet tells us that there is one God, and that we shall live for ever in joy or misery, according as we believe in the Prophet or not. The Buddha says that there is no God, and that we shall be annihilated by and by if we are good enough. Both cannot be infallibly inspired; one or other must have been the victim of a delusion, and thought he knew that which he really did not know. Who shall dare to say which? and how can we justify ourselves in believing that the other was not also deluded?

We are led, then, to these judgments following. The goodness and greatness of a man do not justify us in accepting a belief upon the warrant of his authority, unless there are reasonable grounds for supposing that he knew the truth of what he was saying. And there can be no grounds for supposing that a man knows that which we, without ceasing to be men, could not be supposed to verify.

If a chemist tells me, who am no chemist, that a certain substance can be made by putting together other substances in certain proportions and subjecting them to a known process, I am quite justified in believing this upon his authority, unless I know anything against his character or his judgment. For his professional training is one which tends to encourage veracity and the honest pursuit of truth, and to produce a dislike of hasty conclusions and slovenly investigation. And I have reasonable ground for supposing that he knows the truth of what he is saying, for although I am no chemist, I can be made to understand so much of the methods and processes of the science as makes it conceivable to me that, without ceasing to be man, I might verify the statement. I may never actually verify it, or even see any experiment which goes towards verifying it; but still I have quite reason enough to justify me in believing that the verification is within the reach of human appliances and powers, and in particular that it has been actually performed by my informant. His result, the belief to which he has been led by his inquiries, is valid not only for himself but for others; it is watched and tested by those who are working in the same ground, and who know that no greater service can be rendered to science than the purification of accepted results from the errors which may have crept into them. It is in this way that the result becomes common property, a right object of belief, which is a social affair and matter of public business. Thus it is to be observed that his authority is valid because there are those who question it and verify it; that it is precisely this process of examining and purifying that keeps alive among investigators the love of that which shall stand all possible tests, the sense of public responsibility as of those whose work, if well done, shall remain as the enduring heritage of mankind.

But if my chemist tells me that an atom of oxygen has existed unaltered in weight and rate of vibration throughout all time I have no right to believe this on his authority, for it is a thing which he cannot know without ceasing to be man. He may quite honestly believe that this statement is a fair inference from his experiments, but in that case his judgment is at fault. A very simple consideration of the character of experiments would show him that they never can lead to results of such a kind; that being themselves only approximate and limited, they cannot give us knowledge which is exact and universal. No eminence of character and genius can give a man authority enough to justify us in believing him when he makes statements implying exact or universal knowledge.

Again, an Arctic explorer may tell us that in a given latitude and longitude he has experienced such and such a degree of cold, that the sea was of such a depth, and the ice of such a character. We should be quite right to believe him, in the absence of any stain upon his veracity. It is conceivable that we might, without ceasing to be men, go there and verify his statement; it can be tested by the witness of his companions, and there is adequate ground for supposing that he knows the truth of what he is saying. But if an old whaler tells us that the ice is 300 feet thick all the way up to the Pole, we shall not be justified in believing him. For although the statement may be capable of verification by man, it is certainly not capable of verification by *him*, with any means and appliances which he has possessed; and he must have persuaded himself of the truth of it by some means which does not attach any credit to his testimony. Even if, therefore, the matter affirmed is within the reach of human knowledge, we have no right to accept it upon authority unless it is within the reach of our informant's knowledge.

What shall we say of that authority, more venerable and august than any individual witness, the time-honoured tradition of the human race? An atmosphere of beliefs and conceptions has been formed by the labours and struggles of our forefathers, which enables us to breathe amid the various and complex circumstances of our life. It is around and about us and within us; we cannot think except in the forms and processes of thought which it supplies. Is it possible to doubt and to test it? and if possible, is it right?

We shall find reason to answer that it is not only possible and right, but our bounden duty; that the main purpose of the tradition itself is to supply us with the means of asking questions, of testing and inquiring into things; that if we misuse it, and take it as a collection of cut-and-dried statements to be accepted without further inquiry, we are not only injuring ourselves here, but, by refusing to do our part towards the building up of the fabric which shall be inherited by our children, we are tending to cut off ourselves and our race from the human line.

Let us first take care to distinguish a kind of tradition which especially requires to be examined and called in question, because it especially shrinks from inquiry. Suppose that a medicine-man in Central Africa tells his tribe that a certain powerful medicine in his tent will be propitiated if they kill their cattle, and that the tribe believe him. Whether the medicine was propitiated or not there are no means of verifying, but the cattle are gone. Still the belief may be kept up in the tribe that propitiation has been effected in this way; and in a later generation it will be all the easier for another medicine-man to persuade them to a similar act. Here the only reason for belief is that everybody has believed the thing for so long that it must be true. And yet the belief was founded on fraud, and has been propagated by credulity. That man will undoubtedly do right, and be a friend of men, who shall call it in question and see that there is no evidence for it, help his neighbours to see as he does, and even, if need be, go into the holy tent and break the medicine.

The rule which should guide us in such cases is simple and obvious enough: that the aggregate testimony of our neighbours is subject to the same conditions as the testimony of any one of them. Namely, we have no right to believe a thing true because everybody says so unless there are good grounds for believing that some one person at least has the means of knowing what is true, and is speaking the truth so far as he knows it. However many nations and generations of men are brought into the witness-box they cannot testify to anything which they do not know. Every man who has accepted the statement from somebody, else, without himself testing and verifying it, is out of court; his word is worth nothing at all. And when we get back at last to the true birth and beginning of the statement, two serious questions must be disposed of in regard to him who first made it: was he mistaken in thinking that he *knew* about this matter, or was he lying?

This last question is unfortunately a very actual and practical one even to us at this day and in this country. We have no occasion to go to La Salette, or to Central Africa, or to Lourdes, for examples of immoral and debasing superstition. It is only too possible for a child to grow up in London surrounded by an atmosphere of beliefs fit only for the savage, which have in our own time been founded in fraud and propagated by credulity.

Laying aside, then, such tradition as is handed on without testing by successive generations, let us consider that which is truly built up out of the common experience of mankind. This great fabric is for the guidance of our thoughts, and through them of our actions, both in the moral and in the material world. In the moral world, for example, it gives us the conceptions of right in general, of justice, of truth, of beneficence, and the like. These are given as conceptions, not as statements or propositions; they answer to certain definite instincts which are certainly within us, however they came there. That it is right to be beneficent is matter of immediate personal experience; for when a man retires within himself and there finds something, wider and more lasting than his solitary personality, which says, "I want to do right," as well as, "I want to do good to man," he can verify by direct observation that one instinct is founded upon and agrees fully with the other. And it is his duty so to verify this and all similar statements.

The tradition says also, at a definite place and time, that such and such actions are just, or true, or beneficent. For all such rules a further inquiry is necessary, since they are sometimes established by an authority other than that of the moral sense founded on experience. Until recently, the moral tradition of our own country—and indeed of all Europe—taught that it was beneficent to give money indiscriminately to beggars. But the questioning of this rule, and investigation into it, led men to see that true beneficence is that which helps a man to do the work which he is most fitted for, not that which keeps and encourages him in idleness; and that to neglect this distinction in the present is to prepare pauperism and misery for the future. By this testing and discussion not only has practice been purified and made more beneficent, but the very conception of beneficence has been made wider and wiser. Now here the great social heirloom consists of two parts: the instinct of beneficence, which makes a certain side of our nature, when predominant, wish to do good to men; and the intellectual conception of beneficence, which we can compare with any proposed course of conduct and ask, "Is this beneficent or not?" By the continual asking and answering of such questions the conception grows in breadth and distinctness, and the instinct becomes strengthened and purified. It appears, then, that the great use of the conception, the intellectual part of the heirloom, is to enable us to ask questions; that it grows and is kept straight by means of these questions; and if we do not use it for that purpose we shall gradually lose it altogether, and be left with a mere code of regulations which cannot rightly be called morality at all.

Such considerations apply even more obviously and clearly, if possible, to the store of beliefs and conceptions which our fathers have amassed for us in respect of the material world. We are ready to laugh at the rule of thumb of the Australian who continues to tie his hatchet to the side of the handle, although the Birmingham fitter has made a hole on purpose for him to put the handle in. His people have tied up hatchets so for ages: who is he that he should set himself up against their wisdom? He has sunk so low that he cannot do what some of them must have done in the far distant past—call in question an established usage, and invent or learn something better. Yet here, in the dim beginning of knowledge, where science and art are one, we find only the same simple rule which applies to the highest and deepest growths of that cosmic Tree; to its loftiest flower-tipped branches as well as to the profoundest of its hidden roots; the rule, namely, that what is stored up and handed down to us is rightly used by those who act as the makers acted, when they stored it up; those who use it to ask further questions, to examine, to investigate; who try honestly and solemnly to find out what is the right way of looking at things and of dealing with them.

A question rightly asked is already half answered, said Jacobi; we may add that the method of solution is the other half of the answer, and that the actual result counts for nothing by the side of these two. For an example let us go to the telegraph, where theory and practice, grown each to years of discretion, are marvellously wedded for the fruitful service of men. Ohm found that the strength of an electric current is directly proportional to the strength of the battery which produces it, and inversely as the length of the wire along which it has to travel. This is called Ohm's law; but the result, regarded as a statement to be believed, is not the valuable part of it. The first half is the question: what relation holds good between these quantities? So put, the question involves already the conception of strength of current, and of strength of battery, as quantities to be measured and compared; it hints clearly that these are the things to be attended to in the study of electric currents. The second half is the method of investigation; how to measure these quantities, what instruments are required for the experiment, and how are they to be used? The student who begins to learn about electricity is not asked to believe in Ohm's law: he is made to understand the question, he is placed before the apparatus, and he is taught to verify it. He learns to do things, not to think he knows things, to use instruments and to ask questions, not to accept a traditional statement. The question which required a genius to ask it rightly is answered by a tiro. If Ohm's law were suddenly lost and forgotten by all men, while the question and the method of solution remained, the result could be rediscovered in an hour. But the result by itself, if known to a people who could not comprehend the value of the question or the means of solving it, would be like a watch in the hands of a savage who could not wind it up, or an iron steamship worked by Spanish engineers.

In regard, then, to the sacred tradition of humanity, we learn that it consists, not in propositions or statements which are to be accepted and believed on the authority of the tradition, but in questions rightly asked, in conceptions which enable us to ask further questions, and in methods of answering questions. The value of all these things depends on their being tested day by day. The very sacredness of the precious deposit imposes upon us the duty and the responsibility of testing it, of purifying and enlarging it to the utmost of our power. He who makes use of its results to stifle his own doubts, or to hamper the inquiry of others, is guilty of a sacrilege which centuries shall never be able to blot out. When the labours and questionings of honest and brave men shall have built up the fabric of known truth to a glory which we in this generation can neither hope for nor imagine, in that pure and holy temple he shall have no part nor lot, but his name and his works shall be cast out into the darkness of oblivion for ever.

The Limits of Inference

The question in what cases we may believe that which goes beyond our experience, is a very large and delicate one, extending to the whole range of scientific method, and requiring a considerable increase in the application of it before it can be answered with anything approaching to completeness. But one rule, lying on the threshold of the subject, of extreme simplicity and vast practical importance, may here be touched upon and shortly laid down.

A little reflection will show us that every belief, even the simplest and most fundamental, goes beyond experience when regarded as a guide to our actions. A burnt child dreads the fire, because it believes that the fire will burn it to-day just as it did yesterday; but this belief goes beyond experience, and assumes that the unknown fire of to-day is like the known fire of yesterday. Even the belief that the child was burnt yesterday goes beyond *present* experience, which contains only the memory of a burning, and not the burning itself; it assumes, therefore, that this memory is trustworthy, although we know that a memory may often be mistaken. But if it is to be used as a guide to action, as a hint of what the future is to be, it must assume something about that future, namely, that it will be consistent with the supposition that the burning really took place yesterday; which is going beyond experience. Even the fundamental "I am," which cannot be doubted, is no guide to action until it takes to itself "I shall be," which goes beyond experience. The question is not, therefore, "May we believe what goes beyond experience?" for this is involved in the very nature of belief; but "How far and in what manner may we add to our experience in forming our beliefs?"

And an answer, of utter simplicity and universality, is suggested by the example we have taken: a burnt child dreads the fire. We may go beyond experience by assuming that what we do not know is like what we do know; or, in other words, we may add to our experience on the assumption of a uniformity in nature. What this uniformity precisely is, how we grow in the knowledge of it from generation to generation, these are questions which for the present we lay aside, being content to examine two instances which may serve to make plainer the nature of the rule.

From certain observations made with the spectroscope, we infer the existence of hydrogen in the sun. By looking into the spectroscope when the sun is shining on its slit, we see certain definite bright lines: and experiments made upon bodies on the earth have taught us that when these bright lines are seen hydrogen is the source of them. We assume, then, that the unknown bright lines in the sun are like the known bright lines of the laboratory, and that hydrogen in the sun behaves as hydrogen under similar circumstances would behave on the earth.

But are we not trusting our spectroscope too much? Surely, having found it to be trustworthy for terrestrial substances, where its statements can be verified by man, we are justified in accepting its testimony in other like cases; but not when it gives us information about things in the sun, where its testimony cannot be directly verified by man?

Certainly, we want to know a little more before this inference can be justified; and fortunately we do know this. The spectroscope testifies to exactly the same thing in the two cases; namely, that light-vibrations of a certain rate are being sent through it. Its construction is such that if it were wrong about this in one case, it would be wrong in the other. When we come to look into the matter, we find that we have really assumed the matter of the sun to be like the matter of the earth, made up of a certain number of distinct substances; and that each of these, when very hot, has a distinct rate of vibration, by which it may be recognised and singled out from the rest. But this is the kind of assumption which we are justified in using when we add to our experience. It is an assumption of uniformity in nature, and can only be checked by comparison with many similar assumptions which we have to make in other such cases.

But is this a true belief, of the existence of hydrogen in the sun? Can it help in the right guidance of human action?

Certainly not, if it is accepted on unworthy grounds, and without some understanding of the process by which it is got at. But when this process is taken in as the ground of the belief, it becomes a very serious and practical matter. For if there is no hydrogen in the sun, the spectroscope—that is to say, the measurement of rates of vibration—must be an uncertain guide in recognising different substances; and consequently it ought not to be used in chemical analysis—in assaying, for example—to the great saving of time, trouble, and money. Whereas the acceptance of the spectroscopic method as trustworthy has enriched us not only with new metals, which is a great thing, but with new processes of investigation, which is vastly greater.

For another example, let us consider the way in which we infer the truth of an historical event — say the siege of Syracuse in the Peloponnesian war. Our experience is that manuscripts exist which are said to be and which call themselves manuscripts of the history of Thucydides; that in other manuscripts, stated to be by later historians, he is described as living during the time of the war; and that books, supposed to date from the revival of learning, tell us how these manuscripts had been preserved and were then acquired. We find also that men do not, as a rule, forge books and histories without a special motive; we assume that in this respect men in the past were like men in the present; and we observe that in this case no special motive was present. That is, we add to our experience on the assumption of a uniformity in the characters of men. Because our knowledge of this uniformity is far less complete and exact than our knowledge of that which obtains in physics, inferences of the historical kind are more precarious and less exact than inferences in many other sciences.

But if there is any special reason to suspect the character of the persons who wrote or transmitted certain books, the case becomes altered. If a group of documents give internal evidence that they were produced among people who forged books in the names of others, and who, in describing events, suppressed those things which did not suit them, while they amplified such as did suit them; who not only committed these crimes, but gloried in them as proofs of humility and zeal; then we must say that upon such documents no true historical inference can be founded, but only unsatisfactory conjecture.

We may, then, add to our experience on the assumption of a uniformity in nature; we may fill in our picture of what is and has been, as experience gives it us, in such a way as to make the whole consistent with this uniformity. And practically demonstrative inference—that which gives us a right to believe in the result of it—is a clear showing that in no other way than by the truth of this result can the uniformity of nature be saved.

No evidence, therefore, can justify us in believing the truth of a statement which is contrary to, or outside of, the uniformity of nature. If our experience is such that it cannot be filled up consistently with uniformity, all we have a right to conclude is that there is something wrong somewhere; but the possibility of inference is taken away; we must rest in our experience, and not go beyond it at all. If an event really happened which was not a part of the uniformity of nature, it would have two properties: no evidence could give the right to believe it to any except those whose actual experience it was; and no inference worthy of belief could be founded upon it at all.

Are we then bound to believe that nature is absolutely and universally uniform? Certainly not; we have no right to believe anything of this kind. The rule only tells us that in forming beliefs which go beyond our experience, we may make the assumption that nature is practically uniform so far as we are concerned. Within the range of human action and verification, we may form, by help of this assumption, actual beliefs; beyond it, only those hypotheses which serve for the more accurate asking of questions.

To sum up:—

We may believe what goes beyond our experience, only when it is inferred from that experience by the assumption that what we do not know is like what we know.

We may believe the statement of another person, when there is reasonable ground for supposing that he knows the matter of which he speaks, and that he is speaking the truth so far as he knows it.

It is wrong in all cases to believe on insufficient evidence; and where it is presumption to doubt and to investigate, there it is worse than presumption to believe.

Kierkegaard's Arguments Against Objective Reasoning in Religion

Robert Merrihew Adams

It is sometimes held that there is something in the nature of religious faith itself that renders it useless or undesirable to reason objectively in support of such faith, even if the reasoning should happen to have considerable plausibility. Søren Kierkegaard's *Concluding Unscientific Postscript* is probably the document most commonly cited as representative of this view. In the present essay I shall discuss three arguments for the view. I call them the Approximation Argument, the Postponement Argument, and the Passion Argument; and I suggest they can all be found in the *Postscript*. I shall try to show that the Approximation Argument is a bad argument. The other two will not be so easily disposed of, however. I believe they show that Kierkegaard's conclusion, or something like it, does indeed follow from a certain conception of religiousness—a conception which has some appeal, although for reasons which I shall briefly suggest, I am not prepared to accept it.

Kierkegaard uses the word "objective" and its cognates in several senses, most of which need not concern us here. We are interested in the sense in which he uses it when he says, "it is precisely a misunderstanding to seek an objective assurance," and when he speaks of "an objective uncertainty held fast in the appropriation-process of the most passionate inwardness" (pp. 41, 182).1 Let us say that a piece of reasoning, *R,* is *objective reasoning* just in case every (or almost every) intelligent, fair-minded, and sufficiently informed person would regard *R* as showing or tending to show (in the circumstances in which *R* is used, and to the extent claimed in *R*) that *R's* conclusion is true or probably true. Uses of "objective" and "objectively" in other contexts can be understood from their relation to this one; for example, an objective uncertainty is a proposition which cannot be shown by objective reasoning to be certainly true.

The Approximation Argument

"Is it possible to base an eternal happiness upon historical knowledge?" is one of the central questions in the *Postscript,* and in the *Philosophical Fragments* to which it is a "postscript." Part of Kierkegaard's answer to the question is that it is not possible to base an eternal happiness on objective reasoning about historical facts.

> For nothing is more readily evident than that the greatest attainable certainty with respect to anything historical is merely an *approximation*. And an approximation, when viewed as a basis for an eternal happiness, is wholly inadequate, since the incommensurability makes a result impossible. [p. 25]

Kierkegaard maintains that it is possible, however, to base an eternal happiness on a belief in historical facts that is independent of objective evidence for them, and that that is what one must do in order to be a Christian. This is the Approximation Argument for the proposition that Christian faith cannot be based on objective reasoning.[2] (It is assumed that some belief about historical facts is an essential part of Christian faith, so that if religious faith cannot be based on objective historical reasoning, then Christian faith cannot be based on objective reasoning at all.) Let us examine the argument in detail.

Its first premise is Kierkegaard's claim that "the greatest attainable certainty with respect to anything historical is merely an approximation." I take him to mean that historical evidence, objectively considered, never completely excludes the possibility of error. "It goes without saying," he claims, "that it is impossible in the case of historical problems to reach an objective decision so certain that no doubt could disturb it" (p. 41). For Kierkegaard's purposes it does not matter how small the possibility of error is, so long as it is finitely small (that is, so long as it is not literally infinitesimal). He insists (p. 31) that his Approximation Argument makes no appeal to the supposition that the objective evidence for Christian historical beliefs is weaker than the objective evidence for any other historical belief. The argument turns on a claim about *all* historical evidence. The probability of error in our belief that there was an American Civil War in the nineteenth century, for instance, might be as small as $\frac{1}{10^{2,000,000}}$; that would be a large enough chance of error for Keirkegaard's argument.

It might be disputed, but let us assume for the sake of argument that there is some such finitely small probability of error in the objective grounds for all historical beliefs, as Kierkegaard held, This need not keep us from saying that we "know," and it is "certain," that there was an American Civil War. For such an absurdly small possibility of error is as good as no possibility of error at all, "for all practical intents and purposes," as we might say. Such a possibility of error is too small to be worth worrying about.

But would it be too small to be worth worrying about if we had an *infinite* passionate interest in the question about the Civil War? If we have an infinite passionate interest in something, there is no limit to how important it is to us. (The nature of such an interest will be discussed more fully in section 3 below.) Kierkegaard maintains that in relation to an infinite passionate interest *no* possibility of error is too small to be worth worrying about. "In relation to an eternal happiness, and an infinite passionate interest in its behalf (in which latter alone the former can exist), an iota is of importance, of infinite importance . . ." (p. 28). This is the basis for the second premise of the Approximation Argument, which is Kierkegaard's claim that "an approximation, when viewed as a basis for an eternal happiness, is wholly inadequate" (p. 25). "An approximation is essentially incommensurable with an infinite personal interest in an eternal happiness" (p. 26).

At this point in the argument it is important to have some understanding of Kierkegaard's conception of faith, and the way in which he thinks faith excludes doubt. Faith must be decisive; in fact it seems to consist in a sort of decision-making. "The conclusion of belief is not so much a conclusion as a resolution, and it is for this reason that belief excludes doubt."[3] The decision of faith is a decision to disregard the possibility of error—to act on what is believed, without hedging one's bets to take account of any possibility of error.

To disregard the possibility of error is not to be unaware of it, or fail to consider it, or lack anxiety about it. Kierkegaard insists that the believer must be keenly *aware* of the risk of error. "If I wish to preserve myself in faith I must constantly be intent upon holding fast the objective uncertainty. so as to remain out upon the deep, over seventy thousand fathoms of water, still preserving my faith" (p. 182).

For Kierkegaard, then, to ask whether faith in a historical fact can be based on objective reasoning is to ask whether objective reasoning can justify one in disregarding the possibility of error which (he thinks) historical evidence always leaves. Here another aspect of Kierkegaard's conception of faith plays its part in the argument. He thinks that in all genuine religious faith the believer is *infinitely* interested in the object of his faith. And he thinks it follows that objective reasoning cannot justify him in disregarding *any* possibility of error about the object of faith, and therefore cannot lead him all the way to religious faith where a historical fact is concerned. The farthest it could lead him is to the conclusion that *if* he had only a certain finite (though very great) interest in the matter, the possibility of error would be too small to be worth worrying about and he would be justified in disregarding it. But faith disregards a possibility of error that *is* worth worrying about, since an infinite interest is involved. Thus faith requires a "leap" beyond the evidence, a leap that cannot be justified by objective reasoning (cf. p. 90).

There is something right in what Kierkegaard is saying here, but his Approximation Argument is a bad argument. He is right in holding that grounds of doubt which may be insignificant for most practical purposes can be extremely troubling for the intensity of a religious concern, and that it may require great decisiveness, or something like courage, to overcome them religiously. But he is mistaken in holding that objective reasoning could not justify one in disregarding any possibility of error about something in which one is infinitely interested.

The mistake, I believe, lies in his overlooking the fact that there are at least two different reasons one might have for disregarding a possibility of error. The first is that the possibility is too small to be worth worrying about. The second is that the risk of not disregarding the possibility of error would be greater than the risk of disregarding it. Of these two reasons only the first is ruled out by the infinite passionate interest.

I will illustrate this point with two examples, one secular and one religious. A certain woman has a very great (though not infinite) interest in her husband's love for her. She rightly judges that the objective evidence available to her renders it 99.9% probable that he loves her truly. The intensity of her interest is sufficient to cause her some *anxiety* over the remaining 1/1,000 chance that he loves her not; for her this chance is not too small to be worth worrying about. (Kierkegaard uses a similar example to support his Approximation Argument; see p. 511.) But she (very reasonably) wants to *disregard* the risk of error, in the sense of not hedging her bets, if he does love her. This desire is at least as strong as her desire not to be deceived if he does not love her. Objective reasoning should therefore suffice to bring her to the conclusion that she ought to disregard the risk of error, since by not disregarding it she would run 999 times as great risk of frustrating one of these desires.

Or suppose you are trying to base your eternal happiness on your relation to Jesus, and therefore have an infinite passionate interest in the question whether he declared Peter and his episcopal successors to be infallible in matters of religious doctrine. You want to be committed to whichever is the true belief on this question, disregarding any possibility of error in it. And suppose, just for the sake of argument, that objective historical evidence renders it 99% probable that Jesus did declare Peter and his successors to be infallible—or 99% probable that he did not—for our present discussion it does not matter which. The one per cent chance of error is enough to make you *anxious*, in view of your infinite interest. But objective reasoning leads to the conclusion that you ought to commit yourself to the more probable opinion, *disregarding* the risk of error, if your strongest desire in the matter is to be so committed to be true opinion. For the only other way to satisfy this desire would be to commit yourself to the less probable opinion, disregarding the risk of error in it. The first way will be successful if and only if the more probable opinion is true, and the second way if and only if the less probable opinion is true. Surely it is prudent to do what gives you a 99% chance of satisfying your strong desire, in preference to what gives you only a one per cent chance of satisfying it.

In this argument your strong desire to be committed to the true opinion is presupposed. The reasonableness of this desire may depend on a belief for which no probability can be established by purely historical reasoning, such as the belief that Jesus is God. But any difficulties arising from this point are distinct from those urged in the

Approximation Argument, which itself presupposes the infinite passionate interest in the historical question.

There is some resemblance between my arguments in these examples and Pascal's famous Wager argument. But whereas Pascal's argument turns on weighing an infinite interest against a finite one, mine turn on weighing a large chance of success against a small one. An argument closer to Pascal's will be discussed in section 4 below.

The reader may well have noticed in the foregoing discussion some un-clarity about what sort of justification is being demanded and given for religious beliefs about historical facts. There are at least two different types of question about a proposition which I might try to settle by objective reasoning: (1) Is it probable that the proposition is true? (2) In view of the evidence which I have for and against the proposition, and my interest in the matter, is it prudent for me to have faith in the truth of the proposition, disregarding the possibility of error? Correspondingly, we may distinguish two ways in which a belief can be *based on* objective reasoning. The proposition believed may be the conclusion of a piece of objective reasoning, and accepted because it is that. We may say that such a belief is *objectively probable.* Or one might hold a belief or maintain a religious faith because of a piece of objective reasoning whose conclusion is that it would be prudent, morally right, or otherwise desirable for one to hold that belief or faith. In this latter case let us say that the belief is *objectively advantageous.* It is clear that historical beliefs can be objectively probable; and in the Approximation Argument, Kierkegaard does not deny Christian historical beliefs can be objectively probable. His thesis is, in effect, that in view of an infinite passionate interest in their subject matter, they cannot be objectively advantageous, and therefore cannot be fully justified objectively, even if they are objectively probable. It is this thesis that I have attempted to refute. I have not been discussing the question whether Christian historical beliefs are objectively probable.

The Postponement Argument

The trouble with objective historical reasoning, according to the Approximation Argument, is that it cannot yield complete certainty. But that is not Kierkegaard's only complaint against it as a basis for religious faith. He also objects that objective historical inquiry is never completely finished, so that one who seeks to base his faith on it postpones his religious commitment forever. In the process of historical research "new difficulties arise and are overcome, and new difficulties again arise. Each generation inherits from its predecessor the illusion that the method is quite impeccable, but the learned scholars have not yet succeeded . . . and so forth. . . . The infinite personal passionate interest of the subject . . . vanishes more and more, because the decision is postponed, and postponed as following directly upon the result of the learned inquiry" (p. 28). As soon as we take "an historical document" as "our standard for the determination of Christian truth," we are "involved in a parenthesis whose conclusion is everlastingly prospective" (p. 28)—that is, we are involved in a religious digression which keeps religious commitment forever in the future.[4]

Kierkegaard has such fears about allowing religious faith to rest on *any* empirical reasoning. The danger of postponement of commitment arises not only from the uncertainties of historical scholarship, but also in connection with the design argument for God's existence. In the *Philosophical Fragments* Kierkegaard notes some objections to the attempt to prove God's existence from evidence of "the wisdom in nature, the goodness, the wisdom in the governance of the world," and then says, "even if I began I would never finish, and would in addition have to live constantly in suspense, lest something so terrible should suddenly happen that my bit of proof would be demolished."[5] What we have before us is a quite general sort of objection to the treatment of religious beliefs as empirically testable. On this point many analytical philosophers seem to agree with

Kierkegaard. Much discussion in recent analytical philosophy of religion has proceeded from the supposition that religious beliefs are not empirically testable. I think it is far from obvious that that supposition is correct; and it is interesting to consider arguments that may be advanced to support it.

Kierkegaard's statements suggest an argument that I call the Postponement Argument. Its first premise is that one cannot have an authentic religious faith without being totally committed to it. In order to be totally committed to a belief, in the relevant sense, one must be determined not to abandon the belief under any circumstances that one recognizes as epistemically possible.

The second premise is that one cannot yet be totally committed to any belief which one bases on an inquiry in which one recognizes any possibility of a future need to revise the results. Total commitment to any belief so based will necessarily be postponed. I believe that this premise, suitably interpreted, is true. Consider the position of someone who regards himself as committed to a belief on the basis of objective evidence, but who recognizes some possibility that future discoveries will destroy the objective justification of the belief. We must ask how he is disposed to react in the event, however unlikely, that the objective basis of his belief is overthrown. Is he prepared to abandon the belief in that event? If so, he is not totally committed to the belief in the relevant sense. But if he is determined to cling to his belief even if its objective justification is taken away, then he is not basing the belief on the objective justification—or at least he is not basing it solely on the justification.[6]

The conclusion to be drawn from these two premises is that authentic religious faith cannot be based on an inquiry in which one recognizes any possibility of a future need to revise the results. We ought to note that this conclusion embodies two important restrictions on the scope of the argument.

In the first place, we are not given an argument that authentic religious faith cannot *have* an objective justification that is subject to possible future revision. What we are given is an argument that the authentic believer's holding of his religious belief cannot *depend* entirely on such a justification.

In the second place, this conclusion applies only to those who *recognize* some epistemic possibility that the objective results which appear to support their belief may be overturned. I think it would be unreasonable to require, as part of total commitment, a determination with regard to one's response to circumstances that one does not recognize as possible at all. It may be, however, that one does not recognize such a possibility when one ought to.

Kierkegaard needs one further premise in order to arrive at the conclusion that authentic religious faith cannot without error be based on any objective empirical reasoning. This third premise is that in every objective empirical inquiry there is always, objectively considered, some epistemic possibility that the results of the inquiry will need to be revised in view of new evidence or new reasoning. I believe Kierkegaard makes this assumption; he certainly makes it with regard to historical inquiry. From this premise it follows that one is in error if in any objective empirical inquiry one does not recognize any possibility of a future need to revise the results. But if one does recognize such a possibility, then according to the conclusion already reached in the Postponement Argument, one cannot base an authentic religious faith on the inquiry.

Some philosophers might attack the third premise of this argument; and certainly it is controversial. But I am more inclined to criticize the first premise. There is undoubtedly something plausible about the claim that authentic religious faith must involve a commitment so complete that the believer is resolved not to abandon his belief under any circumstances that he regards as epistemically possible. If you are willing to abandon your ostensibly religious beliefs for the sake of objective inquiry, mightn't we justly say that objective inquiry is your real religion, the thing to which you are most deeply committed?

There is also something plausible to be said on the other side, however. It has commonly been thought to be an important part of religious ethics that one ought to be humble, teachable, open to correction, new inspiration, and growth of insight, even (and perhaps especially) in important religious beliefs. That view would have to be discarded if we were to concede to Kierkegaard that the heart of commitment in religion is an unconditional determination not to change in one's important religious beliefs. In fact I think there is something radically wrong with this conception of religious commitment, Faith ought not to be thought of as unconditional devotion to a belief. For in the first place the object of religious devotion is not a belief or attitude of one's own, but God. And in the second place it may be doubted that religious devotion to God can or should be completely unconditional. God's love for sinners is sometimes said to be completely unconditional, not being based on any excellence or merit of theirs. But religious devotion to God is generally thought to be based on His goodness and love, It is the part of the strong, not the weak, to love unconditionally. And in relation to God we are weak.

The Passion Argument

In Kierkegaard's statements of the Approximation Argument and the Postponement Argument it is assumed that a system of religious beliefs might be objectively probable. It is only for the sake of argument, however, that Kierkegaard allows this assumption. He really holds that religious faith, by its very nature, needs objective *im*probablity. "Anything that is almost probable, or probable, or extremely and emphatically probable, is something [one] can almost know, or as good as know, or extremely and emphatically almost *know*—but it is impossible to *believe*" (p. 189). Nor will Kierkegaard countenance the suggestion that religion ought to go beyond belief to some almost-knowledge based on probability. "Faith is the highest passion in a man. There are perhaps many in every generation who do not even reach it, but no one gets further."[7] It would be a betrayal of religion to try to go beyond faith. The suggestion that faith might be replaced by "probabilities and guarantees" is for the believer "a temptation to be resisted with all his strength" (p. 15). The attempt to establish religious beliefs on a foundation of objective probability is therefore no service to religion, but inimical to religion's true interests. The approximation to certainty which might be afforded by objective probability is rejected, not only for the reasons given in the Approximation Argument and Postponement Argument, but also from a deeper motive, "since on the contrary it behooves us to get rid of introductory guarantees of security, proofs from consequences, and the whole mob of public pawnbrokers and guarantors, so as to permit the absurd to stand out in all its clarity—in order that the individual may believe if he wills it; I merely say that it must be strenuous in the highest degree so to believe" (p. 190).

As this last quotation indicates, Kierkegaard thinks that religious belief ought to be based on a strenuous exertion of the will—a passionate striving. His reasons for thinking that objective probability is religiously undesirable have to do with the place of passion in religion, and constitute what I call the Passion Argument. The first premise of the argument is that the most essential and the most valuable feature of religiousness is passion, indeed an infinite passion, a passion of the greatest possible intensity. The second premise is that an infinite passion requires objective improbability. And the conclusion therefore is that that which is most essential and most valuable in religiousness requires objective improbability.

My discussion of this argument will have three parts. (a) First I will try to clarify, very briefly, what it is that is supposed to be objectively improbable. (b) Then we will consider Kierkegaard's reasons for holding that infinite passion requires objective improbability. In so doing we will also gain a clearer understanding of what a Kierkegaardian infinite passion is. (c) Finally I will discuss the first premise of the argument—although issues will arise at that point which I do not pretend to be able to settle by argument.

a. What are the beliefs whose improbability is needed by religious passion? Kierkegaard will hardly be satisfied with the improbability of just any one belief; it must surely be at least an important belief. On the other hand it would clearly be preposterous to suppose that every belief involved in Christianity must be objectively improbable. (Consider, for example, the belief that the man Jesus did indeed live.) I think that what is demanded in the Passion Argument is the objective improbability of at least one belief which must be true if the goal sought by the religious passion is to be attained.

b. We can find in the *Postscript* suggestions of several reasons for thinking that an infinite passion needs objective improbability. The two that seem to me most interesting have to do with (i) the risks accepted and (ii) the costs paid in pursuance of a passionate interest.

i. One reason that Kierkegaard has for valuing objective improbability is that it increases the *risk* attaching to the religious life, and risk is so essential for the expression of religious passion that "without risk there is no faith" (p. 182). About the nature of an eternal happiness, the goal of religious striving, Kierkegaard says "there is nothing to be said . . . except that it is the good which is attained by venturing everything absolutely" (p. 382).

But what then does it mean to venture? A venture is the precise correlative of an uncertainty; when the certainty is there the venture becomes impossible. . . . If what I hope to gain by venturing is itself certain, I do not risk or venture, but make an exchange. . . . No, if I am in truth resolved to venture, in truth resolved to strive for the attainment of the highest good, the uncertainty must be there, and I must have room to move, so to speak. But the largest space I can obtain, where there is room for the most vehement gesture of the passion that embraces the infinite, is uncertainty of knowledge with respect to an eternal happiness, or the certain knowledge that the choice is in the finite sense a piece of madness: now there is room, now you can venture! [pp. 380–82]

How is it that objective improbability provides the largest space for the most vehement gesture of infinite passion? Consider two cases. (A) You plunge into a raging torrent to rescue from drowning someone you love, who is crying for help. (B) You plunge into a raging torrent in a desperate attempt to rescue someone you love, who appears to be unconscious and *may* already have drowned. In both cases you manifest a passionate interest in saving the person, risking your own life in order to do so. But I think Kierkegaard would say there is more passion in the second case than in the first. For in the second case you risk your life in what is, objectively considered, a smaller chance that you will be able to save your loved one. A greater passion is required for a more desperate attempt.

A similar assessment may be made of the following pair of cases. (A′) You stake everything on your faith in the truth of Christianity, knowing that it is objectively 99% probable that Christianity is true. (B′) You stake everything on your faith in the truth of Christianity, knowing that the truth of Christianity is, objectively, possible but so improbable that its probability is, say, as small as $\frac{1}{10^{2,000,000}}$. There is passion in both cases, but Kierkegaard will say that there is more passion in the second case than in the first. For to venture the same stake (namely, everything) on a much smaller chance of success shows greater passion.

Acceptance of risk can thus be seen as a *measure* of the intensity of passion. I believe this provides us with one way of understanding what Kierkegaard means when he calls religious passion "infinite." An *infinite* passionate interest in x is an interest so strong that it leads one to make the greatest possible sacrifices in order to obtain x, on the smallest possible chance of success. The infinity of the passion is shown in that there is no sacrifice so great one will not make it, and no chance of success so small one will not act on it. A passion which is infinite in this sense requires, by its very nature, a situation of maximum risk for its expression.

It will doubtless be objected that this argument involves a misunderstanding of what a passionate interest is. Such an interest is a disposition. In order to have a great passionate interest it is not necessary actually to make a great sacrifice with a small chance of success; all that is necessary is to have such an intense interest that one *would* do so if an appropriate occasion should arise. It is therefore a mistake to say that there *is* more passion in case (B) than in case (A), or in (B′) than in (A′). More passion is *shown* in (B) than in (A), and in (B′) than in (A′); but an equal passion may exist in cases in which there is no occasion to show it.

This objection may well be correct as regards what we normally mean by "passionate interest." But that is not decisive for the argument. The crucial question is what part dispositions, possibly unactualized, ought to play in religious devotion. And here we must have a digression about the position of the *Postscript* on this question—a position that is complex at best and is not obviously consistent.

In the first place I do not think that Kierkegaard would be prepared to think of passion, or a passionate interest, as primarily a disposition that might remain unactualized. He seems to conceive of passion chiefly as an intensity in what one actually does and feels. "Passion is momentary" (p. 178), although capable of continual repetition. And what is momentary in such a way that it must be repeated rather than protracted is presumably an occurrence rather than a disposition. It agrees with this conception of passion that Kierkegaard idealizes a life of "persistent striving," and says that the religious task is to "exercise" the God-relationship and to give "existential expression" to the religious choice (pp. 110, 364, 367).

All of this supports the view that what Kierkegaard means by "an infinite passionate interest" is a pattern of actual decision-making, in which one continually exercises and expresses one's religiousness by making the greatest possible sacrifices on the smallest possible chance of success. In order to actualize such a pattern of life one needs chances of success that are as small as possible. That is the room that is required for "the most vehement gesture" of infinite passion.

But on the other hand Kierkegaard does allow a dispositional element in the religious life, and even precisely in the making of the greatest possible sacrifices. We might suppose that if we are to make the greatest possible sacrifices in our religious devotion, we must do so by abandoning all worldly interests and devoting all our time and attention to religion. That is what monasticism attempts to do, as Kierkegaard sees it; and (in the *Postscript,* at any rate) he rejects the attempt, contrary to what our argument to this point would have led us to expect of him. He holds that "resignation" (pp. 353, 367) or "renunciation" (pp. 362, 386) of *all* finite ends is precisely the first thing that religiousness requires; but he means a renunciation that is compatible with pursuing and enjoying finite ends (pp. 362–71). This renunciation is the practice of a sort of detachment; Kierkegaard uses the image of a dentist loosening the soft tissues around a tooth, while it is still in place, in preparation for pulling it (p. 367). It is partly a matter of not treating finite things with a desperate seriousness, but with a certain coolness or humor, even while one pursues them (pp. 368, 370).

This coolness is not just a disposition. But the renunciation also has a dispositional aspect. "Now if for any individual an eternal happiness is his highest good, this will mean that all finite satisfactions are volitionally relegated to the status of what may have to be renounced in favor of an eternal happiness" (p. 350). The volitional relegation is not a disposition but an act of choice. The object of this choice, however, appears to be a dispositional state—the state of being such that one *would* forgo any finite satisfaction *if* it *were* religiously necessary or advantageous to do so.

It seems clear that Kierkegaard, in the *Postscript,* is willing to admit a dispositional element at one point in the religious venture, but not at another. It is enough in most cases, he thinks, if one is *prepared* to cease for the sake of religion from pursuing some finite end; but it is not enough that one *would* hold to one's belief in the face of objective improbability. The belief must actually be improbable, although the pursuit of the finite need not actually cease. What is not clear is a reason for this disparity. The following hypothesis, admittedly somewhat speculative as interpretation of the text, is the best explanation I can offer.

The admission of a dispositional element in the religious renunciation of the finite is something to which Kierkegaard seems to be driven by the view that there is no alternative to it except idolatry, For suppose one actually ceases from all worldly pursuits and enters a monastery. In the monastery one would pursue a number of particular ends (such as getting up in the middle of the night to say the offices) which, although religious in a way ("churchy," one might say), are still finite. The absolute *telos* or end of religion is no more to be identified with them than with the ends pursued by an alderman (pp. 362–71). To pretend otherwise would be to make an idolatrous identification of the absolute end with some finite end. An existing person cannot have sacrificed everything by actually having ceased from pursuing *all* finite ends. For as long as he lives and acts he is pursuing some finite end. Therefore his renouncing *everything* finite must be at least partly dispositional.

Kierkegaard does not seem happy with this position. He regards it as of the utmost importance that the religious passion should come to expression. The problem of finding an adequate expression for a passion for an infinite end, in the face of the fact that in every concrete action one will be pursuing some finite end, is treated in the *Postscript* as the central problem of religion (see especially pp. 386–468). If the sacrifice of everything finite must remain largely dispositional, then perhaps it is all the more important to Kierkegaard that the smallness of the chance for which it is sacrificed should be fully actual, so that the infinity of the religious passion may be measured by an actuality in at least one aspect of the religious venture.

ii. According to Kierkegaard, as I have argued, the intensity of a passion is measured in part by the smallness of the chances of success that one acts on. It can also be measured in part by its *costliness*—that is, by how much one gives up or suffers in acting on those chances. This second measure can also be made the basis of an argument for the claim that an infinite passion requires objective improbability. For the objective improbability of a religious belief, if recognized, increases the costliness of holding it. The risk involved in staking everything on an objectively improbable belief gives rise to an anxiety and mental suffering whose acceptance is itself a sacrifice. It seems to follow that if one is not staking everything on a belief one sees to be objectively improbable, one's passion is not infinite in Kierkegaard's sense, since one's sacrifice could be greater if one did adhere to an improbable belief.

Kierkegaard uses an argument similar to this. For God to give us objective knowledge of Himself, eliminating paradox from it, would be "to lower the price of the God-relationship."

And even if God could be imagined willing, no man with passion in his heart could desire it. To a maiden genuinely in love it could never occur that she had bought her happiness too dear, but rather that she had not bought it dear enough. And just as the passion of the infinite was itself the truth, so in the case of the highest value it holds true that the price is the value, that a low price means a poor value.... [p. 207]

Kierkegaard here appears to hold, first, that an increase in the objective probability of religious belief would reduce its costliness, and second, that the value of a religious life is measured by its cost. I take it his reason for the second of these claims is that passion is the most valuable thing in a religious life and passion is measured by its cost. If we grant Kierkegaard the requisite conception of an infinite passion, we seem once again to have a plausible argument for the view that objective improbability is required for such a passion.

    c. We must therefore consider whether infinite passion, as Kierkegaard conceives of it, ought to be part of the religious ideal of life, Such a passion is a striving, or pattern of decision-making, in which, with the greatest possible intensity of feeling, one continually makes the greatest possible sacrifices on the smallest possible chance of success. This seems to me an impossible ideal. I doubt that any human being could have a passion of this sort, because I doubt that one could make a sacrifice so great that a greater could not be made, or have a (nonzero) chance of success so small that a smaller could not be had.

But even if Kierkegaard's ideal is impossible, one might want to try to approximate it. Intensity of passion might still be measured by the greatness of sacrifices made and the smallness of chances of success acted on, even if we cannot hope for a greatest possible or a smallest possible here, And it could be claimed that the most essential and valuable thing in religiousness is a passion that is very intense (though it cannot be infinite) by this standard—the more intense the better. This claim will not support an argument that objective improbability is absolutely required for religious passion. For a passion could presumably be very intense, involving great sacrifices and risks of some other sort, without an objectively improbable belief. But it could still be argued that objectively improbable religious beliefs enhance the value of the religious life by increasing its sacrifices and diminishing its chances of success, whereas objective probability detracts from the value of religious passion by diminishing its intensity.

The most crucial question about the Passion Argument, then, is whether maximization of sacrifice and risk are so valuable in religion as to make objective improbability a desirable characteristic of religious beliefs. Certainly much religious thought and feeling places a very high value on sacrifice and on passionate intensity. But the doctrine that it is desirable to increase without limit, or to the highest possible degree (if there is one) the cost and risk of a religious life is less plausible (to say the least) than the view that *some* degree of cost and risk may add to the value of a religious life. The former doctrine would set the religious interest at enmity with all other interests, or at least with the best of them. Kierkegaard is surely right in thinking that it would be impossible to live without pursuing some finite ends. But even so it would be possible to exchange the pursuit of better finite ends for the pursuit of worse ones—for example, by exchanging the pursuit of truth, beauty, and satisfying personal relationships for the self-flagellating pursuit of pain. And a way of life would be the costlier for requiring such an exchange, Kierkegaard does not, in the *Postscript,* demand it. But the presuppositions of his Passion Argument seem to imply that such a sacrifice would be religiously desirable. Such a conception of religion is demonic. In a tolerable religious ethics some way must be found to conceive of the religious interest as inclusive rather than exclusive of the best of other interests—including, I think, the interest in having well-grounded beliefs.

Pascal's Wager and Kierkegaard's Leap

Ironically, Kierkegaard's views about religious passion suggest a way in which his religious beliefs could be based on objective reasoning—not on reasoning which would show them to be objectively probable, but on reasoning which shows them to be objectively advantageous. Consider the situation of a person whom Kierkegaard would regard as a genuine Christian believer. What would such a person want most of all? He would want above all else to, attain the truth through Christianity. That is, he would desire both that Christianity be true and that he himself be related to it as a genuine believer. He would desire that state of affairs (which we may call S) so ardently that he would be willing to sacrifice everything else to obtain it, given only the smallest possible chance of success.

We can therefore construct the following argument, which has an obvious analogy to Pascal's Wager. Let us assume that there is, objectively, some chance, however small, that Christianity is true. This is an assumption which Kierkegaard accepts (p. 31), and I think it is plausible. There are two possibilities, then: either Christianity is true, or it is false. (Others might object to so stark a disjunction, but Kierkegaard will not.) If Christianity is false it is impossible for anyone to obtain S, since S includes the truth of Christianity. It is only if Christianity is true that anything one does will help one or hinder one in obtaining S. And if Christianity is true, one will obtain S just in case one becomes a genuine Christian believer. It seems obvious that one would increase one's chances of becoming a genuine Christian believer by becoming one now (if one can), even if the truth of Christian beliefs is now objectively uncertain or improbable. Hence it would seem to be advantageous for anyone who can to become a genuine Christian believer now, if he wants S so much that he would be willing to sacrifice everything else for the smallest possible chance of obtaining S. Indeed I believe that the argument I have given for this conclusion is a piece of objective reasoning, and that Christian belief is therefore *objectively* advantageous for anyone who wants S as much as a Kierkegaardian genuine Christian must want it.

Of course this argument does not tend at all to show that it is objectively probable that Christianity is true. It only gives a practical, prudential reason for believing, to someone who has a certain desire. Nor does the argument do anything to prove that such an absolutely overriding desire for S is reasonable.[8] It does show, however, that just as Kierkegaard's position has more logical structure than one might at first think, it is more difficult than he probably realized for him to get away entirely from objective justification.[9]

Robert Merrihew Adams
University of California, Los Angeles

Notes

1. Søren Kierkegaard, *Concluding Unscientific Postscript,* translated by David F. Swenson; introduction, notes, and completion of translation by Walter Lowrie (Princeton: Princeton University Press, 1941). Page references in parentheses in the body of the present paper are to this work.
2. The argument is not original with Kierkegaard. It can be found in works of G.E. Lessing and D.F. Strauss that Kierkegaard had read. See especially Thulstrup's quotation and discussion of a passage from Strauss in the commentary portion of Søren Kierkegaard, *Philosophical Fragments,* translated by David F. Swenson, second edition, translation revised by Howard V. Hong, with introduction and commentary by Niels Thulstrup (Princeton: Princeton University Press, 1962), pp. 149–51.

3. Kierkegaard, *Philosophical Fragments,* p. 104; cf. pp. 102–03.

4. Essentially the same argument can be found in a plea, which has had great influence among more recent theologians, for making Christian faith independent of the results of critical historical study of the Bible: Martin Kähler's famous lecture, first delivered in 1892, *Der sogenannte historische Jesus und der geschichtliche biblische Christus* (München: Christus Kaiser Verlag, 1961), p. 50f.

5. Kierkegaard, *Philosophical Fragments,* p. 52.

6. Kierkegaard notes the possibility that in believing in God's existence "I make so bold as to defy all objections, even those that have not yet been made," But in that case he thinks the belief is not really based on the evidence of God's work in the world; "it is not from the works that I make my proof" (*Philosophical Fragments,* p. 52).

7. Søren Kierkegaard, *Fear and Trembling,* trans. Walter Lowrie, 2d ed. (Princeton: Princeton University Press, 1970; published in one volume with *The Sickness unto Death*), p, 131. Cf. *Postscript,* p. 31f.

8. It is worth noting, though, that a similar argument might still provide some less overriding justification of belief to someone who had a strong, but less overriding, desire for *S.*

9. Versions of this paper have been read to philosophical colloquia at Occidental College and California State University, Fullerton. I am indebted to participants in those discussions, to students in many of my classes, and particularly to Marilyn McCord Adams, Van Harvey, Thomas Kselman, William Laserow, and James Muyskens, for helpful comment on the ideas which are contained in this paper (or which would have been, had it not been for their criticisms).

Chapter 3 Proofs for the Existence of the Theistic God

In this chapter we will cover the most important and well-known proofs for the existence of a theistic God. Since all three proofs we will examine are based in part on logical reasoning, they belong to the tradition which holds that faith and reason can be reconciled. Thus, while these proofs are not designed the replace the attitude of faith, they are intended to complement it with reason.

It is important for you to note that any argument that is designed to prove that God exists must show that there exists a being that satisfies *all* of the above perfections. It is not going to be enough to show, for instance, that there exists something that created the universe including us. For most people, including most atheists, agree that there is something or other that created the universe. Any proof for the existence of God must show that there exists **one, and only one,** being that is omniscient, omnipotent, perfectly-good, omni-benevolent, person-like, necessarily exists (if it exists at all), and that it created the universe including us in it. This is important to keep in mind as you examine the three classical proofs we will discuss.

The three classical proofs for the existence of a theistic God are as follows:

- *Cosmo*-**Logical** Argument;
- *Teleo*-**Logical** Argument;
- *Onto*-**Logical** Argument.

Notice the title of the three classical proofs. Each of these titles is an amalgamation of two words. Thus, we have the *Cosmo*-**logical** proof; the *Teleo*-**logical** proof; and the *Onto*-**logical** proof. As you can see, the title of all three proofs includes the word 'logical'. This is not an accident. Those who proposed these proofs thought that the existence of God, of one and only one perfect being, can be proven by means of *the natural light of reason*. Why did they think that?

In order to answer this question, two points need to be appreciated. First, as I have stated above, religion (including theistic religions) can be characterized as proposing a conception of a reality that transcends the material world. Second, it has been believed since the Greek thinkers that the world has a rational order and that we are capable of understanding this order by relying upon the natural light of reason. Thus, the three classical proofs for the existence of God presuppose the following two assumptions: i.e., that God is part of a transcendent reality and that we possess the cognitive faculty of reason to understanding the facts that governs this reality, including facts about God. Hence, the word 'logical'.

The first word in the title of each proof is a Greek word, which refers to the central factor in the proof. Thus, the word 'Cosmo' refers to the physical or observable universe; 'teleo' comes from the Greek word *telos* which means end or purpose; and, finally, 'onto' means in Greek 'being' or 'existence'. Each of these prefixes offers a hint as to the kind of assumptions the proof in question is going to make.

The three classical arguments for the existence of God can be divided into two groups based on a technical distinction in philosophy between two different kinds of knowledge: i.e., *a-posteriori* and *a-priori*. I will now define for you these terms and then use these definitions to create the two categories into which the three proofs are divided.

A. *a-priori* =df. A proposition P is *a-priori* just in case it can be known independently of any experience.

B. *a-posteriori* = df. A proposition P is *a-posteriori* just in case it can be known only based on experience.

In our context, then, a proof for the existence of God is *a-priori* just in case all its premises can be known or be conceived independently of experience. A proof for the existence of God is *a-posteriori* just in case at least one of its premises can be known only based on experience.

	A-Posteriori	**A-Priori**
Cosmological Argument	X	
Teleological Argument	X	
Ontological Argument		X

Thus, as you can see, the Cosmological and the Teleological arguments are *a-posteriori*; whereas the Ontological argument alone is *a-priori*. This means that the first two arguments depend on something that can be known only by observing some fact in the universe, whereas the last argument depends upon no such observations.

The Cosmological Argument

The Cosmological Argument has several versions, but all of them depend on observing something in the universe. For instance; the *causal* version of the argument requires us to observe at least one event that occurred (it does not matter what is the nature of this event) and then proceed by saying that since the occurrence of this event must have an explanation, there must be another prior event which caused it.

Notice two important things about what I have just said. The argument depends upon the assumption that the occurrence of the event we observed must have a reason and that this reason takes the form of a causal explanation that assumes that a prior event caused it. This principle which is assumed here is called the *Principle of Sufficient Reason* (PSR). This principle (i.e., PSR) says that everything in reality has a reason, unless it constitutes its own reason. The exception stated after the 'unless' is reserved to very few and special cases that are forced upon us by the light of reason itself. That is, if reason dictates that something must exist without something else being the reason for its existence, then this very fact is the reason for its existence. In our case this reason takes the form of a *cause*.

So let us spell out the Cosmological Argument in some detail. I want you to think about any event (it does not matter what kind of event) which you have observed or experienced recently. Let us represent this event which you have recalled by the symbol E_0. By PSR this event must have been caused by some other event. Notice that I did not ask you to produce in your mind the event which caused E_0. For the purpose of our argument, it does not matter whether you know the cause for E_0. It is enough for you to agree that such a cause must exist. Call this cause E_1. So, since E_1 caused E_0, the former must exist as well. Once we have the original event E_0 together with PSR we may repeat the same process over and over again beyond E_1, to produce a series of events E_2, E_3, E_4, ...,etc., (!) Notice the exclamation mark I inserted after the 'etc'. Its purpose is to alert you that the 'etc' may be interpreted in two ways:

A. The series of events E_0, E_1, E_2, E_3, E_4, ..., ***Infinity***; i.e., this series goes on forever.

B. The series of events E_0, E_1, E_2, E_3, E_4, ..., ⬚ ; i.e., this series **stops**.

Call the rounded rectangle representing the stopping point 'Uncaused-Cause'. It is a *cause*, since it started the whole series of events that came before it. It is *uncaused* because nothing came before it to cause it.

Now, which of the two alternatives, A or B, is possible? Many think that alternative A is incoherent. Why? Because the series of events prior to E_4 is infinite: i.e., there are an infinite number of events preceding E_4. But if so, then it will take an infinite amount of time before E_4 will occur. This means that E_4, so the argument goes, will never happen. But, contrary to this conclusion, E_4 did occur and it occurred at a particular time. Hence, A is not possible. But this leaves us with B as the only alternative explanation. Therefore, an uncaused-cause must exist. Call such an uncaused-cause 'God': i.e., uncaused-cause = God. Therefore, God exists.

What do you think about this argument? It is advisable that before we proceed you write down your impressions of this version of the Cosmological Argument as presented here. Let us now critically examine this argument. First, let us ask what exactly does the above argument prove? At best it proves that *at least one* thing, which we labeled the 'uncaused-cause' exists. But notice that the above argument does not prove that *at most one* such uncaused-cause exists. If so, then the above argument fails to prove that there exists one and only one uncaused-cause. In fact, it is perfectly compatible with alternative B that there should be several stopping-points, each of which is necessary to begin the chain of events, but none are sufficient by themselves. Thus, if that were the case, then there would be a multitude of uncaused-causes. However, since there can be **one, and only one**, theistic God, our claim that the uncaused-cause is identical to God (i.e., uncaused-cause = God) cannot be true. This is the first glaring weakness of this version of the Cosmological Argument.

Upon reflection other weaknesses emerge. Even if we allow that there is only one uncaused-cause, this will not prove that this uncaused-cause is God. For we have not proven that the uncaused-cause, even if it exists, is omniscient, omnipotent, perfectly good, omnibenevolent, and person-like. At most we have shown that there is something; i.e., an uncaused-cause, that must have started the chain of events. However, the argument says nothing about whether this uncaused-cause features any of the other perfections that the theistic God must have. Therefore, the Cosmological Argument by itself fails to offer an airtight proof that a theistic God exists.

The Teleological Argument

The first version of the *teleological argument* that we will outline is based upon an analogy between an artifact and the universe. *An argument by analogy is an argument that draws a conclusion based upon relevant similarities between something that is familiar to us and something about which we are trying to prove a claim.* The present version of the teleological argument was made popular by William Pale (1973–1805) and it is become known as The Watch and the Watchmaker.[1]

The first premise of the argument is to observe that the universe contains intelligent life. Hence, this argument is *a-posteriori*. The question in front of us is this: How do we explain the existence of intelligent life?

Consider any artifact with which you are pretty familiar; for instance, an old school (not digital) clock. Its purpose is to tell time. How does it do that? Well, in order to answer this question you need to examine the inner workings of this clock, right! So when you open this clock what do you find? You will undoubtedly find inside a variety of gears and other parts, each of which is designed to cause some other gear or part to function in a certain way. While none of the parts inside the clock by itself tells time, the proper functioning of all the parts results in the clock telling time. Since the functioning of the inner workings of the clock requires a precise coordination in order for the clock to tell time, it had to be designed by an intelligent being which made the parts work just in the right way. Clearly, no one thinks that it is very likely that the clock was assembled by some fluke event such as a storm or the actions of the ocean. Therefore, from the purpose of the clock together with the manner in which the clock fulfills its purpose we conclude that it must have been designed by some intelligent being.

The universe, so the argument goes, is just like this clock. Everything in the universe must function just in the right way in order to produce exactly the right conditions, at exactly the right time, at exactly the right way so as to lead to the existence of intelligent life. However, since the universe is vastly more complicated than our old school clock, the designer of the universe must be vastly more intelligent, knowledgeable, powerful, etc., than the designer of the clock. No other being fits this bill than our theistic God. Therefore, God exists.

What shall we think about this argument? The first thing to note is that the argument is based upon a very outdated *mechanistic* conception of the way the universe works. This is not surprising, since during Pale's time a mechanistic conception of the universe was pretty prevalent. The mechanistic functioning of clocks was a common model for how the universe works. Our current conception of how the universe works is no longer mechanistic. Therefore, one might reject the argument because of an outdated analogy between the mechanistic functioning of a clock and a more modern conception of the way the universe actually works.

Another objection that is common to the above argument relies upon *evolution theory*. The objection might go as follows: evolution theory is a much better explanation of the fact that life, and in particular intelligent life, exists than an explanation that relies upon an intelligent designer such as the theistic God.

The debate between intelligent design and evolution theory may be framed as follows. First, the facts that need explanation are the existence of life and, in particular, the existence of intelligent life. Second, we formulate two hypotheses each of which alleges to explain better how such life came to exist on earth. The first hypothesis, the Intelligent Designer Hypothesis, we represent as HID, whereas the second hypothesis we call HET. Our task is to determine which of the two hypotheses is more *probable*. But how are we to determine probabilities?

Well, we consider numerous conditions that are required in order for life to emerge and assess their individual probabilities as well as their aggregate probabilities. So for instance, in order for life to exist, water is necessary. What is the probability that just the right amount of water exists on earth without any design? Very small, so will those

---

[1] William Pale, (1802), *Natural Theology or Evidences of the Existence and Attributes of the Deity*.

who favor HID argue. Similarly, in order for there to be life on Earth the size of the Sun and Earth must be just the right sizes so that their relative distance from each other is exactly right. Similarly, things would have to be arranged in such a way that Earth is not destroyed prior to the emergence of life by a huge meteor. Moreover, the laws of nature must be exactly the way they are (e.g., the law of gravity) so that Earth does not collide with the Sun or drifts away too far and thus is either destroyed or is unable to benefit from the heat and light that the Sun provides. What is the probability, ask the proponents of HID, that all of these conditions, and many more, happen to exist simultaneously without some designer who guides the process in just the right way so as to bring them about?

The proponents of HET respond that if you give the universe enough time (in fact, close to 14 billion years), these conditions will in fact materialize somewhere; and Earth is just as good a place for them all to happen in just the right way as any other. Hence, all we need to explain the presence of intelligent life on Earth is our theory of the physical universe together with a refined theory of evolution. There is no need to add to all of this an extra being that sets up all of these conditions in motion just so that human beings emerge on the scene. In other words, the probability of all of these conditions happening in just the right way is also a matter of time. And once we allow enough time, it is more likely that these conditions will materialize somewhere. Making such a "modest" assumption, so the argument goes, is much more credible than positing the existence of a divine being that created this complicated and vast universe and set all of these laws in motion just for the purpose of bringing about the existence of human beings. It seems that an omnipotent and omniscient being could have created a much simpler universe; e.g., a universe conforming to the old picture with Earth in the center, if the purpose was merely to create the conditions so as human beings emerge.

And so the debate continues......!

The Ontological Argument

Pay careful attention to this argument and figure out how I did it!

So, I hope we can all agree that *to exist is more perfect than not to exist*. After all, how can this claim be false; in order for it to be false one has to argue that, well, lacking existence is better for some*thing* (say you or me) than having existence. Surely this makes no sense, for after all, how could it be better for me not to have existed at all. Better? What exactly are we comparing my existing with? Me not existing? But me not existing deprives the comparison of one of the sides to make the comparison with. Therefore, existing is more perfect than not existing. Call this the *Existence is a Perfection Assumption*.

Now, let us try to conceive of the most perfect being possible. Remember, that the most perfect being that is possible to conceive must feature *all and only* perfections as its properties. If it lacks any perfection, then it is certainly not the most perfect being that is possible to imagine. And if it includes a property that is not perfection, then it becomes not the most perfect being that is possible to imagine, for it features something that makes it not quite perfect.

e.g., suppose you include height as one of the properties of this being. Any being that features the property of height must have a specific height. But then it is possible to imagine a being that is taller (or shorter) than the one we imagined. Therefore, height cannot be perfection.

There are now two possibilities, so this argument goes. The simple possibility is that you remembered the *Existence as a Perfection Assumption* and therefore included existence as one of the perfections of the most perfect being conceivable that you imagined. Since the being you imagined featured existence, it follows that this being exists. But this being is just God. Therefore, God exists.

The more complex possibility is that you forgot the *Existence as a Perfection Assumption* and, as a result, forgot to include existence as one of the perfections of the most perfect being imaginable. So now I ask you to do so. Once you include existence as one of this being's perfections, this possibility reduces to the simple one previously described. Therefore, the most perfect being conceivable exists. Therefore, since 'God' is the name of such a perfect being, it follows that God exists. QED

How did I do it?[2] I can discern that you feel that this argument is like pulling a rabbit out of thin air. I feel your frustration; trust me. But my question to you is this: How did I do it? i.e., how did I make it seem as if I pulled a rabbit (God) out of thin air (my head)? I sense that you think something like this: merely because we think, imagine, conceive of something it simply does not follow that *it exists*. Well, again I sympathize. But we agreed that to exist is more perfect than not to exist and we also saw that existence must be included as one of the perfections of the most perfect being conceivable. So it seems that we must concede that the most perfect being conceivable must exist. Or do we?

Let me help you out here. First, notice how I went from talk of existence as perfection, to talk about existence as a property of things; that is, in this case of the most perfect being imaginable. And once the most perfect being imaginable in my (or your) head also has the property of existing, then it seems it also must exist outside of our head: i.e., in a mind independent reality. This is the move you feel is illegitimate here. But, how can we block this move?

Here is a way of doing this. First let us distinguish between *concept* and *object*. Think of existence not as a *property* of objects, but rather as a *concept* (or idea, if you will). Let me explain what I mean. Let us consider unicorns. We of course know that unicorns do not exist. That is, there is no real physical horse that also features a horn. Well, now, so how do we come up with the concept or idea of a unicorn? The explanation is simple. We have the **concept of a *horse***, right? We also have the **concept of a *horn***, right? So the concept of a unicorn results from combining three concepts: the concept of *horse* plus the concept of *having* plus the concept of *horn*. That is:

[concept of *horse*] + [concept of *has*] + [concept of *horn*] = **concept of *unicorn***.

Notice that merely obtaining the concept of a *unicorn* in this way does not entail that unicorns must exist. Now, all we need to do is treat *existence as a concept*, somewhat in the same way as we have treated the other concepts of a *horse* and a *horn*. So now we obtain the concept of a most perfect being conceivable as a combination of various concepts of *perfections* (e.g., the concept of *being omnipotent*, the concept of *being omniscient*, the concept of *existing*, etc.) and we thereby obtain the concept of being the most perfect being conceivable:

[concept of *omniscient*] + [concept of *omnipotent*] + ...+ [concept of *existing*] = [concept of *God*].

So what have we accomplished by combining these various perfection concepts? At most we have shown that we have the *concept of* a perfect being expressed by our term 'God'. What this argument fails to demonstrate is that a perfect *object* or entity we name God actually exists outside the realm of concepts or outside the realm of our mind, but *in the external reality*. Yet I am sure that you expected an argument that proves the existence of God to show that such a being actually exists; i.e., exists not merely as a concept or idea,

---

[2] Actually, I learned how to do it from others, specifically from St. Anselm, as you will see as you read the material below.

but as a mind independent object or entity. And your frustration with the ontological argument is traceable to the fact that it seems to fail to do that. You are right! The proponents of the ontological argument will have to overcome this objection. But such a discussion is beyond the scope of the present book.

To sum up: each of the arguments presented above features certain weaknesses. Therefore, none of them individually suffices to prove that a theistic God exists. The question is whether the combination of all three offers a case beyond reasonable doubt that a theistic God exists. I leave this question up to you to decide and invite you to move to the next chapter where we examine one of the most powerful arguments *against* the existence of a theistic God: i.e., The Problem of Evil.

Dialogues Concerning Natural Religion

David Hume

I must own, CLEANTHES, said DEMEA, that nothing can more surprise me, than the light in which you have all along put this argument. By the whole tenor of your discourse, one would imagine that you were maintaining the Being of a God, against the cavils of Atheists and Infidels; and were necessitated to become a champion for that fundamental principle of all religion. But this, I hope, is not by any means a question among us. No man, no man at least of common sense, I am persuaded, ever entertained a serious doubt with regard to a truth so certain and self-evident. The question is not concerning the being, but the nature of God. This, I affirm, from the infirmities of human understanding, to be altogether incomprehensible and unknown to us. The essence of that supreme Mind, his attributes, the manner of his existence, the very nature of his duration; these, and every particular which regards so divine a Being, are mysterious to men. Finite, weak, and blind creatures, we ought to humble ourselves in his august presence; and, conscious of our frailties, adore in silence his infinite perfections, which eye hath not seen, ear hath not heard, neither hath it entered into the heart of man to conceive. They are covered in a deep cloud from human curiosity. It is profaneness to attempt penetrating through these sacred obscurities. And, next to the impiety of denying his existence, is the temerity of prying into his nature and essence, decrees and attributes.

But lest you should think that my piety has here got the better of my philosophy, I shall support my opinion, if it needs any support, by a very great authority. I might cite all the divines, almost, from the foundation of Christianity, who have ever treated of this or any other theological subject: But I shall confine myself, at present, to one equally celebrated for piety and philosophy. It is Father MALEBRANCHE, who, I remember, thus expresses himself [Recherche de la Verite. Liv. 3. Chap.9]. "One ought not so much," says he, "to call God a spirit, in order to express positively what he is, as in order to signify that he is not matter. He is a Being infinitely perfect: Of this we cannot doubt. But in the same manner as we ought not to imagine, even supposing him corporeal, that he is clothed with a human body, as the ANTHROPOMORPHITES asserted, under colour that that figure was the most perfect of any; so, neither ought we to imagine that the spirit of God has human ideas, or bears any resemblance to our spirit, under colour that we know nothing more perfect than a human mind. We ought rather to believe, that as he comprehends the perfections of matter without being material.... he comprehends also the perfections of created spirits without being spirit, in the manner we conceive spirit: That his true name is, He that is; or, in other words, Being without restriction, All Being, the Being infinite and universal."

After so great an authority, DEMEA, replied PHILO, as that which you have produced, and a thousand more which you might produce, it would appear ridiculous in me to add my sentiment, or express my approbation of your doctrine. But surely, where reasonable men treat these subjects, the question can never be concerning the Being, but only the Nature, of the Deity. The former truth, as you well observe, is unquestionable and self-evident. Nothing exists without a cause; and the original cause of this universe (whatever it be) we call God; and piously ascribe to him every species of perfection. Whoever scruples this fundamental truth, deserves every punishment which can be inflicted among philosophers, to wit, the greatest ridicule, contempt, and disapprobation. But as all perfection is entirely relative, we ought never to imagine that we comprehend the attributes of this divine Being, or to suppose that his perfections have any analogy or likeness to the perfections of a human creature. Wisdom, Thought, Design, Knowledge; these we justly ascribe to him; because these words are honourable among men, and we have no other language or other conceptions by which we can express our adoration of him. But let us beware, lest we think that our ideas anywise correspond to his perfections, or that his attributes have any resemblance to these qualities among men. He is infinitely superior to our limited view and comprehension; and is more the object of worship in the temple, than of disputation in the schools.

In reality, CLEANTHES, continued he, there is no need of having recourse to that affected scepticism so displeasing to you, in order to come at this determination. Our ideas reach no further than our experience. We have no experience of divine attributes and operations. I need not conclude my syllogism. You can draw the inference yourself. And it is a pleasure to me (and I hope to you too) that just reasoning and sound piety here concur in the same conclusion, and both of them establish the adorably mysterious and incomprehensible nature of the Supreme Being.

Not to lose any time in circumlocutions, said CLEANTHES, addressing himself to DEMEA, much less in replying to the pious declamations of PHILO; I shall briefly explain how I conceive this matter. Look round the world: contemplate the whole and every part of it: You will find it to be nothing but one great machine, subdivided into an infinite number of lesser machines, which again admit of subdivisions to a degree beyond what human senses and faculties can trace and explain. All these various machines, and even their most minute parts, are adjusted to each other with an accuracy which ravishes into admiration all men who have ever contemplated them. The curious adapting of means to ends, throughout all nature, resembles exactly, though it much exceeds, the productions of human contrivance; of human designs, thought, wisdom, and intelligence. Since, therefore, the effects resemble each other, we are led to infer, by all the rules of analogy, that the causes also resemble; and that the Author of Nature is somewhat similar to the mind of man, though possessed of much larger faculties, proportioned to the grandeur of the work which he has executed. By this argument a posteriori, and by this argument alone, do we prove at once the existence of a Deity, and his similarity to human mind and intelligence.

I shall be so free, CLEANTHES, said DEMEA, as to tell you, that from the beginning, I could not approve of your conclusion concerning the similarity of the Deity to men; still less can I approve of the mediums by which you endeavour to establish it. What! No demonstration of the Being of God! No abstract arguments! No proofs a priori! Are these, which have hitherto been so much insisted on by philosophers, all fallacy, all sophism? Can we reach no further in this subject than experience and probability? I will not say that this is betraying the cause of a Deity: But surely, by this affected candour, you give advantages to Atheists, which they never could obtain by the mere dint of argument and reasoning.

What I chiefly scruple in this subject, said PHILO, is not so much that all religious arguments are by CLEANTHES reduced to experience, as that they appear not to be even the most certain and irrefragable of that inferior kind. That a stone will fall, that fire will burn, that the earth has solidity, we have observed a thousand and a thousand times; and when any new instance of this nature is presented, we draw without hesitation the accustomed inference. The exact similarity of the cases gives us a perfect assurance of a similar event; and a stronger evidence is never desired nor sought after. But wherever you depart, in the least, from the similarity of the cases, you diminish proportionably the evidence; and may at last bring it to a very weak analogy, which is confessedly liable to error and uncertainty. After having experienced the circulation of the blood in human creatures, we make no doubt that it takes place in TITIUS and MAEVIUS. But from its circulation in frogs and fishes, it is only a presumption, though a strong one, from analogy, that it takes place in men and other animals. The analogical reasoning is much weaker, when we infer the circulation of the sap in vegetables from our experience that the blood circulates in animals; and those, who hastily followed that imperfect analogy, are found, by more accurate experiments, to have been mistaken.

If we see a house, CLEANTHES, we conclude, with the greatest certainty, that it had an architect or builder; because this is precisely that species of effect which we have experienced to proceed from that species of cause. But surely you will not affirm, that the universe bears such a resemblance to a house, that we can with the same certainty infer a similar cause, or that the analogy is here entire and perfect. The dissimilitude is so striking, that the utmost you can here pretend to is a guess, a conjecture, a presumption concerning a similar cause; and how that pretension will be received in the world, I leave you to consider.

It would surely be very ill received, replied CLEANTHES; and I should be deservedly blamed and detested, did I allow, that the proofs of a Deity amounted to no more than a guess or conjecture. But is the whole adjustment of means to ends in a house and in the universe so slight a resemblance? The economy of final causes? The order, proportion, and arrangement of every part? Steps of a stair are plainly contrived, that human legs may use them in mounting; and this inference is certain and infallible. Human legs are also contrived for walking and mounting; and this inference, I allow, is not altogether so certain, because of the dissimilarity which you remark; but does it, therefore, deserve the name only of presumption or conjecture?

Good God! cried DEMEA, interrupting him, where are we? Zealous defenders of religion allow, that the proofs of a Deity fall short of perfect evidence! And you, PHILO, on whose assistance I depended in proving the adorable mysteriousness of the Divine Nature, do you assent to all these extravagant opinions of CLEANTHES? For what other name can I give them? or, why spare my censure, when such principles are advanced, supported by such an authority, before so young a man as PAMPHILUS?

You seem not to apprehend, replied PHILO, that I argue with CLEANTHES in his own way; and, by showing him the dangerous consequences of his tenets, hope at last to reduce him to our opinion. But what sticks most with you, I observe, is the representation which CLEANTHES has made of the argument a posteriori; and finding that that argument is likely to escape your hold and vanish into air, you think it so disguised, that you can scarcely believe it to be set in its true light. Now, however much I may dissent, in other respects, from the dangerous principles of CLEANTHES, I must allow that he has fairly represented that argument; and I shall endeavour so to state the matter to you, that you will entertain no further scruples with regard to it.

Were a man to abstract from every thing which he knows or has seen, he would be altogether incapable, merely from his own ideas, to determine what kind of scene the universe must be, or to give the preference to one state or situation of things above another. For as nothing which he clearly conceives could be esteemed impossible or implying a contradiction, every chimera of his fancy would be upon an equal footing; nor could he assign any just reason why he adheres to one idea or system, and rejects the others which are equally possible.

Again; after he opens his eyes, and contemplates the world as it really is, it would be impossible for him at first to assign the cause of any one event, much less of the whole of things, or of the universe. He might set his fancy a rambling; and she might bring him in an infinite variety of reports and representations. These would all be possible; but being all equally possible, he would never of himself give a satisfactory account for his preferring one of them to the rest. Experience alone can point out to him the true cause of any phenomenon.

Now, according to this method of reasoning, DEMEA, it follows, (and is, indeed, tacitly allowed by CLEANTHES himself,) that order, arrangement, or the adjustment of final causes, is not of itself any proof of design; but only so far as it has been experienced to proceed from that principle. For aught we can know a priori, matter may contain the source or spring of order originally within itself, as well as mind does; and there is no more difficulty in conceiving, that the several elements, from an internal unknown cause, may fall into the most exquisite arrangement, than to conceive that their ideas, in the great universal mind, from a like internal unknown cause, fall into that arrangement. The equal possibility of both these suppositions is allowed. But, by experience, we find, (according to CLEANTHES), that there is a difference between them. Throw several pieces of steel together, without shape or form; they will never arrange themselves so as to compose a watch. Stone, and mortar, and wood, without an architect, never erect a house. But the ideas in a human mind, we see, by an unknown, inexplicable economy, arrange themselves so as to form the plan of a watch or house. Experience, therefore, proves, that there is an original principle of order in mind, not in matter. From similar effects we infer similar causes. The adjustment of means to ends is alike in the universe, as in a machine of human contrivance. The causes, therefore, must be resembling.

I was from the beginning scandalised, I must own, with this resemblance, which is asserted, between the Deity and human creatures; and must conceive it to imply such a degradation of the Supreme Being as no sound Theist could endure. With your assistance, therefore, DEMEA, I shall endeavour to defend what you justly call the adorable mysteriousness of the Divine Nature, and shall refute this reasoning of CLEANTHES, provided he allows that I have made a fair representation of it.

When CLEANTHES had assented, PHILO, after a short pause, proceeded in the following manner.

That all inferences, CLEANTHES, concerning fact, are founded on experience; and that all experimental reasonings are founded on the supposition that similar causes prove similar effects, and similar effects similar causes; I shall not at present much dispute with you. But observe, I entreat you, with what extreme caution all just reasoners proceed in the transferring of experiments to similar cases. Unless the cases be exactly similar, they repose no perfect confidence in applying their past observation to any particular phenomenon. Every alteration of circumstances occasions a doubt concerning the event; and it requires new experiments to prove certainly, that the new circumstances are of no moment or importance. A change in bulk, situation, arrangement, age, disposition of the air, or surrounding bodies; any of these particulars may be attended with the most unexpected consequences: And unless the objects be quite familiar to us, it is the highest temerity to expect with assurance, after any of these changes, an event similar to that which before fell under our observation. The slow and deliberate steps of philosophers here, if any where, are distinguished from the precipitate march of the vulgar, who, hurried on by the smallest similitude, are incapable of all discernment or consideration.

But can you think, CLEANTHES, that your usual phlegm and philosophy have been preserved in so wide a step as you have taken, when you compared to the universe houses, ships, furniture, machines, and, from their similarity in some circumstances, inferred a similarity in their causes? Thought, design, intelligence, such as we discover in men and other animals, is no more than one of the springs and principles of the universe, as well as heat or cold, attraction or repulsion, and a hundred others, which fall under daily observation. It is an active cause, by which some particular parts of nature, we find, produce alterations on other parts. But can a conclusion, with any propriety, be transferred from parts to the whole? Does not the great disproportion bar all comparison and inference? From observing the growth of a hair, can we learn any thing concerning the generation of a man? Would the manner of a leaf's blowing, even though perfectly known, afford us any instruction concerning the vegetation of a tree?

But, allowing that we were to take the operations of one part of nature upon another, for the foundation of our judgement concerning the origin of the whole, (which never can be admitted,) yet why select so minute, so weak, so bounded a principle, as the reason and design of animals is found to be upon this planet? What peculiar privilege has this little agitation of the brain which we call thought, that we must thus make it the model of the whole universe? Our partiality in our own favour does indeed present it on all occasions; but sound philosophy ought carefully to guard against so natural an illusion.

So far from admitting, continued PHILO, that the operations of a part can afford us any just conclusion concerning the origin of the whole, I will not allow any one part to form a rule for another part, if the latter be very remote from the former. Is there any reasonable ground to conclude, that the inhabitants of other planets possess thought, intelligence, reason, or any thing similar to these faculties in men? When nature has so extremely diversified her manner of operation in this small globe, can we imagine that she incessantly copies herself throughout so immense a universe? And if thought, as we may well suppose, be confined merely to this narrow corner, and has even there so limited a sphere of action, with what propriety can we assign it for the original cause of all things? The narrow views of a peasant, who makes his domestic economy the rule for the government of kingdoms, is in comparison a pardonable sophism.

But were we ever so much assured, that a thought and reason, resembling the human, were to be found throughout the whole universe, and were its activity elsewhere vastly greater and more commanding than it appears in this globe; yet I cannot see, why the operations of a world constituted, arranged, adjusted, can with any propriety be extended to a world which is in its embryo state, and is advancing towards that constitution and arrangement. By observation, we know somewhat of the economy, action, and nourishment of a finished animal; but we must transfer with great caution that observation to the growth of a foetus in the womb, and still more to the formation of an animalcule in the loins of its male parent. Nature, we find, even from our limited experience, possesses an infinite number of springs and principles, which incessantly discover themselves on every change of her position and situation. And what new and unknown principles would actuate her in so new and unknown a situation as that of the formation of a universe, we cannot, without the utmost temerity, pretend to determine.

A very small part of this great system, during a very short time, is very imperfectly discovered to us; and do we thence pronounce decisively concerning the origin of the whole?

Admirable conclusion! Stone, wood, brick, iron, brass, have not, at this time, in this minute globe of earth, an order or arrangement without human art and contrivance; therefore the universe could not originally attain its order and arrangement, without something similar to human art. But is a part of nature a rule for another part very wide of the former? Is it a rule for the whole? Is a very small part a rule for the universe? Is nature in one situation, a certain rule for nature in another situation vastly different from the former?

And can you blame me, CLEANTHES, if I here imitate the prudent reserve of SIMONIDES, who, according to the noted story, being asked by HIERO, What God was? desired a day to think of it, and then two days more; and after that manner continually prolonged the term, without ever bringing in his definition or description? Could you even blame me, if I had answered at first, that I did not know, and was sensible that this subject lay vastly beyond the reach of my faculties? You might cry out sceptic and railler, as much as you pleased: but having found, in so many other subjects much more familiar, the imperfections and even contradictions of human reason, I never should expect any success from its feeble conjectures, in a subject so sublime, and so remote from the sphere of our observation. When two species of objects have always been observed to be conjoined together, I can infer, by custom, the existence of one wherever I see the existence of the other; and this I call an argument from experience. But how this argument can have place, where the objects, as in the present case, are single, individual, without parallel, or specific resemblance, may be difficult to explain. And will any man tell me with a serious countenance, that an orderly universe must arise from some thought and art like the human, because we have experience of it? To ascertain this reasoning, it were requisite that we had experience of the origin of worlds; and it is not sufficient, surely, that we have seen ships and cities arise from human art and contrivance...

PHILO was proceeding in this vehement manner, somewhat between jest and earnest, as it appeared to me, when he observed some signs of impatience in CLEANTHES, and then immediately stopped short. What I had to suggest, said CLEANTHES, is only that you would not abuse terms, or make use of popular expressions to subvert philosophical reasonings. You know, that the vulgar often distinguish reason from experience, even where the question relates only to matter of fact and existence; though it is found, where that reason is properly analysed, that it is nothing but a species of experience. To prove by experience the origin of the universe from mind, is not more contrary to common speech, than to prove the motion of the earth from the same principle. And a caviller might raise all the same objections to the Copernican system, which you have urged against my reasonings. Have you other earths, might he say, which you have seen to move? Have...

Yes! cried PHILO, interrupting him, we have other earths. Is not the moon another earth, which we see to turn round its centre? Is not Venus another earth, where we observe the same phenomenon? Are not the revolutions of the sun also a confirmation, from analogy, of the same theory? All the planets, are they not earths, which revolve about the sun? Are not the satellites moons, which move round Jupiter and Saturn, and along with these primary planets round the sun? These analogies and resemblances, with others which I have not mentioned, are the sole proofs of the COPERNICAN system; and to you it belongs to consider, whether you have any analogies of the same kind to support your theory.

In reality, CLEANTHES, continued he, the modern system of astronomy is now so much received by all inquirers, and has become so essential a part even of our earliest education, that we are not commonly very scrupulous in examining the reasons upon which it is founded. It is now become a matter of mere curiosity to study the first writers on that subject, who had the full force of prejudice to encounter, and were obliged to turn their arguments on every side in order to render them popular and convincing. But if we peruse GALILEO's famous Dialogues concerning the system of the world, we shall find, that that great genius, one of the sublimest that ever existed, first bent all his endeavours to prove, that there was no foundation for the distinction commonly made between elementary and celestial substances. The schools, proceeding from the illusions of sense, had carried this distinction very far; and had established the latter substances to be ingenerable, incorruptible, unalterable, impassable; and had assigned all the opposite qualities to the former. But GALILEO, beginning with the moon, proved its similarity in every particular to the earth; its convex figure, its natural darkness when not illuminated, its density, its distinction into solid and liquid, the variations of its phases, the mutual illuminations of the earth and moon, their mutual eclipses, the inequalities of the lunar surface, &c. After many instances of this kind, with regard to all the planets, men plainly saw that these bodies became proper objects of experience; and that the similarity of their nature enabled us to extend the same arguments and phenomena from one to the other.

In this cautious proceeding of the astronomers, you may read your own condemnation, CLEANTHES; or rather may see, that the subject in which you are engaged exceeds all human reason and inquiry. Can you pretend to show any such similarity between the fabric of a house, and the generation of a universe? Have you ever seen nature in any such situation as resembles the first arrangement of the elements? Have worlds ever been formed under your eye; and have you had leisure to observe the whole progress of the phenomenon, from the first appearance of order to its final consummation? If you have, then cite your experience, and deliver your theory.

The Ontological Argument
St. Anselm & Guanilo

St. Anselm's Presentation

Truly there is a God, although the fool hath said in his heart, There is no God.

And so, Lord, do thou, who dost give understanding to faith, give me, so far as thou knowest it to be profitable, to understand that thou art as we believe; and that thou art that which we believe. And, indeed, we believe that thou art a being than which nothing greater can be conceived. Or is there no such nature, since the fool hath said in his heart, there is no God? (Psalms xiii, 1). But, at any rate, this very fool, when he hears of this being of which I speak—a being than which nothing greater can be conceived—understands what he hears, and what he understands is in his understanding; although he does not understand it to exist.

For, it is one thing for an object to be in the understanding, and another to understand that the object exists. When a painter first conceives of what he will afterwards perform, he has it in his understanding, but he does not yet understand it to be, because he has not yet performed it. But after he has made the painting, he both has it in his understanding, and he understands that it exists, because he has made it.

Hence, even the fool is convinced that something exists in the understanding, at least, than which nothing greater can be conceived. For, when he hears of this, he understands it. And whatever is understood, exists in the understanding. And assuredly that, than which nothing greater can be conceived, cannot exist in the understanding alone. For, suppose it exists in the understanding alone: then it can be conceived to exist in reality; which is greater.

Therefore, if that, than which nothing greater can be conceived, exists in the understanding alone, the very being, than which nothing greater can be conceived, is one, than which a greater can be conceived. But obviously this is impossible. Hence, there is no doubt that there exists a being, than which nothing greater can be conceived, and it exists both in the understanding and in reality.

God cannot be conceived not to exist.—God is that, than which nothing greater can be conceived.—That which can be conceived not to exist is not God.

And it assuredly exists so truly, that it cannot be conceived not to exist. For, it is possible to conceive of a being which cannot be conceived not to exist; and this is greater than one which can be conceived not to exist. Hence, if that, than which nothing greater

Reprinted from *Anselm's Basic Writings,* translated by S. W. Deane, 2d ed. (La Salle, III.: Open Court Publishing Company, 1962), by permission of the publisher.

can be conceived, can be conceived not to exist, it is not that, than which nothing greater can be conceived. But this is an irreconcilable contradiction. There is, then, so truly a being than which nothing greater can be conceived to exist, that it cannot even be conceived not to exist; and this being thou art, O Lord, our God.

So truly, therefore, dost thou exist, O Lord, my God, that thou canst not be conceived not to exist; and rightly. For, if a mind could conceive of a being better than thee, the creature would rise above the Creator; and this is most absurd. And, indeed, whatever else there is, except thee alone, can be conceived not to exist. To thee alone, therefore, it belongs to exist more truly than all other beings, and hence in a higher degree than all others. For, whatever else exists does not exist so truly, and hence in a less degree it belongs to it to exist. Why, then, has the fool said in his heart, there is no God (Psalms xiii, 1), since it is so evident, to a rational mind, that thou dost exist in the highest degree of all? Why, except that he is dull and a fool?

> *How the fool has said in his heart what cannot be conceived.—A thing may be conceived in two ways: (1) when the word signifying it is conceived: (2) when the thing itself is understood. As far as the word goes, God can be conceived not to exist; in reality he cannot.*

But how has the fool said in his heart what he could not conceive; or how is it that he could not conceive what he said in his heart? since it is the same to say in the heart, and to conceive.

But, if really, nay, since really, he both conceived, because he said in his heart; and did not say in his heart, because he could not conceive; there is more than one way in which a thing is said in the heart or conceived. For, in one sense, an object is conceived, when the word signifying it is conceived; and in another, when the very entity, which the object is, is understood.

In the former sense, then, God can be conceived not to exist; but in the latter, not at all, For no one who understands what fire and water are can conceive fire to be water, in accordance with the nature of the facts themselves, although this is possible according to the words, So, then, no one who understands what God is can conceive that God does not exist; although he says these words in his heart, either without any or with some foreign, signification. For, God is that than which a greater cannot be conceived. And he who thoroughly understands this, assuredly understands that this being so truly exists, that not even in concept can it be non-existent. Therefore, he who understands that God so exists, cannot conceive that he does not exist.

I thank thee, gracious Lord, I thank thee; because what I formerly believed by thy bounty, I now so understand by thine illumination, that if I were unwilling to believe that thou dost exist, I should not be able not to understand this to be true.

Gaunilo's Criticism*

For example: it is said that somewhere in the ocean is an island, which, because of the difficulty, or rather the impossibility, of discovering what does not exist, is called the lost island. And they say that this island has an inestimable wealth of all manner of riches and delicacies in greater abundance than is told of the Islands of the Blest; and that having no owner or inhabitant, it is more excellent than all other countries, which are inhabited by mankind, in the abundance with which it is stored.

Now if some one should tell me that there is such an island, I should easily understand his words, in which there is no difficulty. But suppose that he went on to say, as if

---

*Gaunilo, a monk, was a contemporary of St. Anselm's.

by a logical inference: "You can no longer doubt that this island which is more excellent than all lands exists somewhere, since you have no doubt that it is in your understanding. And since it is more excellent not to be in the understanding alone, but to exist both in the understanding and in reality, for this reason it must exist. For if it does not exist, any land which really exists will be more excellent than it; and so the island already understood by you to be more excellent will not be more excellent."

If a man should try to prove to me by such reasoning that this island truly exists, and that its existence should no longer be doubted, either I should believe that he was jesting, or I know not which I ought to regard as the greater fool: myself, supposing that I should allow this proof; or him, if he should suppose that he had established with any certainty the existence of this island. For he ought to show first that the hypothetical excellence of this island exists as a real and indubitable fact, and in no wise as any unreal object, or one whose existence is uncertain, in my understanding.

St. Anselm's Rejoinder

A criticism of Gaunilo's example, in which he tries to show that in this way the real existence of a lost island might be inferred from the fact of its being conceived.

But, you say, it is as if one should suppose an island in the ocean, which surpasses all lands in its fertility, and which, because of the difficulty, or rather the impossibility, of discovering what does not exist, is called a lost island; and should say that there can be no doubt that this island truly exists in reality, for this reason, that one who hears it described easily understands what he hears.

Now I promise confidently that if any man shall devise anything existing either in reality or in concept alone (except that than which a greater cannot be conceived) to which he can adapt the sequence of my reasoning, I will discover that thing, and will give him his lost island, not to be lost again.

But it now appears that this being than which a greater is inconceivable cannot be conceived not to be, because it exists on so assured a ground of truth; for otherwise it would not exist at all.

Hence, if any one says that he conceives this being not to exist, I say that at the time when he conceives of this either he conceives of a being than which a greater is inconceivable, or he does not conceive at all. If he does not conceive, he does not conceive of the non-existence of that of which he does not conceive. But if he does conceive, he certainly conceives of a being which cannot be even conceived not to exist. For if it could be conceived not to exist, it could be conceived to have a beginning and an end. But this is impossible.

He, then, who conceives of this being conceives of a being which cannot be even conceived not to exist; but he who conceives of this being does not conceive that it does not exist; else he conceives what is inconceivable. The non-existence, then, of that than which a greater cannot be conceived is inconceivable.

An Analysis of the Ontological Argument

William Rowe

It is perhaps best to think of the Ontological Argument not as a single argument but as a family of arguments each member of which begins with a concept of God and, by appealing only to *a priori* principles, endeavors to establish that God actually exists. Within this family of arguments, the most important historically is the argument set forth by Anselm in the second chapter of his *Proslogium* (a discourse).[1] Indeed, it is fair to say that the Ontological Argument begins with Chapter Two of Anselm's *Proslogium.* In an earlier work, *Monologium* (a soliloquy), Anselm had endeavored to establish the existence and nature of God by weaving together several versions of the Cosmological Argument. In the preface to *Proslogium* Anselm remarks that after the' publication of *Monologium* he began to search for a single argument which alone would establish the existence and nature of God. After much strenuous but unsuccessful effort, he reports that he sought to put the project out of his mind in order to turn to more fruitful tasks. The idea, however, continued to haunt him until one day the proof he had so strenuously sought became clear to his mind. It is this proof which Anselm sets forth in the second chapter of *Proslogium.*

Basic Concepts

Before setting forth Anselm's argument in step-by-step fashion, it will be useful to introduce a few concepts that will help us understand some of the central ideas which figure in the argument. Suppose we draw a vertical line in our imagination and imagine that on the left side of our line are all the things which exist, while on the right side of the line are all the things which don't exist. We might then set about to make a list of some of the things on both sides of our imaginary line, a list we might start as follows:

Things Which Exist	Things Which Don't Exist
The Empire State Building	The Fountain of Youth
Dogs	Unicorns
The Planet Mars	The Abominable Snowman

Now, each of the things (or sort of things) listed thus far has the following feature: it logically might have been on the other side of the line. The Fountain of Youth, for example, is on the right side of the line but *logically* there is no absurdity in the idea that it might have been on the left side of the line. Similarly, although dogs do exist, we surely can imagine without logical absurdity that they might not have existed, that they might have been on the right side of the line. Let's then record this feature of the things thus far listed by introducing the idea of a *contingent thing* as a thing that logically might have been on the other side of the line from the side it actually is on. The planet Mars and the abominable snowman are contingent things even though the former happens to exist and the latter does not.

Suppose we add to our list by writing down the phrase "the object which is completely round and completely square at the same time" on the right side of our line. The round square, however, unlike the other things thus far listed on the right side of our line, is something that *logically could not* have been on the left side of the line. Noting this, let's introduce the idea of an *impossible thing* as a thing that is on the right side of the line and logically could not have been on the left side of the line.

Looking again at our list, the question arises as to whether there is anything on the left side of our imaginary line which is such that, unlike the things thus far listed on the left side, it *logically could not* have been on the right side of the line. At this point we don't have to answer this question. But it is useful to have a concept to apply to any such things should there be any. Accordingly, let's introduce the notion of a *necessary thing* as a thing that is on the left side of our imaginary line and logically could not have been on the right side of the line.

Finally, we may introduce the idea of a *possible thing* as any thing that is either on the left side of our imaginary line or logically might have been on the left side of the line. Possible things, then, will be all those things that are not impossible things, that is, all those things that are either contingent or necessary. If there are no necessary things, then all possible things will be contingent and all contingent things will be possible. If there is a necessary thing, however, then there will be a possible thing which is not contingent.

Armed with the concepts just explained we can now proceed to clarify certain important distinctions and ideas in Anselm's thought. The first of these is his distinction between existence in the understanding and existence in reality. Anselm's notion of existence in reality is the same as our notion of existence—that is, being on the left side of our imaginary line. Since the Fountain of Youth is on the right side of the line it does not exist in reality. The things which exist are, to Anselm's phrase, the things which exist in reality. Anselm's notion of existence in the understanding, however, is not the same as any idea we normally employ. But what Anselm means by "existence in the understanding" is not particularly mysterious. When we think of a certain thing, say the Fountain of Youth, then that thing, in Anselm's view, exists in the understanding. So some of the things on both sides of our imaginary line exist in the understanding, but only those on the left side of our line exist in reality. Are there any things that don't exist in the understanding? Undoubtedly there are. For there are things, both existing and nonexisting, of which we have not really thought. Now suppose I assert that the Fountain of Youth does not exist. Since to meaningfully deny the existence of something, I must have that thing in mind, it follows on Anselm's view that whenever someone asserts that some thing does not exist, that thing does exist in the understanding.[2] So in asserting that the Fountain of Youth does not exist I imply that the Fountain of Youth does exist in the understanding. And in asserting that it doesn't exist, I have asserted (on Anselm's view) that it doesn't exist in reality. This means that my simple assertion that the Fountain of Youth doesn't exist amounts to the somewhat more complex claim that the Fountain of Youth exists in the understanding but does not exist in reality—in short, that the Fountain of Youth exists *only* in the understanding.

In view of the above we can now understand why Anselm insists that anyone who hears of God, thinks about God, or even denies the existence of God is, nevertheless, committed to the view that God exists in the understanding. Also, we can understand why Anselm treats what he calls the fool's claim that God does not exist as the claim that God exists *only* in the understanding—that is, that God exists in the understanding but does not exist in reality.

In *Monologium* Anselm sought to prove that among those beings which do exist, there is one which is the greatest, highest, and the best. But in *Proslogium* he undertakes to prove that among those things which exist, there is one which is not just the greatest among existing beings, but is such that no conceivable being is greater. We need to distinguish these two ideas: (i) a being than which *no existing being* is greater, and (ii) a being than which *no conceivable being* is greater. If the only things in existence were a stone, a frog, and a human being, the last of these, the human being, would satisfy our first idea but not our second—for we can conceive of a being (an angel or God) greater than a human. Anselm's idea of God, as he expresses it in *Proslogium*, II, is the same as (ii) above; it is the idea of "a being than which nothing greater can be conceived." It will, I think, facilitate our understanding of Anselm's argument if we make two slight changes in the way he has expressed his idea of God. For his phrase I shall substitute the following: *"the* being than which none greater *is possible."*[3] What this idea says is that if a certain being is God, then no *possible* being can be greater than it; or conversely, if a certain being is such that it is even *possible* for there to be a being greater than it, then that being is not God. What Anselm proposes to prove, then, is that the being than which none greater is possible exists in reality. If he proves this he will have proved that God, as he conceives of him, exists in reality.

But what does Anselm mean by *greatness?* Is a building, for example, greater than a man? Anselm remarks: "But I do not mean physically great, as a material object is great, but that which, the greater it is, is the better or the more worthy—wisdom, for instance."[4] Contrast wisdom with size. Anselm is saying that wisdom is something that contributes to the greatness of a thing. If a thing comes to have more wisdom than it did before (given that its other characteristics remain the same), then that thing has become a greater, better, more worthy thing than it was. Wisdom, Anselm is saying, is a great-making quality. But the mere fact that something increases in size (physical greatness) does not make that thing a better thing than it was before. So size, unlike wisdom, is not a great-making quality. By *greater than* Anselm means *better than, superior to,* or *more worthy than,* and he believes that some characteristics, like wisdom and moral goodness, are great-making characteristics in that anything which has them is a *better thing* than it would be (other characteristics of it remaining the same) were it to lack them.

We come now to what we may call the *key idea* in Anselm's Ontological Argument, Anselm believes that existence *in reality is a great-making quality.* How are we to understand this idea? Does Anselm mean that anything that exists is a greater thing than anything that doesn't? Although he doesn't ask or answer this question, it is perhaps reasonable to believe that Anselm did not mean this. For when he discusses wisdom as a great-making quality he is careful not to say that any wise thing is better than any unwise thing—for he recognizes that a just but unwise person might be a better being than a wise but unjust person.[5] I suggest that what Anselm means is that anything that doesn't exist but might have existed (is on the right side of our line but might have been on the left) would have been a greater thing than it is if it had existed (if it had been on the left side of our line), He is not comparing two different things (one existing and one not existing) and saying that the first is therefore greater than the second. Rather he is talking about one and the same thing and pointing out that if it does not exist but might have existed then *it* would have been a greater thing if it had existed. Using Anselm's distinction between existence in the understanding and existence in reality, we may express the key idea in Anselm's reasoning as follows: If something exists only in the understanding, but might have existed in reality, then it might have been greater than it is. Since the Fountain of Youth, for example, exists only in the understanding but, unlike the round square, might have existed in reality, it follows by Anselm's principle that the Fountain of Youth might have been a greater thing than it is.

Developing Anselm's Ontological Argument

Having looked at some of the important ideas at work in Anselm's Ontological Argument, we can now consider its step-by-step development. In presenting Anselm's argument I shall use the term *God* in place of the longer phrase "the being than which none greater is possible"—wherever the term *God* appears we are to think of it as simply an abbreviation of the longer phrase.

1. God exists in the understanding.

As we've noted, anyone who hears of the being than which none greater is possible is, in Anselm's view, committed to premise 1.

2. God might have existed in reality (God is a possible being).

Anselm, I think, assumes the truth of premise 2 without making it explicit in his reasoning. By asserting 2, I don't mean to imply that God does not exist in reality. All that is meant is that, unlike the round square, God is a possible being.

3. If something exists only in the understanding and might have existed in reality, then it might have been greater than it is.

As we noted earlier this is the key idea in Anselm's Ontological Argument. It is intended as a general principle true of anything.

Steps 1–3 constitute the basic premises of Anselm's Ontological Argument. From these three items it follows, so Anselm believes, that God exists in reality. But how does Anselm propose to convince us that if we accept 1–3 we are committed by the rules of logic to accept his conclusion that God exists in reality? Anselm's procedure is to offer what is called a *reductio ad absurdum* proof of his conclusion. Instead of showing directly that the existence of God follows from 1–3, Anselm invites us to *suppose* that God does not exist (that is, that the conclusion he wants to establish is false) and then shows how this supposition when conjoined with 1–3 leads to an absurd result, a result that couldn't possibly be true because it is contradictory. In short, with the help of 1–3 Anselm shows that the supposition that God does not exist reduces to an absurdity. Since the supposition that God does not exist leads to an absurdity, that supposition must be rejected in favor of the conclusion that God does exist.

Does Anselm succeed in reducing the fool's belief that God does not exist to an absurdity? The best way to answer this question is to follow the steps of his argument.

4. Suppose God exists only in the understanding.

This supposition, as we saw earlier, is Anselm's way of expressing the fool's belief that God does not exist.

5. God might have been greater than he is. (2, 4, and 3)[6]

Step 5 follows from steps 2, 4, and 3. Since 3, if true, is true of anything it will be true of God. Step 3, therefore, implies that if God exists only in the understanding and might have existed in reality, then God might have been greater than he is. If so, then given 2 and 4, 5 must be true. For what 3 says when applied to God is that given 2 and 4 it follows that 5.

6. God is a being than which a greater is possible. (5) Surely if God is such that he logically might have been greater, then he is such than which a greater is possible.

We're now in a position to appreciate Anselm's *reductio* argument. He has shown us that if we accept 1–4 we must accept 6. But 6 is unacceptable; it is the absurdity Anselm was after. For replacing *God* in step 6 with the longer phrase it abbreviates, we see that 6 amounts to the absurd assertion:

7. The being than which none greater is possible is a being than which a greater is possible.

Now since 1–4 have led us to an obviously false conclusion, if we accept Anselm's basic premises 1-3 as true, 4, the supposition that God exists only in the understanding, must be rejected as false. Thus we have shown that

8. It is false that God exists only in the understanding.

But since premise 1 tells us that God does exist in the understanding, and 8 tells us that God does not exist only there, we may infer that

9. God exists in reality as well as in the understanding. (1, 8)

What are we to say of this argument? Most of the philosophers who have considered the argument have rejected it because of a basic conviction that from the logical analysis of a certain idea or concept we can never determine that there exists in reality anything answering to that idea or concept. We may examine and analyze, for example, the idea of an elephant or the idea of a unicorn, but it is only by our experience of the world that we can determine that there exist things answering to our first idea and not to the second. Anselm, however, believes that the concept of God is utterly unique—from an analysis of this concept he believes that it can be determined that there exists in reality a being which answers to it. Moreover, he presents us with an argument to show that it can be done in the case of the idea of God. We can, of course, simply reject his argument on the grounds that it violates the basic conviction noted above. Many critics, however, have sought to prove more directly that Anselm's argument is a bad argument and to point out the particular step in his argument that is mistaken. In what follows we shall examine the three major objections that have been advanced by the argument's critics.

Gaunilo's Criticism

The first major criticism was advanced by a contemporary of Anselm's, a monk named Gaunilo, who wrote a response entitled "On Behalf of the Fool,"[7] Gaunilo sought to prove that Anselm's reasoning is mistaken by applying it to things other than God, things which we know don't exist. He took as his example the island than which none greater is possible. No such island really exists. But, argues Gaunilo, if Anselm's reasoning were correct we could show that such an island really does exist. For since it is greater to exist than not to exist, if the island than which none greater is possible doesn't exist then it is an island than which a greater is possible. But it is impossible for the island than which none greater is possible to be an island than which a greater is possible. Therefore, the island than which none greater is possible must exist. About this argument Gaunilo remarks:

> If a man should try to prove to me by such reasoning that this island truly exists, and that its existence should no longer be doubted, either I should believe that he was jesting, or I know not which I ought to regard as the greater fool: myself, supposing I should allow this proof; or him, if he should suppose that he had established with any certainty the existence of this island.[8]

Gaunilo's strategy is clear. By using the very same reasoning Anselm employs in his argument, we can prove the existence of things we know don't exist. Therefore, Anselm's reasoning in his proof of the existence of God must be mistaken. In his reply to Gaunilo, Anselm insisted that his reasoning applies only to God and cannot be used to establish the existence of things other than God. Unfortunately, Anselm did not explain just why his reasoning cannot be applied to things like Gaunilo's island.

In defense of Anselm against Gaunilo's objection, we should note that the objection supposes that Gaunilo's island is a possible thing. But this requires us to believe that some finite, limited thing (an island) might have unlimited perfections. And it is not at all clear that this is possible. Try to think, for example, of a hockey player than which none greater is possible. How fast would he have to skate? How many goals would such a player have to score in a game? How fast would he have to shoot the puck? Could this player ever fall down, be checked, or receive a penalty? Although the phrase "The hockey player than which none greater is possible" seems meaningful, as soon as we try to get a clear idea of what such a being would be like, we discover that we can't form a coherent idea of it at all. For we are being invited to think of some limited, finite thing—a hockey player or an island—and then to think of it as exhibiting unlimited, infinite perfections. Perhaps, then, since Anselm's reasoning applies only to possible things, Anselm can reject its application to Gaunilo's island on the grounds that the island than which none greater is possible is, like the round square, an impossible thing.

Kant's Criticism

By far the most famous objection to the Ontological Argument was set forth by Immanuel Kant in the eighteenth century. According to this objection, the mistake in the argument is its claim, implicit in premise 3, that existence is a quality or predicate that adds to the greatness of a thing. There are two parts to this claim: (1) existence is a quality or predicate, and (2) existence, like wisdom and unlike physical size, is a great-making quality or predicate. Someone might accept (1) but object to (2). The objection made famous by Kant, however, is directed at (1). According to this objection, existence is not a predicate at all. Therefore, since in its third premise Anselm's argument implies that existence is a predicate, the argument must be rejected.

What is meant by the philosophical doctrine that existence is not a predicate? The central point in this doctrine concerns what we do when we ascribe a certain quality or predicate to something, is for example, when we say of a woman next door that she is intelligent, six feet tall, or thin. In each case we seem to assert or presuppose that there *exists* a woman next door and then go on to ascribe to her a certain predicate—"intelligent," six feet tall," or "thin." And what is claimed by many proponents of the doctrine that existence is not a predicate is that this is a *general feature* of predication. They hold that when we ascribe a quality or predicate to anything, we assert or presuppose that the thing exists and then ascribe the predicate to it. Now, if this is so, then it's clear that existence cannot be a predicate which we may ascribe to or deny of something. For if it were predicate, then when we assert of some thing that it exists we would be asserting or presupposing that it exists and then going on to predicate existence of it. For example, if existence were a predicate, then in asserting "Tigers exist" we would be asserting or presupposing that tigers exist and then going on to predicate existence of them. Furthermore, in asserting "Dragons do not exist" we would be asserting or presupposing, if existence were a predicate, that dragons do exist and then going on to deny that existence attaches to them. In short, if existence were a predicate, the affirmative existential statement "Tigers exist" would be a redundancy, and the negative existential statement "Dragons do not exist" would be contradictory. But clearly "Tigers exist" is not a redundancy and "Dragons do not exist" is true and, therefore, not contradictory. What this shows, according to the proponents of Kant's objection, is that existence is not a genuine predicate.

According to the proponents of the above objection, what we are asserting when we assert that tigers exist and that dragons do not is not that certain things (tigers) have and certain other things (dragons) do not have a peculiar predicate, *existence,* rather, we are saying something about the *concept* of a tiger and the *concept* of a dragon. In the first case we are saying that the concept of a tiger applies to something in the world; in the second case we are saying that the concept of a dragon does not apply to anything in the world.

Although this objection to the Ontological Argument has been widely accepted, it is doubtful that it provides us with a conclusive refutation of the argument. It may be true that existence is not a predicate, that in asserting the existence of something we are not ascribing a certain predicate or attribute to that thing. But the arguments presented for this view seem to rest on mistaken or incomplete claims about the nature of predication. For example, the argument which we stated earlier rests on the claim that when we ascribe a predicate to anything we assert or presuppose that that thing exists. But this claim appears to be mistaken. In asserting that Dr. Doolittle is an animal lover I seem to be ascribing the predicate *animal lover* to Dr. Doolittle, but in doing so I certainly am not asserting or presupposing that Dr. Doolittle actually exists. Dr. Doolittle doesn't exist but it is, nevertheless, true that he is an animal lover. The plain fact is that we can talk about and ascribe predicates to many things which do not and never did exist. Merlin, for example, no less than Houdini, was a magician, although Houdini existed but Merlin did not. If, as these examples suggest, the claim that whenever we ascribe a predicate to something we assert or presuppose that the thing exists is a false claim, then we will need a better argument for the doctrine that existence is not a predicate. There is some question, however, whether anyone has succeeded in giving a really conclusive argument for the view that existence is not a predicate.[9]

A Third Criticism

A third objection against the Ontological Argument calls into question the premise that God might have existed in reality (God is a possible being). As we saw, this premise claims that "the being than which none greater is possible" is not an impossible object. But is this true? Consider the series of positive integers—1, 2, 3, 4 and so on. We know that any integer in this series, no matter how large, is such that a larger than it is possible. Therefore, "the positive integer than which none larger is possible" is an impossible object. Perhaps this is also true of "the being than which none greater is possible." That is, perhaps no matter how great a being may be, it is possible for there to be a being greater than it. If this were so, then, like "the integer than which none larger is possible," Anselm's God would not be a possible object. The mere fact that there are degrees of greatness, however, does not entitle us to conclude that Anselm's God is like "the integer than which none larger is possible." There are, for example, degrees of size in angles — one angle is larger than another—but it is not true that no matter how large an angle is it is possible for there to be an angle larger than it. It is logically impossible for an angle to exceed four right angles. The notion of an angle, unlike the notion of a positive integer, implies a degree of size beyond which it is impossible to go. Is Anselm's God like a largest integer, and therefore impossible, or like a largest angle, and therefore possible? Some philosophers have argued that Anselm's God is impossible.[10] But the arguments for this conclusion are not very compelling. Perhaps, then, this objection is best construed not as proving that Anselm's God is impossible, but as raising the question whether any of us is in a position to know that "the being than which none greater is possible" is a possible object. For Anselm's argument cannot be a successful proof of the existence of God unless its premises are not just true, but are really *known* to be true. Therefore, if we don't know that Anselm's God is a possible object, then his argument cannot prove the existence of God to us, cannot enable us to know that God exists.

A Final Critique

We've had a look at both Anselm's argument, and the three major objections philosophers have raised against it. In this final section I want to present a somewhat different critique of the argument, a critique suggested by the basic conviction noted earlier: namely, that from the mere logical analysis of a certain idea or concept, we can never determine that there exists in reality anything answering to that idea or concept.

Suppose someone comes to us and says:

> I propose to define the term *God* as *an existing, wholly perfect being.* Now since it can't be true that an existing, wholly perfect being does not exist, it can't be true that God, as I've defined him, does not exist. Therefore, God must exist.

This argument appears to be a very simple Ontological Argument. It begins with a particular idea or concept of God and ends by concluding that God, so conceived, must exist. What can we say in response? We might start by objecting to this definition of *God,* claiming (1) that only predicates can be used to define a term, and (2) that existence is not a predicate. But suppose our friend is not impressed by this response—either because he thinks no one has fully explained what a predicate is or proved that existence isn't one, or because he thinks that anyone can define a word in whatever way he pleases. Can we allow our friend to define the word *God* in any way he pleases and still hope to show that it will not follow from that definition that there actually exists something to which this concept of God applies? I think we can. Let's first invite him, however, to consider some concepts other than this peculiar concept of God.

Earlier we noted that the term *magician* may be applied both to Houdini and Merlin, even though the former existed whereas the latter did not. Noting that our friend has used *existing* as part of this definition of *God,* suppose we agree with him that we can define a word in any way we please, and, accordingly, introduce the following words with the following definitions:

> A *magican* is defined as an *existing magician.*
> A *magico* is defined as a *nonexisting magician.*

Here we have introduced two words and used *existing* or *nonexisting* in their definitions. Now something of interest follows from the fact that *existing* is part of our definition of a magican. For while it's true that Merlin was a *magician* it isn't true that Merlin was a *magican.* And something of interest follows from our including *nonexisting* in the definition of a magico. For while it's true that Houdini was a *magician* it isn't true that Houdini was a *magico.* Houdini was a *magician* and a *magican,* but not a *magico,* whereas Merlin was a *magician* and a *magico,* but not a *magican.*

What we have just seen is that introducing *existing* or *nonexisting* into the definition of a concept has a very important implication. If we introduce *existing* into the definition of a concept, it follows that no nonexisting thing can exemplify that concept. And if we introduce *nonexisting* into the definition of a concept, it follows that no existing thing can exemplify that concept. No nonexisting thing can be a *magican* and no existing thing can be a *magico.*

But must some existing thing exemplify the concept *magican?* No! From the fact that *existing* is included in the definition of *magican* it does not follow that some existing thing is a *magican*—all that follows is that no nonexisting thing is a *magican.* If there were no magicians in existence there would be nothing to which the term *magican* would apply. This being so, it clearly does not follow merely from our definition of *magican* that some existing thing is a *magican.* Only if magicians exist will it be true that some existing thing is a *magican.*

We are now in a position to help our friend see that, from the mere fact that *God* is defined as an existing, wholly perfect being, it will not follow that some existing being is God. Something of interest does follow from his definition: namely, that no nonexisting being can be God. But whether some existing thing is God will depend entirely on whether some existing thing is a wholly perfect being. If no wholly perfect being exists there will be nothing to which this concept of God can apply. This being so, it clearly does not follow merely from this definition of *God* that some existing thing is God. Only if a wholly perfect being exists will it be true that God, as our friend conceives of him, exists.

Implications for Anselm's Argument

The implications of these considerations for Anselm's ingenious argument can now be traced. Anselm conceives of God as a being than which none greater is possible. He then claims that existence is a great-making quality, something that has it is greater than it would have been had it lacked existence, Clearly then, no nonexisting thing can exemplify Anselm's concept of God. For if we suppose that some nonexisting thing exemplifies Anselm's concept of God and also suppose that that nonexisting thing might have existed in reality (is a possible thing), then we are supposing that that nonexisting thing (1) might have been a greater thing, and (2) is, nevertheless, a thing than which a greater is not possible. Thus far Anselm's reasoning is, I believe, impeccable. But what follows from it? All that follows from it is that no nonexisting thing can be God (as Anselm conceives of God). All that follows is that given Anselm's concept of God, the proposition "Some nonexisting thing is God" cannot be true. But, as we saw earlier, this is also the case with the proposition "Some nonexisting thing is a magican." What remains to be shown is that some existing thing exemplifies Anselm's concept of God. What really does follow from his reasoning is that the only thing that logically could exemplify his concept of God is something which actually exists. And this conclusion is not without interest. But from the mere fact that nothing but an existing thing could exemplify Anselm's concept of God, it does not follow that some existing thing actually does exemplify his concept of God — no more than it follows from the mere fact that no nonexisting thing can be a magican that some existing thing is a magican.[11]

There is, however, one major difficulty in this critique of Anselm's argument. This difficulty arises when we take into account Anselm's implicit claim that God is a possible thing. To see just what this difficulty is, let's return to the idea of a possible thing. A possible thing, we determined, is any thing that either is on the left side of our imaginary line or logically might have been on the left side of the line. Possible things, then, will be all those things that, unlike the round square, are not impossible things. Suppose we concede to Anselm that God, as he conceives of him, is a possible thing. Now, of course, the mere knowledge that something is a possible thing doesn't enable us to conclude that that thing is an existing thing. For many possible things, like the Fountain of Youth, do not exist. But if something is a possible thing, then it is either an existing thing or a nonexisting thing. The set of possible things can be exhaustively divided into those possible things which actually exist and those possible things which do not exist. Therefore, if Anselm's God is a possible thing, it is either an existing thing or a nonexisting thing. We have concluded, however, that no nonexisting thing can be Anselm's God; therefore, it seems we must conclude with Anselm that some actually existing thing does exemplify his concept of God.

To see the solution to this major difficulty we need to return to an earlier example. Let's consider again the idea of a magican, an existing magician. It so happens that some magicians have existed—Houdini, The Great Blackstone, and others. But, of course, it might have been otherwise. Suppose, for the moment, that no magicians have ever existed. The concept "magician" would still have application, for it would still be true that Merlin was a magician. But what about the concept of a "magican?" Would any possible object be picked out by that concept? No! For no nonexisting thing could exemplify the concept "magican." And on the supposition that no magicians ever existed, no existing thing would exemplify the concept "magican."[12] We then would have a coherent concept "magican" which would not be exemplified by any possible object at all. For if all the possible objects which are magicians are nonexisting things, none of them would be a magican and, since no possible objects which exist are magicians, none of them would be a magican. We then would have a coherent, consistent concept "magican," which in fact is not exemplified by any possible object at all. Put in this way, our result seems paradoxical. For we are inclined to think that only contradictory concepts like "the round square" are not exemplified by any possible things. The truth is, however, that when *existing* is included in or implied by a certain concept, it may be the case that no possible object does in fact exemplify that concept. For no possible object that doesn't exist will exemplify a concept like "magican" in which *existing* is included; and if there are no existing things which exemplify the other features included in the concept—for example, "being a magician" in the case of the concept "magican"—then no possible object that exists will exemplify the concept. Put in its simplest terms, if we ask whether any possible thing is a magican, the answer will depend entirely on whether any existing thing is a magician. If no existing things are magicians, then no possible things are magicans. Some possible object is a magican just in case some actually existing thing is a magician.[13]

Applying these considerations to Anselm's argument we can find the solution to our major difficulty. Given Anselm's concept of God and his principle that existence is a great-making quality, it really does follow that the only thing that logically could exemplify his concept of God is something which actually exists. But, we argued, it doesn't follow from these considerations alone that God actually exists, that some existing thing exemplifies Anselm's concept of God. The difficulty we fell into, however, is that when we add the premise that God is a possible thing, that some possible object exemplifies his concept of God, it really does follow that God actually exists, that some actually existing thing exemplifies Anselm's concept of God. For if some possible object exemplifies his concept of God, that object is either an existing thing or a nonexisting thing. But since no nonexisting thing could exemplify Anselm's concept of God, it follows that the possible object which exemplifies his concept of God must be a possible object that actually exists. Therefore, given (1) Anselm's concept of God, (2) his principles that existence is a great-making quality, and (3) the prmise that God, as conceived by Anselm, is a possible thing, it really does follow that Anselm's God actually exists.

The Generous Grant

But we now can see that in granting Anselm the premise that God is a possible thing we have granted far more than we intended. All we thought we were conceding is that Anselm's concept of God, unlike the concept of a round square, is not contradictory or incoherent. But without realizing it we were in fact granting much more than this, as became apparent when we considered the idea of a "magician" There is nothing contradictory in the idea of a magican, an existing magician. But in asserting that a magican is a possible thing, we are, as we saw, directly implying that some existing thing is a magician. For if no existing thing is a magician, the concept of a magican will apply to no possible object whatever. The same point holds with respect to Anselm's God. Since Anselm's concept of God logically cannot apply to some nonexisting thing, the only possible objects to which it could apply are possible objects which actually exist. Therefore, in granting that Anselm's God is a possible thing, we are granting far more than that his idea of God isn't incoherent or contradictory. Suppose, for example, that every existing being has some defect which it might not have had. Without realizing it, we were denying this when we granted that Anselm's God is a possible being. For if every existing being has a defect it might not have had, then every existing being might have been greater. But if every existing being might have been greater, then Anselm's concept of God will apply to no possible object whatever. Therefore, if we allow Anselm his concept of God and his principle that existence is a great-making quality, then in granting that God, as Anselm conceives of him, is a possible being, we will be granting much more than that his concept of God is not contradictory. We will be granting, for example, that some existing thing is as perfect as it can be. For the plain fact is that Anselm's God is a possible thing only if some *existing* thing is as perfect as it can be.

Our final critique of Anselm's argument is simply this. In granting that Anselm's God is a possible thing, we are in fact granting that Anselm's God actually exists. But since the purpose of the argument is to prove to us that Anselm's God exists, we cannot be asked to grant as a premise a statement which is virtually equivalent to the conclusion that is to be proved. Anselm's concept of God may be coherent and his principle that existence is a great-making quality may be true. But all that follows from this is that no nonexisting thing can be Anselm's God. If we add to all of this the premise that God is a possible thing it will follow that God actually exists. But the additional premise claims more than that Anselm's concept of God isn't incoherent or contradictory. It amounts to the assertion that some existing being is supremely great. And since this is, in part, the point the argument endeavors to prove, the argument begs the question: it assumes the point it is supposed to prove.

If the above critique is correct, Anselm's argument fails as a proof of the existence of God. This is not to say, however, that the argument isn't a work of genius. Perhaps no other argument in the history of thought has raised so many basic philosophical questions and stimulated so much hard thought. Even if it fails as a proof of the existence of God, it will remain as one of the high achievements of the human intellect.

Notes

1. Some philosophers believe that Anselm sets forth a different and more cogent argument in Chapter Three of his *Proslogium.* For this viewpoint see Charles Hartshorne, *Anselm's Discovery* (La Salle, Illinois: Open Court Publishing Co., 1965), and Norman Malcolm, "Anselm's Ontological Arguments," *The Philosophical Review,* LXIX, No. 1 (1960), pp. 41–62. For an illuminating account both of Anselm's intensions in *Proslogium,* II and III and of recent interpretations of Anselm, see Arthur C. McGill's essay "Recent Discussions of Anselm's Argument" in *The Many-faced Argument,* ed. John Hick and Arthur C. McGill (New York: The Macmillan Co., 1967), pp. 33–110.

2. Anselm does allow that someone may assert the sentence "God does not exist" without having in his understanding the object or idea for which the word *God* stands (See *Proslogium,* IV in *Saint Anselm: Basic Writings,* tr. Sidney N. Deane). But when a person does understand the object for which a word stands, then when he uses that word in a sentence denying the existence of that object, he must have that object in his understanding. It is doubtful, however, that Anselm thought that incoherent or contradictory expressions like *round square* stand for objects which may exist in the understanding.

3. Anselm speaks of *a being* rather than *the being* than which none greater can be conceived. His argument is easier to present if we express his idea of God in terms of *the being.* Secondly, to avoid the psychological connotations of *can be conceived* I have substituted *possible.*

4. St. Anselm, *Monologium,* II in *Saint Anselm, Basic Writings,* tr. Sidney N. Deane.

5. See *Monologium,* XV in *Saint Anselm, Basic Writings,* tr. Sidney N. Deane.

6. The numbers in parentheses refer to the earlier steps in the argument from which the present step is derived.

7. Gaunilo's brief essay, Anselm's reply, and several of Anselm's major works, as translated by S. N. Deane, are collected together in *Saint Anselm: Basic Writings* (La Salle, Illinois: Open Court Publishing Co., 1962).

8. Deane, *Saint Anselm: Basic Writings,* p. 151.

9. Perhaps the most sophisticated presentation of the objection that existence is not a predicate is William P. Alston's "The Ontological Argument Revisited" in *The Philosophical Review,* LXIX (1960), pp. 452–74.
10. See, for example, C. D. Broad's discussion of the Ontological Argument in *Religion, Philosophy, and Psychical Research* (New York: Harcourt, Brace & Co., 1953).
11. An argument along the lines just presented may be found in J. Shaffer's illuminating essay, "Existence, Predication and the Ontological Argument," *Mind* LXXI (1962), pp. 307–25.
12. I am indebted to Professor William Wainwright for bringing this point to my attention.
13. In the language of possible worlds, we can say that some object *x* is a *magican* in a possible world *w,* provided (i) *x* is a magician in *w,* and (ii) *x* is a magician in whatever world happens to be actual. For more on this matter, as well as a critical discussion of some other versions of the Ontological Argument, see my essay "Modal Versions of the Ontological Argument" in *Philosophy of Religion,* ed. Louis Pojman (Belmont, CA: Wadsworth, 1987), pp. 69–73.

Chapter 4 The Problem of Evil

In the previous chapter we have explored the three classical **proofs for** the existence of a theistic God; namely, the Cosmological, Teleological, and Ontological Arguments. In the present chapter we are going to cover perhaps the most formidable **argument against** the existence of a theistic God; namely, an argument based on the presence of evil in the world. *The problem of evil* (as it is often called) can be stated succinctly in the form of the following question:

Can a Perfect God co-exist with the existence of Evil?

It is important to remember in the present context that a theistic God is *perfect* in the sense that it features all of the perfections listed in Chapter 1. The intuition behind the problem of evil as stated by the above question then is this: it is difficult to understand and, perhaps, it is even *inconceivable* that a being alleged to be omniscient, omnipotent, morally perfect, omni-benevolent, person-like and creator will allow any evil to exist in the world, let alone so much evil as actually exists.

In is worth emphasizing two points regarding the concept of *evil* as we shall use it in the present context. First, we shall use 'evil' to mean *suffering of innocent persons*, regardless of the cause of the suffering. (Note: We are leaving aside the suffering of innocent animals.) Second, when we talk about evil, in this sense, we talk about several dimensions of evil: i.e., different categories of suffering; the quantity of suffering; the duration of suffering; and the intensity of suffering. Each dimension of suffering listed above must be explained by a theist.

It appears then that the problem of evil arises because there is some sort of *tension* between the following two propositions:

A. A perfect God exists;
B. Evil exists.

The word 'tension' above can be interpreted in two different ways. According to one clear interpretation, the *tension* between propositions A and B means that they are *logically inconsistent.*

There are several ways in which a set of propositions (or sentences) can be logically inconsistent. The simplest way is if the set in questions consists of two contradictory propositions. For instance, the pair of propositions

i   Snow is white.
ii It is not the case that snow is white.

is said to be *explicitly* inconsistent because it contains two contradictory propositions, since (ii) is the negation of (i). Under such conditions, it is immediately clear that (i) and (ii) cannot both be true.

But there are more complicated cases where a set of propositions is said to be logically inconsistent, but the inconsistency is not as simple as in the case of the pair (i)-(ii). Consider a very clear yet simple example offered by William L. Rowe[1]:

    iii This object is red.
    iv   This object is not colored.

It should be obvious to anyone that (iii) and (iv) are logically inconsistent. But in this case the logical inconsistency is not as straightforward as in the case of (i) and (ii) because we do not have here two contradictory propositions. (iii) and (iv) are *implicitly* inconsistent, in the following sense: in order to derive an explicit contradiction from (iii) and (iv) we need an additional propositions so that the resulting triad of propositions will entail an explicit contradiction. What kind of proposition do we need to add in order to derive the desired contradiction? Well, in this case it is relatively easy to identify the particular proposition that will do the trick; it is

    v Everything that is red is colored.

Once we add (v) to (iii) and (iv), we can derive from this triad of propositions an explicit contradiction. But notice that (v) is a *necessary truth*: i.e., it is not possible for there to be an object that is red, but it is not colored. And, of course, we have intuitively relied upon something like (v) when we initially judged the pair of sentences (iii) and (iv) as logically inconsistent.

Now, clearly A and B are not explicitly inconsistent (in the same sense as (i) and (ii) above are). So if they are logically inconsistent at all, they are more like the example of (iii) and (iv). But this means that those who think that the existence of a perfect God is *logically inconsistent* with the existence of evil in the world must produce an additional proposition, call it C, such that:

    a. C in conjunction with A and B entail a contradiction;
    b. C is a necessary truth.

The problem that the logical version of the problem of evil faces is that it is not that easy to produce a sentence C that satisfies *both* conditions (a) and (b). In order to see this, let us make a couple of reasonable assumptions.

First, let us assume that a being that is morally perfect always does what morality requires. This assumption is part of what we mean by God's moral perfection, as stated in Chapter 1. Second, let us also assume (something that should be perfectly obvious) that what is prevented from occurring does not exist. Both of these assumptions are fairly harmless.

> Now, suppose you come up with the following candidate for C:
> C*. A perfect God ought to prevent every instance of evil in the world.

---

[1] Rowe, L. W. (2001), *Philosophy of Religion: An Introduction*, (3rd. edition), pp.93-94, Wadsworth/Thomson Learning, Belmont: CA. See also, Nelson Pike, 'Hume on Evil', *The Philosophical Review*, 72 (1963), pp. 180-97.

If we add C* to A and B, then the set A, B, and C* (together with the two harmless assumptions we have just stated above) entails a contradiction: namely, that Evil exists and that Evil does not exist. So C* satisfies the first requirement expressed in (a) above. But does it satisfy requirement (b)? That is, can we show that C* is a *necessary truth*, in the sense that this proposition could not possibly be false?

The proponents of the logical version of the problem of evil have had a very difficult time showing that C*, or any alternative version that is equivalent to C*, can be considered a necessary truth. Intuitively the problem with coming up with the requisite necessary truth is this. We very frequently encounter in our own experiences cases whereby some evil is necessary either in order to prevent an even worst evil (a visit to the dentist comes to mind) or in order to make it possible that some very important good should come to exist. Under such circumstances, we ourselves would consider allowing such evils to exist as morally justified, provided we are convinced that they are required in one of the two ways just noted. And, now, all we need to do is to apply the very same considerations to God.

It is possible, or at least not yet ruled out, that God is morally justified to allow quite a lot of evil in the world, provided that such evil is necessary either in order to prevent an even worst evil from occurring or in order to allow for a very important good to come about. And due to the fact that human beings, unlike the theistic God, are not omniscient, we cannot, or simply do not, know these connections. But if this concession is made, then the following is true:

> D. There are some cases of evil where it is not morally obligatory for a perfect God to prevent such evils.

But if D is true even just in one case of evil, then C* is false for that particular case. But, then, C* cannot be a necessary truth. Hence, if we concede that even God is morally justified to allow some evils either in order to prevent some worst evils from occurring or in order to bring about some valuable goods, then any attempt to come up with a sentence that renders A and B logically inconsistent and satisfies conditions (a) and (b) is doomed to failure.

It is due to these considerations that ultimately philosophers concluded that the logical version of the problem of evil fails to pose a serious threat to the existence of a theistic God.

So far we have argued that the proponents of the logical problem of evil cannot show that the existence of a theistic perfect God (A) is logically inconsistent with the existence of evil (B) unless they come up with a suitable candidate for a propositions C which satisfies conditions (a) and (b). And this task is not as easy as it has been initially thought. We may describe our efforts on behalf of a perfect theistic God so far as purely negative or better yet as purely *defensive*. In other words, so far we have marshaled arguments that are defensive in character.

But a purely defensive strategy against the logical problem of evil is inherently risky, for it does not show that a suitable candidate for C does not actually exist or that it is not possible for anyone to discover it at some future time. In order to show that such a suitable candidate for C cannot exist, a defender of theism must show that the existence of a perfect theistic God is *logically consistent* with the existence of evil. And this task requires a positive theory which explains how even a perfect God must allow evil to exist in the world. In the language of the philosophy of Religion, such a positive theory is called a *theodicy*. In other words, we need a positive theodicy which proves that evil is *logically consistent* with a perfect God. In other words, a theodicy attempts to provide a positive explanation why an omnipotent, omniscient, morally perfect, omnibenevolent, person-like God would allow so much evil in the world.

Free-Will Theodicy: Several theodicies have been proposed in the literature. The most well-known among these is the so-called the *Free-Will Theodicy*.[2] Since we all agree that free-will is a very valuable thing, we will also grant that a world that contains beings like us that feature free-will is a better world than a world which would lack any such beings altogether. But it is not logically possible even for a perfect being such as God to create beings with free-will and at the same time guarantee that such beings will always choose good and avoid evil. For any such guarantee, so the argument goes, requires God to causally prevent free beings from exercising their free will to choose evil. But such interference deprives free agents from their free-will which defeats the whole point of granting such agents free will in the first place.

The Free-Will theodicy is intended to offer an explanation why a perfect God must allow evil in the world; it does not merely place the burden of proof on the proponents of the logical problem of evil to come up with a suitable candidate for C. And the explanation is that it is logically impossible even for a perfect being such as the theistic God to grant free-will, which is an extremely valuable characteristic to have, and yet guarantee that beings such as us will never use our free will to do evil. Therefore, evil is logically consistent with the existence of a perfect theistic God. This account is supposed to explain why it is not possible to come up with a suitable candidate for C.

The Free-Will theodicy, however, is vulnerable to several objections. The most important of these objections is that even if we grant that the free will theodicy is successful in explaining why a perfect God allows certain types of evil to exist, it leaves a whole other category of evils unexplained. Thus, we need to distinguish between two types of evils.

On the one hand, there are **moral evils** *which are evils caused by intentional choices made by free agents* such as ourselves. On the other hand, there are so-called **natural evils** *which are evils caused by natural phenomena* such as Tsunamis, Hurricanes, Floods, Diseases, Earthquakes, etc. Since the evils caused by these later type of natural events are not caused by intentional choices of moral agents, the free will theodicy fails to explain why a perfect theistic God allows natural evils to occur. Thus, a proponent of the free-will theodicy will have to appeal to another explanation in order to account for why God allows natural evils to occur or else extend somehow the free will theodicy to explain why God allows natural evils. Both of these courses require additional premises, which expose the free will theodicy to further potential objections.

A different type of approach a theist might wish to take to the problem of evil is to argue that *there **cannot** be good without evil*. The intuition advanced here is that good and evil are in some ways are so linked they must appear together. We are familiar with this phenomenon from other examples. For instance, right and left or up and down also are pairs of concepts such that no one of these concepts from each pair makes sense without the other. If this feature of good and evil were true, then the theist can maintain that even a theistic God cannot create a world in which only good occurs without any evil.

Before we can evaluate this claim, we need to distinguish between two ways in which we can understand the proposition: *there cannot be good without evil*. The first interpretation construes the word 'cannot' as pertaining to the manner we happen to be constituted. In other words, we are so constituted that we cannot understand and appreciate good unless we experience evil. The second interpretation construes the word 'cannot' about the world, rather than about us. Namely, according to the second interpretation, there cannot be any possible world such that it contains only good without some instances of evil.

Let us now examine each of these interpretations. The first interpretation fails due to the enormous amount of different kinds of suffering, the sheer quantity of suffering,

---

the duration of suffering, and its intensity. Even if it is true that we cannot understand or appreciate good unless we experience evil, it is still not clear why there is so much evil in the world. Let me try to bring this point home to you with a parable. Suppose God created what I call 'Evil Zoos'. In these Zoos children and adults as well, can watch a variety of different kinds of evil. We can imagine how parents take their children to evil zoos on a weekend so that they can experience some evil and, therefore, learn how to understand and appreciate good. God surely could have so created the world. In other words, there is simply too much suffering in the world; too many kinds of suffering; too many instances of suffering; too many instances where the duration of suffering is unnecessarily long; and too many cases of intense suffering so that all of this is simply allowed by God in order for us to be educated to appreciate good.

Let us now turn to the second interpretation. According to this interpretation, it is not possible for any world to exist in which there are instances of good but no instances of evil. Unfortunately, the theist cannot accept this proposition. For this proposition is incompatible with two important theses the theist holds. The first thesis is that God is perfectly good; i.e., there is no evil in God. The second thesis the theist holds is that while God create the world, God could have created absolutely nothing. Now, in a world which God created nothing, which is certainly a possible world, only God exists, since there is nothing else. And since God is perfectly good, in a world in which God created nothing, there is good without evil. Therefore, the theist is compelled to reject this second interpretation of the proposition that there cannot be good without evil.

To conclude: The first way of interpreting the proposition that there cannot be good without evil fails to explain why there is so much evil in the world. So the thsit cannot take full advantage of this interpretation in order to explain why there is evil in the world. The second interpretation of the proposition that there cannot be good without evil the theist must reject because it turns out to be inconsistent with other important theses the theist holds. Therefore, neither interpretation suffices to rule out the problem of evil.

And so our original question whether a perfect God can co-exist with evil is still debated and most likely will be debated for a long time into the future.

Evil and Omnipotence

J. L. Mackie

The traditional arguments for the existence of God have been fairly thoroughly criticised by philosophers. But the theologian can, if he wishes, accept this criticism. He can admit that no rational proof of God's existence is possible. And he can still retain all that is essential to his position, by holding that God's existence is known in some other, non-rational way. I think, however, that a more telling criticism can be made by way of the traditional problem of evil. Here it can be shown, not that religious beliefs lack rational support, but that they are positively irrational, that the several parts of the essential theological doctrine are inconsistent with one another, so that the theologian can maintain his position as a whole only by a much more extreme rejection of reason than in the former case. He must now be prepared to believe, not merely what cannot be proved, but what can be *disproved* from other beliefs that he also holds.

The problem of evil, in the sense in which I shall be using the phrase, is a problem only for someone who believes that there is a God who is both omnipotent and wholly good. And it is a logical problem, the problem of clarifying and reconciling a number of beliefs: it is not a scientific problem that might be solved by further observations, or a practical problem that might be solved by a decision or an action. These points are obvious; I mention them only because they are sometimes ignored by theologians, who sometimes parry a statement of the problem with such remarks as 'Well, can you solve the problem yourself?' or 'This is a mystery which may be revealed to us later' or 'Evil is something to be faced and overcome, not to be merely discussed'.

In its simplest form the problem is this; God is omnipotent; God is wholly good; and yet evil exists. There seems to be some contradiction between these three propositions, so that if any two of them were true the third would be false. But at the same time all three are essential parts of most theological positions: the theologian, it seems, at once *must* adhere and *cannot consistently* adhere to all three. (The problem does not arise only for theists, but I shall discuss it in the form in which it presents itself for ordinary theism.)

However, the contradiction does not arise immediately; to show it we need some additional premises, or perhaps some quasi-logical rules connecting the terms 'good', 'evil', and 'omnipotent'. These additional principles are that good is opposed to evil, in such a way that a good thing always eliminates evil as far as it can, and that there are no limits to what an omnipotent thing can do. From these it follows that a good omnipotent thing eliminates evil completely, and then the propositions that a good omnipotent thing exists, and that evil exists, are incompatible.

J. L. Mackie, 'Evil and Omnipotence', first published in *Mind,* 64 (1955), pp. 200–12. Reprinted by permission of Oxford University Press.

Adequate Solutions

Now once the problem is fully stated it is clear that it can be solved, in the sense that the problem will not arise if one gives up at least one of the propositions that constitute it. If you are prepared to say that God is not wholly good; or not quite omnipotent, or that evil does not exist, or that good is not opposed to the kind of evil that exists, or that there are limits to what an omnipotent thing can do, then the problem of evil will not arise for you.

There are, then, quite a number of adequate solutions of the problem of evil, and some of these have been adopted, or almost adopted, by various thinkers. For example, a few have been prepared to deny God's omnipotence, and rather more have been prepared to keep the term 'omnipotence' but severely to restrict its meaning, recording quite a number of things that an omnipotent being cannot do. Some have said that evil is an illusion, perhaps because they held that the whole world of temporal, changing things is an illusion, and that what we call evil belongs only to this world, or perhaps because they held that although temporal things *are* much as we see them, those that we call evil are not really evil. Some have said that what we call evil is merely the privation of good, that evil in a positive sense, evil that would really be opposed to good, does not exist. Many have agreed with Pope that disorder is harmony not understood, and that partial evil is universal good. Whether any of these views is *true* is, of course, another question. But each of them gives an adequate solution of the problem of evil in the sense that if you accept it this problem does not arise for you, though you may, of course, have *other* problems to face.

But often enough these adequate solutions are only *almost* adopted. The thinkers who restrict God's power, but keep the term 'omnipotence', may reasonably be suspected of thinking, in other contexts, that his power is really unlimited. Those who say that evil is an illusion may also be thinking, inconsistently, that this illusion is itself an evil. Those who say that 'evil' is merely privation of good may also be thinking, inconsistently, that privation of good is an evil. (The fallacy here is akin to some forms of the 'naturalistic fallacy' in ethics, where some think, for example, that 'good' is just what contributes to evolutionary progress, and that evolutionary progress is itself good.) If Pope meant what he said in the first line of his couplet, that 'disorder' is only harmony not understood, the 'partial evil' of the second line must, for consistency, mean 'that which, taken in isolation, falsely appears to be evil', but it would more naturally mean 'that which, in isolation, really is evil'. The second line, in fact, hesitates between two views, that 'partial evil' isn't really evil, since only the universal quality is real, and that 'partial evil' is really an evil, but only a little one.

In addition, therefore, to adequate solutions, we must recognise unsatisfactory inconsistent solutions, in which there is only a half-hearted or temporary rejection of one of the propositions which together constitute the problem. In these, one of the constituent propositions is explicitly rejected, but it is covertly re-asserted or assumed elsewhere in the system.

Fallacious Solutions

Besides these half-hearted solutions, which explicitly reject but implicitly assert one of the constituent propositions, there are definitely fallacious solutions which explicitly maintain all the constituent propositions, but implicitly reject at least one of them in the course of the argument that explains away the problem of evil.

There are, in fact, many so-called solutions which purport to remove the contradiction without abandoning any of its constituent propositions. These must be fallacious, as we can see from the very statement of the problem, but it is not so easy to see in each case precisely where the fallacy lies. I suggest that in all cases the fallacy has the general form suggested above: in order to solve the problem one (or perhaps more) of its constituent propositions is given up, but in such a way that it appears to have been retained, and can therefore be asserted without qualification in other contexts, Sometimes there is a further complication: the supposed solution moves to and fro between, say, two of the constituent propositions, at one point asserting the first of these but covertly abandoning the second, at another point asserting the second but covertly abandoning the first. These fallacious solutions often turn upon some equivocation with the words 'good' and 'evil', or upon some vagueness about the way in which good and evil are opposed to one another, or about how much is meant by 'omnipotence'. I propose to examine some of these so-called solutions, and to exhibit their fallacies in detail. Incidentally, I shall also be considering whether an adequate solution could be reached by a minor modification of one or more of the constituent propositions, which would, however, still satisfy all the essential requirements of ordinary theism.

1. 'Good cannot exist without evil' or 'Evil is necessary as a counterpart to good.'

It is sometimes suggested that evil is necessary as a counterpart to good, that if there were no evil there could be no good either, and that this solves the problem of evil. It is true that it points to an answer to the question 'Why should there be evil?' But it does so only by qualifying some of the propositions that constitute the problem.

First, it sets a limit to what God can do, saying that God *cannot* create good without simultaneously creating evil, and this means either that God is not omnipotent or that there are *some* limits to what an omnipotent thing can do. It may be replied that these limits are always presupposed, that omnipotence has never meant the power to do what is logically impossible, and on the present view the existence of good without evil would be a logical impossibility. This interpretation of omnipotence may, indeed, be accepted as a modification of our original account which does not reject anything that is essential to theism, and I shall in general assume it in the subsequent discussion. It is, perhaps, the most common theistic view, but I think that some theists at least have maintained that God can do what is logically impossible. Many theists, at any rate, have held that logic itself is created or laid down by God, that logic is the way in which God arbitrarily chooses to think. (This is, of course, parallel to the ethical view that morally right actions are those which God arbitrarily chooses to command, and the two views encounter similar difficulties.) And *this* account of logic is clearly inconsistent with the view that God is bound by logical necessities—unless it is possible for an omnipotent being to bind himself, an issue which we shall consider later, when we come to the Paradox of Omnipotence. This solution of the problem of evil cannot, therefore, be consistently adopted along with the view that logic is self created by God.

But, secondly, this solution denies that evil is opposed to good in our original sense. If good and evil are counterparts, a good thing will not 'eliminate evil as far as it can'. Indeed, this view suggests that good and evil are not strictly qualities of things at all. Perhaps the suggestion is that good and evil are related in much the same way as great and small. Certainly, when the term 'great' is used relatively as a condensation of 'greater than so-and-so', and 'small' is used correspondingly, greatness and smallness are counterparts and cannot exist without each other. But in this sense greatness is not a quality, not an intrinsic feature of anything; and it would be absurd to think of a movement in favour of greatness and against smallness in this sense. Such a movement would be self-defeating, since relative greatness can be promoted only by a simultaneous promotion of relative smallness. I feel sure that no theists would be content to regard God's goodness as analogous to this—as if what he supports were not the *good* but the *better*, and as if he had the paradoxical aim that all things should be better than other things.

This point is obscured by the fact that 'great' and 'small' seem to have an absolute as well as a relative sense. I cannot discuss here whether there is absolute magnitude or not, but if there is, there could be an absolute sense for 'great', it could mean of at least a certain size, and it would make sense to speak of all things getting bigger, of a universe that was expanding all over, and therefore it would make sense to speak of promoting greatness. But in *this* sense great and small are not logically necessary counterparts: either quality could exist without the other. There would be no logical impossibility in everything's being small or in everything's being great.

Neither in the absolute nor in the relative sense, then, of 'great' and 'small' do these terms provide an analogy of the sort that would be needed to support this solution of the problem of evil. In neither case are greatness and smallness *both* necessary counterparts *and* mutually opposed forces or possible objects for support and attack.

It may be replied that good and evil are necessary counterparts in the same way as any quality and its logical opposite: redness can occur, it is suggested, only if non-redness also occurs. But unless evil is merely the privation of good, they are not logical opposites, and some further argument would be needed to show that they are counterparts in the same way as genuine logical opposites. Let us assume that this could be given. There is still doubt of the correctness of the metaphysical principle that a quality must have a real opposite: I suggest that it is not really impossible that everything should be, say, red, that the truth is merely that if everything were red we should not notice redness, and so we should have no word 'red'; we observe and give names to qualities only if they have real opposites. If so, the principle that a term must have an opposite would belong only to our language or to our thought, and would not be an ontological principle, and, correspondingly, the rule that good cannot exist without evil would not state a logical necessity of a sort that God would just have to put up with. God might have made everything good, though *we* should not have noticed it if he had.

But, finally, even if we concede that this *is* an ontological principle, it will provide a solution for the problem of evil only if one is prepared to say, 'Evil exists, but only just enough evil to serve as the counterpart of good.' I doubt whether any theist will accept this. After all, the *ontological* requirement that non-redness should occur would be satisfied even if all the universe, except for a minute speck, were red, and, if there were a corresponding requirement for evil as a counterpart to good, a minute dose of evil would presumably do. But theists are not usually willing to say, in all contexts, that all the evil that occurs is a minute and necessary dose.

2.   'Evil is necessary as a means to good.'

It is sometimes suggested that evil is necessary for good not as a counterpart but as a means. In its simple form this has little plausibility as a solution of the problem of evil, since it obviously implies a severe restriction of God's power. It would be a *causal* law that you cannot have a certain end without a certain means, so that if God has to introduce evil as a means to good, he must be subject to at least some causal laws. This certainly conflicts with what a theist normally means by omnipotence, This view of God as limited by causal laws also conflicts with the view that causal laws are themselves made by God, which is more widely held than the corresponding view about the laws of logic, This conflict would, indeed, be resolved if it were possible for an omnipotent being to bind himself, and this possibility has still to be considered, Unless a favourable answer can be given to this question, the suggestion that evil is necessary as a means to good solves the problem of evil only by denying one of its constituent propositions, either that God is omnipotent or that 'omnipotent' means what it says.

3. 'The universe is better with some evil in it than it could be if there were no evil.'

Much more important is a solution which at first seems to be a mere variant of the previous one, that evil may contribute to the goodness of a whole in which it is found, so that the universe as a whole is better as it is, with some evil in it, than it would be if there were no evil. This solution may be developed in either of two ways. It may be supported by an aesthetic analogy, by the fact that contrasts heighten beauty, that in a musical work, for example, there may occur discords which somehow add to the beauty of the work as a whole. Alternatively, it may be worked out in connexion with the notion of progress, that the best possible organisations of the universe will not be static, but progressive, that the gradual overcoming of evil by good is really a finer thing than would be the eternal unchallenged supremacy of good.

In either case, this solution usually starts from the assumption that the evil whose existence gives rise to the problem of evil is primarily what is called physical evil, that is to say, pain. In Hume's rather half-hearted presentation of the problem of evil, the evils that he stresses are pain and disease, and those who reply to him argue that the existence of pain and disease makes possible the existence of sympathy, benevolence, heroism, and the gradually successful struggle of doctors and reformers to overcome these evils. In fact, theists often seize the opportunity to accuse those who stress the problem of evil of taking a low, materialistic view of good and evil, equating these with pleasure and pain, and of ignoring the more spiritual goods which can arise in the struggle against evils.

But let us see exactly what is being done here. Let us call pain and misery 'first order evil' or 'evil (1)', What contrasts with this, namely, pleasure and happiness, will be called 'first order good' or 'good (1)'. Distinct from this is 'second order good' or 'good (2)' which somehow emerges in a complex situation in which evil (1) is a necessary component—logically, not merely causally, necessary. (Exactly *how* it emerges does not matter: in the crudest version of this solution good (2) is simply the heightening of happiness by the contrast with misery, in other versions it includes sympathy with suffering, heroism in facing danger, and the gradual decrease of first order evil and increase of first order good.) It is also being assumed that second order good is more important than first order good or evil, in particular that it more than outweighs the first order evil it involves.

Now this is a particularly subtle attempt to solve the problem of evil. It defends God's goodness and omnipotence on the ground that (on a sufficiently long view) this is the best of all logically possible worlds, because it includes the important second order goods, and yet it admits that real evils, namely first order evils, exist. But does it still hold that good and evil are opposed? Not, clearly, in the sense that we set out originally: good does not tend to eliminate evil in general. Instead, we have a modified, a more complex pattern. First order good (*e.g.* happiness) *contrasts with* first order evil (*e.g.* misery): these two are opposed in a fairly mechanical way; some second order goods (*e.g.* benevolence) try to maximise first order good and minimise first order evil; but God's goodness is not this, it is rather the will to maximise *second* order good. We might, therefore, call God's goodness an example of a third order goodness, or good (3). While this account is different from our original one, it might well be held to be an improvement on it, to give a more accurate description of the way in which good is opposed to evil, and to be consistent with the essential theist position.

There might, however, be several objections to this solution.

First, some might argue that such qualities as benevolence—and *a fortiori* the third order goodness which promotes benevolence—have a merely derivative value, that they are not higher sorts of good, but merely means to good (1), that is, to happiness, so that it would be absurd for God to keep misery in existence in order to make possible the virtues of benevolence, heroism, etc. The theist who adopts the present solution must, of course, deny this, but he can do so with some plausibility, so I should not press this objection.

Secondly, it follows from this solution that God is not in our sense benevolent or sympathetic: he is not concerned to minimise evil (1), but only to promote good (2); and this might be a disturbing conclusion for some theists.

But, thirdly, the fatal objection is this. Our analysis shows clearly the possibility of the existence of a *second* order evil, an evil (2) contrasting with good (2) as evil (1) contrasts with good (1). This would include malevolence, cruelty, callousness, cowardice, and states in which good (1) is decreasing and evil (1) increasing. And just as good (2) is held to be the important kind of good, the kind that God is concerned to promote, so evil (2) will, by analogy, be the important kind of evil, the kind which God, if he were wholly good and omnipotent, would eliminate. And yet evil (2) plainly exists, and indeed most theists (in other contexts) stress its existence more than that of evil (1). We should, therefore, state the problem of evil in terms of second order evil, and against this form of the problem the present solution is useless.

An attempt might be made to use this solution again, at a higher level, to explain the occurrence of evil (2): indeed the next main solution that we shall examine does just this, with the help of some new notions. Without any fresh notions, such a solution would have little plausibility: for example, we could hardly say that the really important good was a good (3), such as the increase of benevolence in proportion to cruelty, which logically required for its occurrence the occurrence of some second order evil. But even if evil (2) could be explained in this way, it is fairly clear that there would be third order evils contrasting with this third order good: and we should be well on the way to an infinite regress, where the solution of a problem of evil, stated in terms of evil (n), indicated the existence of an evil ($n+1$), and a further problem to be solved.

4. 'Evil is due to human freewill.'

Perhaps the most important proposed solution of the problem of evil is that evil is not to be ascribed to God at all, but to the independent actions of human beings, supposed to have been endowed by God with freedom of the will. This solution may be combined with the preceding one: first order evil (*e.g.* pain) may be justified as a logically necessary component in second order good (*e.g.* sympathy) while second order evil (*e.g.* cruelty) is not *justified,* but is so ascribed to human beings that God cannot be held responsible for it. This combination evades my third criticism of the preceding solution.

The freewill solution also involves the preceding solution at a higher level. To explain why a wholly good God gave men freewill although it would lead to some important evils, it must be argued that it is better on the whole that men should act freely, and sometimes err, than that they should be innocent automata, acting rightly in a wholly determined way. Freedom, that is to say, is now treated as a third order good, and as being more valuable than second order goods (such as sympathy and heroism) would be if they were deterministically produced, and it is being assumed that second order evils, such as cruelty, are logically necessary accompaniments of freedom, just as pain is a logically necessary pre-condition of sympathy.

I think that this solution is unsatisfactory primarily because of the incoherence of the notion of freedom of the will: but I cannot discuss this topic adequately here, although some of my criticisms will touch upon it.

First I should query the assumption that second order evils are logically necessary accompaniments of freedom. I should ask this: if God has made men such that in their free choices they sometimes prefer what is good and sometimes what is evil, why could he not have made men such that they always freely choose the good? If there is no logical impossibility in a man's freely choosing the good on one, or on several, occasions, there cannot be a logical impossibility in his freely choosing the good on every occasion. God was not, then, faced with a choice between making innocent automata and making beings who, in acting freely, would sometimes go wrong: there was open to him the obviously better possibility of making beings who would act freely but always go right, Clearly, his failure to avail himself of this possibility is inconsistent with his being both omnipotent and wholly good.

If it is replied that this objection is absurd, that the making of some wrong choices is logically necessary for freedom, it would seem that 'freedom' must here mean complete randomness or indeterminacy, including randomness with regard to the alternatives good and evil, in other words that men's choices and consequent actions can be 'free' only if they are not determined by their characters. Only on this assumption can God escape the responsibility for men's actions; for if he made them as they are, but did not determine their wrong choices, this can only be because the wrong choices are not determined by men as they are. But then if freedom is randomness, how can it be a characteristic of *will*? And, still more, how can it be the most important good? What value or merit would there be in free choices if these were random actions which were not determined by the nature of the agent?

I conclude that to make this solution plausible two different senses of 'freedom' must be confused, one sense which will justify the view that freedom is a third order good, more valuable than other goods would be without it, and another sense, sheer randomness, to prevent us from ascribing to God a decision to make men such that they sometimes go wrong when he might have made them such that they would always freely go right.

This criticism is sufficient to dispose of this solution. But besides this there is a fundamental difficulty in the notion of an omnipotent God creating men with free will, for if men's wills are really free this must mean that even God cannot control them, that is, that God is no longer omnipotent. It may be objected that God's gift of freedom to men does not mean that he *cannot* control their wills, but that he always *refrains* from controlling their wills. But why, we may ask, should God refrain from controlling evil wills? Why should he not leave men free to will rightly, but intervene when he sees them beginning to will wrongly? If God could do this, but does not, and if he is wholly good, the only explanation could be that even a wrong free act of will is not really evil, that its freedom is a value which outweighs its wrongness, so that there would be a loss of value if God took away the wrongness and the freedom together. But this is utterly opposed to what theists say about sin in other contexts. The present solution of the problem of evil, then, can be maintained only in the form that God has made men so free that he *cannot* control their wills.

This leads us to what I call the Paradox of Omnipotence: can an omnipotent being make things which he cannot subsequently control? Or, what is practically equivalent to this, can an omnipotent being make rules which then bind himself? (These are practically equivalent because any such rules could be regarded as setting certain things beyond his control, and *vice versa*.) The second of these formulations is relevant to the suggestions that we have already met, that an omnipotent God creates the rules of logic or causal laws, and is then bound by them.

It is clear that this is a paradox: the questions cannot be answered satisfactorily either in the affirmative or in the negative. If we answer 'Yes', it follows that if God actually makes things which he cannot control, or makes rules which bind himself, he is not omnipotent once he has made them: there are *then* things which he cannot do. But if we answer 'No', we are immediately asserting that there are things which he cannot do, that is to say that he is already not omnipotent.

It cannot be replied that the question which sets this paradox is not a proper question. It would make perfectly good sense to say that a human mechanic has made a machine which he cannot control: if there is any difficulty about the question it lies in the notion of omnipotence itself.

This, incidentally, shows that although we have approached this paradox from the free will theory, it is equally a problem for a theological determinist. No one thinks that machines have free will, yet they may well be beyond the control of their makers. The determinist might reply that anyone who makes anything determines its ways of acting, and so determines its subsequent behaviour: even the human mechanic does this by his *choice* of materials and structure for his machine, though he does not know all about either of these: the mechanic thus determines, though he may not foresee, his machine's actions. And since God is omniscient, and since his creation of things is total, he both determines and foresees the ways in which his creatures will act. We may grant this, but it is beside the point. The question is not whether God *originally* determined the future actions of his creatures, but whether he can *subsequently* control their actions, or whether he was able in his original creation to put things beyond his subsequent control. Even on determinist principles the answers 'Yes' and 'No' are equally irreconcilable with God's omnipotence.

Before suggesting a solution of this paradox, I would point out that there is a parallel Paradox of Sovereignty. Can a legal sovereign make a law restricting its own future legislative power? For example, could the British parliament make a law forbidding any future parliament to socialise banking, and also forbidding the future repeal of this law itself? Or could the British parliament, which was legally sovereign in Australia in, say, 1899, pass a valid law, or series of laws, which made it no longer sovereign in 1933? Again, neither the affirmative nor the negative answer is really satisfactory. If we were to answer 'Yes', we should be admitting the validity of a law which, if it were actually made, would mean that parliament was no longer sovereign. If we were to answer 'No', we should be admitting that there is a law, not logically absurd, which parliament cannot validly make, that is, that parliament is not now a legal sovereign. This paradox can be solved in the following way. We should distinguish between first order laws, that is laws governing the actions of individuals and bodies other than the legislature, and second order laws, that is laws about laws, laws governing the actions of the legislature itself. Correspondingly, we should distinguish two orders of sovereignty, first order sovereignty (sovereignty (1)) which is unlimited authority to make first order laws, and second order sovereignty (sovereignty (2)) which is unlimited authority to make second order laws. If we say that parliament is sovereign we might mean that any parliament at any time has sovereignty (1), or we might mean that parliament has both sovereignty (1) and sovereignty (2) at present, but we cannot without contradiction mean both that the present parliament has sovereignty (2) and that every parliament at every time has sovereignty (1), for if the present parliament has sovereignty (2) it may use it to take away the sovereignty (1) of later parliaments. What the paradox shows is that we cannot ascribe to any continuing institution legal sovereignty in an inclusive sense.

The analogy between omnipotence and sovereignty shows that the paradox of omnipotence can be solved in a similar way. We must distinguish between first order omnipotence (omnipotence (1)), that is unlimited power to act, and second order omnipotence (omnipotence (2)), that is unlimited power to determine what powers to act things shall have. Then we could consistently say that God all the time has omnipotence (1), but if so no beings at any time have powers to act independently of God, Or we could say that God at one time had omnipotence (2), and used it to assign independent powers to act to certain things, so that God thereafter did not have omnipotence (1). But what the paradox shows is that we cannot consistently ascribe to any continuing being omnipotence in an inclusive sense.

An alternative solution of this paradox would be simply to deny that God is a continuing being, that any times can be assigned to his actions at all. But on this assumption (which also has difficulties of its own) no meaning can be given to the assertion that God made men with wills so free that he could not control them. The paradox of omnipotence can be avoided by putting God outside time, but the freewill solution of the problem of evil cannot be saved in this way, and equally it remains impossible to hold that an omnipotent God *binds himself* by causal or logical laws.

Conclusion

Of the proposed solutions of the problem of evil which we have examined, none has stood up to criticism. There may be other solutions which require examination, but this study strongly suggests that there is no valid solution of the problem which does not modify at least one of the constituent propositions in a way which would seriously affect the essential core of the theistic position.

Quite apart from the problem of evil, the paradox of omnipotence has shown that God's omnipotence must in any case be restricted in one way or another, that unqualified omnipotence cannot be ascribed to any being that continues through time. And if God and his actions are not in time, can omnipotence, or power of any sort, be meaningfully ascribed to him?

Why God Doesn't Intervene to Prevent Evil

B. C. Johnson

HERE IS A COMMON SITUATION: A house catches on fire and a six-month-old baby is painfully burned to death. Could we possibly describe as "good" any person who had the power to save this child and yet refused to do so? God undoubtedly has this power and yet in many cases of this sort he has refused to help. Can we call God "good"? Are there adequate excuses for his behavior?

First, it will not do to claim that the baby will go to heaven. It was either necessary for the baby to suffer or it was not. If it was not, then it was wrong to allow it. The child's ascent to heaven does not change this fact. If it was necessary, the fact that the baby will go to heaven does not explain why it was necessary, and we are still left without an excuse for God's inaction.

It is not enough to say that the baby's painful death would in the long run have good results and therefore should have happened, otherwise God would not have permitted it. For if we know this to be true, then we know—just as God knows—that every action successfully performed must in the end be good and therefore the right thing to do, otherwise God would not have allowed it to happen. We could deliberately set houses ablaze to kill innocent people and if successful we would then know we had a duty to do it. A defense of God's goodness which takes as its foundation duties known only after the fact would result in a morality unworthy of the name. Furthermore, this argument does not explain why God allowed the child to burn to death. It merely claims that there is some reason discoverable in the long run. But the belief that such a reason is within our grasp must rest upon the additional belief that God is good. This is just to counter evidence against such a belief by assuming the belief to be true. It is not unlike a lawyer defending his client by claiming that the client is innocent and therefore the evidence against him must be misleading—that proof vindicating the defendant will be found in the long run. No jury of reasonable men and women would accept such a defense and the theist cannot expect a more favorable outcome.

The theist often claims that man has been given free will so that if he accidentally or purposefully causes fires, killing small children, it is his fault alone. Consider a bystander who had nothing to do with starting the fire but who refused to help even though he could have saved the child with no harm to himself. Could such a bystander be called good? Certainly not. If we would not consider a mortal human being good under these circumstances, what grounds could we possibly have for continuing to assert the goodness of an all-powerful God?

The suggestion is sometimes made that it is best for us to face disasters without assistance, otherwise we would become dependent on an outside power for aid. Should we then abolish modern medical care or do away with efficient fire departments? Are we not dependent on their help? Is it not the case that their presence transforms us into soft, dependent creatures? The vast majority are not physicians or firemen. These people help in their capacity as professional outside sources of aid in much the same way that we would expect God to be helpful. Theists refer to aid from firemen and physicians as cases of man helping himself. In reality, it is a tiny minority of men helping a great many. We can become just as dependent on them as we can on God. Now the existence of this kind of outside help is either wrong or right. If it is right, then God should assist those areas of the world which do not have this kind of help. In fact, throughout history, such help has not been available. If aid ought to have been provided, then God should have provided it. On the other hand, if it is wrong to provide this kind of assistance, then we should abolish the aid altogether. But we obviously do not believe it is wrong.

Similar considerations apply to the claim that if God interferes in disasters, he would destroy a considerable amount of moral urgency to make things right. Once again, note that such institutions as modern medicine and fire departments are relatively recent. They function irrespective of whether we as individuals feel any moral urgency to support them. To the extent that they help others, opportunities to feel moral urgency are destroyed, because they reduce the number of cases which appeal to us for help. Since we have not always had such institutions, there must have been a time when there was greater moral urgency than there is now. If such a situation is morally desirable, then we should abolish modem medical care and fire departments. If the situation is not morally desirable, then God should have remedied it.

Besides this point, we should note that God is represented as one who tolerates disasters, such as infants burning to death, in order to create moral urgency. It follows that God approves of these disasters as a means to encourage the creation of moral urgency. Furthermore, if there were no such disasters occurring, God would have to see to it that they occur. If it so happened that we lived in a world in which babies never perished in burning houses, God would be morally obliged to take an active hand in setting fire to houses with infants in them. In fact, if the frequency of infant mortality due to fire should happen to fall below a level necessary for the creation of maximum moral urgency in our real world, God would be justified in setting a few fires of his own. This may well be happening right now, for there is no guarantee that the maximum number of infant deaths necessary for moral urgency are occurring.

All of this is of course absurd. If I see an opportunity to create otherwise nonexistent opportunities for moral urgency by burning an infant or two, then I should *not* do so. But if it is good to maximize moral urgency, then I *should* do so. Therefore, it is not good to maximize moral urgency. Plainly we do not in general believe that it is a good thing to maximize moral urgency. The fact that we approve of modern medical care and applaud medical advances is proof enough of this.

The theist may point out that in a world without suffering there would be no occasion for the production of such virtues as courage, sympathy, and the like. This may be true, but the atheist need not demand a world without suffering. He need only claim that there is suffering which is in excess of that needed for the production of various virtues, For example, God's active attempts to save six-month-old infants from fires would not in itself create a world without suffering. But no one could sincerely doubt that it would improve the world.

The two arguments against the previous theistic excuse apply here also. "Moral urgency" and "building virtue" are susceptible to the same criticisms. It is worthwhile to emphasize, however that we encourage efforts to eliminate evils; we approve of efforts to promote peace, prevent famine and wipe out disease. In other words, we do value a world with fewer or (if possible) no opportunities for the development of virtue (when "virtue" is understood to mean the reduction of suffering). If we produce such a world for succeeding generations, how will they develop virtues? Without war, disease, and famine, they will not be virtuous. Should we then cease our attempts to wipe out war, disease, and famine? If we do not believe that it is right to cease attempts at improving the world, then by implication we admit that virtue-building is not an excuse for God to permit disasters. For we admit that the development of virtue is no excuse for permitting disasters.

It might be said that God allows innocent people to suffer in order to deflate man's ego so that the latter will not be proud of his apparently deserved good fortune. But this excuse succumbs to the arguments used against the preceding excuses and we need discuss them no further.

Theists may claim that evil is a necessary byproduct of the laws of nature and therefore it is irrational for God to interfere every time a disaster happens. Such a state of affairs would alter the whole causal order and we would then find it impossible to predict anything. But the death of a child caused by an electrical fire could have been prevented by a miracle and no one would ever have known. Only a minor alteration in electrical equipment would have been necessary. A very large disaster could have been avoided simply by producing in Hitler a miraculous heart attack — and no one would have known it was a miracle. To argue that continued miraculous intervention by God would be wrong is like insisting that one should never use salt because ingesting five pounds of it would be fatal. No one is requesting that God interfere all of the time. He should, however, intervene to prevent especially horrible disasters. Of course, the question arises: where does one draw the line? Well, certainly the line should be drawn somewhere this side of infants burning to death. To argue that we do not know where the line should be drawn is no excuse for failing to interfere in those instances that would be called clear cases of evil.

It will not do to claim that evil exists as a necessary contrast to good so that we might know what good is. A very small amount of evil, such as a toothache, would allow that. It is not necessary to destroy innocent human beings.

The claim could be made that God has a "higher morality" by which his actions are to be judged. But it is a strange "higher morality" which claims that what we call "bad" is good and what we call "good" is bad. Such a morality can have no meaning to us. It would be like calling black "white" and white "black." In reply the theist may say that God is the wise Father and we are ignorant children. How can we judge God any more than a child is able to judge his parent? It is true that a child may be puzzled by his parents' conduct, but his basis for deciding that their conduct is nevertheless good would be the many instances of good behavior he has observed. Even so, this could be misleading. Hitler, by all accounts, loved animals and children of the proper race; but if Hitler had had a child, this offspring would hardly have been justified in arguing that his father was a good man. At any rate, God's "higher morality," being the opposite of ours, cannot offer any grounds for deciding that he is somehow good.

Perhaps the main problem with the solutions to the problem of evil we have thus far considered is that no matter how convincing they may be in the abstract, they are implausible in certain particular cases. Picture an infant dying in a burning house and then imagine God simply observing from afar. Perhaps God is reciting excuses in his own behalf. As the child succumbs to the smoke and flames, God may be pictured as saying: "Sorry, but if I helped you I would have considerable trouble deflating the ego of your parents. And don't forget I have to keep those laws of nature consistent. And anyway if you weren't dying in that fire, a lot of moral urgency would just go down the drain. Besides, I didn't start this fire, so you can't blame *me*."

It does no good to assert that God may not be all-powerful and thus not able to prevent evil. He can create a universe and yet is conveniently unable to do what the fire department can do—rescue a baby from a burning building. God should at least be as powerful as a man. A man, if he had been at the right place and time, could have killed Hitler. Was this beyond God's abilities? If God knew in 1910 how to produce polio vaccine and if he was able to communicate with somebody, he should have communicated this knowledge. He must be incredibly limited if he could not have managed this modest accomplishment. Such a God if not dead, is the next thing to it. And a person who believes in such a ghost of a God is practically an atheist. To call such a thing a god would be to strain the meaning of the word.

The theist, as usual, may retreat to faith. He may say that he has faith in God's goodness and therefore the Christian Deity's existence has not been disproved. "Faith" is here understood as being much like confidence in a friend's innocence despite the evidence against him. Now in order to have confidence in a friend one must know him well enough to justify faith in his goodness. We cannot have justifiable faith in the supreme goodness of strangers. Moreover, such confidence must come not just from a speaking acquaintance. The friend may continually assure us with his words that he is good but if he does not act like a good person, we would have no reason to trust him. A person who says he has faith in God's goodness is speaking as if he had known God for a long time and during that time had never seen Him do any serious evil. But we know that throughout history God has allowed numerous atrocities to occur. No one can have justifiable faith in the goodness of such a God.

This faith would have to be based on a close friendship wherein God was never found to do anything wrong. But a person would have to be blind and deaf to have had such a relationship with God. Suppose a friend of yours had always claimed to be good yet refused to help people when he was in a position to render aid. Could you have justifiable faith in his goodness?

You can of course say that you trust God anyway—that no arguments can undermine your faith. But this is just a statement describing how stubborn you are; it has no bearing whatsoever on the question of God's goodness.

The various excuses theists offer for why God has allowed evil to exist have been demonstrated to be inadequate. However, the conclusive objection to these excuses does not depend on their inadequacy.

First, we should note that every possible excuse making the actual world consistent with the existence of a good God could be used in reverse to make that same world consistent with an evil God. For example, we could say that God is evil and that he allows free will so that we can freely do evil things, which would make us more truly evil than we would be if forced to perform evil acts. Or we could say that natural disasters occur in order to make people more selfish and bitter, for most people tend to have a "me-first" attitude in a disaster (note, for example, stampedes to leave burning buildings). Even though some people achieve virtue from disasters, this outcome is necessary if persons are to react freely to disaster—necessary if the development of moral degeneracy is to continue freely. But, enough; the point is made. Every excuse we could provide to make the world consistent with a good God can be paralleled by an excuse to make the world consistent with an evil God. This is so because the world is a mixture of both good and bad.

Now there are only three possibilities concerning God's moral character. Considering the world as it actually is, we may believe: (*a*) that God is more likely to be all evil than he is to be all good; (*b*) that God is less likely to be all evil than he is to be all good; or (*c*) that God is equally as likely to be all evil as he is to be good. In case (*a*) it would be admitted that God is unlikely to be all good. Case (*b*) cannot be true at all, since—as we have seen—the belief that God is all evil can be justified to precisely the same extent as the belief that God is all good. Case (*c*) leaves us with no reasonable excuses for a good God to permit evil. The reason is as follows: if an excuse is to be a reasonable excuse, the circumstances it identifies as excusing conditions must be actual. For example, if I run over a pedestrian and my excuse is that the brakes failed because someone tampered with them, then the facts had better bear this out. Otherwise the excuse will not hold. Now if case (*c*) is correct and, given the facts of the actual world, God is as likely to be all evil as he is to be all good, then these facts do not support the excuses which could be made for a good God permitting evil. Consider an analogous example. If my excuse for running over the pedestrian is that my brakes were tampered with, and if the actual facts lead us to believe that it is no more likely that they were tampered with than that they were not, the excuse is no longer reasonable. To make good my excuse, I must show that it is a fact or at least highly probable that my brakes were tampered with—not that it is just a possibility. The same point holds for God. His excuse must not be a possible excuse, but an actual one. But case (*c*), in maintaining that it is just as likely that God is all evil as that he is all good, rules this out. For if case (*c*) is true, then the facts of the actual world do not make it any more likely that God is all good than that he is all evil. Therefore, they do not make it any more likely that his excuses are good than that they are not. But, as we have seen, good excuses have a higher probability of being true.

Cases (*a*) and (*c*) conclude that it is unlikely that God is all good, and case (*b*) cannot be true. Since these are the only possible cases, there is no escape from the conclusion that it is unlikely that God is all good. Thus the problem of evil triumphs over traditional theism.

The Problem of Evil and Some Varieties of Atheism

William L. Rowe

THIS paper is concerned with three interrelated questions. The first is: Is there an argument for atheism based on the existence of evil that may rationally justify someone in being an atheist? To this first question I give an affirmative answer and try to support that answer by setting forth a strong argument for atheism based on the existence of evil.[1] The second question is: How can the theist best defend his position against the argument for atheism based on the existence of evil? In response to this question I try to describe what may be an adequate rational defense for theism against any argument for atheism based on the existence of evil. The final question is: What position should the informed atheist take concerning the rationality of theistic belief? Three different answers an atheist may give to this question serve to distinguish three varieties of atheism: unfriendly atheism, indifferent atheism, and friendly atheism. In the final part of the paper I discuss and defend the position of friendly atheism.

Before we consider the argument from evil, we need to distinguish a narrow and a broad sense of the terms "theist," "atheist," and "agnostic." By a "theist" in the narrow sense I mean someone who believes in the existence of an omnipotent, omniscient, eternal, supremely good being who created the world. By a "theist" in the broad sense I mean someone who believes in the existence of some sort of divine being or divine reality. To be a theist in the narrow sense is also to be a theist in the broad sense, but one may be a theist in the broad sense—as was Paul Tillich—without believing that there is a supremely good, omnipotent, omniscient, eternal being who created the world. Similar distinctions must be made between a narrow and a broad sense of the terms "atheist" and "agnostic." To be an atheist in the broad sense is to deny the existence of any sort of divine being or divine reality. Tillich was not an atheist in the broad sense. But he was an atheist in the narrow sense, for he denied that there exists a divine being that is all-knowing, all-powerful and perfectly good. In this paper I will be using the terms "theism," "theist," "atheism," "atheist," "agnosticism," and "agnostic" in the narrow sense, not in the broad sense.

---

[1]Some philosophers have contended that the existence of evil is *logically inconsistent* with the existence of the theistic God. No one, I think, has succeeded in establishing such an extravagant claim. Indeed, granted incompatibilism, there is a fairly compelling argument for the view that the existence of evil is logically consistent with the existence of the theistic God. (For a lucid statement of this argument see Alvin Plantinga, *God, Freedom, and Evil* (New York, 1974), pp. 29–59.) There remains, however, what we may call the *evidential* form—as opposed to the *logical* form—of the problem of evil: the view that the variety and profusion of evil in our world, although perhaps not logically inconsistent with the existence of the theistic God, provides, nevertheless, *rational support* for atheism. In this paper I shall be concerned solely with the evidential form of the problem, the form of the problem which, I think, presents a rather severe difficulty for theism.

I

In developing the argument for atheism based on the existence of evil, it will be useful to focus on some particular evil that our world contains in considerable abundance. Intense human and animal suffering, for example, occurs daily and in great plenitude in our world. Such intense suffering is a clear case of evil. Of course, if the intense suffering leads to some greater good, a good we could not have obtained without undergoing the suffering in question, we might conclude that the suffering is justified, but it remains an evil nevertheless. For we must not confuse the intense suffering in and of itself with the good things to which it sometimes leads or of which it may be a necessary part. Intense human or animal suffering is in itself bad, an evil, even though it may sometimes be justified by virtue of being a part of, or leading to, some good which is unobtainable without it. What is evil in itself may sometimes be good as a means because it leads to something that is good in itself. In such a case, while remaining an evil in itself, the intense human or animal suffering is, nevertheless, an evil which someone might be morally justified in permitting.

Taking human and animal suffering as a clear instance of evil which occurs with great frequency in our world, the argument for atheism based on evil can be stated as follows:

1. There exist instances of intense suffering which an omnipotent, omniscient being could have prevented without thereby losing some greater good or permitting some evil equally bad or worse.[2]
2. An omniscient, wholly good being would prevent the occurrence of any intense suffering it could, unless it could not do so without thereby losing some greater good or permitting some evil equally bad or worse.
3. There does not exist an omnipotent, omniscient, wholly good being.

What are we to say about this argument for atheism, an argument based on the profusion of one sort of evil in our world? The argument is valid; therefore, if we have rational grounds for accepting its premises, to that extent we have rational grounds for accepting atheism. Do we, however, have rational grounds for accepting the premises of this argument?

Let's begin with the second premise. Let $s1$ be an instance of intense human or animal suffering which an omniscient, wholly good being could prevent. We will also suppose that things are such that $s1$ will occur unless prevented by the omniscient, wholly good (OG) being. We might be interested in determining what would be a *sufficient* condition of OG failing to prevent $s1$. But, for our purpose here, we need only try to state a *necessary* condition for OG failing to prevent $s1$. That condition, so it seems to me, is this:

---

[2]If there is some good, G, greater than any evil, (1) will be false for the trivial reason that no matter what evil. E, we pick the conjunctive good state of affairs consisting of G and E will outweigh E and be such that an omnipotent being could not obtain it without permitting E. (See Alvin Plantinga, *God and Other Minds* [Ithaca, 1967], p. 167.) To avoid this objection we may insert "unreplaceable" into our premises (1) and (2) between "some" and "greater." If E isn't required for G, and G is better than G plus E, then the good conjunctive state of affairs composed of G and E would be *replaceable* by the greater good of G alone. For the sake of simplicity, however, I will ignore this complication both in the formulation and discussion of premises (1) and (2).

Either (i) there is some greater good, *G*, such that *G* is obtainable by *OG* only if *OG* permits s_1[3],

or (ii) there is some greater good, *G*, such that *G* is obtainable by *OG* only if *OG* permits either s_1 or some evil equally bad or worse,

or (iii) s_1 is such that it is preventable by *OG* only if *OG* permits some evil equally bad or worse.

It is important to recognize that (iii) is not included in (i). For losing a good greater than *s*1 is not the same as permitting an evil greater than *s*1. And this because the *absence* of a good state of affairs need not itself be an evil state of affairs. It is also important to recognize that *s*1 might be such that it is preventable by *OG without* losing *G* (so condition (i) is not satisfied) but also such that if *OG* did prevent it, *G* would be loss *unless OG* permitted some evil equal to or worse than *s*1. If this were so, it does not seem correct to require that *OG* prevent *s*1. Thus, condition (ii) takes into account an important possibility not encompassed in condition (i).

Is it true that if an omniscient, wholly good being permits the occurrence of some intense suffering it could have prevented, then either (i) or (ii) or (iii) obtains? It seems to me that it is true. But if it is true then so is premise (2) of the argument for atheism. For that premise merely states in more compact form what we have suggested must be true if an omniscient, wholly good being fails to prevent some intense suffering it could prevent. Premise (2) says that an omniscient, wholly good being would prevent the occurrence of any intense suffering it could, unless it could not do so without thereby losing some greater good or permitting some evil equally bad or worse. This premise (or something not too distant from it) is, I think, held in common by many atheists and nontheists. Of course, there may be disagreement about whether something is good, and whether, if it is good, one would be morally justified in permitting some intense suffering to occur in order to obtain it. Someone might hold, for example, that no good is great enough to justify permitting an innocent child to suffer terribly.[4] Again, someone might hold that the mere fact that a given good outweighs some suffering and would be loss if the suffering were prevented, is not a morally sufficient reason for permitting the suffering. But to hold either of these views is not to deny (2). For (2) claims only that *if* an omniscient, wholly good being permits intense suffering *then* either there is some greater good that would have been loss, or some equally bad or worse evil that would have occurred, had the intense suffering been prevented. (2) does not purport to describe what might be a *sufficient* condition for an omniscient, wholly good being to permit intense suffering, only what is a *necessary* condition. So stated, (2) seems to express a belief that accords with our basic moral principles, principles shared by both theists and nontheists. If we are to fault the argument for atheism, therefore, it seems we must find some fault with its first premise.

Suppose in some distant forest lightning strikes a dead tree, resulting in a forest fire. In the fire a fawn is trapped, horribly burned, and lies in terrible agony for several days before death relieves its suffering. So far as we can see, the fawn's intense suffering is

---

[3]Three clarifying points need to be made in connection with (i). First, by "good" I don't mean to exclude the fulfillment of certain moral principles. Perhaps preventing *s*1 would preclude certain actions prescribed by the principles of justice. I shall allow that the satisfaction of certain principles of justice may be a good that outweighs the evil of *s*1. Second, even though (i) may suggest it, I don't mean to limit the good in question to something that would *follow in time* the occurrence of *s*1. And, finally, we should perhaps not fault *OG* if the good *G*, that would be loss were *s*1 prevented, is not actually greater than *s*1, but merely such that allowing *s*1 and *G*, as opposed to preventing *s*1 and thereby losing *G*, would not alter the balance between good and evil. For reasons of simplicity, I have left this point out in stating (i), with the result that (i) is perhaps a bit stronger than it should be.

[4]See Ivan's speech in Book V, Chapter IV of *The Brothers Karamazov*.

pointless. For there does not appear to be any greater good such that the prevention of the fawn's suffering would require either the loss of that good or the occurrence of an evil equally bad or worse. Nor does there seem to be any equally bad or worse evil so connected to the fawn's suffering that it would have had to occur had the fawn's suffering been prevented. Could an omnipotent, omniscient being have prevented the fawn's apparently pointless suffering? The answer is obvious, as even the theist will insist. An omnipotent, omniscient being could have easily prevented the fawn from being horribly burned, or, given the burning, could have spared the fawn the intense suffering by quickly ending its life, rather than allowing the fawn to lie in terrible agony for several days. Since the fawn's intense suffering was preventable and, so far as we can see, pointless, doesn't it appear that premise (1) of the argument is true, that there do exist instances of intense suffering which an omnipotent, omniscient being could have prevented without thereby losing some greater good or permitting some evil equally bad or worse.

It must be acknowledged that the case of the fawn's apparently pointless suffering does not *prove* that (1) is true. For even though we cannot see how the fawn's suffering is required to obtain some greater good (or to prevent some equally bad or worse evil), it hardly follows that it is not so required. After all, we are often surprised by how things we thought to be unconnected turn out to be intimately connected. Perhaps, for all we know, there is some familiar good outweighing the fawn's suffering to which that suffering is connected in a way we do not see. Furthermore, there may well be unfamiliar goods, goods we haven't dreamed of, to which the fawn's suffering is inextricably connected. Indeed, it would seem to require something like omniscience on our part before we could lay claim to *knowing* that there is no greater good connected to the fawn's suffering in such a manner than an omnipotent, omniscient being could not have achieved that good without permitting that suffering or some evil equally bad or worse. So the case of the fawn's suffering surely does not enable us to *establish* the truth of (1).

The truth is that we are not in a position to prove that (1) is true. We cannot know with certainty that instances of suffering of the sort described in (1) do occur in our world. But it is one thing to *know* or *prove* that (1) is true and quite another thing to have *rational grounds* for believing (1) to be true. We are often in the position where in the light of our experience and knowledge it is rational to believe that a certain statement is true, even though we are not in a position to prove or to know with certainty that the statement is true. In the light of our past experience and knowledge it is, for example, very reasonable to believe that neither Goldwater nor McGovern will ever be elected President, but we are scarcely in the position of knowing with certainty that neither will ever be elected President. So, too, with (1), although we cannot know with certainty that it is true, it perhaps can be rationally supported, shown to be a rational belief.

Consider again the case of the fawn's suffering. Is it reasonable to believe that there is some greater good so intimately connected to that suffering that even an omnipotent, omniscient being could not have obtained that good without permitting that suffering or some evil at least as bad? It certainly does not appear reasonable to believe this. Nor does it seem reasonable to believe that there is some evil at least as bad as the fawn's suffering such that an omnipotent being simply could not have prevented it without permitting the fawn's suffering. But even if it should somehow be reasonable to believe either of these things of the fawn's suffering, we must then ask whether it is reasonable to believe either of these things of *all* the instances of seemingly pointless human and animal suffering that occur daily in our world. And surely the answer to this more general question must be no. It seems quite unlikely that *all* the instances of intense suffering occurring daily in our world are intimately related to the occurrence of greater goods or the prevention of evils at least as bad; and even more unlikely, should they somehow all be so related, than an omnipotent, omniscient being could not have achieved at least some of those goods (or prevented some of those evils) without permitting the instances of intense suffering that are supposedly related to them. In the light of our experience and knowledge of the variety and scale of human and animal suffering in our world, the idea that none of this suffering could have been prevented by an omnipotent being without thereby losing a greater good or permitting an evil at least as bad seems an extraordinary absurd idea, quite beyond our belief. It seems then that although we cannot *prove* that (1) is true, it is, nevertheless, altogether *reasonable* to believe that (1) is true, that (1) is a *rational* belief.[5]

Returning now to our argument for atheism, we've seen that the second premise expresses a basic belief common to many theists and nontheists. We've also seen that our experience and knowledge of the variety and profusion of suffering in our world provides *rational support* for the first premise. Seeing that the conclusion, "There does not exist an omnipotent, omniscient, wholly good being" follows from these two premises, it does seem that we have *rational support* for atheism, that it is reasonable for us to believe that the theistic God does not exist.

II

Can theism be rationally defended against the argument for atheism we have just examined? If it can, how might the theist best respond to that argument? Since the argument from (1) and (2) to (3) is valid, and since the theist, no less than the nontheist, is more than likely committed to (2), it's clear that the theist can reject this atheistic argument only by rejecting its first premise, the premise that states that there are instances of intense suffering which an omnipotent, omniscient being could have prevented without thereby losing some greater good or permitting some evil equally bad or worse. How, then, can the theist best respond to this premise and the considerations advanced in its support?

There are basically three responses a theist can make. First, he might argue not that (1) is false or probably false, but only that the reasoning given in support of it is in some way *defective*. He may do this either by arguing that the reasons given in support of (1) are *in themselves* insufficient to justify accepting (1), or by arguing that there are other things we know which, when taken in conjunction with these reasons, do not justify us in accepting (1). I suppose some theists would be content with this rather modest response to the basic argument for atheism. But given the validity of the basic argument and the theist's likely acceptance of (2), he is thereby committed to the view that (1) is false, not just that we have no good reasons for accepting (1) as true. The second two responses are aimed at showing that it is reasonable to believe that (1) is false. Since

---

[5]One might object that the conclusion of this paragraph is stronger than the reasons given warrant. For it is one thing to argue that it is unreasonable to think that (1) is false and another thing to conclude that we are therefore justified in accepting (1) as true. There are propositions such that believing them is much more reasonable than disbelieving them, and yet are such that *withholding judgment* about them is more reasonable than believing them. To take an example of Chisholm's: it is more reasonable to believe that the Pope will be in Rome (on some arbitrarily picked future date) than to believe that he won't; but it is perhaps more reasonable to suspend judgment on the question of the Pope's whereabouts on that particular date, than to believe that he will be in Rome. Thus, it might be objected, that while we've shown that believing (1) is more reasonable than disbelieving (1), we haven't shown that believing (1) is more reasonable than withholding belief. My answer to this objection is that there are things we know which render (1) probable to the degree that it is more reasonable to believe (1) than to suspend judgment on (1). What are these things we know? First, I think, is the fact that there is an enormous variety and profusion of intense human and animal suffering in our world. Second, is the fact that much of this suffering seems quite unrelated to any greater goods (or the absence of equal or greater evils) that might justify it. And, finally, there is the fact that such suffering as is related to greater goods (or the absence of equal or greater evils) does not, in many cases, seem so intimately related as to require its permission by an omnipotent being bent on securing those goods (the absence of those evils). These facts, I am claiming, make it more reasonable to accept (1) than to withhold judgment on (1).

the theist is committed to this view I shall focus the discussion on these two attempts, attempts which we can distinguish as "the direct attack" and "the indirect attack."

By a direct attack, I mean an attempt to reject (1) by pointing out goods, for example, to which suffering may well be connected, goods which an omnipotent, omniscient being could not achieve without permitting suffering. It is doubtful, however, that the direct attack can succeed. The theist may point out that some suffering leads to moral and spiritual development impossible without suffering. But it's reasonably clear that suffering often occurs in a degree far beyond what is required for character development. The theist may say that some suffering results from free choices of human beings and might be preventable only by preventing some measure of human freedom. But, again, it's clear that much intense suffering occurs not as a result of human free choices. The general difficulty with this direct attack on premise (1) is twofold. First, it cannot succeed, for the theist does not know what greater goods might be served, or evils prevented, by each instance of intense human or animal suffering. Second, the theist's own religious tradition usually maintains that in this life it is not given to us to know God's purpose in allowing particular instances of suffering. Hence, the direct attack against premise (1) cannot succeed and violates basic beliefs associated with theism.

The best procedure for the theist to follow in rejecting premise (1) is the indirect procedure. This procedure I shall call "the G. E. Moore shift," socalled in honor of the twentieth century philosopher, G. E. Moore, who used it to great effect in dealing with the arguments of the skeptics. Skeptical philosophers such as David Hume have advanced ingenious arguments to prove that no one can know of the existence of any material object. The premises of their arguments employ plausible principles, principles which many philosophers have tried to reject directly, but only with questionable success. Moore's procedure was altogether different. Instead of arguing directly against the premises of the skeptic's arguments, he simply noted that the premises implied, for example, that he (Moore) did not know of the existence of a pencil. Moore then proceeded indirectly against the, skeptic's premises by arguing:

I do know that this pencil exists.

If the skeptic's principles are correct I cannot know of the existence of this pencil.

The skeptic's principles (at least one) must be incorrect.

Moore then noted that his argument is just as valid as the skeptic's, that both of their arguments contain the premise "If the skeptic's principles are correct Moore cannot know of the existence of this pencil," and concluded that the only way to choose between the two arguments (Moore's and the skeptic's) is by deciding which of the first premises it is more rational to believe—Moore's premise "I do know that this pencil exists" or the skeptic's premise asserting that his skeptical principles are correct, Moore concluded that his own first premise was the more rational of the two.[6]

Before we see how the theist may apply the G. E. Moore shift to the basic argument for atheism, we should note the general strategy of the shift. We're given an argument: *p, q*, therefore, *r*. Instead of arguing directly against *p*, another argument is constructed—not-*r, q*, therefore, not-*p*—which begins with the denial of the conclusion of the first argument, keeps its second premise, and ends with the denial of the first premise as its conclusion.

Compare, for example, these two:

I. *p*   II. *not-r*
   q   *q*
   r   *not-p*

---

[6]See, for example, the two chapters on Hume in G. E. Moore, *Some Main Problems of Philosophy* (London, 1953).

It is a truth of logic that If I is valid II must be valid as well. Since the arguments are the same so far as the second premise is concerned, any choice between them must concern their respective first premises. To argue against the first premise (*p*) by constructing the counter argument II is to employ the G. E. Moore shift.

Applying the G. E. Moore shift against the first premise of the basic argument for atheism, the theist can argue as follows:

> not-3. There exists an omnipotent, omniscient, wholly good being.

2. An omniscient, wholly good being would prevent the occurrence of any intense suffering it could, unless it could not do so without thereby losing some greater good or permitting some evil equally bad or worse. therefore, not-1. It is not the case that there exist instances of intense suffering which an omnipotent, omniscient being could have prevented without thereby losing some greater good or permitting some evil equally bad or worse.

We now have two arguments: the basic argument for atheism from (1) and (2) to (3), and the theist's best response, the argument from (not-3) and (2) to (not-1). What the theist then says about (1) is that he has rational grounds for believing in the existence of the theistic God (not-3), accepts (2) as true, and sees that (not-1) follows from (not-3) and (2). He concludes, therefore, that he has rational grounds for rejecting (1). Having rational grounds for rejecting (1), the theist concludes that the basic argument for atheism is mistaken.

III

We've had a look at a forceful argument for atheism and what seems to be the theist's best response to that argument. If one is persuaded by the argument for atheism, as I find myself to be, how might one best view the position of the theist. Of course, he will view the theist as having a false belief,

just as the theist will view the atheist as having a false belief. But what position should the atheist take concerning the *rationality* of the theist's belief? There are three major positions an atheist might take, positions which we may think of as some varieties of atheism. First, the atheist may believe that no one is rationally justified in believing that the theistic God exists. Let us call this position "unfriendly atheism." Second, the atheist may hold no belief concerning whether any theist is or isn't rationally justified in believing that the theistic God exists. Let us call this view "indifferent atheism." Finally, the atheist may believe that some theists are rationally justified in believing that the theistic God exists. This view we shall call "friendly atheism." In this final part of the paper I propose to discuss and defend the position of friendly atheism.

If no one can be rationally justified in believing a false proposition then friendly atheism is a paradoxical, if not incoherent position. But surely the truth of a belief is not a necessary condition of someone's being rationally justified in having that belief. So in holding that someone is rationally justified in believing that the theistic God exists, the friendly atheist is not committed to thinking that the theist has a true belief. What he is committed to is that the theist has rational grounds for his belief, a belief the atheist rejects and is convinced he is rationally justified in rejecting. But is this possible? Can someone, like our friendly atheist, hold a belief, be convinced that he is rationally justified in holding that belief, and yet believe that someone else is equally justified in believing the opposite? Surely this is possible. Suppose your friends see you off on a flight to Hawaii. Hours after take-off they learn that your plane has gone down at sea. After a twenty-four hour search, no survivors have been found. Under these circumstances they are rationally justified in believing that you have perished. But it is hardly rational for you to believe this, as you bob up and down in your life vest, wondering why the search planes have failed to spot you. Indeed, to amuse yourself while awaiting your fate, you might very well reflect on the fact that your friends are rationally justified in believing that you are now dead, a proposition you disbelieve and are rationally justified in disbelieving. So, too, perhaps an atheist may be rationally justified in his atheistic belief and yet hold that some theists are rationally justified in believing just the opposite of what he believes.

What sort of grounds might a theist have for believing that God exists. Well, he might endeavor to justify his belief by appealing to one or more of the traditional arguments: Ontological, Cosmological, Teleological, Moral, etc. Second, he might appeal to certain aspects of religious experience, perhaps even his own religious experience. Third, he might try to justify theism as a plausible theory in terms of which we can account for a variety of phenomena. Although an atheist must hold that the theistic God does not exist, can he not also believe, and be justified in so believing, that some of these "justifications of theism" do actually rationally justify some theists in their belief that there exists a supremely good, omnipotent, omniscient being? It seems to me that he can.

If we think of the long history of theistic belief and the special situations in which people are sometimes placed, it is perhaps as absurd to think that no one was ever rationally justified in believing that the theistic God exists as it is to think that no one was ever justified in believing that human being would never walk on the moon. But in suggesting that friendly atheism is preferable to unfriendly atheism, I don't mean to rest the case on what some human beings might reasonably have believed in the eleventh or thirteenth century. The more interesting question is whether some people in modern society, people who are aware of the usual grounds for belief and disbelief and are acquainted to some degree with modern science, are yet rationally justified in accepting theism. Friendly atheism is a significant position only if it answers this question in the affirmative.

It is not difficult for an atheist to be friendly when he has reason to believe that the theist could not reasonably be expected to be acquainted with the grounds for disbelief that he (the atheist) possesses. For then the atheist may take the view that some theists are rationally justified in holding to theism, but would not be so were they to be acquainted with the grounds for disbelief—those grounds being sufficient to tip the scale in favor of atheism when balanced against the reasons the theist has in support of his belief.

Friendly atheism becomes paradoxical, however, when the atheist contemplates believing that the theist has all the grounds for atheism that he, the atheist, has, and yet is rationally justified in maintaining his theistic belief. But even so excessively friendly a view as this perhaps can be held by the atheist if he also has some reason to think that the grounds for theism are not as telling as the theist is justified in taking them to be.[7]

In this paper I've presented what I take to be a strong argument for atheism, pointed out what I think is the theist's best response to that argument, distinguished three positions an atheist might take concerning the rationality of theistic belief, and made some remarks in defense of the position called "friendly atheism." I'm aware that the central

---

[7]Suppose that I add a long sum of numbers three times and get result x. I inform you of this so that you have pretty much the same evidence I have for the claim that the sum of the numbers is *x*. You then use your calculator twice over and arrive at result *y*. You, then, are justified in believing that the sum of the numbers is *not x*. However, knowing that your calculator has been damaged and is therefore unreliable, and that you have no reason to think that it is damaged, *I* may reasonably believe not only that the sum of the numbers is *x,* but also that you are justified in believing that the sum is not *x*. Here is a case, then, where you have all of my evidence for *p,* and yet I can reasonably believe that you are justified in believing not-*p*—for I have reason to believe that your grounds for not-*p* are not as telling as you are justified in taking them to be.

points of the paper are not likely to be warmly received by many philosophers. Philosophers who are atheists tend to be tough minded—holding that there are no good reasons for supposing that theism is true. And theists tend either to reject the view that the existence of evil provides rational grounds for atheism or to hold that religious belief has nothing to do with reason and evidence at all. But such is the way of philosophy.[8]

Purdue University
Received July 13, 1978

[8]I am indebted to my colleagues at Purdue University, particularly to Ted Ulrich and Lilly Russow, and to philosophers at The University of Nebraska, Indiana State University, and The University of Wisconsin at Milwaukee for helpful criticisms of earlier versions of this paper.

Part II The Meaning of Life: What is the Meaning of Life?

Chapter 1 General Introduction

The purpose of this preliminary chapter on the topic of the meaning of life (henceforth, MOL) is to introduce you to the reason(s), significance, and meaning of the question of the meaning of life. The question of the meaning of life is one of the most vital and basic questions about the human condition which any self-reflective person could ever ponder. Exploring this question in some depth promises to pose complex challenges. Before we even set out to examine various prospective answers to our question, we must confront three principal challenges:

I. First, we need to be clear about the nature of the question: i.e., what exactly do we mean when we ask the question "What is the *meaning* of *life*?"
II. Second, we need to distinguish between two different reasons or motivations for asking the question: the *psychological motivation* and the *philosophical motivation*.
III. Third, we need to be clear about the type of considerations about the human condition that provoke a *self-reflective conscious person* to ask the *philosophical question*.

In this chapter we will focus on these three principal tasks.

I. **What do we mean by the question "What is the *meaning* of *life*?"**

There are several levels to the meaning-of-life question depending upon what is meant by 'life'. Let us delineate these different possible layers:

a. What is the meaning of **my** existence as a conscious person?
b. What is the meaning of the existence of **human life**?
c. What is the meaning of the existence of **any life** whatsoever?
d. What is the meaning of the existence of **anything** at all?

Our primary focus will be on (a) with occasional reference to (b).

Our next task is to clarify what is meant by 'meaning' in the context of our question. In other words, we are looking for appropriate **components** that make the question about the meaning of our lives more exact. I suggest the following test that will help identify appropriate candidates. Take the question "What is the *meaning* of life?" and replace the word 'meaning' in it with your proposed candidate. If this replacement retains the sense of the question (i.e., if you feel that the resulting question is part of our original question), then your candidate is a suitable component of the original question; otherwise, your candidate is not an appropriate component of the original question.

Example: Suppose you think that the term 'cause' is a suitable candidate as a component of our original question "What is the meaning of life?" Following the above test, replace the word 'meaning' with 'cause' and you get: "What is the *cause* of life?" Clearly, the resulting question fails to retain the original sense of our question, for when we inquire about the meaning of our life; we are not primarily interested in our life's causal origins.

I suggest that the following two candidates are appropriate components of our original question: **purpose** and **value**. I recommend that you run the proposed test and confirm for yourself the claim I have just made. Let us assume for now that **purpose** (or any other synonymous concept) and **value** are indeed the two primary components of the meaning of life question. It turns out that each of these can be further divided into two different categories.

Purpose: If the question about the meaning of my life involves essentially a question about a purpose of my life, then it seems that such a purpose can be determined in two different ways: **externally** and **internally**. A widely accepted contender for an *externally determined purpose* is God, for instance, who is thought by some people to have created us in order to worship it. An alternative contender might be an alien species which brought about my existence for some end that may be unknown to me. On the other hand, an *internally determined purpose* for my life would be a purpose that flows inevitably from an essential fact about me: i.e., about my very nature. For instance, if we do have free-will and having free will is an essential feature of what it is to be a human agent, then purposes chosen by certain application of my free will may qualify as an internally determined purpose. It is important to note that the two ways in which purpose can be determined; i.e., externally and internally, need not exclude each other. For instance, it is quite possible that we were created by a God to worship it (i.e., externally determined purpose), yet upon deep reflection I freely choose as the purpose of my life to worship God (i.e., internally chosen purpose). Of course, there are other situations in which the externally determined purpose and the internally determined purpose exclude each other.

Value: It has been customary in value theory to distinguish between **objective** vs. **subjective** values. Objective values, like objective facts, are independent from our beliefs, opinions and preferences; subjective values, by contrast, are entirely dependent upon our subjective preferences (here think about a preference someone might have for chocolate ice-cream over vanilla ice-cream; this preference is entirely a matter of taste).

We can now represent the above distinctions within our concept of 'meaning' in the meaning of life question in the form of the following diagram:

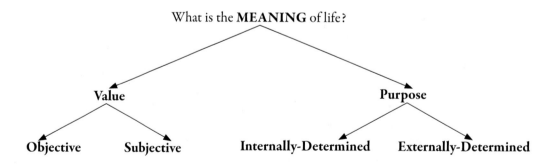

II.   **What is the kind of Motivations for asking the Question?**

What is the meaning of *my* life or *my* existence? Under what circumstances would one pose this question? Two such circumstances come to mind:

Psychological Reasons: We often face circumstances that have a deep impact upon our emotional life such as a tragedy or a situation that leaves us with a sense of helplessness or failure. This emotional upheaval results in an unstable state of mind which we find difficult to alter or control. In desperation we often find ourselves reacting to these conditions by declaring that life is not *worth* living or alternatively asking "Why this happens to *me*?" or "What is the point or meaning of *my* life?" and by that we mean that life has no meaning in light of the suffering one must endure.

It is important to recognize the exact *function* of questioning the meaning of life when posed under the circumstances described. The role of such questions is not to initiate an impersonal and serious *inquiry* into the meaning of life. Rather their function is to *express* a sense of psychological distress and helplessness. Questioning the meaning of life under these conditions, then, is a *symptom caused by psychological distress*. The remedy in such cases is to treat the underlying conditions that cause the psychological distress. The idea is that once the psychological conditions are removed, then in time the symptoms will vanish as well. Relief from the agony caused by the psychological conditions is expected to remove the compulsion to ask the question. Henceforth, we shall refer to this mode of asking the question as the *psychological question*.

Philosophical Reasons: An alternative motivation to raise the meaning of life question is *philosophical*. The hallmark of a philosophically motivated inquiry into the meaning of life is *the pursuit of truth*. Truth about what? About the objective *facts*, if there are any, that constitute the meaning of life or the lack of such meaning.

It is important to recognize the *generality* of such a pursuit. When the question of the meaning of life is philosophical rather than psychological, then the reference to *me* or *I* is no longer an essential component of the question. Replacing the reference to *me* in the question with *anyone* similarly situated retains whatever significance or import the question enjoyed prior to such replacement. Thus, the identity of the person who asks the question and their particular circumstance is only tangentially relevant to the inquiry into the question. From a purely philosophical point of view, the distinction between the person who confronts the philosophical question of the meaning of life and anyone else is not a fundamental difference. A philosophical answer to the question of what is the meaning of my life, if one is to be found, applies to anyone who is similar in the relevant respects to the person who embarks upon an inquiry into this question.

Thus, while the psychological question is inextricably (i.e., inseparably) linked to a particular *person* and the *individual circumstances* that prompted them to question the meaning of their life, the philosophical question is detached from any particular person and their unique circumstances. The inquiry into the philosophical question must proceed in the same manner regardless of the identity of the person who happens to ask the question and the character of their particular circumstance in life. Henceforth, we shall refer to this mode of asking the question as the *philosophical question*.

Hybrid Reason: It is imaginable that initially a person begins to question the meaning of their life due to some psychological reasons only to gradually recognize the generality and the impersonal character of the question. When such a person becomes engrossed in the philosophical pursuit of the question, then the unique conditions which initially prompted them to ask the psychological question become incidental to the philosophical inquiry and serve merely as an illustration of the import of the question.

The sharp distinction we have drawn above between the psychological question and the philosophical question entails that a solution to one is not necessarily an adequate or satisfactory solution to the other. In particular, it is important to recognize that a philosophical answer to the question of the meaning of life, if there is one, may not be satisfying psychologically; and vice versa.

While our primary focus is on the *philosophical* question of the meaning of life and various proposed solutions to *this* question, we cannot ignore the psychological question altogether. For we cannot rule out in advance to our philosophical inquiry the possibility that the philosophical question cannot be answered. If it turns out that the philosophical question is ill phrased or that it is impossible to answer, then the sentiments that give rise to the question of the meaning of life have only a psychological basis. In other words, under such circumstances, the only question about the meaning of life that remains is the psychological question.

III. **Motivations for Asking the *Philosophical* Question.**

So, how exactly does the ***philosophical question*** arise?
Remember: Even if ***you*** happen to begin the inquiry with the psychological question, once you move to the philosophical realm the reasons for asking the question are very different. This question focuses exclusively on the rationale, if any, that motivates asking the philosophical question. Remember also the ***generality criterion*** for the philosophical question: i.e., once you ask the philosophical question, then the fact that it is ***you*** who asks the question is not essential to the inquiry. The question and, therefore, the answer (if one is available) are both applicable to ***any*** person similarly situated whether or not they have ever contemplated the philosophical question as you now do. Thus, in some sense when ***you*** contemplate the philosophical question you do so on behalf of every human person or even every person ever lived, currently lives, and will live in the future.

The philosophical question arises once we become aware that certain beliefs we hold about the world and the human condition are *incompatible*, or at least severely *challenge*, our implicit or explicit beliefs about life's meaningfulness. Let us describe in detail how this incompatibility, or tension, might arise.

Subjective/Internal/Personal Point of View

As you are preoccupied in the goings on of your daily life you are at the same time immersed in a sea of meaning, purpose, and value. Much that makes a difference to your experience of life is so because you see in it some value, meaning, or purpose. You are so accustomed seeing everything in your surrounding as ripe with meaning, value, or purpose that you do not even notice the significance of this fact: you simply take it for granted.

Objective/External/Impersonal Point of View

While we contemplate the nature of the universe around us and make some progress in understanding its nature, we find that it is governed by laws that are completely *indifferent* to meaning, purpose, and value. Rocks, mountains, rivers, planets, meteors, galaxies, plants, electrons do not have a point of view from which they choose a purpose or assign value. The Sun does not furnish light and heat ***in order*** for us to survive. The Sun has no purposes, worthwhile or not. The order of causation is rather the other way around: life on Earth is made possible, among other things, ***because*** the Sun provides heat and light. The same goes for plants and animals. A meteor which is on a path to destroy Earth does not change its trajectory ***in order*** to spare life on Earth including that of the human race. If it does change its trajectory, then that lucky break for life on Earth is due to ***causal*** factors quite independent from purposes, meanings, or things we might value. Nature on its own is thoroughly indifferent to our fate, to life, and to anything we might deem worthwhile in life. I shall call this posture which nature has toward meaning, value, and purpose ***radical indifference***.[1]

---

1 The difference between the subjective versus the objective perspectives and its relevance to the meaning of life is inspired by Thomas Nagel's excellent work on the subject. See his "The Absurd", reprinted in *Mortal Questions*, (1979), Cambridge University Press; originally published in "Journal of Philosophy", LXVIII, no. 20 (1971).

This radical indifference of nature to everything that we value from our subjective, internal, and personal point of view is precisely the way the universe is depicted from the objective standpoint of ***modern science.*** Matters, however, are even worst, for this radical indifference appears to extend to the very beginning of our own life and to its end.

Our life begins with a sequence of chance occurrences culminating with the random chase, a chase that lacks any ***built-in*** meaning, purpose, or value. Conception does not happen ***in order*** for you or I to be endowed with the gift of life. We are endowed with the gift of life ***because*** of a sequence of chance occurrences culminating with the random chase that happens to conclude with you and I.

And then of course there is the matter of the inevitability of death. Death is annihilation of life as we know it during life. Between the beginning of life and its end there is a mix of satisfying experiences and there is also much suffering, both psychological and physical.

Moreover, our individual existence as well as humanity's very existence including all its achievements, regardless of its temporary prominence, is in the end always ***imperfect, transitory, finite,*** and in the long run ***immaterial.*** In the long run not a trace of them will be left. It is in this way that objective/external/impersonal reflections challenge the subjective/external/personal belief that life is meaningful. The elements of this challenge are as follows:

   i. Nature on its own is radically indifferent;
   ii. Human life begins without build-in meaning, purpose, or value. It just happens by chance;
  iii. Death is inevitable;
  iv. Individual existence as well as humanity's existence is imperfect, transitory, finite, vulnerable, and in the long run immaterial.

The philosophical question about the meaning of life arises because the objective facts about the transitory, finite, and temporary nature of our life conflict with our beliefs about the meaningfulness of our life, our goals, desires, and aspirations.

Chapter 2 Theistic Basis of the Meaning of Life

Tolstoy was a superb novelist and wrote several classic novels.[1] However, in this essay, "My Confessions", Tolstoy ventures into the question of the meaning of life not only from a novelist perspective, but also from a more philosophical point of view. It is, however, imperative to remember that Tolstoy is first and foremost a novelist, not a philosopher. Therefore, his treatment of the question of the meaning of life is literal and occasionally dramatic. Yet despite the literal treatment of the problem, there is an underlying philosophical argument.

It is not always clear whether Tolstoy's motivation to ask the question of the meaning of life is psychological, philosophical, or a hybrid. I will assume here that at the least Tolstoy's motivation includes a heavy emphasis on philosophical considerations. So what is the philosophical motivation for Tolstoy's inquiry into the meaning of life question? Tolstoy seems to rely heavily on the observation that our life is temporary and all our efforts and achievements are transitory. Tolstoy employs a very interesting strategy in his inquiry. He concludes that if there is an answer to the question of the meaning of life, then this answer must be found in the following three fields: Science; Philosophy; and Religion. The three areas Tolstoy chooses here seem to be very reasonable, since all three areas purport to provide us with *general truths* about the world. Next, Tolstoy divides the three areas into two categories: the *rational* category which includes science and philosophy, on the one hand, and the *non-rational* category that contains religion.[2] So we can present this in the following diagram:

	Rational	Non-Rational
Science	X	
Philosophy	X	
Religion		X

The strategy now is to try to rule out two of the three areas. If there is an answer to the question of the meaning of life, then the answer is going to be contained in the area that was not ruled out. Tolstoy thinks that the rational disciplines of science and

---

[1] Several well know novels written by Leo Tolstoy are: *War and Peace; Anna Karenina; The Death of Ivan Ilyich*. I recommend that you read these novels; they will undoubtedly enhance you.
[2] While Tolstoy uses the phrase 'irrational', I prefer to use 'non-rational' instead because of the later more neutral connotation.

philosophy are ruled out as capable of answering the question of the meaning of life because of their very *method*.

Consider science first. Every science must include some *quantitative element essentially* either in the very formulation of its *laws* (physics, for instance) or by employing *measurements* in the course of observation or experimentation (e.g., statistical inference in psychology) or both. But, if you recall one of the two components of the meaning of life diagram in Chapter 1 was *value*. And value, as it turns out, is an *essentially qualitative* feature. Therefore, Tolstoy reasons, since every science is quantitative, whereas the value of life is qualitative, science cannot provide a cogent answer to the question of the meaning of life.

Next consider philosophy. The fundamental method of philosophy is *reasoning*. But reasoning requires that every philosophical claim is supported by an argument. And arguments have premises and a conclusion, where the former support the later. Therefore, a philosophical answer to the meaning of life must take the form of an argument in which certain premises are asserted in order to support a conclusion about what is the meaning of life. Unfortunately, at least one or more of the said premises can always be challenged, which inevitably leads to the necessity to present another argument, featuring additional premises that aim to support the challenged premises. And this process does not seem to have an ending point whereby we can be certain about a philosophical answer to the meaning of life. Therefore, Tolstoy concludes, philosophy is also ruled out by its very method.

Since both rational disciplines were ruled out, that leaves us with religion as the sole non-rational area to seek an answer. And, indeed, religion does offer us an answer to the philosophical question of the meaning of life: namely, immortality in afterlife. If one has religious faith, then such faith includes the promise of immortality in afterlife. And this promise, Tolstoy maintains, resolves the original philosophical motivation for his inquiry, namely, the temporary and transitory nature of our life.

I invite you to ponder the following problem with Tolstoy's answer. Does Tolstoy *non-philosophical solution* to the question of the meaning of life properly match the *philosophical motivation* that drove him to ask the question in the first place?

Let us now turn to Pojman. Pojman's essay can be divided into four clear parts. In the first part Pojman narrates an encounter with an atheist woman who makes certain statements about the relationship between autonomy and the meaning of life provided by religion. Her comments, however, seem to be primarily metaphorical. The question that you need to ask yourself is this: What do these metaphors actually mean?

The second part of Pojman's article consists of two *theses* which he claims summarize what the atheist woman meant to say. I ask you at this point to *provisionally* accept Pojman's two theses as an interpretation of what the atheist woman meant to say; but remember that the validity of his interpretation may be subject to challenge at a later point. The third part of Pojman's article consists of an argument he offers against each thesis. You need to identify each argument and then critically examine whether it refutes the thesis it is intended to refute. The fourth part of Pojman's article consists of eight reasons why you should believe that religion offers truths about the world. This part is intended as a defense of one of the premises of his argument against the second thesis. Once you have identified each of the arguments and evaluated whether they are cogent, you can now reexamine whether Pojman's interpretation of what the atheist woman meant to say with her metaphorical narrative is accurate. I leave this determination to your own judgment.

My Confession

Leo Tolstoy

Although I regarded authorship as a waste of time, I continued to write during those fifteen years. I had tasted of the seduction of authorship, of the seduction of enormous monetary remunerations and applauses for my insignificant labour, and so I submitted to it, as being a means for improving my material condition and for stifling in my soul all questions about the meaning of my life and life in general.

In my writings I advocated, what to me was the only truth, that it was necessary to live in such a way as to derive the greatest comfort for oneself and one's family.

Thus I proceeded to live, but five years ago something very strange began to happen with me: I was overcome by minutes at first of perplexity and then of an arrest of life, as though I did not know how to live or what to do, and I lost myself and was dejected. But that passed, and I continued to live as before. Then those minutes of perplexity were repeated oftener and oftener, and always in one and the same form. These arrests of life found their express ion in ever the same questions: "Why? Well, and then?"

At first I thought that those were simply aimless, inappropriate questions. It seemed to me that that was all well known and that if I ever wanted to busy myself with their solution, it would not cost me much labour;—that now I had no time to attend to them, but that if I wanted to I should find the proper answers. But the questions began to repeat themselves oftener and oftener, answers were demanded more and more persistently, and, like dots that fall

on the same spot, these questions, without any answers, thickened into one black blotch.

There happened what happens with any person who falls ill with a mortal internal disease. At first there appear insignificant symptoms of indisposition, to which the patient pays no attention; then these symptoms are repeated more and more frequently and blend into one temporally indivisible suffering. The suffering keeps growing, and before the patient has had time to look around, he becomes conscious that what he took for an indisposition is the most significant thing in the world to him,—is death.

The same happened with me. I understood that it was not a passing indisposition, but something very important, and that, if the questions were going to repeat themselves, it would be necessary to find an answer for them. And I tried to answer them. The questions seemed to be so foolish, simple, and childish. But the moment I touched them and tried to solve them, I became convinced, in the first place, that they were not childish and foolish, but very important and profound questions in life, and, in the second, that, no matter how much I might try, I should not be able to answer them. Before attending to my Samára estate, to my son's education, or to the writing of a book, I ought to know

From Leo Tolstoy, *My Confession,* trans. Leo Wiener (London: J. M. Dent & Sons, 1905); reprinted by permission of J. M. Dent & Sons Ltd.

why I should do that. So long as I did not know why, I could not do anything. I could not live. Amidst my thoughts of farming, which interested me very much during that time, there would suddenly pass through my head a question like this: "All right, you are going to have six thousand desyatínas of land in the Government of Samára, and three hundred horses,—and then?" And I completely lost my senses and did not know what to think farther. Or, when I thought of the education of my children, I said to myself: "Why?" Or, reflecting on the manner in which the masses might obtain their welfare, I suddenly said to myself: "What is that to me?" Or, thinking of the fame which my works would get me, I said to myself: "All right, you will be more famous than Gógol, Púshkin, Shakespeare, Molière, and all the writers in the world,—what of it?" And I was absolutely unable to make any reply. The questions were not waiting, and I had to answer them at once; if I did not answer them, I could not live.

I felt that what I was standing on had given way, that I had no foundation to stand on, that that which I lived by no longer existed, and that I had nothing to live by. . . .

All that happened with me when I was on every side surrounded by what is considered to be complete happiness. I had a good, loving, and beloved wife, good children, and a large estate, which grew and increased without any labour on my part. I was respected by my neighbours and friends, more than ever before, was praised by strangers, and, without any self-deception, could consider my name famous. With all that, I was not deranged or mentally unsound,—on the contrary, I was in full command of my mental and physical powers, such as I had rarely met with in people of my age: physically I could work in a field, mowing, without falling behind a peasant; mentally I could work from eight to ten hours in succession, without experiencing any consequences from the strain. And while in such condition I arrived at the conclusion that I could not live, and, fearing death, I had to use cunning against myself, in order that I might not take my life.

This mental condition expressed itself to me in this form: my life is a stupid, mean trick played on me by somebody. Although I did not recognize that "somebody" as having created me, the form of the conception that some one had played a mean, stupid trick on me by bringing me into the world was the most natural one that presented itself to me.

Involuntarily I imagined that there, somewhere, there was somebody who was now having fun as he looked down upon me and saw me, who had lived for thirty or forty years, learning, developing, growing in body and mind, now that I had become strengthened in mind and had reached that summit of life from which it lay all before me, standing as a complete fool on that summit and seeing clearly that there was nothing in life and never would be. And that was fun to him—

But whether there was or was not that somebody who made fun of me, did not make it easier for me, I could not ascribe any sensible meaning to a single act, or to my whole life. I was only surprised that I had not understood that from the start. All that had long ago been known to everybody. Sooner or later there would come diseases and death (they had come already) to my dear ones and to me, and there would be nothing left but stench and worms. All my affairs, no matter what they might be, would sooner or later be forgotten, and I myself should not exist. So why should I worry about all these things? How could a man fail to see that and live,—that was surprising! A person could live only so long as he was drunk; but the moment he sobered up, he could not help seeing that all that was only a deception, and a stupid deception at that! Really, there was nothing funny and ingenious about it, but only something cruel and stupid.

Long ago has been told the Eastern story about the traveller who in the steppe is overtaken by an infuriated beast. Trying to save himself from the animal, the traveller jumps into a waterless well, but at its bottom he sees a dragon who opens his jaws in order to swallow him. And the unfortunate man does not dare climb out, lest he perish from the infuriated beast, and does not dare jump down to the bottom of the well, lest he be devoured by the dragon, and so clutches the twig of a wild bush growing in a cleft of the well and holds on to it. His hands grow weak and he feels that soon he shall have to surrender to the peril which awaits him at either side; but he still holds on and sees two mice, one white, the other black, in even measure making a circle around the main trunk of the bush to which he is clinging, and nibbling at it on all sides. Now, at any moment, the bush will break and tear off, and he will fall into the dragon's jaws. The traveller sees that and knows that he will inevitably perish; but while he is still clinging, he sees some drops of honey hanging on the leaves of the bush, and so reaches out for them with his tongue and licks the leaves. Just so I hold on to the branch of life, knowing that the dragon of death is waiting inevitably for me, ready to tear me to pieces, and I cannot understand why I have fallen on such suffering. And I try to lick that honey which used to give me pleasure; but now it no longer gives me joy, and the white and the black mouse day and night nibble at the branch to which I am holding on. I clearly see the dragon, and the honey is no longer sweet to me. I see only the inevitable dragon and the mice, and am unable to turn my glance away from them. That is not a fable, but a veritable, indisputable, comprehensible truth.

The former deception of the pleasures of life, which stifled the terror of the dragon, no longer deceives me. No matter how much one should say to me, "You cannot understand the meaning of life, do not think, live!" I am unable to do so, because I have been doing it too long before. Now I cannot help seeing day and night, which run and lead me up to death. I see that alone, because that alone is the truth. Everything else is a lie.

The two drops of honey that have longest turned my eyes away from the cruel truth, the love of family and of authorship, which I have called an art, are no longer sweet to me.

"My family—" I said to myself, "but my family, my wife and children, they are also human beings. They are in precisely the same condition that I am in: they must either live in the lie or see the terrible truth. Why should they live? Why should I love them, why guard, raise, and watch them? Is it for the same despair which is in me, or for dulness of perception? Since I love them, I cannot conceal the truth from them,—every step in cognition leads them up to this truth. And the truth is death."

"Art, poetry?" For a long time, under the influence of the success of human praise, I tried to persuade myself that that was a thing which could be done, even though death should come and destroy everything, my deeds, as well as my memory of them; but soon I came to see that that, too, was a deception. It was clear to me that art was an adornment of life, a decoy of life. But life lost all its attractiveness for me. How, then, could I entrap others? So long as I did not live my own life, and a strange life bore me on its waves; so long as I believed that life had some sense, although I was not able to express it,—the reflections of life of every description in poetry and in the arts afforded me pleasure, and I was delighted to look at life through this little mirror of art; but when I began to look for the meaning of life, when I experienced the necessity of living myself, that little mirror became either useless, superfluous, and ridiculous, or painful to me. I could no longer console myself with what I saw in the mirror, namely, that my situation was stupid and desperate. It was all right for me to rejoice so long as I believed in the depth of my soul that life had some sense. At that time the play of lights—of the comical, the tragical, the touching, the beautiful, the terrible in life—afforded me amusement. But when I knew that life was meaningless and terrible, the play in the little mirror could no longer amuse me. No sweetness of honey could be sweet to me, when I saw the dragon and the mice that were nibbling down my support. . . .

In my search after the question of life I experienced the same feeling which a man who has lost his way in the forest may experience.

He comes to a clearing, climbs a tree, and clearly sees an unlimited space before him; at the same time he sees that there are no houses there, and that there can be none; he goes back to the forest, into the darkness, and he sees darkness, and again there are no houses.

Thus I blundered in this forest of human knowledge, between the clearings of the mathematical and experimental sciences, which disclosed to me clear horizons, but such in the direction of which there could be no house, and between the darkness of the speculative sciences, where I sunk into a deeper darkness, the farther I proceeded, and I convinced myself at last that there was no way out and could not be.

By abandoning myself to the bright side of knowledge I saw that I only turned my eyes away from the question. No matter how enticing and clear the horizons were that were disclosed to me, no matter how enticing it was to bury myself in the infinitude of this knowledge, I comprehended that these sciences were the more clear, the less I needed them, the less they answered my question.

"Well, I know," I said to myself, "all which science wants so persistently to know, but there is no answer to the question about the meaning of my life." But in the speculative sphere I saw that, in spite of the fact that the aim of the knowledge was directed straight to the answer of my question, or because of that fact, there could be no other answer than what I was giving to myself: "What is the meaning of my life?"—"None." Or, "What will come of my life?"—"Nothing." Or, "Why does everything which exists exist, and why do I exist?"—"Because it exists."

Putting the question to the one side of human knowledge, I received an endless quantity of exact answers about what I did not ask: about the chemical composition of the stars, about the movement of the sun toward the constellation of Hercules, about the origin of species and of man, about the forms of infinitely small, imponderable particles of ether; but the answer in this sphere of knowledge to my question what the meaning of my life was, was always: "You are what you call your life; you are a temporal, accidental conglomeration of particles. The interrelation, the change of these particles, produces in you that which you call life. This congeries will last for some time; then the interaction of these particles will cease, and that which you call life and all your questions will come to an end. You are an accidentally cohering globule of something. The globule is fermenting. This fermentation the globule calls its life. The globule falls to pieces, and all fermentation and all questions will come to an end." Thus the clear side of knowledge answers, and it cannot say anything else, if only it strictly follows its principles.

With such an answer it appears that the answer is not a reply to the question. I want to know the meaning of my life, but the fact that it is a particle of the infinite not only gives it no meaning, but even destroys every possible meaning.

Those obscure transactions, which this side of the experimental, exact science has with speculation, when it says that the meaning of life consists in evolution and the coöperation with this evolution, because of their obscurity and inexactness cannot be regarded as answers.

The other side of knowledge, the speculative, so long as it sticks strictly to its fundamental principles in giving a direct answer to the question, everywhere and at all times has answered one and the same: "The world is something infinite and incomprehensible. Human life is an incomprehensible part of this incomprehensible *all*. . . ."

I lived for a long time in this madness, which, not in words, but in deeds, is particularly characteristic of us, the most liberal and learned of men. But, thanks either to my strange, physical love for the real working class, which made me understand it and see that it is not so stupid as we suppose, or to the sincerity of my conviction, which was that I could know nothing and that the best that I could do was to hang myself,—I felt that if I wanted to live and understand the meaning of life, I ought naturally to look for it, not among those who had lost the meaning of life and wanted to kill themselves, but among those billions departed and living men who had been carrying their own lives and ours upon their shoulders. And I looked around at the enormous masses of deceased and living men,—not learned and wealthy, but simple men,—and I saw something quite different. I saw that all these billions of men that lived or had lived, all, with rare exceptions, did not fit into my subdivisions,* and that I could not recognize them as not understanding the question, because they themselves put it and answered it with surprising clearness. Nor could I recognize them as Epicureans, because their lives were composed rather of privations and suffering than of enjoyment. Still less could I recognize them as senselessly living out their meaningless lives, because every act of theirs and death itself was explained by them. They regarded it as the greatest evil to kill themselves. It appeared, then, that all humanity was in possession of a knowledge of the meaning of life, which I did not recognize and which I contemned. It turned out that rational knowledge did not give any meaning to life, excluded life, while the meaning which by billions of people, by all humanity, was ascribed to life was based on some despised, false knowledge.

The rational knowledge in the person of the learned and the wise denied the meaning of life, but the enormous masses of men, all humanity, recognized this meaning in an irrational knowledge. This irrational knowledge was faith, the same that I could not help but reject. That was God as one and three, the creation in six days, devils and angels, and all that which I could not accept so long as I had not lost my senses.

My situation was a terrible one. I knew that I should not find anything on the path of rational knowledge but the negation of life, and there, in faith, nothing but the negation of reason, which was still more impossible than the negation of life. From the rational knowledge it followed that life was an evil and men knew it,—it depended on men whether they should cease living, and yet they lived and continued to live, and I myself lived, though I had known long ago that life was meaningless and an evil. From faith it followed that, in order to understand life, I must renounce reason, for which alone a meaning was needed.

There resulted a contradiction, from which there were two ways out: either what I called rational was not so rational as I had thought; or that which to me appeared irrational was not so irrational as I had thought. And I began to verify the train of thoughts of my rational knowledge.

In verifying the train of thoughts of my rational knowledge, I found that it was quite correct. The deduction that life was nothing was inevitable; but I saw a mistake. The mistake was that I had not reasoned in conformity with the question put by me. The question was, "Why should I live?" that is, "What real, indestructible essence will come from my phantasmal, destructible life? What meaning has my finite existence in this infinite world?" And in order to answer this question, I studied life.

The solutions of all possible questions of life apparently could not satisfy me, because my question, no matter how simple it appeared in the beginning, included the necessity of explaining the finite through the infinite, and vice versa.

I asked, "What is the extra-temporal, extra-causal, extra-spatial meaning of life?" But I gave an answer to the question, "What is the temporal, causal, spatial meaning of my life?" The result was that after a long labour of mind I answered, "None."

In my reflections I constantly equated, nor could I do otherwise, the finite with the finite, the infinite with the infinite, and so from that resulted precisely what had to

---

* Tolstoy previously observed that each of his peers assumed one of four attitudes toward life; They lived in ignorance of the problem of life's meaning; ignored the problem and pursued whatever pleasures possible; acknowledged the meaninglessness of life and committed suicide; or, acknowledged the meaninglessness, but lived on aimlessly, usually lacking the fortitude to take their own lives. See Chapter Seven of *My Confession*. [Eds.]

result: force was force, matter was matter, will was will, infinity was infinity, nothing was nothing,—and nothing else could come from it.

There happened something like what at times takes place in mathematics: you think you are solving an equation, when you have only an identity. The reasoning is correct, but you receive as a result the answer: $a = a$, or $x = x$, or $0 = 0$. The same happened with my reflection in respect to the question about the meaning of my life. The answers given by all science to that question are only identities.

Indeed, the strictly scientific knowledge, that knowledge which, as Descartes did, begins with a full doubt in everything, rejects all knowledge which has been taken on trust, and builds everything anew on the laws of reason and experience, cannot give any other answer to the question of life than what I received,—an indefinite answer. It only seemed to me at first that science gave me a positive answer,—Schopenhauer's answer: "Life has no meaning, it is an evil." But when I analyzed the matter, I saw that the answer was not a positive one, but that it was only my feeling which expressed it as such. The answer, strictly expressed, as it is expressed by the Brahmins, by Solomon, and by Schopenhauer, is only an indefinite answer, or an identity, $0 = 0$, life is nothing. Thus the philosophical knowledge does not negate anything, but only answers that the question cannot be solved by it, that for philosophy the solution remains insoluble.

When I saw that, I understood that it was not right for me to look for an answer to my question in rational knowledge, and that the answer given by rational knowledge was only an indication that the answer might be got if the question were differently put, but only when into the discussion of the question should be introduced the question of the relation of the finite to the infinite, I also understood that, no matter how irrational and monstrous the answers might be that faith gave, they had this advantage that they introduced into each answer the relation of the finite to the infinite, without which there could be no answer.

No matter how I may put the question, "How must I live?" the answer is, "According to God's law." "What real result will there be from my life?"—"Eternal torment or eternal bliss." "What is the meaning which is not destroyed by death?"—"The union with infinite God, paradise."

Thus, outside the rational knowledge, which had to me appeared as the only one, I was inevitably led to recognize that all living humanity had a certain other irrational knowledge, faith, which made it possible to live.

All the irrationality of faith remained the same for me, but I could not help recognizing that it alone gave to humanity answers to the questions of life, and, in consequence of them, the possibility of living.

The rational knowledge brought me to the recognition that life was meaningless,—my life stopped, and I wanted to destroy myself. When I looked around at people, at all humanity, I saw that people lived and asserted that they knew the meaning of life. I looked back at myself: I lived so long as I knew the meaning of life. As to other people, so even to me, did faith give the meaning of life and the possibility of living.

Looking again at the people of other countries, contemporaries of mine and those passed away, I saw again the same. Where life had been, there faith, ever since humanity had existed, had given the possibility of living, and the chief features of faith were everywhere one and the same.

No matter what answers faith may give, its every answer gives to the finite existence of man the sense of the infinite,—a sense which is not destroyed by suffering, privation, and death. Consequently in faith alone could we find the meaning and possibility of life. What, then, was faith? I understood that faith was not merely an evidence of things not seen, and so forth, not revelation (that is only the description of one of the symptoms of faith), not the relation of man to man (faith has to be defined, and then God, and not first God, and faith through him), not merely an agreement with what a man was told, as faith was generally understood,—that faith was the knowledge of the meaning of human life, in consequence of which man did not destroy himself, but lived. Faith is the power of life. If a man lives he believes in something. If he did not believe that he ought to live for some purpose, he would not live. If he does not see and understand the phantasm of the finite, he believes in that finite; if he understands the phantasm of the finite, he must believe in the infinite. Without faith one cannot live. . . .

In order that all humanity may be able to live, in order that they may continue living, giving a meaning to life, they, those billions, must have another, a real knowledge of faith, for not the fact that I, with Solomon and Schopenhauer, did not kill myself convinced me of the existence of faith, but that these billions had lived and had borne us, me and Solomon, on the waves of life.

Then I began to cultivate the acquaintance of the believers from among the poor, the simple and unlettered folk, of pilgrims, monks, dissenters, peasants. The doctrine of these people from among the masses was also the Christian doctrine that the quasi-believers of our circle professed. With the Christian truths were also mixed in very many superstitions, but there was this difference: the superstitions of our circle were quite unnecessary to them, had no connection with their lives, were only a kind of an Epicurean amusement, while the superstitions of the believers from among the labouring classes were to such an extent blended with their life that it would have been impossible to imagine it without these superstitions,—it was a necessary condition of that life. I began to examine closely the lives and beliefs of these people, and the more I examined them, the more did I become convinced that they had the real faith, that their faith was necessary for them, and that it alone gave them a meaning and possibility of life. In contradistinction to what I saw in our circle, where life without faith was possible, and where hardly one in a thousand professed to be a believer, among them there was hardly one in a thousand who was not a believer. In contradistinction to what I saw in our circle, where all life passed in idleness, amusements, and tedium of life, I saw that the whole life of these people was passed in hard work, and that they were satisfied with life. In contradistinction to the people of our circle, who struggled and murmured against fate because of their privations and their suffering, these people accepted diseases and sorrows without any perplexity or opposition, but with the calm and firm conviction that it was all for good. In contradistinction to the fact that the more intelligent we are, the less do we understand the meaning of life and the more do we see a kind of a bad joke in our suffering and death, these people live, suffer, and approach death, and suffer in peace and more often in joy. In contradistinction to the fact that a calm death, a death without terror or despair, is the greatest exception in our circle, a restless, insubmissive, joyless death is one of the greatest exceptions among the masses. And of such people, who are deprived of everything which for Solomon and for me constitutes the only good of life, and who withal experience the greatest happiness, there is an enormous number. I cast a broader glance about me. I examined the life of past and present vast masses of men, and I saw people who in like manner had understood the meaning of life, who had known how to live and die, not two, not three, not ten, but hundreds, thousands, millions. All of them, infinitely diversified as to habits, intellect, culture, situation, all equally and quite contrary to my ignorance knew the meaning of life and of death, worked calmly, bore privations and suffering, lived and died, seeing in that not vanity, but good.

I began to love those people. The more I penetrated into their life, the life of the men now living, and the life of men departed, of whom I had read and heard, the more did I love them, and the easier it became for me to live. Thus I lived for about two years, and within me took place a transformation, which had long been working within me, and the germ of which had always been in me. What happened with me was that the life of our circle,—of the rich and the learned,—not only disgusted me, but even lost all its meaning. All our acts, reflections, sciences, arts,—all that appeared to me in a new light.

I saw that all that was mere pampering of the appetites, and that no meaning could be found in it; but the life of all the working masses, of all humanity, which created life, presented itself to me in its real significance. I saw that that was life itself and that the meaning given to this life was truth, and I accepted it.

Religion Gives Meaning to Life

Louis P. Pojman

In this essay Louis Pojman argues that religion, specifically theistic religion, gives special meaning to life, unavailable in secular world views. Furthermore, the autonomy that secularists prize (sometimes value it beyond its worth) is not significantly diminished by religious faith.

Study Questions

1. What are the two theses that the atheist holds, and how does Pojman argue against them?
2. What are his definitions of "meaning" and "autonomy"?
3. What is the relationship of meaning to freedom or autonomy?
4. Which of Pojman's eight theses on the value of religious faith do you agree with and which do you disagree with?

Several years ago during a class break, I was discussing the significance of religion in our society with a few students in the college lounge. I, at that time an agnostic, was conceding to a devout Christian that it would be nice if theism were true, for then the world would not be simply a matter of chance and necessity, a sad tale with a sadder ending. Instead, "the world would be personal, a gift from our heavenly Father, who provides a basis for meaning and purpose." A mature woman from another class, whom I knew to be an atheist, overheard my remarks, charged through a group of coffee drinkers and angrily snapped at me, "That is the most disgusting thing I've ever heard!" I inquired why she thought this, and she replied, "Religion keeps humans from growing up. We don't need a big Daddy in the sky. We need to grow up and become our own parents."

I recalled Nietzsche's dictum that now that "God is dead," now that we have killed the Holy One, we must ourselves become gods to seem worthy of the deed. The atheist woman was prizing autonomy over meaning and claiming that religion did just the opposite.

In other words, she held two theses:

1. It is more important to be free or autonomous than to have a grand meaning or purpose to life.
2. Religion provides a grand meaning or purpose to life, but it does not allow humans to be free or autonomous.

This article first appeared in Philosophy: The Quest for Truth, *1st edition (Wadsworth Publishing co., 1989), Copyright © 2002 by Louis P. Pojman. Reprinted by permission of family. Originally published under the pseudonym Lois Hope Walker.*

I've thought a lot about that woman's response over the years. I think that she is wrong on both counts. In this essay I will defend religion against her two theses and try to show that meaning and autonomy are both necessary or important ingredients for an ideal existence and that they are compatible within a religious framework.

Let me begin with the first thesis, that it is more important to be free than that there be meaning in life. First let us define our terms. By "autonomy" I mean self-governing, the ability to make choices on the basis of good reasons rather than being coerced by threats or forces from without.

By "meaning" in life I mean that life has a purpose. There is some intrinsic rationale or plan to it. Now this purpose can be good, bad, or indifferent. An example of something with a bad purpose is the activity of poisoning a reservoir on which a community depends for its sustenance. An example of something with an indifferent purpose might be pacing back and forth to pass the time of day (it is arguable that this is bad or good depending on the options and context, and if you think that then either choose your own example or dismiss the category of indifferent purpose). An example of a good purpose is digging a well in order to provide water to a community in need of water.

Now it seems to be the case that, as a value, autonomy is superior to indifferent and bad purposes, since it has positive value while these other two categories do not. Autonomy may be more valuable to us than some good purposes, but it does not seem to be superior to *all* good purposes. While it may be more valuable to be free than to have this or that incidental purpose in life, freedom cannot really be understood apart from the notion of purposiveness. To be free is to be able to do some act *A*, when you want to, in order to reach some goal *G*. So the two ideas are related.

But the atheist woman meant more than this. She meant that if she had to choose whether to have free will or to live in a world that had a governing providential hand, she would choose the former. But this seems to make two mistakes. (1) It makes autonomy into an unjustified absolute and (2) it creates a false dilemma.

(1) Consider two situations: In situation A you are as free as you are now (say you have 100 units of autonomy—call these units "autonotoms") but are deeply miserable because you are locked in a large and interesting room which is being slowly filled with poisonous gas. You can do what ever you want for five more minutes but then you will be dead. In situation B, however, you have only 95 autonotoms (that is, there are a few things that you are unable to do in this world—say commit adultery or kill your neighbor) but the room is being filled with sunshine and fresh air. Which world would you choose? I would choose situation B, for autonomy, it seems to me, is not the only value in the universe, nor is it always the overriding value. I think most of us would be willing to give up a few autonotoms for an enormous increase in happiness. And I think that a world with a good purpose would be one in which we would be willing to give up a few bits of freedom. If we were told that we could eliminate poverty, crime, and great suffering in the world by each sacrificing one autonotom, wouldn't we do this? If so, then autonomy is not an absolute which always overrides every other value. It is one important value among others.

I turn to the atheist's second thesis, that religion always holds purpose, as superior to autonomy. I think that this is a misunderstanding of what the best types of religion try to do. As Jesus said in John 8 : 32, "Ye shall know the truth and the truth shall set you free." Rather than seeing freedom and meaning as opposites, theism sees them as inextricably bound together. Since it claims to offer us the truth about the world, and since having true beliefs is important in reaching one's goals, it follows that our autonomy is actually heightened in having the truth about the purpose of life. If we know why we are here and what the options in our destiny really are, we will be able to choose more intelligently than the blind who lead the blind in ignorance.

Indeed theistic religion (I have in mind Judaism, Christianity, and Islam, but this could apply to many forms of Hinduism and African religions as well) claims to place before us options of the greatest importance, so that if it is true the world is far better (infinitely better?) than if it is not.

Let me elaborate on this point. If theism is true and there is a benevolent supreme being governing the universe, the following eight theses are true:

1. We have a satisfying explanation of the origin and sustenance of the universe. We are the product not of chance and necessity or an impersonal Big Bang, but of a Heavenly Being who cares about us. As William James says, if religion is true, "the universe is no longer a mere *It* to us, but a *Thou* . . . and any relation that may be possible from person to person might be possible here." We can take comfort in knowing that the visible world is part of a more spiritual universe from which it draws its meaning and that there is, in spite of evil, an essential harmonious relationship between our world and the transcendent reality.

2. Good will win out over evil—we're not fighting alone, but God is on our side in the battle. So, you and I are not fighting in vain—we'll win eventually. This thought of the ultimate victory of Goodness gives us confidence to go on in the fight against injustice and cruelty when others calculate that the odds against righteousness are too great to fight against.

3. God loves and cares for us—His love compels us (II Corinthians 5 : 7), so that we have a deeper motive for morally good actions, including high altruism. We live deeply moral lives because of deep gratitude to One who loves us and whom we love. Secularism lacks this sense of cosmic love, and it is, therefore, no accident that it fails to produce moral saints like Jesus, St. Francis, Gandhi, Martin Luther King, and Mother Teresa. You need special love to leave a world of comfort in order to go to a desolate island to minister to lepers, as Father Damian did.

4. We have an answer to the problem why be moral—it's clearly in your interest. Secular ethics has a severe problem with the question, Why be moral when it is not in your best interest, when you can profitably advance yourself by an egoistic act? But such a dilemma does not arise in religious ethics, for Evil really is bad for you and the Good good for you.

5. Cosmic Justice reigns in the universe. The scales are perfectly balanced so that everyone will get what he or she deserves, according to their moral merit. There is no moral luck (unless you interpret the grace which will finally prevail as a type of "luck"), but each will be judged according to how one has used one's talents (Matthew, chapter 25).

6. All persons are of equal worth. Since we have all been created in the image of God and are His children, we are all brothers and sisters. We are family and ought to treat each other benevolently as we would family members of equal worth. Indeed, modern secular moral and political systems often assume this equal worth of the individual without justifying it. But without the Parenthood of God it makes no sense to say that all persons are innately of equal value. From a perspective of intelligence and utility, Aristotle and Nietzsche are right: there are enormous inequalities, and why shouldn't the superior persons use the baser types to their advantage? In this regard, secularism, in rejecting inegalitarianism, seems to be living off of the interest of a religious capital which it has relinquished.

7. Grace and forgiveness—a happy ending for all. All's well that ends well (the divine comedy). The moral guilt which we experience, even for the most heinous acts, can be removed, and we can be redeemed and given a new start. This is true moral liberation.

8. There is life after death, Death is not the end of the matter, but we shall live on, recognizing each other in a better world. We have eternity in our souls and are destined for a higher existence. (Of course, hell is a problem here—which vitiates the whole idea somewhat, but many variations of theism [e.g., varieties of theistic Hinduism and the Christian theologians Origen (in the second century), F. Maurice, and Karl Barth] hold to universal salvation in the end. Hell is only a temporary school in moral education—I think that this is a plausible view.) So if Hebraic-Christian theism is true, the world is a friendly home in which we are all related as siblings in one family, destined to live forever in cosmic bliss in a reality in which good defeats evil.

If theism is false and secularism is true, then there is no obvious basis for human equality, no reason to treat all people with equal respect, no simple and clear answer to the question, Why be moral even when it is not in my best interest? no sense of harmony and purpose in the universe, but "Whirl has replaced Zeus and is king" (Sophocles).

Add to this the fact that theism doesn't deprive us of any autonomy that we have in non-theistic systems. If we are equally free to choose the good or the evil whether or not God exists (assuming that the notions of good and evil make sense in a non-theistic universe)—then it seems clear that the world of the theist is far better and more satisfying to us than one in which God does not exist.

Of course, the problem is that we probably do not know if theism, let alone our particular religious version of it, is true. Here I must use a Pascalean argument to press my third point that we may have an obligation or, at least, it may be a good thing, to live *as if* theism is true. That is, unless you think that theism is so improbable that we should not even consider it as a candidate for truth, we should live in such a way as to allow the virtues of theism to inspire our lives and our culture. The theistic world view is so far superior to the secular that—even though we might be agnostics or weak atheists—it is in our interest to live as though it were true, to consider each person as a child of God, of high value, to work as though God is working with us in the battle of Good over evil, and to build a society based on these ideas. It is good then to gamble on God. Religion gives us a purpose to life and a basis for morality that is too valuable to dismiss lightly, It is a heritage that we may use to build a better civilization and one which we neglect at our own peril.

Chapter 3 The Absurdity of Life

During the 17th and 18th centuries several monumental revolutions occurred in the Western World. The most well-known of these revolutions is the so-called Scientific Revolution. The scientific revolution changed the manner in which we understand the world, thereby, undermining the previous explanatory regime primarily fueled by theistic religion. As a result the hold which theistic religion had on our inquiry of the world was diluted and eventually completely replaced by the scientific method. However, the scientific revolution did more than that.[1]

Prior to the 17th Century both religious and secular conceptions of the world included the idea that the concept of *purpose* is central and essential in our understanding of the way the world works. According to the pre 17th century conception, shared by both religious and secular thinkers, *everything has a purpose*. The disagreement between the religious and secular thinking was about whom or what determined the purpose of each thing. According to religious thinkers, it was the theistic God which determined the purpose of each thing. According to the secular conception, it was nature which determined the purpose of each thing. They both agreed, however, that *everything has a purpose*. And of course if everything has a purpose, then so do we. Purpose, according to the pre 17th century worldview, was part of the very fabric of reality. *Value* was thought also to be part of objective reality and it was determined based on the extent to which each thing fulfilled its purpose. Thus, if the more extensively something fulfills its purpose, then more valuable it is. Thus, value too was thought to be part of the very fabric of reality.

The broader revolution of the 17th century *replaced the concept of purpose as central to our understanding of the world with the concept of cause or causal law*. During and after the 17th century scientists no longer looked for the purpose of things in order to explain their behavior; instead they were seeking to find *causes* or *causal laws*.

Once the concept of purpose was replaced as an explanatory concept with the concept of cause, the very question of the meaning of life became threatened. The new worldview no longer considered purposes and values as objective aspects of reality. Therefore, the two principal components of the meaning of life (as illustrated by the Meaning of Life Diagram in Chapter 1) were no longer viewed as part of objective reality. This change has monumental significance for the very meaningfulness of an objective conception of the meaning of life. If meaning of life can no longer be viewed as an objective aspect of reality, then perhaps there is no objective meaning to our life.

---

[1] The present account is based upon an excellent essay by Walter T. Stace, "Man Against Darkness", (1948), The Atlantic Monthly Company, Boston Massachusetts. Unfortunately, as of the printing of the first edition of the present book we were unable to identify who currently holds the copyrights for this paper and so we were unable to include it in this book.

And once this move is made, the only alternative is to seek a subjective and internally determined purpose and value. The selections below explore various ways in which we may identify an internally chosen purpose joined with a subjective value. The meaning of life, thus, become, internalized and no longer was viewed as an objective aspect of our life.

The Meaning of Life

Richard Taylor

The question whether life has any meaning is difficult to interpret, and the more one concentrates his critical faculty on it the more it seems to elude him, or to evaporate as any intelligible question. One wants to turn it aside, as a source of embarrassment, as something that, if it cannot be abolished, should at least be decently covered. And yet I think any reflective person recognizes that the question it raises is important, and that it ought to have a significant answer.

If the idea of meaningfulness is difficult to grasp in this context, so that we are unsure what sort of thing would amount to answering the question, the idea of meaninglessness is perhaps less so. If, then, we can bring before our minds a clear image of meaningless existence, then perhaps we can take a step toward coping with our original question by seeing to what extent our lives, as we actually find them, resemble that image, and draw such lessons as we are able to from the comparison.

Meaningless Existence

A perfect image of meaninglessness, of the kind we are seeking, is found in the ancient myth of Sisyphus. Sisyphus, it will be remembered, betrayed divine secrets to mortals, and for this he was condemned by the gods to roll a stone to the top of a hill, the stone then immediately to roll back down, again to be pushed to the top by Sisyphus, to roll down once more, and so on again and again, *forever*. Now in this we have the picture of meaningless, pointless toil, of a meaningless existence that is absolutely *never* redeemed. It is not even redeemed by a death that, if it were to accomplish nothing more, would at least bring this idiotic cycle to a close. If we were invited to imagine Sisyphus struggling for awhile and accomplishing nothing, perhaps eventually falling from exhaustion, so that we might suppose him then eventually turning to something having some sort of promise, then the meaninglessness of that chapter of his life would not be so stark. It would be a dark and dreadful dream, from which he eventually awakens to sunlight and reality. But he does not awaken, for there is nothing for him to awaken to. His repetitive toil is his life and reality, and it goes on forever, and it is without any meaning whatever. Nothing ever comes of what he is doing, except simply, more of the same. Not by one step, nor by a thousand, nor by ten thousand does he even expiate by the smallest token the sin against the gods that led him into this fate. Nothing comes of it, nothing at all.

This ancient myth has always enchanted men, for countless meanings can be read into it. Some of the ancients apparently thought it symbolized the perpetual rising and setting of the sun, and others the repetitious crashing of the waves upon the shore. Probably the commonest interpretation is that it symbolizes man's eternal struggle and unquenchable spirit, his determination always to try once more in the face of overwhelming discouragement. This interpretation is further supported by that version of the myth according to which Sisyphus was commanded to roll the stone *over* the hill, so that it would finally roll down the other side, but was never quite able to make it.

I am not concerned with rendering or defending any interpretation of this myth, however. I have cited it only for the one element it does unmistakably contain, namely, that of a repetitious, cyclic activity, that never comes to anything. We could contrive other images of this that would serve just as well, and no myth-makers are needed to supply the materials of it. Thus, we can imagine two persons transporting a stone—or even a precious gem, it does not matter—back and forth, relay style. One carries it to a near or distant point where it is received by the other; it is returned to its starting point, there to be recovered by the first, and the process is repeated over and over. Except in this relay nothing counts as winning, and nothing brings the contest to any close, each step only leads to a repetition of itself. Or we can imagine two groups of prisoners, one of them engaged in digging a prodigious hole in the ground that is no sooner finished than it is filled in again by the other group, the latter then digging a new hole that is at once filled in by the first group, and so on and on endlessly.

Now what stands out in all such pictures as oppressive and dejecting is not that the beings who enact these roles suffer any torture or pain, for it need not be assumed that they do. Nor is it that their labors are great, for they are no greater than the labors commonly undertaken by most men most of the time. According to the original myth, the stone is so large that Sisyphus never quite gets it to the top and must groan under every step, so that his enormous labor is all for nought. But this is not what appalls. It is not that his great struggle comes to nothing, but that his existence itself is without meaning. Even if we suppose, for example, that the stone is but a pebble that can be carried effortlessly, or that the holes dug by the prisoners are but small ones, not the slightest meaning is introduced into their lives. The stone that Sisyphus moves to the top of the hill, whether we think of it as large or small, still rolls back every time, and the process is repeated forever. Nothing comes of it, and the work is simply pointless. That is the element of the myth that I wish to capture.

Again, it is not the fact that the labors of Sisyphus continue forever that deprives them of meaning. It is, rather, the implication of this: that they come to nothing. The image would not be changed by our supposing him to push a different stone up every time, each to roll down again. But if we supposed that these stones, instead of rolling back to their places as if they had never been moved, were assembled at the top of the hill and there incorporated, say, in a beautiful and enduring temple, then the aspect of meaninglessness would disappear. His labors would then have a point, something would come of them all, and although one could perhaps still say it was not worth it, one could not say that the life of Sisyphus was devoid of meaning altogether. Meaningfulness would at least have made an appearance, and we could see what it was.

That point will need remembering. But in the meantime, let us note another way in which the image of meaninglessness can be altered by making only a very slight change. Let us suppose that the gods, while condemning Sisyphus to the fate just described, at the same time, as an afterthought, waxed perversely merciful by implanting in him a strange and irrational impulse; namely, a compulsive impulse to roll stones. We may if we like, to make this more graphic, suppose they accomplish this by implanting in him some substance that has this effect on his character and drives. I call this perverse, because from our point of view there is clearly no reason why anyone should have a persistent and insatiable desire to do something so pointless as that. Nevertheless, suppose that is Sisyphus' condition. He has but one obsession, which is to roll stones, and it is an obsession that is only for the moment appeased by his rolling them—he no sooner gets a stone rolled to the top of the hill than he is restless to roll up another.

Now it can be seen why this little afterthought of the gods, which I called perverse, was also in fact merciful. For they have by this device managed to give Sisyphus precisely what he wants—by making him want precisely what they inflict on him. However it may appear to us, Sisyphus' fate now does not appear to him as a condemnation, but the very reverse. His one desire in life is to roll stones, and he is absolutely guaranteed its endless fulfillment, Where otherwise he might profoundly have wished surcease, and even welcomed the quiet of death to release him from endless boredom and meaninglessness, his life is now filled with mission and meaning, and he seems to himself to have been given an entry to heaven. Nor need he even fear death, for the gods have promised him an endless opportunity to indulge his single purpose, without concern or frustration. He will be able to roll stones *forever*.

What we need to mark most carefully at this point is that the picture with which we began has not really been changed in the least by adding this supposition. Exactly the same things happen as before. The only change is in Sisyphus' view of them. The picture before was the image of meaningless activity and existence. It was created precisely to be an image of that. It has not lost that meaninglessness, it has now gained not the least shred of meaningfulness. The stones still roll back as before, each phase of Sisyphus' life still exactly resembles all the others, the task is never completed, nothing comes of it, no temple ever begins to rise, and all this cycle of the same pointless thing over and over goes on forever in this picture as in the other. The *only* thing that has happened is this: Sisyphus has been reconciled to it, and indeed more, he has been led to embrace it. Not, however, by reason or persuasion, but by nothing more rational than the potency of a new substance in his veins.

The Meaninglessness of Life

I believe the foregoing provides a fairly clear content to the idea of meaninglessness and, through it, some hint of what meaningfulness, in this sense, might be. Meaninglessness is essentially endless pointlessness, and meaningfulness is therefore the opposite. Activity, and even long, drawn out and repetitive activity, has a meaning if it has some significant culmination, some more or less lasting end that can be considered to have been the direction and purpose of the activity. But the descriptions so far also provide something else; namely, the suggestion of how an existence that is objectively meaningless, in this sense, can nevertheless acquire a meaning for him whose existence it is.

Now let us ask: Which of these pictures does life in fact resemble? And let us not begin with our own lives, for here both our prejudices and wishes are great, but with the life in general that we share with the rest of creation. We shall find, I think, that it all has a certain pattern, and that this pattern is by now easily recognized.

We can begin anywhere, only saving human existence for our last consideration. We can, for example, begin with any animal. It does not matter where we begin, because the result is going to be exactly the same.

Thus, for example, there are caves in New Zealand, deep and dark, whose floors are quiet pools and whose walls and ceilings are covered with soft light. As one gazes in wonder in the stillness of these caves it seems that the Creator has reproduced there in microcosm the heavens themselves, until one scarcely remembers the enclosing presence of the walls. As one looks more closely, however, the scene is explained. Each dot of light identifies an ugly worm, whose luminous tail is meant to attract insects from the surrounding darkness. As from time to time one of these insects draws near it becomes entangled in a sticky thread lowered by the worm, and is eaten. This goes on month after month, the blind worm lying there in the barren stillness waiting to entrap an occasional bit of nourishment that will only sustain it to another bit of nourishment until.... Until what? What great thing awaits all this long and repetitious effort and makes it worthwhile? Really nothing. The larva just transforms itself finally to a tiny winged adult that lacks even mouth parts to feed and lives only a day or two. These adults, as soon as they have mated and laid eggs, are themselves caught in the threads and are devoured by the cannibalist worms, often without having ventured into the day, the only point to their existence having now been fulfilled. This has been going on for millions of years, and to no end other than that the same meaningless cycle may continue for another millions of years.

All living things present essentially the same spectacle. The larva of a certain cicada burrows in the darkness of the earth for seventeen years, through season after season, to emerge finally into the daylight for a brief flight, lay its eggs, and die—this all to repeat itself during the next seventeen years, and so on to eternity. We have already noted, in another connection, the struggles of fish, made only that others may do the same after them and that this cycle, having no other point than itself, may never cease. Some birds span an entire side of the globe each year and then return, only to insure that others may follow the same incredibly long path again and again. One is led to wonder what the point of it all is, with what great triumph this ceaseless effort, repeating itself through millions of years, might finally culminate, and why it should go on and on for so long, accomplishing nothing, getting nowhere. But then one realizes that there is no point to it at all, that it really culminates in nothing, that each of these cycles, so filled with toil, is to be followed only by more of the same. The point of any living thing's life is, evidently, nothing but life itself.

This life of the world thus presents itself to our eyes as a vast machine, feeding on itself, running on and on forever to nothing. And we are part of that life. To be sure, we are not just the same, but the differences are not so great as we like to think; many are merely invented, and none really cancels the kind of meaninglessness that we found in Sisyphus and that we find all around, wherever anything lives. We are conscious of our activity. Our goals, whether in any significant sense we choose them or not, are things of which we are at least partly aware and can therefore in some sense appraise. More significantly, perhaps, men have a history, as other animals do not, such that each generation does not precisely resemble all those before. Still, if we can in imagination disengage our wills from our lives and disregard the deep interest each man has in his own existence, we shall find that they do not so little resemble the existence of Sisyphus. We toil after goals, most of them—indeed every single one of them—of transitory significance and, having gained one of them, we immediately set forth for the next, as if that one had never been, with this next one being essentially more of the same. Look at a busy street any day, and observe the throng going hither and thither. To what? Some office or shop, where the same things will be done today as were done yesterday, and are done now so they may be repeated tomorrow. And if we think that, unlike Sisyphus, these labors do have a point, that they culminate in something lasting and, independently of our own deep interests in them, very worthwhile, then we simply have not considered the thing closely enough. Most such effort is directed only to the establishment and perpetuation of home and family; that is, to the begetting of others who will follow in our steps to do more of the same. Each man's life thus resembles one of Sisyphus' climbs to the summit of his hill, and each day of it one of his steps; the difference is that whereas Sisyphus himself returns to push the stone up again, we leave this to our children. We at one point imagined that the labors of Sisyphus finally culminated in the creation of a temple, but for this to make any difference it had to be a temple that would at least endure, adding beauty to the world for the remainder of time. Our achievements, even though they are often beautiful, are mostly bubbles; and those that do last, like the sand-swept pyramids, soon become mere curiosities while around them the rest of mankind continues its perpetual toting of rocks, only to see them roll down. Nations are built upon the bones of their founders and pioneers, but only to decay and crumble before long, their rubble then becoming the foundation for others directed to exactly the same fate. The picture of Sisyphus is the picture of existence of the individual man, great or unknown, of nations, of the race of men, and of the very life of the world.

On a country road one sometimes comes upon the ruined hulks of a house and once extensive buildings, all in collapse and spread over with weeds, A curious eye can in imagination reconstruct from what is left a once warm and thriving life, filled with purpose. There was the hearth, where a family once talked, sang, and made plans; there were the rooms, where people loved, and babes were born to a rejoicing mother; there are the musty remains of a sofa, infested with bugs, once bought at a dear price to enhance an ever-growing comfort, beauty, and warmth. Every small piece of junk fills the mind with what once, not long ago, was utterly real, with children's voices, plans made, and enterprises embarked upon. That is how these stones of Sisyphus were rolled up, and that is how they became incorporated into a beautiful temple, and that temple is what now lies before you. Meanwhile other buildings, institutions, nations, and civilizations spring up all around, only to share the same fate before long. And if the question "What for?" is now asked, the answer is clear: so that just this may go on forever.

The two pictures—of Sisyphus and of our own lives, if we look at them from a distance—are in outline the same and convey to the mind the same image. It is not surprising, then, that men invent ways of denying it, their religions proclaiming a heaven that does not crumble, their hymnals and prayer books declaring a significance to life of which our eyes provide no hint whatever.1 Even our philosophies portray some permanent and lasting good at which all may aim, from the changeless forms invented by Plato to the beatific vision of St. Thomas and the ideals of permanence contrived by the moderns. When these fail to convince, then earthly ideals such as universal justice and brotherhood are conjured up to take their places and give meaning to man's seemingly endless pilgrimage, some final state that will be ushered in when the last obstacle is removed and the last stone pushed to the hilltop. No one believes, of course, that any such state will be final, or even wants it to be in case it means that human existence would then cease to be a struggle; but in the meantime such ideas serve a very real need.

The Meaning of Life

We noted that Sisyphus' existence would have meaning if there were some point to his labors, if his efforts ever culminated in something that was not just an occasion for fresh labors of the same kind. But that is precisely the meaning it lacks. And human existence resembles his in that respect. Men do achieve things—they scale their towers and raise their stones to their hilltops—but every such accomplishment fades, providing only an occasion for renewed labors of the same kind.

But here we need to note something else that has been mentioned, but its significance not explored, and that is the state of mind and feeling with which such labors are undertaken. We noted that if Sisyphus had a keen and unappeasable desire to be doing just what he found himself doing, then, although his life would in no way be changed, it would nevertheless have a meaning for him. It would be an irrational one, no doubt, because the desire itself would be only the product of the substance in his veins, and not any that reason could discover, but a meaning nevertheless.

And would it not, in fact, be a meaning incomparably better than the other? For let us examine again the first kind of meaning it could have. Let us suppose that, without having any interest in roiling stones, as such, and finding this, in fact, a galling toil, Sisyphus did nevertheless have a deep interest in raising a temple, one that would be beautiful and lasting. And let us suppose he succeeded in this, that after ages of dreadful toil, all directed at this final result, he did at last complete his temple, such that now he could say his work was done, and he could rest and forever enjoy the result. Now what? What picture now presents itself to our minds? It is precisely the picture of infinite boredom! Of Sisyphus doing nothing ever again, but contemplating what he has already wrought and can no longer add anything to, and contemplating it for an eternity! Now in this picture we have a meaning for Sisyphus' existence, a point for his prodigious labor, because we have put it there; yet, at the same time, that which is really worthwhile seems to have slipped away entirely. Where before we were presented with the nightmare of eternal and pointless activity, we are now confronted with the hell of its eternal absence.

Our second picture, then, wherein we imagined Sisyphus to have had inflicted on him the irrational desire to be doing just what he found himself doing, should not have been dismissed so abruptly. The meaning that picture lacked was no meaning that he or anyone could crave, and the strange meaning it had was perhaps just what we were seeking.

At this point, then, we can reintroduce what has been until now, it is hoped, resolutely pushed aside in an effort to view our lives and human existence with objectivity; namely, our own wills, our deep interest in what we find ourselves doing. If we do this we find that our lives do indeed still resemble that of Sisyphus, but that the meaningfulness they thus lack is precisely the meaningfulness of infinite boredom. At the same time, the strange meaningfulness they possess is that of the inner compulsion to be doing just what we were put here to do, and to go on doing it forever. This is the nearest we may hope to get to heaven, but the redeeming side of that fact is that we do thereby avoid a genuine hell.

If the builders of a great and flourishing ancient civilization could somehow return now to see archaeologists unearthing the trivial remnants of what they had once accomplished with such effort—see the fragments of pots and vases, a few broken statues, and such tokens of another age and greatness—they could indeed ask themselves what the point of it all was, if this is all it finally came to. Yet, it did not seem so to them then, for it was just the building, and not what was finally built, that gave their life meaning. Similarly, if the builders of the ruined home and farm that I described a short while ago could be brought back to see what is left, they would have the same feelings. What we construct in our imaginations as we look over these decayed and rusting pieces would reconstruct itself in their very memories, and certainly with unspeakable sadness. The piece of a sled at our feet would revive in them a warm Christmas. And what rich memories would there be in the broken crib? And the weed-covered remains of a fence would reproduce the scene of a great herd of livestock, so laboriously built up over so many years. What was it all worth, if this is the final result? Yet, again, it did not seem so to them through those many years of struggle and toil, and they did not imagine they were building a Gibraltar. The things to which they bent their backs day after day, realizing one by one their ephemeral plans, were precisely the things in which their wills were deeply involved, precisely the things in which their interests lay, and there was no need then to ask questions. There is no more need of them now—the day was sufficient to itself, and so was the life.

This is surely the way to look at all of life—at one's own life, and each day and moment it contains; of the life of a nation; of the species; of the life of the world; and of everything that breathes. Even the glow worms I described, whose cycles of existence over the millions of years seem so pointless when looked at by us, will seem entirely different to us if we can somehow try to view their existence from within. Their endless activity, which gets nowhere, is just what it is their will to pursue. This is its whole justification and meaning. Nor would it be any salvation to the birds who span the globe every year, back and forth, to have a home made for them in a cage with plenty of food and protection, so that they would not have to migrate any more. It would be their condemnation, for it is the doing that counts for them, and not what they hope to win by it. Flying these prodigious distances, never ending, is what it is in their veins to do, exactly as it was in Sisyphus' veins to roll stones, without end, after the gods had waxed merciful and implanted this in him.

A human being no sooner draws his first breath than he responds to the will that is in him to live. He no more asks whether it will be worthwhile, or whether anything of significance will come of it, than the worms and the birds. The point of his living is simply to be living, in the manner that it is his nature to be living. He goes through his life building his castles, each of these beginning to fade into time as the next is begun; yet, it would be no salvation to rest from all this. It would be a condemnation, and one that would in no way be redeemed were he able to gaze upon the things he has done, even if these were beautiful and absolutely permanent, as they never are. What counts is that one should be able to begin a new task, a new castle, a new bubble. It counts only because it is there to be done and he has the will to do it. The same will be the life of his children, and of theirs; and if the philosopher is apt to see in this a pattern similar to the unending cycles of the existence of Sisyphus, and to despair, then it is indeed because the meaning and point he is seeking is not there—but mercifully so. The meaning of life is from within us, it is not bestowed from without, and it far exceeds in both its beauty and permanence any heaven of which men have ever dreamed or yearned for.

Note

1. A popular Christian hymn, sung often at funerals and typical of many hymns, expresses this thought:

    Swift to its close ebbs out life's little day;
    Earth's joys grow dim, its glories pass away;
    Change and decay in all around I see:
    O thou who changest not, abide with me.

The Far Side of Despair

Hazel E. Barnes

Among the accusing adjectives which hostile critics have attached to humanistic existentialism, one of the most frequently heard is "nihilistic." Existentialists, it appears, believe in *nothing;* hence nothing stands to block their destructive impulses, and we may expect *anything* from them. Whether spoken naively or formulated with philosophical sophistication, this attitude contains an important assumption: that there is a logical connection between what one believes about ultimate reality, one's sense of purpose, one's values, and one's concrete action. . . .

It is generally assumed that a lack of higher meaning or over-all purpose in the Universe is a terribly bad thing. Even Sartre has remarked that it would be much better if God the Father existed. Our forlornness is due to our discovery that He is not there. It is worthwhile to ask ourselves just what this hypothesis of higher meaning and purpose really does and has meant to man and why he has felt the necessity to project it. Most of the time I believe it has been bound up with the hope for immortality. Certainly in traditional Christianity, as in any religion which promises a personal afterlife, the significant part of the idea of historical development is not that God and His Universe are infinitely good and eternal but that the individual shares in this destiny. Most important of all for our present selves is the thought that the specific role we play in this far future is determined by the way we conduct ourselves here and now. This life on earth is our trial and test, and the grade we receive indicates the eternal class we go into. The undeniable positive element here is the conviction that

what we do matters forever. If taken literally—or as near to literally as today's fundamentalist is willing to take it—the pragmatic value of this doctrine is overwhelming. Meaning, purpose, and progress toward some definite destination are clearly defined and omnipresent. The catch is that the more concrete and specific the positive promise, the darker the negative side. The Medieval Heaven gains part of its shining light from the contrast with the smoky darkness of the Hell which lies below it. "Here pity or here piety must die," says Dante; and I, for one, would at this point bid piety a hasty adieu. A God who would for eternity subject even one person to horrors surpassing those of Buchenwald, a Creator who would create souls capable of deserving such punishment seems to me to echo man's ignoble desire for vengeance more than his aspirations for an understanding Justice. Of course very few people today believe in everlasting punishment, and it is easy to see why. Only the most hardened sinner could bear to live with this sort of anticipation for any of his acquaintances—let alone the fear of being condemned himself.

In a more acceptable form, Christianity for today's average believer stresses the mercy of God. Although it may not be put in quite this way, the idea seems to be that since

---

Excerpted from Hazel E. Barnes, *An Existentialist Ethic* (1967), pp. 98, 102–5, 106–9, and 113–15; reprinted by permission of Alfred A. Knopf, Inc. and Hazel E. Barnes.

God views each life from within, He sees each man's good intentions. "*Tout comprendre, c'est tout pardonner.*" Hell isn't left quite empty, but like the Greeks' realm of Hades, it is reserved for the really great sinners—like Hitler, perhaps—who are condemned by almost everybody and sufficiently remote so as not to concern us. Heaven and Hell are less concrete and precisely located than they used to be. If one gets liberal enough in his Christian commitment, he may think of Heaven as simply the eternal consciousness of God's presence and Hell as the painful awareness of His absence. At this point, even if individual immortality is not lost, we are in danger of floating off into a vague pantheism which is no longer specifically Christian. In itself, this makes no difference for our present discussion. The issue is not specifically between existentialism and Christianity. Yet we may note that the more the old idea of Heaven and Hell is subjected to ethical purification and intellectual criticism, the feebler becomes any specific hypothesis as to the meaning and ultimate goal of the individual life. If Christianity reaches the point of no longer postulating any afterlife for the specific person, then we may well ask what remains of what centuries have found most valuable—the infinite value of every human soul, its eternal existence, and its freedom of choice to determine the quality of that existence.

Not all hypotheses of the existence of a higher meaning necessarily postulate eternal life for the individual consciousness, whether separate or absorbed in some ultimate Unity. Aristotelianism does not—despite the First Cause, the Unmoved Mover which thinks itself and by its very presence draws all other forms upward toward pure Thought. The Hebrew prophets, too, speak of no future life for man. It is in the present that man must walk humbly and righteously in the sight of the Just God, who will champion those whose cause is right. These interpretations of reality are not oriented toward any eternal Future, but they do serve as some sort of absolute guarantee and point of reference. If the Universe is rationally organized, whether ordered by a Deist Creator, or simply sustained by an Unmoved Mover, it at least serves as a mirror for man wherein he can find himself and his proper place. If the order of the Universe both corresponds to human reason and exists independently of it, one may conclude, at the very least, that Reason is our essence and guide, that to develop it to its greatest extent is our highest good. It is an easy step from there to the notion that Reason may discover absolutes in the ethical sphere as well and that the ultimate attainment of rationality will be a culmination of all that is best in ourselves and a steadfast bond between us and the outside world. Similarly, the belief that the structure of things is permeated with the spirit of Justice offers a sustenance and guarantee to man which come from outside himself. Not only will God reward the Just. He furnishes the assurance that we *ought* to be just and that we may know what Justice is.

Existentialism rejects all of these blandishments. In the early writing of French existentialists, man's recognition that he stood alone in an irrational world without God was expressed in an attitude in which revolt and despair were equally mingled. Things ought not to be this way, was the cry. We will never accept our fate with resignation, but we will live it—in our own way—against the Universe. At the end of *The Flies,* Orestes declares: "On the far side of despair, life begins." But the life which was to start involved no change in the view of things which precipitated Orestes' self-chosen exile. Camus said that his thought had gone beyond what he formulated early in *The Myth of Sisyphus,* but he added that he had never renounced the vision of the absurd which led him to ask, "Can I live without appeal? Can Thought live in this desert?" It is important not to forget this tragic vision of man against the Universe. Humanistic existentialism finds no divine presence, no ingrained higher meaning, no reassuring Absolute. At the same time, no humanistic existentialist will allow that the only alternative is despair and irresponsibility. Camus has pointed out the fallacy involved in leaping from the premise "The Universe has no higher meaning" to the conclusion, "Therefore my life is not worth living." The individual life may have an intrinsic value, both to the one who lives it and to those in the sphere of his influence, whether the Universe knows what it is doing or not.

Merleau Ponty has remarked, "Life makes no sense, but it is ours to make sense of." In a popular lecture, Sartre expressed somewhat the same idea, explaining in simple terms both what he means by creating or "inventing" values and by value itself.

To say that we invent values means nothing except this: life has no meaning a priori. Before you live it, life is nothing, but it is for you to give it a meaning. Value is nothing other than this meaning which you choose.[1]

. . . In contrasting traditional and existentialist attitudes toward the question of the meaning of life, I should like to use a homely example as an illustration. Let us imagine reality to have the shape of a gigantic Chinese checkerboard—without even the logically arranged spacing of the regularly shaped holes as in the usual game board, and with various-sized marbles, only some of which will fit into the spaces provided. The traditional attitude of religion and philosophy has been that we faced two alternatives. Theological and rational positions have assumed that there exists some correct pattern, impressed into the board itself, which can be discovered and which will then show us how we may satisfactorily and correctly arrange the piles of marbles near us. They have assumed—and so have the Nihilists—that if there is no such pattern, then there is no reason to play at all. If there is no motive for making a particular pattern, they have concluded that one might as well destroy the patterns set up by others or commit suicide. Existentialism holds that there is a third possibility. There is no pre-existing pattern. No amount of delving into the structure of the board will reveal one inscribed there in matter. Nor is it sensible to hope for some nonmaterial force which might magnetically draw the marbles into their correct position if we put ourselves in touch with such a power by prayer or drugs or any other device which man might think of. But while this lack deprives man of guide and certain goal, it leaves him free to create his own pattern. It is true that there is no external model according to which one may pronounce the new pattern good or bad, better or worse. There are only the individual judgments by him who makes it and by those who behold it, and these need not agree. If the maker finds value in his own creation, if the process of making is satisfying, if the end result compares sufficiently favorably with the intention, then the pattern *has* value and the individual life has been worthwhile. I must quickly add that no such pattern exists alone. Although its unique form and color remain distinctly perceptible, it is intermeshed with the edges of the patterns of others—like the design of a paisley print. The satisfaction in a life may well result in large part from the sense that these intermeshings have positive significance for the individual pattern. There is another kind of satisfaction—that which comes from the knowledge that other persons have declared one's pattern good. Still a third derives from the realization that what one has done has helped make it easier for others to live patterns intrinsically satisfying to them.

That a positive value is present in experiencing a delight in what one has created and in the approval of others cannot be denied. For many people this is not enough. The sense that there is something missing is sufficient to undermine any quiet content with what one has. We hear most frequently three basic complaints, and these refer respectively to (1) the starting point, (2) the here and now, and (3) the farther on. First, there is the feeling that we need some sort of eternal archetype or measuring stick. Existentialism admits that there is nothing of the sort and that life is harder without it. Yet we may well ask whether the privilege of having such an authority would not come at too high a price, and cost more than it is worth. Pragmatically, the over-all destiny and purpose of the Universe play a small part in the daily projects of Western man—with the possible exception of those remaining fundamentalists who still take the promise of Heaven and Hell quite literally. Mostly it is there as a kind of consolation at moments of failure, cheering our discouragement with the idea that things may be better sometime in a way

---

[1] Sartre; *L'Existentialisme est un humanisme*, pp. 89–90.

that we cannot begin to comprehend. I do not deny the psychic refreshment of such comfort. But if the belief in any such authority and plan is sufficiently specific to be more than a proud hope, it must be restrictive as well. If man can be sure that he is right by any nonhuman standard, then his humanity is strictly confined by the nonhuman. He is not free to bring anything new into the world. His possibilities are those of the slave or the well-bred child. Higher meaning is itself a limitation for a being-who-is-a-process. Such a future is not open but prescribed. Man as a tiny being in an impersonal world may be without importance from the theoretical but nonexistent point of view of an omniscient objective observer. Man in the theological framework of the medieval man-centered Universe has only the dignity of the child, who must regulate his life by the rules laid down by adults. The human adventure becomes a conducted tour. It is in this sense that I seriously question the sincerity or the wisdom of Sartre's statement that it would be better if God the Father existed. The time has come for man to leave his parents and to live in his own right by his own judgments.

The second disturbing aspect of a life of self-created patterns emerges when we compare ourselves with our fellow man. Obviously some people are satisfied with patterns which others regard as deplorable. Can we allow this chaos of judgments and still cling to the belief in the positive value of whatever patterns we ourselves have made? Is the result not such an anarchy of the arbitrary that to speak of pattern at all is nonsense? Here existentialism begins by saying that up to a point, arbitrariness, inconsistency, and the simultaneous existence of divergent value systems are not to be lamented but welcomed. The creative freedom to choose and structure one's own pattern would be worthless if we were to agree that we would all work in the same way toward the same end. Just as we expect persons to differ in their specific projects, so we should allow for those individual over-all orientations which bestow upon the project its significance and which are, in turn, colored by it. Sartre has declared that the creation of a value system by which one is willing to live and to judge one's life is man's most important creative enterprise. This means more than the working out of standards of right and wrong and the regulation of one's own demands in the light of our relations with others. It involves the whole context of what we might call "the style" of a life—not just the moral but the aesthetic, the temperamental—everything which goes to make up the personality which continues, with varying degrees of modification, until death and which even then will leave behind it an objectified "Self for Others." Every such life is unique, no matter how hard the one who lives it may have tried to mold himself after the pattern of his contemporaries. Existentialism prizes this uniqueness and resists all attempts to reduce it to the lowest possible minimum. Existentialism recognizes and exults in the fact that since everyone *is* a point of view, there is no more possibility of all persons becoming the same than there is of reducing to one perspective the views of two people looking at a landscape from different spots. . . .

The absence of any discernible higher meaning in the Universe takes on a new and special significance when we confront the future, not merely my own but that of the world as a whole. What difference does it make, some will ask, whether I fashion one kind of pattern rather than another or none at all? All patterns will be blotted out as though they had never been. If this world is all, how can one attach any significance whatsoever to the individual life in the face of the immensity of space, the staggering infinity of Time? "We are sick with space!" cries Robert Frost. The French keep reminding us of the futility of all endeavor "from the point of view of Sirius." Again, I feel that we suffer still from Christianity's insistence that all of us together and the Universe with us are going somewhere definite and that the destination bestows its meaning on the present mile of the journey. Deprived of this forward voyaging, we find no delight in the nonpurposeful development of an impersonal cosmos which has no prearranged destination. Whether this drifting Universe will eventually become cold and lifeless, or whether there will occur once again—or many times—the coming together of organized matter and the appearance of other forms of consciousness, it seems unlikely that man will be remembered any more than we have reason to think that all of this present world of matter was put here for his express benefit.

Is there any reason *why* we should try to adopt the point of view of Sirius? We should realize that observation of a dead planet through a telescope is neither more nor less true as a vision of the Universe than is the examination of living organisms through a microscope. To see the big without the small is to exclude much of reality just as surely as to stay within the limits of the microscopic. If there is a falsification of boundaries at the one end, there is a blurring of details and elimination of foreground at the other. William James has commented that inasmuch as death comes at the end to cut off all human projects, every life is finally a failure. The point of view of Sirius reveals the same message on the cosmic scale. Yet if it were possible for one to stand on Sirius at the instant before the final disappearance of all life, that moment of conclusion would be no more real or significant than any one of the moments preceding it. If there is an absolute negative quality in the absence of what will not be, then there is a corresponding positive value in what will have been. This last awareness might just as well take pride in what had been there as despair in the knowledge that it will no longer be. One does not choose to eat something bitter today simply because tomorrow it will make no difference which food one has chosen. The addition of positive moments does not add up to zero even if the time arrives when nothing more is added to the series. One might say that there is never any adding up of the sum, but this is not quite true. The new digits carry the weight of those which have gone before.

It is illogical to conclude that human values and meanings are unreal and of no importance simply because they do not originate in the structure of the nonhuman Universe. It is enough that the world serves to support these subjective structures for the consciousness which lives them. At the same time it is only natural that an individual man, whose being is a self-projection, should rebel at the prospect of seeing his projects suddenly brought to a stop. If the patterns and meanings which a consciousness creates were restricted to those experiences which we can live directly, then despair would in truth seem to be our only proper response. But man's being is that of a creature who is always about-to-be. In a peculiar sense also, he is, in his being, always outside or beyond himself, out there in the objects of his intentions or—more accurately—in his projects in the world. An impersonal Universe cannot sustain these subjective structures. But we do not exist in an impersonal Universe. We live in a human world where multitudes of other consciousnesses are ceaselessly imposing their meanings upon Being-in-itself and confronting the projects which I have introduced. It is in the future of these intermeshed human activities that I most fully transcend myself. In so far as "I" have carved out my being in his human world, "I" go on existing in its future.

The Absurd

Thomas Nagel

Most people feel on occasion that life is absurd, and some feel it vividly and continually. Yet the reasons usually offered in defense of this conviction are patently inadequate: they *could* not really explain why life is absurd. Why then do they provide a natural expression for the sense that it is?

I

Consider some examples. It is often remarked that nothing we do now will matter in a million years. But if that is true, then by the same token, nothing that will be the case in a million years matters now. In particular, it does not matter now that in a million years nothing we do now will matter. Moreover, even if what we did now *were* going to matter in a million years, how could that keep our present concerns from being absurd? If their mattering now is not enough to accomplish that, how would it help if they mattered a million years from now?

Whether what we do now will matter in a million years could make the crucial difference only if its mattering in a million years depended on its mattering, period. But then to deny that whatever happens now will matter in a million years is to beg the question against its mattering, period; for in that sense one cannot know that it will not matter in a million years whether (for example) someone now is happy or miserable, without knowing that it does not matter, period.

What we say to convey the absurdity of our lives often has to do with space or time: we are tiny specks in the infinite vastness of the universe; our lives are mere instants even on a geological time scale, let alone a cosmic one; we will all be dead any minute. But of course none of these evident facts can be what *makes* life absurd, if it is absurd. For suppose we lived for ever; would not a life that is absurd if it lasts seventy years be infinitely absurd if it lasted through eternity? And if our lives are absurd given our present size, why would they be any less absurd if we filled the universe (either because we were larger or because the universe was smaller)? Reflection on our minuteness and brevity appears to be intimately connected with the sense that life is meaningless; but it is not clear what the connection is.

Another inadequate argument is that because we are going to die, all chains of justification must leave off in mid-air: one studies and works to earn money to pay for clothing, housing, entertainment, food, to sustain oneself from year to year, perhaps to support a family and pursue a career – but to what final end? All of it is an elaborate journey leading nowhere. (One will also have some effect on other people's lives, but that simply reproduces the problem, for they will die too.)

There are several replies to this argument. First, life does not consist of a sequence of activities each of which has as its purpose some later member of the sequence. Chains of justification come repeatedly to an end within life, and whether the process as a whole can be justified has no bearing on the finality of these end-points. No further justification is needed to make it reasonable to take aspirin for a headache, attend an exhibition of the work of a painter one admires, or stop a child from putting his hand on a hot stove. No larger context or further purpose is needed to prevent these acts from being pointless.

Even if someone wished to supply a further justification for pursuing all the things in life that are commonly regarded as self-justifying, that justification would have to end somewhere too. If *nothing* can justify unless it is justified in terms of something outside itself, which is also justified, then an infinite regress results, and no chain of justification can be complete. Moreover, if a finite chain of reasons cannot justify anything, what could be accomplished by an infinite chain, each link of which must be justified by something outside itself?

Since justifications must come to an end somewhere, nothing is gained by denying that they end where they appear to, within life – or by trying to subsume the multiple, often trivial ordinary justifications of action under a single, controlling life scheme. We can be satisfied more easily than that. In fact, through its misrepresentation of the process of justification, the argument makes a vacuous demand. It insists that the reasons available within life are incomplete, but suggests thereby that all reasons that come to an end are incomplete. This makes it impossible to supply any reasons at all.

The standard arguments for absurdity appear therefore to fail as arguments. Yet I believe they attempt to express something that is difficult to state, but fundamentally correct.

II

In ordinary life a situation is absurd when it includes a conspicuous discrepancy between pretension or aspiration and reality: someone gives a complicated speech in support of a motion that has already been passed; a notorious criminal is made president of a major philanthropic foundation; you declare your love over the telephone to a recorded announcement; as you are being knighted, your pants fall down.

When a person finds himself in an absurd situation, he will usually attempt to change it, by modifying his aspirations, or by trying to bring reality into better accord with them, or by removing himself from the situation entirely. We are not always willing or able to extricate ourselves from a position whose absurdity has become clear to us. Nevertheless, it is usually possible to imagine some change that would remove the absurdity – whether or not we can or will implement it. The sense that life as a whole is absurd arises when we perceive, perhaps dimly, an inflated pretension or aspiration which is inseparable from the continuation of human life and which makes its absurdity inescapable, short of escape from life itself.

Many people's lives are absurd, temporarily or permanently, for conventional reasons having to do with their particular ambitions, circumstances, and personal relations. If there is a philosophical sense of absurdity, however, it must arise from the perception of something universal – some respect in which pretension and reality inevitably clash for us all. This condition is supplied, I shall argue, by the collison between the seriousness with which we take our lives and the perpetual possibility of regarding everything about which we are serious as arbitrary, or open to doubt.

We cannot live human lives without energy and attention, nor without making choices which show that we take some things more seriously than others. Yet we have always available a point of view outside the particular form of our lives, from which the seriousness appears gratuitous. These two inescapable viewpoints collide in us, and that is what makes life absurd. It is absurd because we ignore the doubts that we know cannot be settled, continuing to live with nearly undiminished seriousness in spite of them.

This analysis requires defense in two respects: first as regards the unavoidability of seriousness; second as regards the inescapability of doubt.

We take ourselves seriously whether we lead serious lives or not and whether we are concerned primarily with fame, pleasure, virtues, luxury, triumph, beauty, justice, knowledge, salvation, or mere survival. If we take other people seriously and devote ourselves to them, that only multiplies the problem. Human life is full of effort, plans, calculation, success and failure: we *pursue* our lives, with varying degrees of sloth and energy.

It would be different if we could not step back and reflect on the process, but were merely led from impulse to impulse without self-consciousness. But human beings do not act solely on impulse. They are prudent, they reflect, they weigh consequences, they ask whether what they are doing is worth while. Not only are their lives full of particular choices that hang together in larger activities with temporal structure: they also decide in the broadest terms what to pursue and what to avoid, what the priorities among their various aims should be, and what kind of people they want to be or become. Some men are faced with such choices by the large decisions they make from time to time; some merely by reflection on the course their lives are taking as the product of countless small decisions. They decide whom to marry, what profession to follow, whether to join the Country Club, or the Resistance; or they may just wonder why they go on being salesmen or academics or taxi drivers, and then stop thinking about it after a certain period of inconclusive reflection.

Although they may be motivated from act to act by those immediate needs with which life presents them, they allow the process to continue by adhering to the general system of habits and the form of life in which such motives have their place – or perhaps only by clinging to life itself. They spend enormous quantities of energy, risk, and calculation on the details. Think of how an ordinary individual sweats over his appearance, his health, his sex life, his emotional honesty, his social utility, his self-knowledge, the quality of his ties with family, colleagues, and friends, how well he does his job, whether he understands the world and what is going on in it. Leading a human life is a full-time occupation, to which everyone devotes decades of intense concern.

This fact is so obvious that it is hard to find it extraordinary and important. Each of us lives his own life – lives with himself twenty-four hours a day. What else is he supposed to do – live someone else's life? Yet humans have the special capacity to step back and survey themselves, and the lives to which they are committed, with that detached amazement which comes from watching an ant struggle up a heap of sand. Without developing the illusion that they are able to escape from their highly specific and idiosyncratic position, they can view it *sub specie aeternitatis* – and the view is at once sobering and comical.

The crucial backward step is not taken by asking for still another justification in the chain, and failing to get it. The objections to that line of attack have already been stated; justifications come to an end. But this is precisely what provides universal doubt with its object. We step back to find that the whole system of justification and criticism, which controls our choices and supports our claims to rationality, rests on responses and habits that we never question, that we should not know how to defend without circularity, and to which we shall continue to adhere even after they are called into question.

The things we do or want without reasons, and without requiring reasons – the things that define what is a reason for us and what is not – are the starting points of our skepticism. We see ourselves from outside, and all the contingency and specificity of our aims and pursuits become clear. Yet when we take this view and recognize what we do as arbitrary, it does not disengage us from life, and there lies our absurdity: not in the fact that such an external view can be taken of us, but in the fact that we ourselves can take it, without ceasing to be the persons whose ultimate concerns are so coolly regarded.

III

One may try to escape the position by seeking broader ultimate concerns, from which it is impossible to step back – the idea being that absurdity results because what we take seriously is something small and insignificant and individual. Those seeking to supply their lives with meaning usually envision a role or function in something larger than themselves. They therefore seek fulfillment in service to society, the state, the revolution, the progress of history, the advance of science, or religion and the glory of God.

But a role in some larger enterprise cannot confer significance unless that enterprise is itself significant. And its significance must come back to what we can understand, or it will not even appear to give us what we are seeking. If we learned that we were being raised to provide food for other creatures fond of human flesh, who planned to turn us into cutlets before we got too stringy – even if we learned that the human race had been developed by animal breeders precisely for this purpose – that would still not give our lives meaning, for two reasons. First, we would still be in the dark as to the significance of the lives of those other beings; second, although we might acknowledge that this culinary role would make our lives meaningful to them, it is not clear how it would make them meaningful to us.

Admittedly, the usual form of service to a higher being is different from this. One is supposed to behold and partake of the glory of God, for example, in a way in which chickens do not share in the glory of coq au vin. The same is true of service to a state, a movement, or a revolution. People can come to feel, when they are part of something bigger, that it is part of them too. They worry less about what is peculiar to themselves, but identify enough with the larger enterprise to find their role in it fulfilling.

However, any such larger purpose can be put in doubt in the same way that the aims of an individual life can be, and for the same reasons. It is as legitimate to find ultimate justification there as to find it earlier, among the details of individual life. But this does not alter the fact that justifications come to an end when we are content to have them end – when we do not find it necessary to look any further. If we can step back from the purposes of individual life and doubt their point, we can step back also from the progress of human history, or of science, or the success of a society, or the kingdom, power, and glory of God, and put all these things into question in the same way. What seems to us to confer meaning, justification, significance, does so in virtue of the fact that we need no more reasons after a certain point.

What makes doubt inescapable with regard to the limited aims of individual life also makes it inescapable with regard to any larger purpose that encourages the sense that life is meaningful. Once the fundamental doubt has begun, it cannot be laid to rest.

Camus maintains in *The Myth of Sisyphus* that the absurd arises because the world fails to meet our demands for meaning. This suggests that the world might satisfy those demands if it were different. But now we can see that this is not the case. There does not appear to be any conceivable world (containing us) about which unsettlable doubts could not arise. Consequently the absurdity of our situation derives not from a collison between our expectations and the world, but from a collision within ourselves.

IV

It may be objected that the standpoint from which these doubts are supposed to be felt does not exist – that if we take the recommended backward step we will land on thin air, without any basis for judgment about the natural responses we are supposed to be surveying. If we retain our usual standards of what is important, then questions about the significance of what we are doing with our lives will be answerable in the usual way. But if we do not, then those questions can mean nothing to us, since there is no longer any content to the idea of what matters, and hence no content to the idea that nothing does.

But this objection misconceives the nature of the backward step. It is not supposed to give us an understanding of what is *really* important, so that we see by contrast that our lives are insignificant. We never, in the course of these reflections, abandon the ordinary standards that guide our lives. We merely observe them in operation, and recognize that if they are called into question we can justify them only by reference to themselves, uselessly. We adhere to them because of the way we are put together; what seems to us important or serious or valuable would not seem so if we were differently constituted.

In ordinary life, to be sure, we do not judge a situation absurd unless we have in mind some standards of seriousness, significance, or harmony with which the absurd can be contrasted. This contrast is not implied by the philosophical judgment of absurdity, and that might be thought to make the concept unsuitable for the expression of such judgments. This is not so, however, for the philosophical judgment depends on another contrast which makes it a natural extension from more ordinary cases. It departs from them only in contrasting the pretensions of life with a larger context in which *no* standards can be discovered, rather than with a context from which alternative, overriding standards may be applied.

V

In this respect, as in others, philosophical perception of the absurd resembles epistemological skepticism. In both cases the final, philosophical doubt is not contrasted with any unchallenged certainties, though it is arrived at by extrapolation from examples of doubt within the system of evidence or justification, where a contrast with other certainties *is* implied. In both cases our limitedness joins with a capacity to transcend those limitations in thought (thus seeing them as limitations, and as inescapable).

Skepticism begins when we include ourselves in the world about which we claim knowledge. We notice that certain types of evidence convince us, that we are content to allow justifications of belief to come to an end at certain points, that we feel we know many things even without knowing or having grounds for believing the denial of others which, if true, would make what we claim to know false.

For example, I know that I am looking at a piece of paper, although I have no adequate grounds for claiming I know that I am not dreaming; and if I am dreaming then I am not looking at a piece of paper. Here an ordinary conception of how appearance may diverge from reality is employed to show that we take our world largely for granted; the certainty that we are not dreaming cannot be justified except circularly, in terms of those very appearances which are being put in doubt. It is somewhat far-fetched to suggest I may be dreaming; but the possibility is only illustrative. It reveals that our claims to knowledge depend on our not feeling it necessary to exclude certain incompatible alternatives, and the dreaming possibility or the total-hallucination possibility are just representatives for limitless possibilities most of which we cannot even conceive.[1]

Once we have taken the backward step to an abstract view of our whole system of beliefs, evidence, and justification, and seen that it works only, despite its pretensions, by taking the world largely for granted, we are *not* in a position to contrast all these appearances with an alternative reality. We cannot shed our ordinary responses, and if we could it would leave us with no means of conceiving a reality of any kind.

---

[1] I am aware that skepticism about the external world is widely thought to have been refuted, but I have remained convinced of its irrefutability since being exposed at Berkeley to Thompson Clarke's largely unpublished ideas on the subject.

It is the same in the practical domain. We do not step outside our lives to a new vantage point from which we see what is really, objectively significant. We continue to take life largely for granted while seeing that all our decisions and certainties are possible only because there is a great deal we do not bother to rule out.

Both epistemological skepticism and a sense of the absurd can be reached via initial doubts posed within systems of evidence and justification that we accept, and can be stated without violence to our ordinary concepts. We can ask not only why we should believe there is a floor under us, but also why we should believe the evidence of our senses at all – and at some point the framable questions will have outlasted the answers. Similarly, we can ask not only why we should take aspirin, but why we should take trouble over our own comfort at all. The fact that we shall take the aspirin without waiting for an answer to this last question does not show that it is an unreal question. We shall also continue to believe there is a floor under us without waiting for an answer to the other question. In both cases it is this unsupported natural confidence that generates skeptical doubts; so it cannot be used to settle them.

Philosophical skepticism does not cause us to abandon our ordinary beliefs, but it lends them a peculiar flavor. After acknowledging that their truth is incompatible with possibilities that we have no grounds for believing do not obtain – apart from grounds in those very beliefs which we have called into question – we return to our familiar convictions with a certain irony and resignation. Unable to abandon the natural responses on which they depend, we take them back, like a spouse who has run off with someone else and then decided to return; but we regard them differently (not that the new attitude is necessarily inferior to the old, in either case).

The same situation obtains after we have put in question the seriousness with which we take our lives and human life in general and have looked at ourselves without presuppositions. We then return to our lives, as we must, but our seriousness is laced with irony. Not that irony enables us to escape the absurd. It is useless to mutter: 'Life is meaningless; life is meaningless . . .' as an accompaniment to everything we do. In continuing to live and work and strive, we take ourselves seriously in action no matter what we say.

What sustains us, in belief as in action, is not reason or justification, but something more basic than these – for we go on in the same way even after we are convinced that the reasons have given out.[2] If we tried to rely entirely on reason, and pressed it hard, our lives and beliefs would collapse – a form of madness that may actually occur if the inertial force of taking the world and life for granted is somehow lost. If we lose our grip on that, reason will not give it back to us.

VI

In viewing ourselves from a perspective broader than we can occupy in the flesh, we become spectators of our own lives. We cannot do very much as pure spectators of our own lives, so we continue to lead them, and devote ourselves to what we are able at the same time to view as no more than a curiosity, like the ritual of an alien religion.

This explains why the sense of absurdity finds its natural expression in those bad arguments with which the discussion began. Reference to our small size and short

---

[2] As Hume says in a famous passage of the *Treatise*: 'Most fortunately it happens, that since reason is incapable of dispelling these clouds, nature herself suffices to that purpose, and cures me of this philosophical melancholy and delirium, either by relaxing this bent of mind, or by some avocation, and lively impression of my senses, which obliterate all these chimeras. I dine, I play a game of backgammon. I converse, and am merry with my friends; and when after three or four hours' amusement, I would return to these speculations, they appear so cold, and strain'd, and ridiculous, that I cannot find in my heart to enter into them any farther' (bk I, pt IV, sect. 7; Selby-Bigge, p. 269).

lifespan and to the fact that all of mankind will eventually vanish without a trace are metaphors for the backward step which permits us to regard ourselves from without and to find the particular form of our lives curious and slightly surprising. By feigning a nebula's-eye view, we illustrate the capacity to see ourselves without presuppositions, as arbitrary, idiosyncratic, highly specific occupants of the world, one of countless possible forms of life.

Before turning to the question whether the absurdity of our lives is something to be regretted and if possible escaped, let me consider what would have to be given up in order to avoid it.

Why is the life of a mouse not absurd? The orbit of the moon is not absurd either, but that involves no strivings or aims at all. A mouse, however, has to work to stay alive. Yet he is not absurd, because he lacks the capacities for self-consciousness and self-transcendence that would enable him to see that he is only a mouse. If that *did* happen, his life would become absurd, since self-awareness would not make him cease to be a mouse and would not enable him to rise above his mousely strivings. Bringing his new-found self-consciousness with him, he would have to return to his meager yet frantic life, full of doubts that he was unable to answer, but also full of purposes that he was unable to abandon.

Given that the transcendental step is natural to us humans, can we avoid absurdity by refusing to take that step and remaining entirely within our sublunar lives? Well, we cannot refuse consciously, for to do that we would have to be aware of the viewpoint we were refusing to adopt. The only way to avoid the relevant self-consciousness would be either never to attain it or to forget it – neither of which can be achieved by the will.

On the other hand, it is possible to expend effort on an attempt to destroy the other component of the absurd – abandoning one's earthly, individual, human life in order to identify as completely as possible with that universal viewpoint from which human life seems arbitrary and trivial. (This appears to be the ideal of certain Oriental religions.) If one succeeds, then one will not have to drag the superior awareness through a strenuous mundane life, and absurdity will be diminished.

However, insofar as this self-etiolation is the result of effort, will-power, asceticism, and so forth, it requires that one take oneself seriously as an individual – that one be willing to take considerable trouble to avoid being creaturely and absurd. Thus one may undermine the aim of unworldliness by pursuing it too vigorously. Still, if someone simply allowed his individual, animal nature to drift and respond to impulse, without making the pursuit of its needs a central conscious aim, then he might, at considerable dissociative cost, achieve a life that was less absurd than most. It would not be a meaningful life either, of course; but it would not involve the engagement of a transcendent awareness in the assiduous pursuit of mundane goals. And that is the main condition of absurdity – the dragooning of an unconvinced transcendent consciousness into the service of an immanent, limited enterprise like a human life.

The final escape is suicide; but before adopting any hasty solutions, it would be wise to consider carefully whether the absurdity of our existence truly presents us with a *problem*, to which some solution must be found – a way of dealing with *prima facie* disaster. That is certainly the attitude with which Camus approaches the issue, and it gains support from the fact that we are all eager to escape from absurd situations on a smaller scale.

Camus – not on uniformly good grounds – rejects suicide and the other solutions he regards as escapist. What he recommends is defiance or scorn. We can salvage our dignity, he appears to believe, by shaking a fist at the world which is deaf to our pleas, and continuing to live in spite of it. This will not make our lives un-absurd, but it will lend them a certain nobility.[3]

This seems to me romantic and slightly self-pitying. Our absurdity warrants neither that much distress nor that much defiance. At the risk of falling into romanticism by a different route, I would argue that absurdity is one of the most human things about us: a manifestation of our most advanced and interesting characteristics. Like skepticism in epistemology, it is possible only because we possess a certain kind of insight – the capacity to transcend ourselves in thought.

If a sense of the absurd is a way of perceiving our true situation (even though the situation is not absurd until the perception arises), then what reason can we have to resent or escape it? Like the capacity for epistemological skepticism, it results from the ability to understand our human limitations. It need not be a matter for agony unless we make it so. Nor need it evoke a defiant contempt of fate that allows us to feel brave or proud. Such dramatics, even if carried on in private, betray a failure to appreciate the cosmic unimportance of the situation. If *sub specie aeternitatis* there is no reason to believe that anything matters, then that does not matter either, and we can approach our absurd lives with irony instead of heroism or despair.

---

[3] 'Sisyphus, proletarian of the gods, powerless and rebellious, knows the whole extent of his wretched condition: it is what he thinks of during his descent. The lucidity that was to constitute his torture at the same time crowns his victory. There is no fate that cannot be surmounted by scorn' (*The Myth of Sisyphus*, trans. Justin O'Brien (New York: Vintage, 1959), p. 90; first published, Paris: Gallimard, 1942).

PART III METAPHYSICS: WHAT EXISTS?
Chapter 1 General Introduction

In this part of the book you will explore a number of intriguing, ultimate, yet extremely difficult questions. Let me first introduce you to the sub-discipline of philosophy called 'Metaphysics'. The label 'metaphysics' originates from a somewhat historical accident; the "accident" here refers to the manner in which Aristotle's work happened to be ordered. It so happens that the books about the *nature of existence* were placed by the original editors of Aristotle's books right after the books on physics (or nature). Thus, the name 'meta-physics' stuck, which means *after* physics: i.e., the book right after the books on physics. Hence, the name 'meta-physics' came to refer to the general philosophical subject about the fundamental nature of existence.

The subject matter of metaphysics is the study of the most general features of reality; *all of reality*. It is the inquiry into the most fundamental *kinds of entities* that must exist so as to provide an adequate explanation of the *appearances* or our *experience* of reality. For instance, around us we regularly experience colors, shapes, sounds, textures, smells. But we may wonder whether there are such entities as colors, shapes, sounds, etc., over and above the things that are colored, have a shape, etc? We cannot help but be aware of our consciousness, our mind, and the self. But a little reflection should lead us to inquire about the nature of consciousness; about the nature of the mind; and the nature of the self. We may wonder whether we are the same *thing*, or *person*, as we were some years ago or what really happens to us after the dreaded end which we know we will have to face at some point. Is there survival after death? If so, what is the nature of this survival? Or are we doomed to total annihilation? If the later, then we may ask: what is the difference between the life we are so familiar with and annihilation? We think of ourselves as beings that make choices and deliberate. Hence, we are often responsible for what we do and think. But is there really such a thing as *free will* or is our experience of free will some kind of *illusion* that our mind plays upon us?

These are the sort of questions that you will be invited to explore in this part of the book. These are very difficult questions. They are intriguing, yet very complex and often puzzling. Often you will feel as if you are spinning your wheels while trying to think them through. This is not an unusual experience. Many who tackle these questions often feel just like you. There are even some philosophers who concluded that even the very questions themselves make no sense. So you are in good company. Perhaps, you might think that too. However, I urge you to arrive at such a conclusion only after you educate yourselves in the nature of the questions and some of the answers that philosophers gave to them. If after you become familiar with these questions and several answers to them you conclude that these ultimate and fundamental questions about the human condition are themselves ill formed, then you have arrived at these conclusions intelligently and upon sincere reflection.

In this chapter you will explore one of the most fundamental philosophical questions about the nature of existence; namely, the general question of the difference between *appearance* and *reality*. Is reality similar in nature to the manner in which we experience it or is it totally different and alien to our experiences? Consider the table in front of you. It has a color, a shape; it has a solid texture; and it appears to you to be continuous, rigid, and compressed. But modern physics tells us that the table actually consists of an untold number of atoms with mostly empty space. Which table is the *real* table? Is the real table the one you experience, the one that appears to your senses, or is the real table the one which modern physics proclaims to be the thing in front of you? Read the two selections below and find out the answer (or perhaps that there is no clear answer!).

The Nature of the Physical World

A. S. Eddington

Introduction

I have settled down to the task of writing these lectures and have drawn up my chairs to my two tables. Two tables! Yes; there are duplicates of every object about me- tables, two chairs, two pens.

This is not a very profound beginning to a course which ought to reach transcendent levels of scientific philosophy. But we cannot touch bedrock immediately; we must scratch a bit at the surface of things first. And whenever I begin to scratch the first thing I strike is— my two tables.

One of them has been familiar to me from earliest years. It is a commonplace object of that environment which I call the world. How shall I describe it? It has extension; it is comparatively permanent; it is coloured; above all it is *substantial*. By substantial I do not merely mean that it does not collapse when I lean upon it; I mean that it is constituted of "substance" and by that word I am trying to convey to you some conception of its intrinsic nature. It is a *thing*; not like space, which is a mere negation; nor like time, which is—Heaven knows what! But that will not help you to my meaning because it is the distinctive characteristic of a "thing" we have this substantiality, and I do not think substantially can be described better than by saying that it is the kind of nature exemplified by an ordinary table. And so we go round in circles. After all if you are a plain commonsense man, not too much worried with scientific scruples you will be confident that you understand the nature of an ordinary table. I have even heard of plain men who had the idea that they could better understand the mystery of their own nature if scientists would discover a way of explaining it in terms of the easily comprehensible nature of a table.

Table No. 2 is my scientific table. It is a more recent acquaintance and I do not feel so familiar with it. It does not belong to the world previously mentioned—that world which spontaneously appears around me when I open my eyes, though how much of it is objective and how much subjective I do not here consider. It is part of a world which in more devious ways has forced itself on my attention. My scientific table is mostly emptiness. Sparsely scattered in that emptiness are numerous electric charges rushing about with great speed; but their combined bulk amounts to less than a billionth of the bulk of the table itself. Notwithstanding its strange construction it turns out to be an entirely efficient table. It supports my writing paper as satisfactorily as table No. 1; for when I lay the paper on it the little electric particles with their headlong speed keep on hitting the underside, so that the paper is maintained in shuttlecock fashion at a nearly steady level. If I lean upon this table I shall not go through; or, to be strictly accurate, the chance of my scientific elbow going through my scientific table is so excessively small that it can be neglected in practical life. Reviewing their properties one by one, there seems to be nothing to choose between the two tables for ordinary purposes; but when abnormal circumstances befall, then my scientific table shows to advantage. If the house catches fire my scientific table will dissolve quite naturally into scientific smoke, whereas my familiar table undergoes a metamorphosis of its substantial nature which I can only regard as miraculous.

There is nothing *substantial* about my second table. It is nearly all empty space—space pervaded, it is true, by fields of force, but these are assigned to the category of "influences", not of "things". Even in the minute part which is not empty we must not transfer the old notion of substance. In dissecting matter into electric charges we have travelled far from that picture of it which first gave rise to the conception of substance, and the meaning of that conception—if it ever had any—has been lost by the way. The whole trend of modern scientific views is to break down the separate categories of "things", "influences", "forms", etc., and to substitute a common background of all experience. Whether we are studying a material object, a magnetic field, a geometrical figure, or a duration of time, our scientific information is summed up in measures; neither the apparatus of measurement nor the mode of using it suggests that there is anything essentially different in these problems The measures themselves afford no ground for a classification by categories. We feel it necessary to concede some background to the measures—an external world; but the attributes of this world, except in so far as they are reflected in the measures, are outside scientific scrutiny. Science has at last revolted against attaching the exact knowledge contained in these measurements to a traditional picture-gallery of conceptions which convey no authentic information of the background and obtrude irrelevancies into the scheme of knowledge.

I will not here stress further the non-substantiality of electrons, since it is scarcely necessary to the present line of thought. Conceive them as substantially as you will, there is a vast difference between my scientific table with its substance (if any) thinly scattered in specks in a region mostly empty and the table of everyday conception which we regard as the type of solid reality—an incarnate protest against Berkleian subjectivism. It makes all the difference in the world whether the paper before me is poised as it were on a swarm of flies and sustained in shuttlecock fashion by a series of tiny blows from the swarm underneath, or whether it is supported because there is substance below it, it being the intrinsic nature of substance to occupy space to the exclusion of other substance; all the difference in conception at least, but no difference to my practical task of writing on the paper.

I need not tell you that modern physics has by delicate test and remorseless logic assured me that my second scientific table is the only one which is really there—wherever "there" may be. On the other hand I need not tell you that modern physics will never succeed in exorcising that first table—strange compound of external nature, mental imagery and inherited prejudice—which lies visible to my eyes and tangible to my grasp. We must bid good-bye to it for the present for we are about to turn from the familiar world to the scientific world revealed by physics. This is, or is intended to be, a wholly external world.

"You speak paradoxically of two worlds. Are they not really two aspects or two interpretations of one and the same world?"

Yes, no doubt they are ultimately to be identified after some fashion. But the process by which the external world of physics is transformed into a world of familiar acquaintance in human consciousness is outside the scope of physics. And so the world studied according to the methods of physics remains detached from the world familiar to consciousness, until after the physicist has finished his labours upon it. Provisionally, therefore, we regard the table which is the subject of physical research as altogether separate from the familiar table prejudging the question of their ultimate identification. It is true that the whole scientific inquiry from the familiar world and in the end it must return to the familiar world; but the part of the journey over which the physicist has charge is in foreign territory.

Until recently there was a much closer linkage; the physicist used to borrow the raw material of his world from familiar world, but he does so no longer. His raw materials are aether, electrons, quanta, potentials, Hamiltonian functions, etc., and he is nowadays scrupulously careful to guard these from contamination by conceptions borrowed from the other world. There is a familiar table parallel to the scientific table, but there is no familiar electron, quantum or potential parallel to the scientific electron, quantum or potential. We do not even desire to manufacture a familiar counterpart to these things or, as we should commonly say, to "explain" the electron. After the physicist has quite finished his world-building a linkage or identification is allowed; but premature attempts at linkage have been found to be entirely mischievous.

Science aims at constructing a world which shall be symbolic of the world of commonplace experience. It is not at all necessary that every individual symbol that is used should represent something in common experience or even something explicable in terms of common experience. The man in the street is always making this demand for concrete explanation of the things referred to in science; but of necessity he must be disappointed. It is like our experience in learning to read. That which is written in a book is symbolic of a story in real life. The whole intention of the book is that ultimately a reader will identify some symbol, say BREAD, with one of the conceptions of familiar life. But it is mischievous to attempt such identifications prematurely, before the letters are strung into words and the words into sentences. The symbol A is not the counterpart of anything in familiar life. To the child the letter A would seem horribly abstract; so we give him a familiar conception along with it. "A was an Archer who shot at a frog." This tides over his immediate difficulty; but he cannot make serious progress with word-building so long as Archers, Butchers, Captains, dance round the letters. The letters are abstract, and sooner or later he has to realise it. In physics we have outgrown archer and apple-pie definitions of the fundamental symbols. To a request to explain what an electron really is supposed to be we can only answer, "It is part of the A B C of physics".

The external world of physics has thus become a world of shadows. In removing our illusions we have removed the substance, for indeed we have seen that substance is one of the greatest of our illusions. Later perhaps we may inquire whether in our zeal to cut out all that is unreal we may not have used the knife too ruthlessly. Perhaps, indeed, reality is a child which cannot survive without its nurse illusion. But if so, that is of little concern to the scientist, who has good and sufficient reasons for pursuing his investigations in the world of shadows and is content to leave to the philosopher the determination of its exact status in regard to reality. In the world of physics we watch a shadowgraph performance of the drama of familiar life. The shadow of my elbow rests on the shadow table as the shadow ink flows over the shadow paper. It is all symbolic, and as a symbol the physicist leaves it. Then comes the alchemist Mind who transmutes the symbols. The sparsely spread nuclei of electric force become a tangible solid their restless agitation becomes the warmth of summer; the octave of aethereal vibrations becomes a gorgeous rainbow. Nor does the alchemy stop here. In the transmuted world new significances arise which are scarsely to be traced in the world of symbols; so that it becomes a world of beauty and purpose—and, alas, suffering and evil.

The frank realization that physical science is concerned with a world of shadows is one of the most significant of recent advances. I do not mean that physicists are to any extent preoccupied with the philosophical implications of this. From their point of view it is not so much a withdrawal of untenable claims as an assertion of freedom for autonomous development. At the moment I am not insisting on the shadowy and symbolic character of the world of physics because of its bearing on philosophy, but because the aloofness from familiar conceptions will be apparent in the scientific theories I have to describe. If you are not prepared for this aloofness you are likely to be out of sympathy with modern scientific theories, and may even think them ridiculous—as, I daresay, many people do.

It is difficult to school ourselves to treat the physical world as purely symbolic. We are always relapsing and mixing with the symbols incongruous conceptions taken from the world of consciousness. Untaught by long experience we stretch a hand to grasp the shadow, instead of accepting its shadowy nature. Indeed, unless we confine ourselves altogether to mathematical symbolism it is hard to avoid dressing our symbols in deceitful clothing. When I think of an electron there rises to my mind a hard, red, tiny ball; the proton similarly is neutral grey. Of course the colour is absurd—perhaps not more absurd than the rest of the conception— but I am incorrigible. I can well understand that the younger minds are finding these pictures too concrete and are striving to construct the world out of Hamiltonian functions and symbols so far removed from human preconception that they do not even obey the laws of orthodox arithmetic. For myself I find some difficulty in rising to that plane of thought; but I am convinced that it has got to come.

In these lectures I propose to discuss some of the results of modern study of the physical world which give most food for philosophic thought. This will include new conceptions in science and also new knowledge. In both respects we are led to think of the material universe in a way very different from that prevailing at the end of the last century. I shall not leave out of sight the ulterior object which must be in the mind of a Gifford Lecturer, the problem of relating these purely physical discoveries to the wider aspects and Interests of our human nature. These relations cannot but have undergone change, since our whole conception of the physical world has radically changed. I am convinced that a just appreciation of the physical world as it is understood to-day carries with it a feeling of open-mindedness towards a wider significance transcending scientific measurement, which might have seemed illogical a generation ago; and in the later lectures I shall try to focus that feeling and make inexpert efforts to find where it leads. But I should be untrue to science if I did not insist that its study is an end in itself. The path of science must be pursued for its own sake, irrespective of the views it may afford of a wider landscape; in this spirit we must follow the path it leads to the hill of vision or the tunnel of obscurity Therefore till the last stage of the course is reached you must be content to follow with me the beaten track of science, nor scold me too severely for loitering among its wayside flowers. That is to be the understanding between us. Shall we set forth?

The Problems of Philosophy

Bertrand Russell

Appearance and Reality

Is there any knowledge in the world which is so certain that no reasonable man could doubt it? This question, which at first sight might not seem difficult, is really one of the most difficult that can be asked. When we have realized the obstacles in the way of a straightforward and confident answer, we shall be well launched on the study of philosophy—for philosophy is merely the attempt to answer such ultimate questions, not carelessly and dogmatically, as we do in ordinary life and even in the sciences, but critically, after exploring all that makes such questions puzzling, and after realizing all the vagueness and confusion that underlie our ordinary ideas.

In daily life, we assume as certain many things which, on a closer scrutiny, are found to be so full of apparent contradictions that only a great amount of thought enables us to know what it is that we really may believe. In the search for certainty, it is natural to begin with our present experiences, and in some sense, no doubt, knowledge is to be derived from them. But any statement as to what it is that our immediate experiences make us know is very likely to be wrong. It seems to me that I am now sitting in a chair, at a table of a certain shape, on which I see sheets of paper with writing or print. By turning my head I see out of the window buildings and clouds and the sun. I believe that the sun is about ninety-three million miles from the earth; that it is a hot globe many times bigger than the earth; that, owing to the earth's rotation, it rises every morning, and will continue to do so for an indefinite time in the future. I believe that, if any other normal person comes into my room, he will see the same chairs and tables and books and papers as I see, and that the table which I see is the same as the table which I feel pressing against my arm. All this seems to be so evident as to be hardly worth stating, except in answer to a man who doubts whether I know anything. Yet all this may be reasonably doubted, and all of it requires much careful discussion before we can be sure that we have stated it in a form that is wholly true.

To make our difficulties plain, let us concentrate attention on the table. To the eye it is oblong, brown and shiny, to the touch it is smooth and cool and hard; when I tap it, it gives out a wooden sound. Any one else who sees and feels and hears the table will agree with this description, so that it might seem as if no difficulty would arise; but as soon as we try to be more precise our troubles begin. Although I believe that the table is 'really' of the same colour all over, the parts that reflect the light look much brighter than the other parts, and some parts look white because of reflected light. I know that, if I move, the parts that reflect the light will be different, so that the apparent distribution of colours on the table will change. It follows that if several people are looking at the table at the same moment, no two of them will see exactly the same distribution of colours, because no two can see it from exactly the same point of view, and any change in the point of view makes some change in the way the light is reflected.

For most practical purposes these differences are unimportant, but to the painter they are all-important: the painter has to unlearn the habit of thinking that things seem to have the colour which common sense says they 'really' have, and to learn the habit of seeing things as they appear. Here we have already the beginning of one of the distinctions that cause most trouble in philosophy—the distinction between 'appearance' and 'reality', between what things seem to be and what they are. The painter wants to know what things seem to be, the practical man and the philosopher want to know what they are; but the philosopher's wish to know this is stronger than the practical man's, and is more troubled by knowledge as to the difficulties of answering the question.

To return to the table. It is evident from what we have found, that there is no colour which preeminently appears to be *the* colour of the table, or even of any one particular part of the table—it appears to be of different colours from different points of view, and there is no reason for regarding some of these as more really its colour than others. And we know that even from a given point of view the colour will seem different by artificial light, or to a colour-blind man, or to a man wearing blue spectacles, while in the dark there will be no colour at all, though to touch and hearing the table will be unchanged. This colour is not something which is inherent in the table, but something depending upon the table and the spectator and the way the light falls on the table. When, in ordinary life, we speak of *the* colour of the table, we only mean the sort of colour which it will seem to have to a normal spectator from an ordinary point of view under usual conditions of light. But the other colours which appear under other conditions have just as good a right to be considered real; and therefore, to avoid favouritism, we are compelled to deny that, in itself, the table has any one particular colour.

The same thing applies to the texture. With the naked eye one can see the grain, but otherwise the table looks smooth and even. If we looked at it through a microscope, we should see roughnesses and hills and valleys, and all sorts of differences that are imperceptible to the naked eye. Which of these is the 'real' table? We are naturally tempted to say that what we see through the microscope is more real, but that in turn would be changed by a still more powerful microscope. If, then, we cannot trust what we see with the naked eye, why should we trust what we see through a microscope? Thus, again, the confidence in our senses with which we began deserts us.

The shape of the table is no better. We are all in the habit of judging as to the 'real' shapes of things, and we do this so unreflectingly that we come to think we actually see the real shapes. But, in fact, as we all have to learn if we try to draw, a given thing looks different in shape from every different point of view. If our table is 'really' rectangular, it will look, from almost all points of view, as if it had two acute angles and two obtuse angles. If opposite sides are parallel, they will look as if they converged to a point away from the spectator; if they are of equal length, they will look as if the nearer side were longer. All these things are not commonly noticed in looking at a table, because experience has taught us to construct the 'real' shape from the apparent shape, and the 'real' shape is what interests us as practical men. But the 'real' shape is not what we see; it is something inferred from what we see. And what we see is constantly changing in shape as we move about the room; so that here again the senses seem not to give us the truth about the table itself, but only about the appearance of the table.

Similar difficulties arise when we consider the sense of touch. It is true that the table always gives us a sensation of hardness, and we feel that it resists pressure. But the sensation we obtain depends upon how hard we press the table and also upon what part of the body we press with; thus the various sensations due to various pressures or various parts of the body cannot be supposed to reveal *directly* any definite property of the table, but at most to be *signs* of some property which perhaps *causes* all the sensations, but is not actually apparent in any of them. And the same applies still more obviously to the sounds which can be elicited by rapping the table.

Thus it becomes evident that the real table, if there is one, is not the same as what we immediately experience by sight or touch or hearing. The real table, if there is one, is not *immediately* known to us at all, but must be an inference from what is immediately known. Hence, two very difficult questions at once arise; namely, (1) Is there a real table at all? (2) If so, what sort of object can it be?

It will help us in considering these questions to have a few simple terms of which the meaning is definite and clear. Let us give the name of 'sense-data' to the things that are immediately known in sensation: such things as colours, sounds, smells, hardnesses, roughnesses, and so on. We shall give the name 'sensation' to the experience of being immediately aware of these things. Thus, whenever we see a colour, we have a sensation *of* the colour, but the colour itself is a sense-datum, not a sensation. The colour is that *of* which we are immediately aware, and the awareness itself is the sensation. It is plain that if we are to know anything about the table, it must be by means of the sense-data—brown colour, oblong shape, smoothness, etc.—which we associate with the table; but, for the reasons which have been given, we cannot say that the table is the sense-data, or even that the sense-data are directly properties of the table. Thus a problem arises as to the relation of the sense-data to the real table, supposing there is such a thing.

The real table, if it exists, we will call a 'physical object'. Thus we have to consider the relation of sense-data to physical objects. The collection of all physical objects is called 'matter'. Thus our two questions may be re-stated as follows: (1) Is there any such thing as matter? (2) If so, what is its nature?

The philosopher who first brought prominently forward the reasons for regarding the immediate objects of our senses as not existing independently of us was Bishop Berkeley (1685-1753). His *Three Dialogues between Hylas and Philonous, in Opposition to Sceptics and Atheists,* undertake to prove that there is no such thing as matter at all, and that the world consists of nothing but minds and their ideas. Hylas has hitherto believed in matter, but he is no match for Philonous, who mercilessly drives him into contradictions and paradoxes, and makes his own denial of matter seem, in the end, as if it were almost common sense. The arguments employed are of very different value: some are important and sound, others are confused or quibbling. But Berkeley retains the merit of having shown that the existence of matter is capable of being denied without absurdity, and that if there are any things that exist independently of us they cannot be the immediate objects of our sensations.

There are two different questions involved when we ask whether matter exists, and it is important to keep them clear. We commonly mean by 'matter' something which is opposed to 'mind', something which we think of as occupying space and as radically incapable of any sort of thought or consciousness. It is chiefly in this sense that Berkeley denies matter; that is to say, he does not deny that the sense-data which we commonly take as signs of the existence of the table are really signs of the existence of *something* independent of us, but he does deny that this something is non-mental, that it is neither mind nor ideas entertained by some mind. He admits that there must be something which continues to exist when we go out of the room or shut our eyes, and that what we call seeing the table does really give us reason for believing in something which persists even when we are not seeing it. But he thinks that this something cannot be radically different in nature from what we see, and cannot be independent of seeing altogether, though it must be independent of *our* seeing. He is thus led to regard the 'real' table as an idea in the mind of God. Such an idea has the required permanence and independence of ourselves, without being—as matter would otherwise be—something quite unknowable, in the sense that we can only infer it, and can never be directly and immediately aware of it.

Other philosophers since Berkeley have also held that, although the table does not depend for its existence upon being seen by me, it does depend upon being seen (or otherwise apprehended in sensation) by *some* mind—not necessarily the mind of God, but more often the whole collective mind of the universe. This they hold, as Berkeley does, chiefly because they think there can be nothing real—or at any rate nothing known to be real except minds and their thoughts and feelings. We might state the argument by which they support their view in some such way as this: 'Whatever can be thought of is an idea in the mind of the person thinking of it; therefore nothing can be thought of except ideas in minds; therefore anything else is inconceivable, and what is inconceivable cannot exist.'

Such an argument, in my opinion, is fallacious; and of course those who advance it do not put it so shortly or so crudely. But whether valid or not, the argument has been very widely advanced in one form or another; and very many philosophers, perhaps a majority, have held that there is nothing real except minds and their ideas. Such philosophers are called 'idealists'. When they come to explaining matter, they either say, like Berkeley, that matter is really nothing but a collection of ideas, or they say, like Leibniz (1646–1716), that what appears as matter is really a collection of more or less rudimentary minds.

But these philosophers, though they deny matter as opposed to mind, nevertheless, in another sense, admit matter. It will be remembered that we asked two questions; namely, (1) Is there a real table at all? (2) If so, what sort of object can it be? Now both Berkeley and Leibniz admit that there is a real table, but Berkeley says it is certain ideas in the mind of God, and Leibniz says it is a colony of souls. Thus both of them answer our first question in the affirmative, and only diverge from the views of ordinary mortals in their answer to our second question. In fact, almost all philosophers seem to be agreed that there is a real table: they almost all agree that, however much our sense-data— colour, shape, smoothness, etc.—may depend upon us, yet their occurrence is a sign of something existing independently of us, something differing, perhaps, completely from our sense-data, and yet to be regarded as causing those sense-data whenever we are in a suitable relation to the real table.

Now obviously this point in which the philosophers are agreed—the view that there *is* a real table, whatever its nature may be—is vitally important, and it will be worth while to consider what reasons there are for accepting this view before we go on to the further question as to the nature of the real table. Our next chapter, therefore, will be concerned with the reasons for supposing that there is a real table at all.

Before we go farther it will be well to consider for a moment what it is that we have discovered so far. It has appeared that, if we take any common object of the sort that is supposed to be known by the senses, what the senses *immediately* tell us is not the truth about the object as it is apart from us, but only the truth about certain sense-data which, so far as we can see, depend upon the relations between us and the object. Thus what we directly see and feel is merely 'appearance', which we believe to be a sign of some 'reality' behind. But if the reality is not what appears, have we any means of knowing whether there is any reality at all? And if so, have we any means of finding out what it is like?

Such questions are bewildering, and it is difficult to know that even the strangest hypotheses may not be true. Thus our familiar table, which has roused but the slightest thoughts in us hitherto, has become a problem full of surprising possibilities. The one thing we know about it is that it is not what it seems. Beyond this modest result, so far, we have the most complete liberty of conjecture. Leibniz tells us it is a community of souls: Berkeley tells us it is an idea in the mind of God; sober science, scarcely less wonderful, tells us it is a vast collection of electric charges in violent motion.

Among these surprising possibilities, doubt suggests that perhaps there is no table at all. Philosophy, if it cannot *answer* so many questions as we could wish, has at least the power of *asking* questions which increase the interest of the world, and show the strangeness and wonder lying just below the surface even in the commonest things of daily life.

Chapter 2 The Mind-Body Problem

In the present chapter we will deal with one of the most important topics in metaphysics: i.e., the mind-body problem. The *mind-body problem* is first and foremost about two fundamental questions:

A. **What is the nature of our mind?**
B. **What is the relationship between the mind and the body?**

However, before we can even begin exploring answers to these two questions, an important preliminary issue must be discussed: What types of phenomena are included in the sphere of the mind? There are three fundamental *mental categories* that have prominence in the discussions about the mind-body problem:

i. *Propositional Attitudes*: propositional attitudes can be viewed as expressing a relation between a *believer* and a *proposition* (hence the name "propositional attitudes"). Examples of propositional attitudes are: thinking, believing, hoping, doubting, wishing, wanting, desiring, etc. These are attitudes that relate a believer to a proposition. For instance: "Mary **believes** *that John went shopping*" is a propositional attitude *sentence* in which 'Mary' refers to a believer; *John went shopping* expresses a proposition; and **believes that** relates Mary to this proposition.

ii. *Emotions*: emotions are enduring states of a person that impact their overall condition, can cause certain actions, and have ramifications to their overall psychological well-being. Examples of emotions are: anger, hatred, love, depression, sadness, despair, elation, joy, happiness, euphoria, etc.

iii. *Sensations (or Qualia)*: sensations (or in a more technical vocabulary 'qualia') are the familiar quality of a physiologically related phenomena such as toothache, itches, irritation, throbbing, aching, etc. The qualitative nature of sensations, or qualia, can be gestured at by the question: "what does this feel like?"

The most important characteristic of propositional attitudes (e.g., belief) is the fact that such attitudes relate a believer to a proposition. And the most important feature of propositions is the fact that they are true or false. Hence, an important fact about propositional attitudes; e.g., beliefs, is that they are true or false (hence, we say that beliefs are either true or false).

The most important philosophical positions regarding the nature of the mind and its relationship to the body (which in the present context includes the brain) are the following: Dualism; Materialism (or identity theory); Functionalism; and Eliminative Materialism (EM). I will discuss EM last.

In order to understand the crucial differences between Dualism, Materialism, and Functionalism we first need to ask what sort of entity is the mind. This is a clear example of a metaphysical question. Is the mind, like the body, a *thing/substance* or is it a totally different kind of item? There are two different positions on this matter and this difference is crucial in order to understand the three views presently considered: i.e., Dualism, Materialism, and Functionalism.

According to one view, the mind belongs to the category of ***things*** (or substances). One of the most important characteristics of ***thing-logic*** (if I may be allowed to use an anachronistic term) is that *items that belong to the category of things can be distinguished or identified in terms of their properties*. Therefore, items that belong to the category of ***things are the same if (and only if) they share all properties***. Otherwise, they are different. This feature of ***thing-logic*** will turn out to be very important.

The three views under present consideration divide as follows:

(a) **Dualism** and **Materialism** share the *assumption* that mental items belong to the category of ***things***; therefore, ***thing-logic*** applies to all mental items. It follows then that mental items are the same if (and only if) they share all properties;

(b) **Functionalism**, by contrast, denies that mental items belong to the category of ***things***. Therefore, according to Functionalists, ***thing-logic*** does not apply to mental items.

We may diagram this breakdown of the main positions as follows:

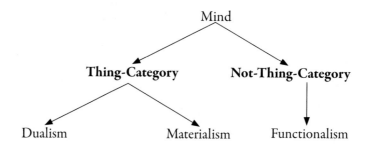

Everyone agrees that material things such as our bodies belong to the category of things; therefore, ***thing-logic*** applies to material things such as our bodies. Now, if one thinks that mental items also belong to the *thing-category*, then it would make sense to ask the following question:

(Q) Are mental items identical to some material items (e.g., items in the brain)?

If, on the other hand, one denies that mental items belong to the *thing-category*, then Q above makes no sense. This is exactly how Functionalists think about Q: the question of whether mental items are identical to, or different from, physical items (e.g., some process in the brain) makes no sense because mental items do not belong to the *thing-category*.

Dualists and Materialist agree that Q makes sense, but they differ about the answer to this question. Dualists think that *no mental item* can ever be identical to *any physical item*, including any physical process in the brain. Materialists, by contrast, think that *every mental item* is identical to *some physical item* or process in the brain (or somewhere in our body). So now we may complete our diagram of mind-body theories:

Descartes' Dualist View: Descartes is considered the first philosopher to focus our attention on the nature of the mind and its relation to the body as a distinct philosophical problem. Descartes thinks that mental items such as thoughts, beliefs, etc., cannot be identical to anything physical because they feature completely different properties.

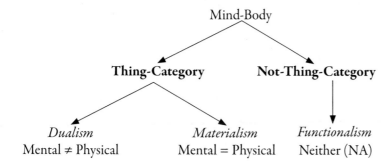

Therefore, Descartes offers three important criteria in order to distinguish the mental from the physical:

i. All mental items feature **consciousness**; no physical item (including our brain) can feature the property of consciousness;
ii. All mental items are in *time* but **not in space**; all physical items are both in time and in space;
iii. We have **privileged access** to our mental items, but not to our physical states.

It is important to emphasize that every one of these criteria of the mental has been challenged in some form or another. For instance, Freud is well-known for introducing the concept of the *un-conscious*. According to Freud, our unconscious goings on are perhaps the most important aspect of our mental life. Therefore, if Freud is right, then there are some mental events that are not conscious. Such a result will certainly undermine Descartes first, and perhaps most important, criterion for distinguishing between the mental and the physical.

Now consider Descartes second criterion. No one ventures to deny that there is a causal connection between mental events and physical events. For instance, I intend to raise my arm in order to illustrate a point and that mental event causes my hand to move. In this case, a mental event (i.e., my intentions) caused a physical event (i.e., my arm moving). Similar examples can be given of how physical events cause mental events. Moreover, our ordinary notion of causation demands that the cause and the effect are both in space and time. But Descartes' second criterion maintains that mental events are not in space. This raises a problem: How can something that is not in space (i.e., a mental event) cause, and be caused by, something that is in space (i.e., a physical event)? One solution that is available to a proponent of Descartes' views (i.e., a Cartesian) is to introduce a variant of our concept of causation that allows for items that are not in space to causally interact with items that are in space. However, such a novel conception might not be as easy as one might think.

Consider now Descartes' third criterion; i.e., that we have privileged access to our mental life. The intuition behind the privileged-access criterion is best illustrated with sensations such as toothaches. Imagine that a friend of yours has a toothache. How would you know that? Well, there are several ways: perhaps your friend tells you that she has a toothache and if you believe her, then you could *infer* from her communication that she has a toothache; or perhaps you see your friend in a pose indicating agony typical of toothache pain (such as for instance holding her face in a certain way). From this you may *infer* that she has a toothache. Notice the word 'infer' in both of the above scenarios. Your knowledge that your friend has a toothache is in both cases **inferential**, and not **direct**.

Now compare the above with how do you know that you have a toothache. Do you know this by *inferring* it from something you say to yourself or by looking at a mirror to see your pose? Certainly not! You know that you have a toothache directly because you experience it directly. This is Descartes' intuition about the privileged-access criterion of the mental.

One of the most severe consequences of this view is the so-called *the problem of other minds*. So while one knows that one has a mind directly, one cannot know that anyone or anything else has a mind in a similar way. All such knowledge, if there is such knowledge at all, must be inferential; i.e., indirect knowledge. But since knowledge of other minds must be inferential, it is always possible that one is wrong. Perhaps, your friend is lying to you when she says that she has a toothache; or perhaps she is practicing a part in a dental-movie and you fail to know that. This problem has been discussed in the literature at length, but here I simply wanted to bring your attention to the problem and leave it to you to ponder the question.

Materialism: Materialists think that all there is in the world are material items, such as our bodies and brains. This metaphysical view has been extremely fruitful in guiding our scientific inquiry. It is useful to think of materialism as consisting of two theses:

(a) *Materialism as a Research Paradigm*: Materialism as a research paradigm is a general approach to scientific inquiry. It means that in order to explain a phenomenon; any phenomenon including mental phenomena, *look for physical causes*. This approach to scientific inquiry has been extremely successful in all areas of knowledge; medicine, neuroscience (science of the brain), understanding of the physical world, and even in anthropology and archeology.

(b) *Materialism as Mind-Body Identity*: Since materialists think that only material or physical entities exist in the universe, the materialist has two options: either deny that there are mental items at all or identify each mental item with some physical process in the brain. The identity-theory materialist opts for the second alternative. Hence, for identity-theory materialism each mental item must be identical to some physical process in the brain. Neuroscience has identified many correlations between various mental functions and processes in the brain. However, we need to view these results with caution. For correlations do not amount to identity; they even cannot entail causation. Therefore, the identity-theory materialist project is very difficult to establish. One must admit, however, that identity-theory materialism has been a very fruitful *research paradigm*.

Eliminative Materialism (EM) agrees with identity-theory materialism that all there is in the world are various configurations of material objects. Our brain is a very complicated such material configuration. But proponents of EM do not think that the identity-theory materialist project is achievable in ways it is required by the theory. Thus, EM opts for the first option in the beginning of the previous paragraph. Proponents of EM suggest that there is no need to try to reduce each mental item to some physical items, thereby showing that they are identical. Instead, the proponents of EM argue that our mental vocabulary (the so-called the vocabulary of Folk-Psychology) belongs to an antiquated theory of behavior and we simply should replace it with a better a newer theory: namely, neuroscience. This proposal is very similar to the replacement of Ptolemy's astronomy with the much better Newtonian astronomy.

Functionalism: The best way of understanding Functionalism is by modeling the mind and its relationship to the brain to the relationship between *software* and *hardware*. According to functionalism, mental categories (or cognitive categories, in a more modern lingo) are to be viewed as **codes that process input to yield a certain output**. A code, in turn, is a set of instructions that are determined by a sequence of zeros and ones. Hence, one can think of a code as an abstract structure that is realized in different computers. Similarly mental categories, according to functionalism, are codes that are realized in different brains. It is for this reason that functionalists do not think that mental (or cognitive) categories can be usefully thought of as belonging to the *thing-category* of items. The brain according to Functionalism is analogous to the hardware that processes the code and yields a certain output (e.g., a word file).

This completes my review of the most important positions about the nature of the mind and its relationship to the body (brain). The selections below cover all of these positions. I hope you enjoy the readings.

Meditations on First Philosophy

Rene Decartes

Section I: Epistomology

Good sense is, of all things among men, the most equally distributed; for every one thinks himself so abundantly provided with it, that those even who are the most difficult to satisfy in everything else, do not usually desire a larger measure of this quality than they already possess. And in this it is not likely that all are mistaken the conviction is rather to be held as testifying that the power of judging aright and of distinguishing truth from error, which is properly what is called good sense or reason, is by nature equal in all men; and that the diversity of our opinions, consequently, does not arise from some being endowed with a larger share of reason than others, but solely from this, that we conduct our thoughts along different ways, and do not fix our attention on the same objects. For to be possessed of a vigorous mind is not enough; the prime requisite is rightly to apply it. The greatest minds, as they are capable of the highest excellences, are open likewise to the greatest aberrations; and those who travel very slowly may yet make far greater progress, provided they keep always to the straight road, than those who, while they run, forsake it.

For myself, I have never fancied my mind to be in any respect more perfect than those of the generality; on the contrary, I have often wished that I were equal to some others in promptitude of thought, or in clearness and distinctness of imagination, or in fullness and readiness of memory. And besides these, I know of no other qualities that contribute to the perfection of the mind; for as to the reason or sense, inasmuch as it is that alone which constitutes us men, and distinguishes us from the brutes, I am disposed to believe that it is to be found complete in each individual; and on this point to adopt the common opinion of philosophers, who say that the difference of greater and less holds only among the accidents, and not among the forms or natures of individuals of the same species.

I will not hesitate, however, to avow my belief that it has been my singular good fortune to have very early in life fallen in with certain tracks which have conducted me to considerations and maxims, of which I have formed a method that gives me the means, as I think, of gradually augmenting my knowledge, and of raising it by little and little to the highest point which the mediocrity of my talents and the brief duration of my life will permit me to reach. For I have already reaped from it such fruits that, although I have been accustomed to think lowly enough of myself, and although when I look with the eye of a philosopher at the varied courses and pursuits of mankind at large, I find scarcely one which does not appear in vain and useless, I nevertheless derive the highest satisfaction from the progress I conceive myself to have already made in the search after truth, and cannot help entertaining such expectations of the future as to believe that if, among the occupations of men as men, there is any one really excellent and important, it is that which I have chosen.

After all, it is possible I may be mistaken; and it is but a little copper and glass, perhaps, that I take for gold and diamonds. I know how very liable we are to delusion in what relates to ourselves, and also how much the judgments of our friends are to be suspected when given in our favor. But I shall endeavor in this discourse to describe the paths I have followed, and to delineate my life as in a picture, in order that each one may also be able to judge of them for himself, and that in the general opinion entertained of them, as gathered from current report, I myself may have a new help towards instruction to be added to those I have been in the habit of employing.

My present design, then, is not to teach the method which each ought to follow for the right conduct of his reason, but solely to describe the way in which I have endeavored to conduct my own. They who set themselves to give precepts must of course regard themselves as possessed of greater skill than those to whom they prescribe; and if they err in the slightest particular, they subject themselves to censure. But as this tract is put forth merely as a history, or, if you will, as a tale, in which, amid some examples worthy of imitation, there will be found, perhaps, as many more which it were advisable not to follow, I hope it will prove useful to some without being hurtful to any, and that my openness will find some favor with all.

From my childhood, I have been familiar with letters; and as I was given to believe that by their help a clear and certain knowledge of all that is useful in life might be acquired, I was ardently desirous of instruction. But as soon as I had finished the entire course of study, at the close of which it is customary to be admitted into the order of the learned, I completely changed my opinion. For I found myself involved in so many doubts and errors, that I was convinced I had advanced no farther in all my attempts at learning, than the discovery at every turn of my own ignorance. And yet I was studying in one of the most celebrated schools in Europe, in which I thought there must be learned men, if such were anywhere to be found. I had been taught all that others learned there; and not contented with the sciences actually taught us, I had, in addition, read all the books that had fallen into my hands, treating of such branches as are esteemed the most curious and rare. I knew the judgment which others had formed of me; and I did not find that I was considered inferior to my fellows, although there were among them some who were already marked out to fill the places of our instructors. And, in fine, our age appeared to me as flourishing, and as fertile in powerful minds as any preceding one. I was thus led to take the liberty of judging of all other men by myself, and of concluding that there was no science in existence that was of such a nature as I had previously been given to believe.

I still continued, however, to hold in esteem the studies of the schools. I was aware that the languages taught in them are necessary to the understanding of the writings of the ancients; that the grace of fable stirs the mind; that the memorable deeds of history elevate it; and, if read with discretion, aid in forming the judgment; that the perusal of all excellent books is, as it were, to interview with the noblest men of past ages, who have written them, and even a studied interview, in which are discovered to us only their choicest thoughts; that eloquence has incomparable force and beauty; that poesy has its ravishing graces and delights; that in the mathematics there are many refined discoveries eminently suited to gratify the inquisitive, as well as further all the arts an lessen the labour of man; that numerous highly useful precepts and exhortations to virtue are contained in treatises on morals; that theology points out the path to heaven; that philosophy affords the means of discoursing with an appearance of truth on all matters, and commands the admiration of the more simple; that jurisprudence, medicine, and the other sciences, secure for their cultivators honors and riches; and, in fine, that it is useful to bestow some attention upon all, even upon those abounding the most in superstition and error, that we may be in a position to determine their real value, and guard against being deceived.

But I believed that I had already given sufficient time to languages, and likewise to the reading of the writings of the ancients, to their histories and fables. For to hold converse with those of other ages and to travel, are almost the same thing. It is useful to know something of the manners of different nations, that we may be enabled to form a more correct judgment regarding our own, and be prevented from thinking that everything contrary to our customs is ridiculous and irrational, a conclusion usually come to by those whose experience has been limited to their own country. On the other hand, when too much time is occupied in traveling, we become strangers to our native country; and the over curious in the customs of the past are generally ignorant of those of the present. Besides, fictitious narratives lead us to imagine the possibility of many events that are impossible; and even the most faithful histories, if they do not wholly misrepresent matters, or exaggerate their importance to render the account of them more worthy of perusal, omit, at least, almost always the meanest and least striking of the attendant circumstances; hence it happens that the remainder does not represent the truth, and that such as regulate their conduct by examples drawn from this source, are apt to fall into the extravagances of the knight-errants of romance, and to entertain projects that exceed their powers.

I esteemed eloquence highly, and was in raptures with poesy; but I thought that both were gifts of nature rather than fruits of study. Those in whom the faculty of reason is predominant, and who most skillfully dispose their thoughts with a view to render them clear and intelligible, are always the best able to persuade others of the truth of what they lay down, though they should speak only in the language of Lower Brittany, and be wholly ignorant of the rules of rhetoric; and those whose minds are stored with the most agreeable fancies, and who can give expression to them with the greatest embellishment and harmony, are still the best poets, though unacquainted with the art of poetry.

I was especially delighted with the mathematics, on account of the certitude and evidence of their reasonings; but I had not as yet a precise knowledge of their true use; and thinking that they but contributed to the advancement of the mechanical arts, I was astonished that foundations, so strong and solid, should have had no loftier superstructure reared on them. On the other hand, I compared the disquisitions of the ancient moralists to very towering and magnificent palaces with no better foundation than sand and mud: they laud the virtues very highly, and exhibit them as estimable far above anything on earth; but they give us no adequate criterion of virtue, and frequently that which they designate with so fine a name is but apathy, or pride, or despair, or parricide.

I revered our theology, and aspired as much as any one to reach heaven: but being given assuredly to understand that the way is not less open to the most ignorant than to the most learned, and that the revealed truths which lead to heaven are above our comprehension, I did not presume to subject them to the impotency of my reason; and I thought that in order competently to undertake their examination, there was need of some special help from heaven, and of being more than man.

Of philosophy I will say nothing, except that when I saw that it had been cultivated for many ages by the most distinguished men, and that yet there is not a single matter within its sphere which is not still in dispute, and nothing, therefore, which is above doubt, I did not presume to anticipate that my success would be greater in it than that of others; and further, when I considered the number of conflicting opinions touching a single matter that may be upheld by learned men, while there can be but one true, I reckoned as well-nigh false all that was only probable.

As to the other sciences, inasmuch as these borrow their principles from philosophy, I judged that no solid superstructures could be reared on foundations so infirm; and neither the honor nor the gain held out by them was sufficient to determine me to their cultivation: for I was not, thank Heaven, in a condition which compelled me to make merchandise of science for the bettering of my fortune; and though I might not profess to scorn glory as a cynic, I yet made very slight account of that honor which I hoped to acquire only through fictitious titles. And, in fine, of false sciences I thought I knew the worth sufficiently to escape being deceived by the professions of an alchemist, the predictions of an astrologer, the impostures of a magician, or by the artifices and boasting of any of those who profess to know things of which they are ignorant.

For these reasons, as soon as my age permitted me to pass from under the control of my instructors, I entirely abandoned the study of letters, and resolved no longer to seek any other science than the knowledge of myself, or of the great book of the world. I spent the remainder of my youth in traveling, in visiting courts and armies, in holding intercourse with men of different dispositions and ranks, in collecting varied experience, in proving myself in the different situations into which fortune threw me, and, above all, in making such reflection on the matter of my experience as to secure my improvement. For it occurred to me that I should find much more truth in the reasonings of each individual with reference to the affairs in which he is personally interested, and the issue of which must presently punish him if he has judged amiss, than in those conducted by a man of letters in his study, regarding speculative matters that are of no practical moment, and followed by no consequences to himself, farther, perhaps, than that they foster his vanity the better the more remote they are from common sense; requiring, as they must in this case, the exercise of greater ingenuity and art to render them probable. In addition, I had always a most earnest desire to know how to distinguish the true from the false, in order that I might be able clearly to discriminate the right path in life, and proceed in it with confidence.

It is true that, while busied only in considering the manners of other men, I found here, too, scarce any ground for settled conviction, and remarked hardly less contradiction among them than in the opinions of the philosophers. So that the greatest advantage I derived from the study consisted in this, that, observing many things which, however extravagant and ridiculous to our apprehension, are yet by common consent received and approved by other great nations, I learned to entertain too decided a belief in regard to nothing of the truth of which I had been persuaded merely by example and custom; and thus I gradually extricated myself from many errors powerful enough to darken our natural intelligence, and incapacitate us in great measure from listening to reason. But after I had been occupied several years in thus studying the book of the world, and in essaying to gather some experience, I at length resolved to make myself an object of study, and to employ all the powers of my mind in choosing the paths I ought to follow, an undertaking which was accompanied with greater success than it would have been had I never quitted my country or my books.

The Nature of Mind

David M. Armstrong

David M. Armstrong (1926–) is Emeritus Professor of Philosophy at the University of Sydney. His publications include *Perception and the Physical World, A Materialist Theory of the Mind,* and *Universals and Scientific Realism.*

MEN have minds, that is to say, they perceive, they have sensations, emotions, beliefs, thoughts, purposes, and desires.[1] What is it to have a mind? What is it to perceive, to feel emotion, to hold a belief, or to have a purpose? In common with many other modern philosophers, I think that the best clue we have to the nature of mind is furnished by the discoveries and hypotheses of modern science concerning the nature of man.

What does modern science have to say about the nature of man? There are, of course, all sorts of disagreements and divergencies in the views of individual scientists. But I think it is true to say that one view is steadily gaining ground, so that it bids fair to become established scientific doctrine. This is the view that we can give a complete account of man *in purely physico-chemical terms.* This view has received a tremendous impetus in the last decade from the new subject of molecular biology, a subject which promises to unravel the physical and chemical mechanisms which lie at the basis of life. Before that time, it received great encouragement from pioneering work in neurophysiology pointing to the likelihood of a purely electro-chemical account of the working of the brain. I think it is fair to say that those scientists who still reject the physico-chemical account of man do so primarily for philosophical, or moral, or religious reasons, and only secondarily, and halfheartedly, for reasons of scientific detail.

This is not to say that in the future new evidence and new problems may not come to light which will force science to reconsider the physico-chemical view of man. But at present the drift of scientific thought is clearly set towards the physico-chemical hypothesis. And we have nothing better to go on than the present.

For me, then, and for many philosophers who think like me, the moral is clear. We must try to work out an account of the nature of mind which is compatible with the view that man is nothing but a physico-chemical mechanism.

And . . . I shall be concerned to do just this: to sketch (in barest outline) what may be called a **Materialist** or **Physicalist** account of the mind.

But before doing this I should like to go back and consider a criticism of my position which must inevitably occur to some. What reason have I, it may be asked, for taking my stand on science? Even granting that I am right about what is the currently dominant scientific view of man, why should we concede science a special authority to decide questions about the nature of man? What of the authority of philosophy, of religion, of

From *The Nature of Mind and Other Essays.* Copyright © 1980 by University of Queensland Press, St. Lucia. Reprinted by permission of the publisher.

morality, or even of literature and art? Why do I set the authority of science above all these? Why this "scientism"?

It seems to me that the answer to this question is very simple. If we consider the search for truth, in all its fields, we find that it is only in science that men versed in their subject can, after investigation that is more or less prolonged, and which may in some cases extend beyond a single human lifetime, reach substantial agreement about what is the case. It is only as a result of scientific investigation that we ever seem to reach an intellectual consensus about controversial matters.

In the Epistle Dedicatory to his *De Corpore* Hobbes wrote of William Harvey, the discoverer of the circulation of the blood, that he was "the only man I know, that conquering envy, hath established a new doctrine in his life-time."

Before Copernicus, Galileo and Harvey, Hobbes remarks, "there was nothing certain in natural philosophy." And, we might add, with the exception of mathematics, there was nothing certain in any other learned discipline.

These remarks of Hobbes are incredibly revealing. They show us what a watershed in the intellectual history of the human race the seventeenth century was. Before that time inquiry proceeded, as it were, in the dark. Men could not hope to see their doctrine *established,* that is to say, accepted by the vast majority of those properly versed in the subject under discussion. There was no intellectual consensus. Since that time, it has become a commonplace to see new doctrines, sometimes of the most farreaching kind, established to the satisfaction of the learned, often within the lifetime of their first proponents. Science has provided us with a method of deciding disputed questions. This is not to say, of course, that the consensus of those who are learned and competent in a subject cannot be mistaken. Of course such a consensus can be mistaken, Sometimes it has been mistaken. But, granting fallibility, what better authority have we than such a consensus?

Now this is of the utmost importance. For in philosophy, in religion, in such disciplines as literary criticism, in moral questions in so far as they are thought to be matters of truth and falsity, there has been a notable failure to achieve an intellectual consensus about disputed questions among the learned. Must we not then attach a peculiar authority to the discipline that can achieve a consensus? And if it presents us with a certain vision of the nature of man, is this not a powerful reason for accepting that vision?

I will not take up here the deeper question *why* it is that the methods of science have enabled us to achieve an intellectual consensus about so many disputed matters. That question, I think, could receive no brief or uncontroversial answer. I am resting my argument on the simple and uncontroversial fact that, as a result of scientific investigation, such a consensus has been achieved.

It may be replied—it often is replied—that while science is all very well in its own sphere—the sphere of the physical, perhaps—there are matters of fact on which it is not competent to pronounce. And among such matters, it may be claimed, is the question what is the whole nature of man. But I cannnot see that this reply has much force. Science has provided us with an island of truths, or, perhaps or should say, a raft of truths, to bear us up on the sea of our disputatious ignorance. There may have to be revisions and refinements, new results may set old findings in a new perspective, but what science has given us will not be altogether superseded. Must we not therefore appeal to these relative certainties for guidance when we come to consider uncertainties elsewhere? Perhaps science cannot help us to decide whether or not there is a God, whether or not human beings have immortal souls, or whether or not the will is free. But if science cannot assist us, what can? I conclude that it is the scientific vision of man, and not the philosophical or religious or artistic or moral vision of man, that is the best clue we have to the nature of man. And it is rational to argument from the best evidence we have.

Having in this way attempted to justify my procedure I turn back to my subject: the attempt to work out an account of mind, or, if you prefer, of mental process within the framework of the physico-chemical as we may call it, the Materialist view of man.

Now there is one account of mental process that is at once attractive to any philosopher sympathic to a Materialist view of man: this is Behavior Formulated originally by a psychologist, J. B. Watson it attracted widespread interest and considerable support from scientifically oriented philosophy. Traditional philosophy had tended to think of the mind as a rather mysterious inward arena that lay behind, and was responsible for, the outward or physical behaviour of our bodies. Descartes thought of this inner arena as a *spiritual substance,* and it was this conception of the mind as spiritual object that Gilbert Ryle attacked, apparently in the interest Behaviourism, in his important book *The Conce*ption Mind. He ridiculed the Cartesian view as the dogma of "the ghost in the machine." The mind was not something behind the behaviour of the body, it was simply part of that physical behaviour. My anger with you is not some modification of a spiritual substance which somehow brings about aggressive behaviour; rather it is the aggressive behaviour itself; my addressing strong words to you, striking you, turning my back on you, and so on. Thought is not an inner process that lies behind, and brings about, the words I speak and write: it is my speaking and writing. The mind is not an inner arena, it is outward act.

It is clear that such a view of mind fits in very well with a completely Materialistic or Physicalist view of man. If there is no need to draw a distinction beween mental processes and their expression in physical behaviour, but if instead the mental processes are identified with their so-called "expressions," then the existence of mind stands in no conflict with the view that man is nothing but a physico-chemical mechanism.

However, the version of Behaviourism that I have just sketched is a very crude version, and its crudity lays it open to obvious objections. One obvious difficulty is that it is our common experience that there can be mental processes going on although there is no behaviour occurring that could possibly be treated as expressions of these processes. A man may be angry, but give no bodily sign; he may think, but say or do nothing at all.

In my view, the most plausible attempt to refine Behaviourism with a view to meeting this objection was made by introducing the notion of *a disposition to behave.* (Dispositions to behave play a particularly important part in Ryle's account of the mind.) Let us connsider the general notion of disposition first, Brittleness is a disposition, a disposition possessed by materials like glass. Brittle materials are those which, when subjected to relatively small forces, break or shatter easily. But breaking and shattering easily is not brittleness, rather it is the *manifestation* of brittleness. Brittleness itself is the tendency or liability of the material to break or shatter easily. A piece of glass may never shatter or break throughout its whole history, but it is still the case that it is brittle: it is liable to shatter or break if dropped quite a small way or hit quite lightly. Now a disposition to *behave* is simply a tendency or liability of a person to behave in a certain way under certain circumstances. The brittleness of glass is a disposition that the glass retains throughout its history, but clearly there could also be dispositions that come and go. The dispositions to behave that are of interest to the Behaviourist are, for the most part, of this temporary character.

Now how did Ryle and others use the notion of a disposition to behave to meet the obvious objection to Behaviourism that there can be mental processes going on although the subject is engaging in no relevant behaviour? Their strategy was to argue that in such cases, although the subject was not behaving in any relevant way, he or she was *disposed* to behave in some relevant way. The glass does not shatter, but it is still brittle. The man does not behave, but he does have a disposition to behave, We can say he thinks although he does not speak or act because at that time he was disposed to speak or act in a certain way. *If* he had been asked, perhaps, he would have spoken or acted. We can say he is angry although he does not behave angrily, because he is disposed so to behave. *If* only one more word had been addressed to him, he would have burst out. And so on. In this way it was hoped that Behaviourism could be squared with the obvious facts.

It is very important to see just how these thinkers conceived of disposition. I quote from Ryle

> To possess a dispositional property *is not to be in a particular state, or to undergo a particular change*; it is to be bound or liable to be in a particular state, or to undergo a particular change, when a particular condition is realised. (*The Concept of Mind*, p. 43, my italics.)

So to explain the breaking of a lightly struck glass on a particular occasion by saying it was brittle is, on this view of dispositions, simply to say that the glass broke because it is the sort of thing that regularly breaks when quite lightly struck. The breaking was the normal behaviour, or not abnormal behaviour, of such a thing. The brittleness is not to be conceived of as a *cause* for the breakage, or even, more vaguely, a *factor* in bringing about the breaking. Brittleness is just the fact that things of that sort break easily.

But although in this way the Behaviourists did something to deal with the objection that mental processes can occur in the absence of behaviour, it seems clear, now that the shouting and the dust have died, that they did not do enough. When I think, but my thoughts do not issue in any action, it seems as obvious as anything is obvious that there is something actually going on in me which constitutes my thought. It is not simply that I would speak or act if some conditions that are unfulfilled were to be fulfilled. Something is currently going on, in the strongest and most literal sense of "going on," and this something is my thought. Rylean Behaviourism denies this, and so it is unsatisfactory as a theory of mind. Yet I know of no version of Behaviourism that is more satisfactory. The moral of those of us who wish to take a purely physicalistic view of man is that we must look for some other account of the nature of mind and of mental processes.

But perhaps we need not grieve too deeply about the failure of Behaviourism to produce a satisfactory theory of mind. Behaviourism is a profoundly unnatural account of mental processes. If somebody speaks and acts in certain ways it is natural to speak of this speech and action as the *expression* of his thought. It is not at all natural to speak of his speech and action as identical with his thought. We naturally think of the thought as something quite distinct from the speech and action which, under suitable circumstances, brings the speech and action about. Thoughts are not to be identified with behaviour, we think, they lie behind behaviour. A man's behaviour constitutes the *reason* we have for attributing certain mental processes to him, but the behaviour cannot be identified with the mental processes.

This suggests a very interesting line of thought about the mind. Behaviourism is certainly wrong, but perhaps it is not altogether wrong. Perhaps the Behaviorists are wrong in identifying the mind and mental occurrences with behaviour, but perhaps they are right in thinking that our notion of a mind and of individual mental states is *logically tied to behaviour*. For perhaps what we mean by a mental state is some state of the person which, under suitable circumstances, *brings about* a certain range of behaviour. Perhaps mind can be defined not as behaviour, but rather as the inner *cause* of certain behaviour. Thought is not speech under suitable circumstances, rather it is something within the person which, in suitable circumstances brings about speech. And, in fact, I believe that this is the true account, or, at any rate, a true first account, of what we mean by a mental state.

How does this line of thought link up with a purely physicalist view of man? The position is, I think, that while it does not make such a physicalist view inevitable, it does make it *possible.* It does not entail, but it is compatible with, a purely physicalist view of man. For if our notion of the mind and mental states is nothing but that of a cause within the person of certain ranges of behaviour, then it becomes a scientific question, and not a question of logical analyze what in fact the intrinsic nature of that cause is. The cause might be, as Descartes thought it was, a spiritual substance working through the pineal gland to produce the complex bodily behaviour of which men are capable. It might be breath, or specially smooth and mobile atoms dispersed throughout the body might be many other things. But in fact the verdict in modern science seems to be that the sole cause as mind-betokening behaviour in man and the higher animals is the physico-chemical workings of the central nervous system. And so, assuming we have all rectly characterized our concept of a mental state as nothing but the cause of certain sorts of behavious then we can identify these mental states with pure physical states of the central nervous system.

At this point we may stop and go back to the behaviourists' dispositions. We saw that, according to them, the brittleness of glass or, to take another example, the elasticity of rubber, is not a state of the glass or the rubber, but is simply the fact that things of that sort behave in the way they do. But now let us consider how a scientist would think about brittleness or elasticity. Faced with the phenomenal breakage under relatively small impacts, or the phenomenon of stretching when a force is applied followed by contraction when the force is removed, it will assume that there is some current *state* of the glass or the rubber which is responsible for the <characteristic behaviour of samples of these two materials. At the beginning he will not know what the state is, but he will endeavor to find out, and he may succeed in finding out. And when he has found out he will very likely make remarks of this sort: "We have discovered that the brittleness of glass is in fact a certain sort of pattern in the molecules of the glass." That is to say, he will *identify* brittleness with the state of the glass that is responsible for the liability of the glass to break. For him, a disposition of an object is a state of the object. What makes the state a state of brittleness is the fact that it gives rise to the chararacteristic manifestations of brittleness? But the disposition itself is distinct from its manifestation: it is the state of the glass that gives rise to these manifestations in suitable circumstances.

You will see that this way of looking at dispositions is very different from that of Ryle and the Behaviourists. The great difference is this: If we treat dispositions as actual states, as I have suggested that scientists do, even if states whose intrinsic nature may yet have to be discovered, then we can say that dispositions are actual *causes,* or causal factors, which, in suitable circumstances, actually bring about those happenings which are the manifestations of the disposition. A certain molecular constitution of glass which constitutes its brittleness is actually *responsible* for the fact that, when the glass is struck, it breaks.

Now I shall not argue the matter here, because the detail of the argument is technical and difficult,[2] but I believe that the view of dispositions as states, which is the view that is natural to science, is the correct one. I believe it can be shown quite strictly that, to the extent that we admit the notion of dispositions at all, we are committed to the view that they are actual *states* of the object that has the disposition. I may add that I think that the same holds for the closely connected notions of capacities and powers. Here I will simply assume this step in my argument.

But perhaps it can be seen that the rejection of the idea that mind is simply a certain range of man's behaviour in favour of the view that mind is rather the inner *cause* of that

range of man's behaviour is bound up with the rejection of the Rylean view of dispositions in favour of one that treats dispositions as states of objects and so as having actual
causal power. The Behaviourists were wrong to identify the mind with behaviour. They
were not so far off the mark when they tried to deal with cases where mental happenings
occur in the absence of behaviour by saying that these are dispositions to behave. But
in order to reach a correct view, I am suggesting, they would have to conceive of these
dispositions as actual *states* of the person who has the disposition, states that have actual
power to bring about behaviour in suitable circumstances. But to do this is to abandon
the central inspiration of Behaviourism: that in talking about the mind we do not have
to go behind outward behaviour to inner states.

And so two separate but interlocking lines of thought have pushed me in the same
direction. The first line of thought is that it goes profoundly against the grain to think of
the mind as behaviour. The mind is, rather, that which stands behind and brings about
our complex behaviour. The second line of thought is that the Behaviourists' dispositions, properly conceived, are really states that underlie behaviour, and, under suitable
circumstances, bring about behaviour. Putting these two together, we reach the conception of a mental state as *a state of the person apt for producing certain ranges of behaviour.*
This formula: a mental state is a state of the person apt for producing certain ranges of
behaviour, I believe to be a very illuminating way of looking at the concept of a mental
state. I have found it very fruitful in the search for detailed logical analyses of the individual mental concepts.

Now, I do not think that Hegel's dialectic has much to tell us about the nature of
reality. But I think that human thought often moves in a dialectical way, from thesis to
antithesis and then to the synthesis. Perhaps thought about the mind is a case in point. I
have already said that classical philosophy tended to think of the mind as an inner arena
of some sort. This we may call the Thesis. Behaviourism moved to the opposite extreme:
the mind was seen as outward behaviour. This is the Antithesis. My proposed Synthesis is
that the mind is properly conceived as an inner principle, but a principle that is identified
in terms of the outward behaviour it is apt for bringing about. This way of looking at the
mind and mental states does not itself entail a Materialist or Physicalist view of man, for
nothing is said in this analysis about the intrinsic nature of these mental states. But is we
have, as I have asserted that we do have, general scientific grounds for thinking that man
is nothing but a physical mechanism, we can go on to argue that the mental states are in
fact nothing but physical states of the central nervous system.

Along these lines, then, I would look for an account of the mind that is compatible with a purely Materialist theory of man. I have tried to carry out this programme
in detail in *A Materialist Theory of the Mind.* There are, as may be imagined, all sorts of
powerful objections that can be made to this view. But [in what follows] . . . I propose to
do only one thing. I will develop one very important objection to my view of the mind—
an objection felt by many philosophers—and then try to show how the objection should
be met.

The view that our notion of mind is nothing but that of an inner principle apt for
bringing about certain sorts of behaviour may be thought to share a certain weakness
with Behaviourism. Modern philosophers have put the point about Behaviourism by saying that although Behaviourism may be a satisfactory account of the mind from an *other-
person point of view,* it will not do as a *first-person* account. To explain. In our encounters
with other people, all we ever observe is their behaviour: their actions, their speech, and
so on. And so, if we simply consider other people, Behaviourism might seem to do full
justice to the facts. But the trouble about Behaviourism is that it seems so unsatisfactory
as applied to our *own* case. In our own case, we seem to be aware of so much more than
mere behaviour.

Suppose that now we conceive of the mind as an inner principle apt for bringing about certain sorts of behaviour. This again fits the other-person cases very well. Bodily behaviour of a very sophisticated sort is observed, quite different from the behaviour that ordinary physical objects display. It is inferred that this behaviour must spring from a very special sort of inner cause in the object that exhibits this behaviour. This inner cause is christened "the mind," and those who take a physicalist view of man argue that it is simply the central nervous system of the body observed. Compare this with the case of glass. Certain characteristic behaviour is observed: the breaking and shattering of the material when acted upon by relatively small forces. A special inner state of the glass is postulated to explain this behaviour. Those who take a purely physicalist view of glass then argue that this state is a *natural* state of the glass. It is, perhaps, an arrangement of its molecules, and not, say, the peculiarly malevolent disposition of the demons that dwell in glass.

But when we turn to our own case, the position may seem less plausible. We are conscious, we have experiences. Now can we say that to be conscious, we have experiences, is simply for something to go on within us apt for the causing of certain sorts of behaviour? Such an account does not seem to do in justice to the phenomena. And so it seems that our account of the mind, like Behaviourism, will fail to do justice to the first-person case.

In order to understand the objection better it may be helpful to consider a particular case. If you have driven for a very long distance without a break, you may have had experience of a curious state of automatism, which can occur in these conditions. One can suddenly "come to" and realize that one has driven for long distances without being aware of what one was doing, or, indeed, without being aware of anything. One has kept the car on the road, used the brake and the clutch perhaps, yet all all out any awareness of what one was doing.

Now, if we consider this case it is obvious that in *some sense* mental processes are still going on when one is in such an automatic state. Unless one's will was still operating in some way, and unless one was still perceiving in some way, the car would not still be on the road. Yet, of course, *something* mentally lacking. Now, I think, when it is alleged that an account of mind as an inner principle apt for the production of certain sorts of behaviour leaves our consciousness or experience, what is alleged to have been left out is just whatever is missing in the automatic driving case. It is conceded that an accountof mental processes as states of the person apt for the production of certain sorts of behaviour may very possibly be adequate to deal with such cases as that of automatic driving. It may be adequate to deal with most of the mental processes of animals, who perhaps spend a good deal of their lives in this state of automatism. But, it is contended, it cannot deal with the consciousness that we normally enjoy.

I will now try to sketch an answer to this important and powerful objection. Let us begin in an apparently unlikely place, and consider the way that an account of mental processes of the sort I am giving would deal with *sense-perception*.

Now psychologists, in particular, have long realised that there is a very close logical tie between sens-perception and *selective behaviour*. Suppose we want to decide whether an animal can perceive the difference between red and green. We might give the animal a choice between two pathways, over one of which a red light shines and over the other of which a green light shines. If the animal happens by chance to choose the green pathway we reward it; if happens to choose the other pathway we do not reward it. If, after some trials, the animal systematically takes the green-lighted pathway, and if we become assured that the only relevant differences in the two pathways are the differences in the colour of the lights, we are entitled to say that the animal can see this colour difference. Using its eyes, it selects between red-lighted and green-lighted pathways. So we say it can see the difference between red and green.

Now a Behaviourist would be tempted to say that the animal's regularly selecting the green-lighted pathway *was* its perception of the colour difference. But this is unsatisfactory, because we all want to say that perception is something that goes on within the person or animal—within its mind—although, of course, this mental event is normally *caused* by the operation of the environment upon the organism. suppose, however, that we speak instead of *capaci*ties for selective behaviour towards the current environment, and suppose we think of these capacities, like dispositions, as actual inner states of the organism. We can then think of the animal's perception as a state within the animal apt, if the animal is so impelled, for selective behaviour between the red- and green-lighted pathways.

In general, we can think of perceptions as inner states or events apt for the production of certain sorts of selective behaviour towards our environment. To perceive is like acquiring a key to a door, You do not have to use the key: you can put it in your pocket and never bother about the door. But if you do want to open the door the key may be essential. The blind man is a man who does not acquire certain keys, and, as a result, is not able to operate in his environment in the way that somebody who has his sight can operate. It seems, then, a very promising view to take of perceptions that they are inner states defined by the sorts of selective behaviour that they enable the perceiver to exhibit, if so impelled.

Now how is this discussion of perception related to the question of consciousness of experience, the sort of thing that the driver who is in a state of automatism has not got, but which we normally do have? Simply this. My proposal is that consciousness, in this sense of the word, is nothing but *perception or awareness of the state of our own mind.* The driver in a state of automatism perceives, or is aware of, the road. If he did not, the car would be in a ditch. But he is not currently aware of this awareness of the road. He perceives the road, but he does not perceive his perceiving, or anything else that is going on in his mind. He is not, as we normally are, conscious of what is going on in his mind.

And so I conceive of consciousness or experience, in this sense of the words, in the way that Locke and Kant conceived it, as like perception. Kant, in a striking phrase, spoke of "inner sense." We cannot directly observe the minds of others, but each of us has the power to observe directly our own minds, and "perceive" what is going on there. The driver in the automatic state is one whose "inner eye" is shut: who is not currently aware of what is going on in his own mind.

Now if this account is along the right lines, why should we not give an account of this inner observation along the same lines as we have already given of perception? Why should we not conceive of it as an inner state, a state in this case directed towards other inner states and not to the environment, which enables us, if we are so impelled, to behave in a selective way *towards our own states of mind?* One who is aware, or conscious, of his thoughts or his emotions is one who has the capacity to make discriminations between his different mental states. His capacity might be exhibited in words. He might say that he was in an angry state of mind when, and only when, he *was* in an angry state of mind, But such verbal behaviour would be the mere *expression* or *result* of the awareness. The awareness itself would be an inner state: the sort of inner state that gave the man a capacity for such behavioural expressions.

So I have argued that consciousness of our own mental state may be assimilated to *perception* of our own mental state, and that, like other perceptions, it may then be conceived of as an inner state or event giving a capacity for selective behaviour, in this case selective behaviour towards our own mental state. All this is meant to be simply a logical analysis of consciousness, and none of it entails, although it does not rule out, a purely physicalist account of what these inner states are. But if we are convinced, on general scientific grounds, that a purely physical account of man is likely to be the true one, then there seems to be no bar to our identifying these inner states with purely physical states of the central nervous system. And so consciousness of our own mental state becomes simply the scanning of one part of our central nervous system by another. Consciousness is a self-scanning mechanism in the central nervous system.

As I have emphasised before, I have done no more than sketch a programme for a philosophy of mind. There are all sorts of expansions and elucidations to be made, and all sorts of doubts and difficulties to be stated and overcome. But I hope I have done enough to show that a purely physicalist theory of the mind is an exciting and plausible intellectual option.

Notes

1. Inaugural lecture of the Challis Professor of Philosophy at the University of Sydney (1965); slightly amended (1968).
2. It is presented in my book *A Materialist Theory of the Mind* (1968) ch. 6, see. VI.

The Dependence of Consciousness on the Brain

Paul Edwards

IN THIS ARTICLE I will discuss the case against survival after death based on what is known about the dependence of consciousness on the brain. This may be called the body – mind dependence argument. I shall try to bring out what a formidable argument it is. Among other things I shall try to show that the various replies to it by philosophers and theologians are unsound.

I will make two assumptions which are favorable to the case for survival. By this I mean that without them one of the major forms of survival-belief would be ruled out from the start. I will assume, first, that some form of dualism is true, i.e., that a person is a body and a mind in a sense in which the mind cannot be identified with any bodily processes or behavior. I will also assume that when we talk about personal identity, bodily continuity is not an essential ingredient in what we mean. The view that bodily continuity is an essential ingredient in personal identity has sometimes been referred to as "corporealism" and I will here assume that corporealism is false.

The Scope of the Argument

In a rudimentary form the argument can already be found in Lucretius and Pomponazzi and, since Bishop Butler expressly argued against it in the first chapter of his *Analogy of Religion,* we may infer that it was current among English free-thinkers in the early years of the eighteenth century. However, the first full statement with which I am familiar occurs in Hume's posthumous essay on immortality:

Where any two objects are so closely connected that all alterations which we have ever seen in the one are attended with proportionable alterations in the other; we ought to conclude, by all rules of analogy, that, when there are still greater alterations produced in the former, and it is totally dissolved, there follows a total dissolution of the latter. . . . The weakness of the body and that of the mind in infancy are exactly proportioned; their vigour in manhood, their sympathetic disorder in sickness; their common gradual decay in old age. The step further seems unavoidable; their common dissolution in death. The last symptoms which the mind discovers, are disorder, weakness, insensibility, and stupidity; the forerunners of its annihilation. The further progress of the same causes increasing, the same effects totally extinguish it.[1]

Some of Hume's detailed observations are of course quite indefensible. There is surely no "exact" proportionality between physical and mental development or between bodily and mental "decay." Nor is it true that all human beings are "insensible" and "stupid"

---

[1] "On the Immortality of the Soul." [See this volume, p. 138.]

Some of the material contained in this article first appeared in "The Case Against Reincarnation, part 3," *Free Inquiry,* Spring 1987.

immediately before their death. Hume was also handicapped by the undeveloped state of brain physiology in the eighteenth century. Nevertheless his statement conveys very vividly the basic idea of the argument.

More recent defenders have placed heavy emphasis on information about the relation between the brain and our mental states and processes. Unlike Hume Professor J. J. C. Smart rejects dualism. As a materialist he maintains that mental states are identical with brain states, but he nevertheless endorses the body–mind dependence argument as valid within a dualistic framework.

Even if some form of philosophical dualism is accepted and the mind is thought of as something over and above the body, the empirical evidence in favor of an invariable correlation between mental states and brain states is extremely strong: that is, the mind may be thought of as in some sense distinct from the body but also as fundamentally dependent upon physical states. Without oxygen or under the influence of anesthetics or soporific drugs, we rapidly lose consciousness. Moreover, the quality of our consciousness can be influenced in spectacular ways by appropriate drugs or by mechanical stimulation of different areas of the brain. In the face of all the evidence that is being accumulated by modern research in neurology, it is hard to believe that after the dissolution of the brain there could be any thought or conscious experience whatever.[2]

I will add one other recent formulation which states the argument simply and forcefully and is based on the most recent evidence from neurology. "What we call 'the mind,'" writes Colin McGinn, is in fact made up of a great number of sub-capacities, and each of these depends upon the functioning of the brain.

Now, the facts of neurology compellingly demonstrate . . . that everything about the mind, from the sensory-motor periphery to the inner sense of self, is minutely controlled by the brain: if your brain lacks certain chemicals or gets locally damaged, your mind is apt to fall apart at the seams. . . . If parts of the mind depend for their existence upon parts of the brain, then the whole of the mind must so depend too. Hence the soul dies with the brain, which is to say it is mortal.[3]

It should be emphasized that the argument does *not* start from the premise that after a person is dead he never again acts in the world. A correspondent in the *London Review* replied to McGinn by observing that we do not need his or the neuropathologist's "assistance to learn that all behavior stops at death." Similarly, John Stuart Mill in his chapter on "Immortality" in *Three Essays on Religion* thought the argument inconclusive on the ground that the absence of any acts by an individual after his death is as consistent with the view that he will "recommence" his existence "elsewhere" as it is with the assumption that he has been extinguished forever. Such remarks are due to a misunderstanding. The absence of any actions by the dead is certainly not irrelevant, but the argument is primarily based on the observed dependence of our mental states and processes on what goes on in the brain.

At first sight it may seem that, if valid, the argument merely rules out the survival of the disembodied mind and leaves other forms of survival untouched. In fact, however, it equally rules out reincarnation and the more sophisticated or replica-version of resurrectionism. This is so because the conclusion of the argument is that my mind depends on my brain. It does not merely support the less specific conclusion that my mind needs *some* brain as its foundation. If my mind is finished when my brain dies, then it cannot transmigrate to any other body. Similarly, if God created a duplicate of my body containing a duplicate of my brain, *my* mind would not be able to make use of it since it stopped

[2]"Religion and Science," *The Encyclopedia of Philosophy* (New York and London: Macmillan, 1967), volume 7, p. 161.
[3]*London Review of Books,* January 23, 1986, pp. 24–25.

existing with the death of my original body. The argument does not refute belief in the literal resurrection of the body. For on this view God will reconstitute our *original* bodies and hence also our original brains on the Day of Judgment. There are indeed vast numbers of fundamentalists and also a few pious philosophers who believe or say that they believe in resurrection in this literal sense, but to the great majority of scientists and philosophers and of educated persons generally it seems totally incredible. However, if anybody does believe in survival in *this* sense our argument has no bearing on his view.

Alzheimer's Disease and Comas

The literature on survival contains a number of standard rejoinders to the body–mind dependence argument. Before turning to them, I will consider two concrete instances of body–mind dependence which will help to bring out the full force of the argument. The first is Alzheimer's disease, a dreadful affliction that ruins the last years of a sizable percentage of the world's population. Almost everybody above the age of thirty has known some elderly relative or friend afflicted with this illness. I can therefore be brief in my description of what happens to Alzheimer patients. In the early stages the person misses appointments, he constantly loses and mislays objects, and he frequently cannot recall events in the recent past. As the illness progresses he can no longer read or write and his speech tends to be incoherent. In nursing homes Alzheimer patients commonly watch television, but there is no evidence that they understand what is happening on the screen. The decline in intellectual function is generally accompanied by severe emotional symptoms, such as extreme irritability and violent reactions to persons in the environment, as well as hallucinations and paranoid fears. In the final stages the patient is totally confused, frequently incontinent, and quite unable to recognize anybody, including the closest relatives and friends. At present Alzheimer's is incurable and, unlike in the case of Parkinson's disease, there are no known means of slowing down the deterioration. It is also as yet a mystery why Alzheimer's strikes certain individuals while sparing the majority of old people. However, a great deal is known about what goes on in the brains of Alzheimer patients. Alois Alzheimer, the neurologist after whom the disease is named, found in 1906 that the cerebral cortex and the hippocampus of his patients contained twisted tangles and filaments as well as abnormal neurites known as "neuritic" or "senile plaques." It has since been determined that the density of these abnormal components is directly proportional to the severity of the disorder. Autopsies have shown that Alzheimer victims have a vastly reduced level of an enzyme called "choline acetyltransferase," which is needed for producing the neurotransmitter acetylcholine. Although the reduced level of the enzyme and the neurotransmitter appear in the cortex, the origin of the trouble lies in another region of the brain, the nucleus basalis, which is situated just above the place where the optic nerves meet and cross. Autopsies have revealed a dramatic loss of neurons from the nucleus basalis in Alzheimer victims, and this explains why so little of the enzyme is manufactured in their brains.

The information just summarized has been culled from articles about Alzheimer's that have appeared in magazines and popular science monthlies in recent years. The authors of these articles are evidently not concerned with the question of survival after death, but they invariably use such phrases as "destruction of the mind" in describing what happens to the victims. In an article in *Science 84* entitled "The Clouded Mind," the author, Michael Shodell, speaks of Alzheimer's as "an illness that destroys the mind, leaving the body behind as a grim reminder of the person who once was there." Similarly, the cover story in *Newsweek* of December 3, 1984, which contained many heart-rending illustrations and listed some of the famous men and women who are suffering from Alzheimer's, was entitled "A Slow Death of the Mind." I think that these descriptions are entirely appropriate: A person who can no longer read or write, whose memory has largely disappeared, whose speech is incoherent, and who is totally indifferent to his environment has in effect lost all or most of what we normally call his mind. The relevance of this to our discussion is obvious. While still alive, an Alzheimer patient's brain is severely damaged and most of his mind has disappeared. After his death his brain is not merely damaged but completely destroyed. It is surely logical to conclude that now his mind is also gone. It seems preposterous to assert that, when the brain is completely destroyed, the mind suddenly returns intact, with its emotional and intellectual capacities, including its memory, restored. How does the *complete* destruction of the brain bring about a cure that has so far totally eluded medical science?

The same obviously applies to people in irreversible comas. Karen Ann Quinlan lay in a coma for over ten years before she finally died. The damage to her brain had made her, in the phrase used by the newspapers, nothing more than a "vegetable." Her E.E.G. was flat; she was unable to speak or write; visits by her foster parents did not register the slightest response. A more recent widely publicized case was that of the great American tenor Jan Peerce. Peerce had amazed the musical public by singing right into his seventies with only a slight decline in his vocal powers. In the end, however, he was felled by two severe strokes, and he spent the last year of his life in an irreversible coma. Relatives and friends could get no response of any kind. Peerce died in December 1984, and Karen Ann Quinlan in June 1985. Did the total destruction of the bodies of these individuals suddenly bring back their emotional and intellectual capacities? If so, where were these during the intervening periods?

The Body as the Instrument of the Mind

The first of the rejoinders I will consider does not dispute the manifold dependence of mental functions on brain processes. It is claimed, however, that these facts are not inconsistent with survival. They are indeed compatible with the view that the mind is annihilated at death, but they are also compatible with the very different position that the mind continues to exist but has lost its "instrument" for acting in the world, and more specifically, for communicating with people who are still alive. An excellent illustration of what the supporters of this rejoinder have in mind is supplied by Father John A. O'Brien in his pamphlet: *The Soul— What Is It?*[4] In order to carve a statue, Father O'Brien writes, a sculptor needs his tools, his hammer and chisel. If the tools are seriously damaged, the quality of his work will be correspondingly impaired, but this does not mean that the sculptor cannot exist if the tools are completely destroyed.

Variants of this argument are found in numerous Protestant theologians, in Catholic philosophers who have frequently relied on the distinction between what they call "extrinsic" and "intrinsic" dependence, and in several secular philosophers, including Descartes, Kant, James, Schiller and McTaggart. "I do not agree with you," writes Descartes to Gassendi in his "Reply to the Fifth Objection" to his *Meditations,* that the mind waxes and wanes with the body; for from the fact that it does not work equally well in the body of a child and in that of a grown man, and that its actions are often impeded by wine and other bodily things, it follows merely that while it is united to the body is uses the body as an instrument in its normal operations.[5]

Have we any reason, asks McTaggart, to suppose that "a body is essential to a self"? Not at all. The facts support the very different proposition that "while a self has a body,

---

[4]New York: The Paulist Press, 1946.
[5]My attention to this passage was called by Jonathan Bennett who quotes it on p. 132 of *A Study of Spinoza's Ethics* (Indianapolis: Hackett, 1984).

that body is essentially connected with the self's mental life." A self needs "sufficient data" for its mental activity. In this life the material is given in the form of sensations, and these can only be obtained by means of a body. It does not follow, however, that "it would be impossible for a self without a body to get data in some other way." McTaggart then offers an analogy which has frequently been quoted by believers in survival:

If a man is shut up in a house, the transparency of the windows is an essential condition of his seeing the sky. But it would not be prudent to infer that, if he walked out of the house, he could not see the sky because there was no longer any glass through which he might see it.[6]

McTaggart is totally unimpressed by the evidence from brain physiology which, it is safe to say, he did not study in detail and which was very extensive even in 1906 when his book was published. He does not dispute that "diseases or mutilations of the brain affect the course of thought," but "the fact that an abnormal state of the brain may affect our thought does not prove that the normal states of the brain are necessary for thought."[7]

It may be instructive at this stage to consider some of the exchanges between Professor Ian Stevenson, the well-known champion of reincarnation, and two of his skeptical interrogators in the course of a BBC program that took place in the spring of 1976. The program dealt with the claims of Edward Ryall, an elderly Englishman who in May 1970 had written a letter to the *Daily Express* in which he mentioned his clear and extensive memories of a life in the seventeenth century as a West Country farmer by the name of John Fletcher. Stevenson corresponded with Ryall and became convinced of the authenticity of his recollections. He encouraged Ryall to write a book about his previous life. *Second Time Around* appeared in 1974, with an introduction and supplementary notes by Stevenson. Besides Stevenson and Ryall, the participants in the BBC program were John Taylor, professor of mathematics at London University, and John Cohen, professor of psychology at Manchester. Here are some of the exchanges that are relevant to our discussion.

> Cohen: . . . memories are tied to a particular brain tissue. If you take away the brain, there is no memory.
>
> Stevenson: I think that's an assumption. Memories may exist in the brain and exist elsewhere also.
>
> Cohen: But we have not the slightest evidence, even a single case, of a memory existing without a brain. We have plenty of slight damage to a brain which destroys memory, but not the other way around.
>
> Stevenson: I feel that's one of the issues here—whether memories can, in fact, survive the destruction of the brain.
>
> Taylor: Professor Stevenson, do you have any evidence, other than these reincarnation cases, that memories can survive the destruction of physical tissue?
>
> Stevenson: No. I think the best evidence comes from the reincarnation cases.[8]
>
> Taylor then brought up the well-known case of people who lose all or most of their memories as a result of brain injuries, Stevenson was not fazed.
>
> Stevenson: Well, it's possible that what is affected is his ability to express memories that he may still have.
>
> Taylor: But are you suggesting, in fact, that memories themselves are in some way nonphysically bound up, and can be stored in a nonphysical manner?
>
> Stevenson: Yes, I'm suggesting that there might be a nonphysical process of storage.

---

[6] *Some Dogmas of Religion* (London: Edward Arnold, 1906), p. 105.
[7] Ibid.
[8] *The Listener,* June 3, 1976, p. 698.

Taylor: What does that mean? Nonphysical storage of what?

Stevenson: The potentiality for the reproduction of an image memory.

Taylor: But information itself involves energy. Is there such a thing as nonphysical energy?

Stevenson: I think there may be, yes.

Taylor: How can you define it? Nonphysical energy, to me, is a complete contradiction in terms. I can's conceive how on earth you could ever conceive of such a quantity. . . .

Stevenson: Well, it might be in some dimension of which we are just beginning to form crude ideas, through the study of what we parapsychologists call paranormal phenomena. We are making an assumption of some kind of process that is not, and maybe cannot be, understood in terms of current physical concepts. That is a jump, a gap, I freely admit.[9]

These exchanges bring out very clearly what is at issue between those who accept the body–mind dependence argument and the supporters of the instrument theory.

It has on occasion been suggested that we have no way of deciding between these two rival explanations of the relevant facts. I see no reason to accept such an agnostic conclusion. It seems to me that by retrodictive extrapolation to cases like Alzheimer patients or people in comas we can see that the alternative to annihilation proposed by the instrument theory is absurd. Let us consider the behavior of Alzheimer patients in, the later stages of their affliction. The more specific the case, the clearer the implications of the rival views will appear. The mother of a close friend of mine, Mrs. D., recently died from Alzheimer's after suffering from the disease for about eight years. Mrs. D. was a prosperous lady from Virginia, the widow of a banker. In her pre-Alzheimer days she was a courteous and well-behaved person, and she had of course no difficulty recognizing her daughter or any of her other relatives or friends. I do not know what her feelings were about paralyzed people, but my guess is that she pitied them and certainly had no wish to beat them up. As her illness progressed she was put into a nursing home run by nuns who were renowned for their gentle and compassionate ways. She shared a room with an older lady who was paralyzed. For the first year or so Mrs. D, did not become violent. Then she started hitting the nurses. At about the time when she could no longer recognize her daughter, she beat up the paralyzed lady on two or three occasions. From then on she had to be confined to the "seventh floor," which was reserved for violent and exceptionally difficult patients.

Let us now see what the survival theorists would have to say about Mrs. D.'s behavior. It should be remembered that on this view Mrs, D., after her death, will exist with her mind intact and will only lack the means of communicating with people on earth. This view implies that throughout her affliction with Alzheimer's Mrs. D.'s mind *was* intact. She recognized her daughter but had lost her ability to express this recognition. She had no wish to beat up an inoffensive paralyzed old woman. On the contrary, "inside" she was the same considerate person as before the onset of the illness. It is simply that her brain disease prevented her from acting in accordance with her true emotions. I must insist that these *are* the implications of the theory that the mind survives the death of the brain and that the brain is only an instrument for communication. Surely these consequences are absurd: The facts are that Mrs. D. no longer recognized her daughter and that she no longer had any compassionate feelings about paralyzed old women. At any rate, we have the same grounds for saying this as we do in any number of undisputed cases in which people do not suffer from Alzheimer's and fail to recognize other human beings or fail to feel compassion.

---

[9] Ibid.

The guards in Argentine dungeons who tortured and killed libera's had no compassion for their victims, and neither of course did the Nazis who rounded up and then shot Jews in Poland and elsewhere. We have exactly the same kind of evidence for concluding that Mrs. D., who probably did feel compassion for paralyzed people before she suffered from Alzheimer's, no longer felt compassion when beating up her paralyzed roommate. As for memories, all of us sometimes cannot place a familiar tune or remember the name of a person we know well; and in such cases it makes good sense to say that the memories are still there. Even when the name never comes back there is a suspicion that the memory may not have been lost: it is entirely possible that one could bring it back under hypnosis. However, the memory loss in Alzheimer's is totally different, and the same of course applies to people in irreversible comas. It is surely fantastic to maintain that during his last months Jan Peerce did recognize his wife and children and simply could not express his recognition. If anybody makes such a claim it can only be for ulterior metaphysical reasons and not because it is supported by the slightest evidence.

Mill, Butler, Ewing—The Absense of Direct Negative Evidence

Mill's posthumously published essay on "Theism" contains a chapter on immortality in which he surveys and evaluates all the major arguments on both sides that were known to him. Mill finds all of them defective and concludes on a note of complete agnosticism. We have here, he writes, "one of those very rare cases in which there is really a total absence of evidence on either side" and "in which the absence of evidence for the affirmative does not, as in so many other cases, create a strong presumption in favor of the negative."[10]

Mill discusses in some detail the evidence from brain physiology. It supplies us with "sufficient evidence that cerebral action is, if not the cause, at least, in our present state of existence, a condition *sine qua non* of mental operations." We are entitled to conclude that the death of the brain would put a stop to all mental function and "remand it [the mind] to unconsciousness unless and until some other set of conditions supervenes, capable of recalling it into activity." The facts of brain physiology most emphatically do not prove that the mind cannot exist after death. "The same thoughts, emotions, volitions, and even sensations which we have here" may, for all we can tell, "persist or recommence somewhere else under other conditions." This is no less possible than that "other thoughts and sensations may exist under other conditions in other parts of the universe."[11] What Mill evidently seems to require in order to establish the negative case is that we observe the nonexistence of the thoughts, volitions, and sensations of the dead person; and this the body–mind dependence argument does not give us.

Independently of this argument, Bishop Butler insists on the same requirement and regards its nonfulfillment as a fatal flaw in the unbeliever's position. Not only do we never directly observe the nonexistence of human minds, but the same is also true of animals. We never "find anything throughout the whole analogy of nature" that could afford us "even the slightest presumption, that animals ever lose their living powers." This is so because we have "no faculties wherewith to trace any beyond or through death to see what becomes of them,"[12] In the case of human beings and animals alike death only destroys "the sensible proof which we had before their death of their being possessed of

---

[10] *Three Essays on Religion* (London: Longman's Green, Reader and Dyer, 1876), p. 203.
[11] Op. cit., p. 200. [See this volume, p. 173.]
[12] *The Analogy of Nature,* Chapter 1. [See this volume, p. 123.]

living powers," but it does not "afford the least reason" for supposing that death causes the extinction of their minds.

A much more recent philosopher, the late A. C. Ewing, used the same kind of reasoning to rebut the unbeliever's argument. Ewing first observes that there is no logically necessary connection between bodily and mental events, something that all dualists would endorse. This means that no deductive argument is available to the unbeliever. At the same time he is also unable to mount an inductive argument. He cannot do this because "we have never observed a mind being annihilated at death."[13] The only one who could do this is the person himself. "No one could observe this," Ewing writes, "but the mind in question itself, and even that could not because it was annihilated, so, if a phenomenon, it is certainly an unobservable one."[14] Ewing is happy to note that once we have disposed of the argument from the connection between body and mind the field is left open "for any empirical evidence drawn from psychical research and any arguments for survival there may be based on ethics and religion."[15]

Butler deserves credit for realizing that his reasoning applies to animals and not only to human beings. It is not clear that either Mill or Ewing saw this. However, not even Butler carried the argument far enough. What reason do we have for denying that purely inanimate objects have an "inner" psychic life? What evidence do I have that the chocolate cream puff I am about to eat does not bitterly resent this murderous activity on my part and how do I know that a tennis ball I am about to serve does not acutely suffer as a result of being hit? For that matter how do I know that the tennis ball does not enjoy the experience of being hit? Since we have no access to the inner life of tennis balls, if they have any, we cannot know either that the tennis ball does or does not like being hit. Not only cannot we know that tennis balls do not have an inner life. We also cannot know that they, or any other inanimate objects, do not continue to have an inner, psychical life after the death of their bodies, whether as disembodied minds or in conjunction with replicas that will be produced in a resurrection world. It is true that we have no evidence that such an inner life will continue after the death of their bodies, but we equally have none that it will not. A complete suspense of judgment is the only defensible attitude.

All who regard panpsychism as either false or meaningless will surely regard the fact that the rejoinder here under discussion can be extended to inanimate objects as its *reductio ad absurdum*. Others will go further and treat the entire rejoinder as a *reductio ad absurdum* of dualism. For clearly we do know that tennis balls and cream puffs do not have an inner life and we can and do know that human beings and animals have certain feelings or sensations. However, we have agreed to accept dualism throughout this article, and it can be shown that the rejoinder is invalid even within a dualistic framework. After all, dualists allow that although we cannot inspect the minds of others we can frequently know that they have certain experiences. We can know that another person is in pain or that he is angry, and we can at least have strong evidence that he has certain thoughts. Now, the same *kind* of evidence is available to us that other people do *not* have these experiences. We can know that somebody has ceased to be in pain, that his anger is gone, or that he no longer thinks about a certain subject. I do not have to be the other person to know that he is no longer in pain or angry. By the same token I do not have to be Mrs. D., the Alzheimer patient herself, to know that her memory is gone and I equally do not have to be Jan Peerce in his coma to know that he no longer recognizes his family. In such cases we surely have the right to assert more than that the memories and thoughts have been "remanded to unconsciousness." This description fits a person under general

---

[13] *Non-Linguistic Philosophy* (London: Allen and Unwin, 1968), p. 173.
[14] Ibid.
[15] Ibid.

anesthesia or during dreamless sleep who may very well return to full consciousness, but it is highly misleading about people in a coma or with advanced Alzheimer's. The only description that is fitting in such cases is that the thoughts and memories have been destroyed; and if they have been destroyed then they cannot be "recalled into activity" when a "different set of conditions supervenes."

Ducasse's Rejoinder

Perhaps the ablest defender of belief in survival in recent decades, at least among those who attempt to judge the issue in terms of evidence and do not simply appeal to faith, was Professor C. J. Ducasse. In almost all of his many discussions of the subject he took note of the argument with which we are concerned in this article. He invariably rejects it on the ground that it logically presupposes epiphenomenalism and that epiphenomenalism is plainly false. As Ducasse states it quite fairly, epiphenomenalism asserts that mental events are by-products or automatic accompaniments of cerebral activity but do not in turn "cause or affect the latter."[16] Such a theory implies that "mental states and activities cannot possibly continue after the life of the brain has ceased." Ducasse does not dispute that many mental events are physically caused. This is particularly obvious in the case of "the several kinds of sensations" which "can, at will, be caused by appropriate stimulation of the body."[17] But although it cannot be denied that "sensations and some other mental states can be so caused," we have "equally good and abundant evidence that mental states can cause various bodily events." Ducasse quotes John Laird who offers a long list of illustrations including "the fact that merely willing to raise one's arm normally suffices to cause it to rise and . . . that certain thoughts cause tears, pallor, blushing, or fainting." The evidence we have that in such cases mental states have bodily effects "is exactly the same here as where bodily processes cause mental states."[18] To the extent to which it constitutes a search for the physical causes of mental phenomena, epiphenomenalism may be a "legitimate research program," but the philosophers who support it have "arbitrarily transmuted it into a materialistic metaphysical dogma."[19] Ducasse concludes that the body–mind–dependence argument fails. "So far as anything that epiphenomenalists have shown to the contrary," he writes, "after-death mental life—at least of certain kinds—remains both a theoretical and an empirical possibility."[20]

The answer to Ducasse is that somebody who maintains that consciousness cannot exist without an intact brain *may* advocate epiphenomenalism but is in no way committed to it. He maintains that the brain is a *necessary* condition for the existence of all conscious states and processes, but this does not imply that conscious states and processes are incapable of influencing behavior. Ducasse mentions the standard example supporting mind–body interaction, namely "the fact that merely willing to raise one's arm normally suffices to cause it to rise." This is a very incomplete account of the facts of the case even if one accepts interactionism. If at the moment when the individual decided to raise his arm he had suffered a stroke, or if the brain had been damaged in certain other ways, the arm would not have gone up. This is all that the defender of the indispensability of an intact brain is committed to. He need not in the least deny that willing to raise the arm is causally relevant, i.e., that it is part of what in the context is the sufficient condition

---

[16] *A Critical Examination of the Belief in Life After Death* (Springfield, Ill.; Charles C. Thomas, 1961), p. 75.
[17] *Nature, Mind and Death* (La Salle, Ill.: Open Court, 1951), p. 455.
[18] Ibid.
[19] "Life After Death Conceived as Reincarnation," The 1960 Garvin Lecture, printed in the collection of Garvin Lectures, *In Search of God and Immortality* (Boston: Beacon Press, 1961), p. 148.
[20] *A Critical Examination of the Belief in Life After Death,* op, cit., p. 80.

of the arm's movement. The scholastic philosophers distinguished between what they called a "*causa in fieri*" which literally means "cause in becoming" but is more accurately rendered as "productive cause" and "*causa in esse*" or sustaining cause. My parents are my *causa in fieri* or at least a major part of it. The air I breathe and the food I eat are a part of my *causa in esse*: they keep me alive but they did not produce me. Using this terminology we may express Ducasse's confusion by saying that his opponent is committed to the assertion that an intact brain is a *cause in esse* of all conscious states and not to the much stronger claim that it is their *causa in fieri*.

The preceding remarks are quite sufficient as an answer to Ducasse's objection. It should be added for the record, however, that various of his statements obscure the situation concerning the causal relations between the body and the mind. It may in fact be the case that the mind affects the body just as much as the body affects the mind, but there is an important asymmetry. If a mental state like a desire precedes a certain action of which it is taken to be the cause, it is always accompanied by a physical fact, namely a state of the brain. We already noted that the brain state is a necessary condition of the action, but it is at least conceivable that it, or it in conjunction with other bodily states, is the sufficient condition as well; and if this is so then the desire, if it is interpreted as a purely mental fact, is causally irrelevant. On the other hand, the physical antecedents of mental states which are regarded as their causes are *not* accompanied by mental antecedents corresponding to the brain states which are present in the putative mind–body interactions. Here therefore there is no alternative to the physical antecedent as cause of the mental state. If the situation were really as symmetrical as Ducasse maintains, there surely would never have been any epiphenomenalists. Epiphenomenalism may be false, but it is not *obviously* false, and epiphenomenalists are not simply deluded fools.

"Extra-Cerebral" Memories

It will be recalled that in the exchanges in the BBC discussion of the Ryall case the question came up whether memories can exist without the brain. Professors Cohen and Taylor regarded the notion of extra-cerebral memories as totally absurd. Professor Stevenson vehemently disagreed. "Memories may exist in the brain," he said, and "exist elsewhere also." The best evidence that they may exist elsewhere, Stevenson continued, comes from his own reincarnation research. On the question of the "storage" of memories he remarked that there "might be a non-physical process of storage." The memories "might be in some dimension . . . which cannot be understood in terms of current physical concepts."[21]

Unlike Stevenson the late Professor H. H. Price did not believe in reincarnation but he took communications from or through mediums very seriously. As far as I know he remained an agnostic on the subject of survival, but he insisted that if brain physiology supplies us with evidence against the existence of extra-cerebral memories, certain of the data assembled by parapsychologists provide evidence in its favor. "It will, of course, be objected," Price wrote, "that memories cannot exist in the absence of a physical brain, nor yet desires, nor images either." Against this it must be emphasized that "any evidence which directly supports the Survival Hypothesis (and there is quite a lot of evidence which does) . . . is *pro tanto* evidence against the Materialistic conception of human personality,"[22] by which Price here simply means the view that consciousness depends on the brain for its existence.

---

[21] *The Listener*, op. cit., p. 686.

[22] "Survival and the Idea of 'Another World,'" in J. R. Smythies, Ed., *Brain and Mind* (London: Routledge, 1965), p. 18.

I will confine myself to two brief comments. First, Price is quite right in maintaining that the issue is one of weighing the evidence from brain physiology against that from parapsychology. For my own part I do not see how any rational person can hesitate in regarding the former evidence as *vastly* more impressive. I spent the better part of two years studying Stevenson's evidence and found it exceedingly weak if not indeed utterly worthless. I hesitate to speak about mediumistic communications but most of these, by the almost common consent of the more respectable students of the subject, have a tendency to break down on close examination, Some impressive cases remain but even they do not compare in solidity with the careful, controlled studies of brain physiologists. Next, it should be pointed out that many parapsychologists are not supporters of belief in any kind of survival and, what is perhaps more the the point, rejection of extra-cerebral memories has no logical bearing on the "this-worldly" phenomena studied in parapsychology. Telepathic communications, to take one example, are between persons who have brains; and if these communications really occur they do not have the slightest tendency to support the existence of any extra-cerebral mental processes. As for Stevenson's nonphysical storage depot of extra-cerebral memories—"the dimension which cannot be understood in terms of current physical concepts"—it must surely be dismissed as nothing but a vague picture which is of no scientific value whatsoever.

The Mind and the Soul

The last rejoinder to be considered involves a distinction between the mind, which is identical with the phenomenal or empirical self whose existence is not disputed by Hume and other empiricists, and another nonphysical entity to which various labels have been applied. It is the immaterial or spiritual substance of Clarke, Butler, and Reid and numerous other philosophers, past and present, it is the Atman of the Hindu version of reincarnation, the noumenal self of Kant, and the soul (in one of its senses) of the Christian and Jewish traditions. It is argued that, although the mind may indeed so closely depend on the body that it must cease with the body's death, the same is not true of the soul. The soul is the "I" that "owns" both the body and the mind. I am five feet seven inches tall, I weigh one hundred and fifty pounds, I have blue eyes and brown hair; but I also have certain sensations and feelings and thoughts. I have various physical skills and I also possess certain emotional and intellectual dispositions. It is this underlying "I"—the subject of both the body and the mind—that has not been shown to require a body for its existence.

There are two objections to this rejoinder, each of them fatal. In the first place, although the way we speak in certain contexts suggests an underlying subject of both body and mind, there is no reason to suppose that it exists. Hume's theory that human beings are nothing but "bundles of impressions and ideas" is seriously inadequate. Each of us, at least while he is sane, has a sense of himself, more specifically, a sense of himself as continuing the same person from moment to moment. However, what this consists in is not the totally unchanging metaphysical entity that Hume rightly rebelled against. It is a sense of continuity in certain bodily sensations (especially of our limbs and certain muscle groups) and of our various tastes, opinions, and habits—more generally of our emotional and intellectual dispositions. These, together with our bodies, make us the kinds of persons we are. Although our emotional and intellectual dispositions are subject to change, unlike our moods and sensations, they are relatively stable. If this is what is meant by "soul," there is no reason to deny that we have a soul; but the soul in this sense is just as dependent on the body and the brain as any particular sensations, feelings, and thoughts.

The second objection to this rejoinder is that if there were such a thing as the spiritual substance or the metaphysical soul, it would not be what anybody means by "I."

Human beings who are afraid of death dread the annihilation of their *empirical* selves and it is these empirical selves which they would like to survive. This is true of Western and Eastern believers alike. The great seventeenth-century philosopher Pierre Gassendi, who was both a Catholic priest and an atomistic materialist, professed belief in the metaphysical soul. He also believed that insanity was a brain disease. Since the soul or reason (Gassendi preferred the latter word) did not depend on the body, he concluded quite consistently that the soul or reason remained sane even when the individual had become insane. Gassendi's consistency led to a *reductio ad absurdum* of his position. If I go mad and if at the same time my soul remains sane then I and my soul are not the same thing.

Eliminative Materialism

Paul M. Churchland

The identity theory was called into doubt not because the prospects for a materialist account of our mental capacities were thought to be poor but because it seemed unlikely that the arrival of an adequate materialist theory would bring with it the nice one-to-one match-ups, between the concepts of folk psychology and the concepts of theoretical neuroscience, that intertheoretic reduction requires. The reason for that doubt was the great variety of quite different physical systems that could instantiate the required functional organization. *Eliminative materialism* also doubts that the correct neuroscientific account of human capacities will produce a neat reduction of our common-sense framework but here the doubts arise from a quite different source.

As the eliminative materialists see it, the one-to-one match-ups will not be found, and our common-sense psychological framework will nolt enjoy an intertheoretic reduction, *because our common-sense psychological framework is a false and radically misleading conception of the causes of human behavior and the nature of cognitive activity.* On this view, folk psychology is not just an incomplete representation of our inner natures; it is an outright *mis*representation of our internal states and activities. Consequently, we cannot expect a truly adequate neuroscientific account of our inner lives to provide theoretical categories that match up nicely with the categories of our common-sense frame-work Accordingly, we must expect that the older framework will simply be eliminated, rather than be reduced, by a matured neuroscience.

Historical Parallels

As the identity theorist can point to historical cases of successful intertheoretic reduction, so the eliminative materialist can point to historical cases of the outright elimination of the ontology of an older theory in favor of the ontology of a new and superior theory. For most of the eighteenth and nineteenth centuries, learned people believed that heat was a subtle *fluid* held in bodies, much in the way water is held in a sponge. A fair body of moderately successful theory described the way this fluid substance—called "caloric"—flowed within a body, or from one body to another, and how it produced thermal expansion, melting, boiling, and so forth. But by the end of the last century it had become abundantly clear that heat was not a substance at all, but just the energy of motion of the trillions of jostling molecules that make up the heated body itself. The new theory—the "corpuscular/kinetic theory of matter and heat"—was much more successful than the old in explaining and predicting the thermal behavior of bodies. And since we were unable to *identify* caloric fluid with kinetic energy (according to the old theory, caloric is a material *substance*; according to the new theory, kinetic energy is a form of *motion*), it was finally agreed that there is *no such thing* as caloric. Caloric was simply eliminated from our accepted ontology.

A second example. It used to be thought that when a piece of wood burns, or a piece of metal rusts, a spiritlike substance called "phlogiston" was being released: briskly, in the former case, slowly in the latter. Once gone, that 'noble' substance left only a base pile of ash or rust. It later came to be appreciated that both processes involve, not the loss of something, but the *gaining* of a substance taken from the atmosphere: oxygen. Phlogiston emerged, not as an incomplete description of what was going on, but as a radical misdescription. Phlogiston was therefore not suitable for reduction to or identification with some notion from within the new oxygen chemistry, and it was simply eliminated from science.

Admittedly, both of these examples concern the elimination of something nonobservable, but our history also includes the elimination of certain widely accepted 'observables'. Before Copernicus' views became available, almost any human who ventured out at night could look up at *the starry sphere of the heavens,* and if he stayed for more than a few minutes he could also see that it *turned,* around an axis through Polaris. What the sphere was made of (crystal?) and what made it turn (the gods?) were theoretical questions that exercised us for over two millennia. But hardly anyone doubted the existence of what everyone could observe with their own eyes. In the end, however, we learned to reinterpret our visual experience of the night sky within a very different conceptual framework, and the turning sphere evaporated.

Witches provide another example. Psychosis is a fairly common affliction among humans, and in earlier centuries its victims were standardly seen as cases of demonic possession, as instances of Satan's spirit itself, glaring malevolently out at us from behind the victims' eyes. That witches exist was not a matter of any controversy. One would occasionally see them, in any city or hamlet, engaged in incoherent, paranoid, or even murderous behavior. But observable or not, we eventually decided that witches simply do not exist. We concluded that the concept of a witch is an element in a conceptual framework that misrepresents so badly the phenomena to which it was standardly applied that literal application of the notion should be permanently withdrawn, Modern theories of mental dysfunction led to the elimination of witches from our serious ontology.

The concepts of folk psychology—belief, desire, fear, sensation, pain, joy, and so on—await a similar fate, according to the view at issue. And when neuroscience has matured to the point where the poverty of our current conceptions is apparent to everyone, and the superiority of the new framework is established, we shall then be able to set about reconceiving our internal states and activities, within a truly adequate conceptual framework at last. Our explanations of one another's behavior will appeal to such things as our neuropharmacological states, the neural activity in specialized anatomical areas, and whatever other states are deemed relevant by the new theory. Our private introspection will also be transformed, and may be profoundly enhanced by reason of the more accurate and penetrating framework it will have to work with—just as the astronomer's perception of the night sky is much enhanced by the detailed knowledge of modern astronomical theory that he or she possesses.

The magnitude of the conceptual revolution here suggested should not be minimized: it would be enormous. And the benefits to humanity might be equally great. If each of us possessed an accurate neuroscientific understanding of (what we now conceive dimly as) the varieties and causes of mental illness, the factors involved in learning, the neural basis of emotions, intelligence, and socialization, then the sum total of human misery might be much reduced. The simple increase in mutual understanding that the new framework made possible could contribute substantially toward a more peaceful and humane society. Of course, there would be dangers as well: increased knowledge means increased power, and power can always be misused.

Arguments for Eliminative Materialism

The arguments for eliminative materialism are diffuse and less than decisive, but they are stronger than as widely supposed. The distinguishing feature of this position is its denial that a smooth intertheoretic reduction is to be expected—even a species-specific reduction—of the framework of folk psychology to the framework of a matured neuroscience. The reason for this denial is the eliminative materialist's conviction that folk psychology is a hopelessly primitive and deeply confused conception of our internal activities. But why this low opinion of our common-sense conceptions?

There are at least three reasons. First, the eliminative materialist will point to the widespread explanatory, predictive, and manipulative failures of folk psychology. So much of what is central and familiar to us remains a complete mystery from within folk psychology. We do not know what *sleep* is, or why we have to have it, despite spending a full third of our lives in that condition. (The answer, "For rest," is mistaken. Even if people are allowed to rest continuously, their need for sleep is undiminished. Apparently, sleep serves some deeper functions, but we do not yet know what they are.) We do not understand how *learning* transforms each of us from a gaping infant to a cunning adult, or how differences in *intelligence* are grounded. We have not the slightest idea how *memory* works, or how we manage to retrieve relevant bits of information instantly from the awesome mass we have stored. We do not know what *mental illness* is, nor how to cure it.

In sum, the most central things about us remain almost entirely mysterious from within folk psychology. And the defects noted cannot be blamed on inadequate time allowed for their correction, for folk psychology has enjoyed no significant changes or advances in well over 2,000 years, despite its manifest failures, Truly successful theories may be expected to reduce, but significantly unsuccessful theories merit no such expectation.

This argument from explanatory poverty has a further aspect. So long as one sticks to normal brains, the poverty of folk psychology is perhaps not strikingly evident. But as soon as one examines the many perplexing behavioral and cognitive deficits suffered by people with *damaged* brains, one's descriptive and explanatory resources start to claw the air (see, for example chapter 7.3, p. 143). As with other humble theories asked to operate successfully in unexplored extensions of their old domain (for example, Newtonian mechanics in the domain of velocities close to the velocity of light, and the classical gas law in the domain of high pressures or temperatures), the descriptive and explanatory inadequacies of folk psychology become starkly evident.

The second argument tries to draw an inductive lesson from our conceptual history. Our early folk theories of motion were profoundly confused, and were eventually displaced entirely by more sophisticated theories. Our early folk theories of the structure and activity of the heavens were wildly off the mark, and survive only as historical lessons in how wrong we can be. Our folk theories of the nature of fire, and the nature of life, were similarly cockeyed. And one could go on, since the vast majority of our past folk conceptions have been similarly exploded. All except folk psychology, which survives to this day and has only recently begun to feel pressure. But the phenomenon of conscious intelligence is surely a more complex and difficult phenomenon than any of those just listed. So far as accurate understanding is concerned, it would be a *miracle* if we had got *that* one right the very first time, when we fell down so badly on all the others. Folk psychology has survived for so very long, presumably, not because it is basically correct in its representations, but because the phenomena addressed are so surpassingly difficult that any useful handle on them, no matter how feeble, is unlikely to be displaced in a hurry.

A third argument attempts to find an a priori advantage for eliminative materialism over the identity theory and functionalism. It attempts to encounter the common intuition that eliminative materialism is distantly possible, perhaps, but is much less probable than either the identity theory or functionalism. The focus again is on whether the concepts of folk psychology will find vindicating match-ups in a matured neuroscience. The eliminativist bets no; the other two bet yes. (Even the functionalist bets yes, but expects the match-ups to be only species-specific, or only person-specific. Functionalism, recall, denies the existence only of *universal* type/type identities.)

The eliminativist will point out that the requirements on a reduction are rather demanding. The new theory must entail a set of principles and embedded concepts that mirrors very closely the specific conceptual structure to be reduced. And the fact is, there are vastly many more ways of being an explanatorily successful neuroscience while *not* mirroring the structure of folk psychology, than there are ways of being an explanatorily successful neuroscience while also *mirroring* the very specific structure of folk psychology. Accordingly, the a priori probability of eliminative materialism is not lower, but substantially *higher* than that of either of its competitors. One's initial intuitions here are simply mistaken.

Granted, this initial a priori advantage could be reduced if there were a very strong presumption in favor of the truth of folk psychology—true theories are better bets to win reduction. But according to the first two arguments, the presumptions on this point should run in precisely the opposite direction.

Arguments against Eliminative Materialism

The initial plausibility of this rather radical view is low for almost everyone, since it denies deeply entrenched assumptions. That is at best a question-begging complaint, of course, since those assumptions are precisely what is at issue. But the following line of thought does attempt to mount a real argument.

Eliminative materialism is false, runs the argument, because one's introspection reveals directly the existence of pains, beliefs, desires, fears, and so forth. Their existence is as obvious as anything could be.

The eliminative materialist will reply that this argument makes the same mistake that an ancient or medieval person would be making if he insisted that he could just see with his own eyes that the heavens form a turning sphere, or that witches exist. The fact is, all observation occurs within some system of concepts, and our observation judgments are only as good as the conceptual framework in which they are expressed. In all three cases—the starry sphere, witches, and the familiar mental states—precisely what is challenged is the integrity of the background conceptual frameworks in which the observation judgments are expressed. To insist on the validity of one's experiences, *traditionally interpreted,* is therefore to beg the very question at issue, For in all three cases, the question is whether we should *re*conceive the nature of some familiar observational domain.

A second criticism attempts to find an incoherence in the eliminative materialist's position. The bald statement of eliminative materialism is that the familiar mental states do not really exist. But that statement is meaningful, runs the argument, only if it is the expression of a certain *belief,* and an *intention* to communicate, and a *knowledge* of the language, and so forth. But if the statement is true, then no such mental states exist, and the statement is therefore a meaningless string of marks or noises, and cannot be true. Evidently, the assumption that eliminative materialism is true entails that it cannot be true.

The hole in this argument is the premise concerning the conditions necessary for a statement to be meaningful. It begs the question. If eliminative materialism is true, then meaningfulness must have some different source. To insist on the 'old' source is to insist on the validity of the very framework at issue, Again, an historical parallel may be helpful here. Consider the medieval theory that being biologically *alive* is a matter of being ensouled by an immaterial *vital spirit.* And consider the following response to someone who has expressed disbelief in that theory.

My learned friend has stated that there is no such thing as vital spirit. But this statement is incoherent. For if it is true, then my friend does not have vital spirit, and must therefore be *dead.* But if he is dead, then his statement is just a string of noises, devoid of meaning or truth. Evidently, the assumption that antivitalism is true entails that it cannot be true! Q.E.D.

This second argument is now a joke, but the first argument begs the question in exactly the same way.

A final criticism draws a much weaker conclusion, but makes a rather stronger case. Eliminative materialism, it has been said, is making mountains out of molehills. It exaggerates the defects in folk psychology, and underplays its real successes. Perhaps the arrival of a matured neuroscience will require the elimination of the occasional folk-psychological concept, continues the criticism, and a minor adjustment in certain folk-psychological principles may have to be endured. But the large-scale elimination forecast by the eliminative materialist is just an alarmist worry or a romantic enthusiasm.

Perhaps this complaint is correct. And perhaps it is merely complacent. Whichever, it does bring out the important point that we do not confront two simple and mutually exclusive possibilities here: pure reduction versus pure elimination. Rather, these are the end points of a smooth spectrum of possible outcomes, between which there are mixed cases of partial elimination and partial reduction. Only empirical research (see chapter 7) can tell us where on that spectrum our own case will fall. Perhaps we should speak here, more liberally, of "revisionary materialism", instead of concentrating on the more radical possibility of an across-the-board elimination. Perhaps we should. But it has been my aim in this section to make it at least intelligible to you that our collective conceptual destiny lies substantially toward the revolutionary end of the spectrum.

Suggested Readings

Feyerabend, Paul, "Comment: 'Mental Events and the Brain,'" *Journal of Philosophy,* vol. LX (1963). Reprinted in *The Mind/Brain Identity Theory,* ed. C. V. Borst (London: Macmillan, 1970).

Feyerabend, Paul, "Materialism and the Mind-Body Problem," *Review of Metaphysics,* vol. XVII (1963). Reprinted in *The Mind/Brain Identity Theory,* ed. C. V. Borst (London: Macmillan, 1970).

Rorty Richard, "Mind-Body Identity, Privacy, and Categories," *Review of Metaphysics,* vol. XIX (1965). Reprinted in *Materialism and the Mind-Body Problem,* ed. D. M. Rosenthal (Englewood Cliffs, NJ: Prentice-Hall, 1971).

Rorty, Richard, "In Defense of Eliminative Materialism," *Review of Metaphysics,* vol. XXIV (1970). Reprinted in *Materialism and the Mind-Body Problem,* ed. D. M. Rosenthal (Englewood Cliffs, NJ: Prentice-Hall, 1971).

Churchland, Paul, "Eliminative Materialism and the Propositional Attitudes," *Journal of Philosophy,* vol. LXXVIII, no. 2 (1981).

Dennett, Daniel, "Why You Can't Make a Computer that Feels Pain," in *Brainstorms* (Montgomery, VT: Bradford, 1978).

Functionalism

Paul M. Churchland

According to *functionalism,* the essential or defining feature of any type of mental state is the set of causal relations it bears to (1) environmental effects on the body, (2) other types of mental states, and (3) bodily behavior, Pain, for example, characteristically results from some bodily damage or trauma; it causes distress, annoyance, and practical reasoning aimed at relief; and it causes wincing, blanching, and nursing of the traumatized area. Any state that plays exactly that functional role is a pain, according to functionalism. Similarly, other types of mental states (sensations, fears, beliefs, and so on) are also defined by their unique causal roles in a complex economy of internal states mediating sensory inputs and behavioral outputs.

This view may remind the reader of behaviorism, and indeed it is the heir to behaviorism, but there is one fundamental difference between the two theories. Where the behaviorist hoped to define each type of mental state solely in terms of environmental input and behavioral output, the functionalist denies that this is possible. As he sees it, the adequate characterization of almost any mental state involves an ineliminable reference to a variety of other mental states with which it is causally connected, and so a reductive definition solely in terms of publicly observable inputs and outputs is quite impossible. Functionalism is therefore immune to one of the main objections against behaviorism.

Thus the difference between functionalism and behaviorism, The difference between functionalism and the identity theory will emerge from the following argument raised against the identity theory.

Imagine a being from another planet, says the functionalist, a being with an alien physiological constitution, a constitution based on the chemical element silicon, for example, instead of on the element carbon, as ours is. The chemistry and even the physical structure of the alien's brain would have to be systematically different from ours. But even so, that alien brain could well sustain a functional economy of internal states whose mutual *relations* parallel perfectly the mutual relations that define our own mental states. The alien may have an internal state that meets all the conditions for being a pain state, as outlined earlier. That state, considered from a purely physical point of view, would have a very different makeup from a human pain state, but it could nevertheless be identical to a human pain state from a purely functional point of view. And so for all of his functional states.

If the alien's functional economy of internal states were indeed *functionally isomorphic* with our own internal economy—if those states were causally connected to inputs, to one another, and to behavior in ways that parallel our own internal connections—then the alien would have pains, and desires, and hopes, and fears just as fully as we, despite the differences in the physical system that sustains or realizes those functional states. What is important for mentality is not the matter of which the creature is made, but the structure of the internal activities which that matter sustains.

If we can think of one alien constitution, we can think of many, and the point just made can also be made with an artificial system. Were we to create an electronic system—a computer of some kind—whose internal economy were functionally isomorphic with our own in all the relevant ways, then it too would be the subject of mental states.

What this illustrates is that there are almost certainly many more ways than one for nature, and perhaps even for man, to put together a thinking, feeling, perceiving creature. And this raises a problem for the identity theory, for it seems that there is no single type of physical state to which a given type of mental state must always correspond. Ironically, there are *too many* different kinds of physical systems that can realize the functional economy characteristic of conscious intelligence. If we consider the universe at large, therefore, and the future as well as the present, it seems quite unlikely that the identity theorist is going to find the one-to-one match-ups between the concepts of our common-sense mental taxonomy and the concepts of an overarching theory that encompasses all of the relevant physical systems. But that is what intertheoretic reduction is standardly said to require. The prospects for universal identities, between types of mental states and types of brain states, are therefore slim.

If the functionalists reject the traditional 'mental-type = physical type' identity theory, virtually all of them remain committed to a weaker 'mental token = physical token' identity theory, for they still maintain that each *instance* of a given type of mental state is numerically identical with some specific physical state in some physical system or other. It is only universal (type/type) identities that are rejected. Even so, this rejection is typically taken to support the claim that the science of psychology is or should be *methodologically autonomous* from the various physical sciences such as physics, biology, and even neurophysiology. Psychology, it is claimed, has its own irreducible laws and its own abstract subject matter.

As this book is written, functionalism is probably the most widely held theory of mind among philosophers, cognitive psychologists, and artificial intelligence researchers. Some of the reasons are apparent from the preceding discussion, and there are further reasons as well. In characterizing mental states as essentially functional states, functionalism places the concerns of psychology at a level that abstracts from the teeming detail of a brain's neurophysiological (or crystallographic, or microelectronic) structure. The science of psychology, it is occasionally said, is methodologically autonomous from those other sciences (biology, neuroscience, circuit theory) whose concerns are with what amount to engineering details. This provides a rationale for a great deal of work in cognitive psychology and artificial intelligence, where researchers postulate a system of abstract functional states and then test the postulated system, often by way of its computer simulation, against human behavior in similar circumstances. The aim of such work is to discover in detail the functional organization that makes us what we are. (Partly in order to evaluate the prospects for a functionalist philosophy of mind, we shall examine some of the recent research in artificial intelligence in chapter 6.)

Arguments against Functionalism

Current popularity aside, functionalism also faces difficulties. The most commonly posed objection cites an old friend: sensory qualia. Functionalism may escape one of behaviorism's fatal flaws, it is said, but it still falls prey to the other. By attempting to make its *relational* properties the definitive feature of any mental state, functionalism ignores the 'inner' or qualitative nature of our mental states. But their qualitative nature is the essential feature of a great many types of mental state (pain, sensations of color, of temperature, of pitch, and so on), runs the objection, and functionalism is therefore false.

The standard illustration of this apparent failing is called "the inverted spectrum thought-experiment". It is entirely conceivable, runs the story, that the range of color sensations that I enjoy upon viewing standard objects is simply inverted relative to the color sensations that you enjoy. When viewing a tomato, I may have what is really a sensation-of-green where you have the normal sensation-of-red; when viewing a banana, I may have what is really sensation-of-blue where you have the normal sensation-of-yellow; and so forth. But since we have no way of comparing our inner qualia, and since I shall make all the same observational discriminations among objects that you will, there is no way to tell whether my spectrum is inverted relative to yours.

The problem for functionalism arises as follows. Even if my spectrum is inverted relative to yours, we remain functionally isomorphic with one another. My visual sensation upon viewing a tomato is *functionally* identical with your visual sensation upon viewing a tomato. According to functionalism, therefore, they are the very same type of state, and it does not even make sense to suppose that my sensation is 'really' a sensation-of-green. If it meets the functional conditions for being a sensation-of-red, then by definition it is a sensation-of-red, According to functionalism, apparently, a spectrum inversion of the kind described is ruled out by definition. But such inversions are entirely conceivable, concludes the objection, and if functionalism entails that they are not conceivable, then functionalism is false.

Another qualia-related worry for functionalism is the so-called "absent qualia problem". The functional organization characteristic of conscious intelligence can be instantiated (= realized or instanced) in a considerable variety of physical systems, some of them radically different from a normal human. For example, a giant electronic computer might instantiate it, and there are more radical possibilities still. One writer asks us to imagine the people of China—all 10^9 of them—organized into an intricate game of mutual interactions so that collectively they constitute a giant brain which exchanges inputs and outputs with a single robot body. That system of the robot-plus-10^9-unit-brain could presumably instantiate the relevant functional organization (though no doubt it would be much slower in its activities than a human or a computer), and would therefore be the subject of mental states, according to functionalism. But surely, it is urged, the complex states that there play the functional roles of pain, pleasure, and sensations-of-color would not have intrinsic qualia as ours do, and would therefore fail to be genuine mental states. Again, functionalism seems at best an incomplete account of the nature of mental states.

It has recently been argued that both the inverted-qualia and the absent-qualia objections can be met, without violence to functionalism and without significant violence to our common-sense intuitions about qualia. Consider the inversion problem first. I think the functionalist is right to insist that the type-identity of our visual sensations be reckoned according to their functional role. But the objector is also right in insisting that a relative inversion of two people's qualia, without functional inversion, is entirely conceivable. The apparent inconsistency between these positions can be dissolved by insisting that (1) our functional states (or rather, their physical realizations) do indeed have an intrinsic nature on which our introspective identification of those states depends; while also insisting that (2) such intrinsic natures are nevertheless not essential to the type-identity of a given mental state, and may indeed *vary* from instance to instance of the same type of mental state.

What this means is that the qualitative character of your sensation-of-red might be different from the qualitative character of my sensation-of-red, slightly or substantially, and a third person's sensation-of-red might be different again. But so long as all three states are standardly caused by red objects and standardly cause all three of us to believe that something is red, then all three states are sensations-of-red, whatever their intrinsic qualitative character. Such intrinsic qualia merely serve as salient features that permit the quick introspective identification of sensations, as black-on-orange stripes serve as a salient feature for the quick visual identification of tigers. But specific qualia are not essential to the type-identity of mental states, any more than black-on-orange stripes are essential to the type-identity of tigers.

Plainly, this solution requires the functionalist to admit the *reality* of qualia, and we may wonder how there can be room for qualia in his materialist world-picture, Perhaps they can be fit in as follows: *identify* them with physical properties of whatever physical states instantiate the mental (functional) states that display them. For example, identify the qualitative nature of your sensations-of-red with that physical feature (of the brain state that instantiates it) to which your mechanisms of introspective discrimination are in fact responding when you judge that you have a sensation-of-red. If materialism is true, then there must *be* some internal physical feature or other to which your discrimination of sensations-of-red is keyed: *that* is the quale of your sensations-of-red. If the pitch of a sound can turn out to be the frequency of an oscillation in air pressure, there is no reason why the quale of a sensation cannot turn out to be, say, a spiking frequency in a certain neural pathway, ('Spikes' are the tiny electrochemical pulses by which our brain cells communicate.)

This entails that creatures with a constitution different from ours may have qualia different from ours, despite being psychologically isomorphic with us. It does not entail that they *must* have different qualia, however. If the qualitative character of my sensation-of-red is really a spiking frequency of 90 hertz in a certain neural pathway, it is possible that an electromechanical robot might enjoy the very same qualitative character if, in reporting sensations-of-red, the robot were responding to a spiking frequency of 90 hertz in a corresponding *copper* pathway. It might be the spiking frequency that matters to our respective mechanisms of discrimination, not the nature of the medium that carries it.

This proposal also suggests a solution to the absent qualia problem. So long as the physical system at issue is functionally isomorphic with us, to the last detail, then it will be equally capable of subtle introspective discriminations among its sensations. Those discriminations must be made on some systematic physical basis, that is, on some characteristic physical features of the states being discriminated. Those features at the objective focus of the system's discriminatory mechanisms, *those* are its sensory qualia—though the alien system is no more likely to appreciate their true physical nature than we appreciate the true physical nature of our own qualia. Sensory qualia are therefore an inevitable concomitant of any system with the kind of functional organization at issue. It may be difficult or impossible to 'see' the qualia in an alien system, but it is equally difficult to 'see' them even when looking into a human brain.

I leave it to the reader to judge the adequacy of these responses. If they are adequate, then, given its other virtues, functionalism must be conceded a very strong position among the competing contemporary theories of mind. It is interesting, however, that the defense offered in the last paragraph found it necessary to take a leaf from the identity theorist's book (types of quale are reduced to or identified with types of physical state), since the final objection we shall consider also tends to blur the distinction between functionalism and reductive materialism.

Consider the property of *temperature,* runs the objection. Here we have a paradigm of a physical property, one that has also been cited as the paradigm of a successfully *reduced* property, as expressed in the intertheoretic identity

"temperature = mean kinetic energy of constituent molecules".

Strictly speaking, however, this identity is true only for the temperature of a gas, where simple particles are free to move in ballistic fashion. In a *solid,* temperature is realized differently, since the interconnected molecules are confined to a variety of vibrational motions. In a *plasma,* temperature is something else again, since a plasma has no constituent molecules; they, and their constituent atoms, have been ripped to pieces. And even a *vacuum* has a so-called 'blackbody' temperature—in the distribution of electromagnetic waves coursing through it. Here temperature has nothing to do with the kinetic energy of particles.

It is plain that the physical property of temperature enjoys 'multiple instantiations' no less than do psychological properties. Does this mean that thermodynamics (the theory of heat and temperature) is an 'autonomous science', separable from the rest of physics, with its own irreducible laws and its own abstract nonphysical subject matter?

Presumably not. What it means, concludes the objection, is that *reductions are domain-specific*:

temperature-in-a-gas = the mean kinetic energy of the gas's molecules,

whereas

temperature-in-a-vacuum = the blackbody distribution of the vacuum's transient radiation.

Similarly, perhaps

joy-in-a-human = resonances in the lateral hypothalamus,

whereas

joy-in-a-Martian = something else entirely.

This means that we may expect some type/type reductions of mental states to physical states after all, though they will be much narrower than was first suggested. Furthermore, it means that functionalist claims concerning the radical autonomy of psychology cannot be sustained. And last, it suggests that functionalism is not so profoundly different from the identity theory as was first made out.

As with the defense of functionalism outlined earlier, I leave the evaluation of this criticism to the reader. We shall have occasion for further discussion of functionalism in later chapters. At this point, let us turn to the final materialist theory of mind, for functionalism is not the only major reaction against the identity theory.

Suggested Readings

Putnam, Hilary, "Minds and Machines," in *Dimensions of Mind,* ed. Sidney Hook (New York: New York University Press, 1960).

Putnam, Hilary, "Robots: Machines or Artificially Created Life?" *Journal of Philosophy,* vol. LXI, no. 21 (1964).

Putnam, Hilary, "The Nature of Mental States," in *Materialism and the Mind-Body Problem,* ed. David Rosenthal (Englewood Cliffs, NJ: Prentice-Hall, 1971).

Fodor, Jerry, *Psychological Explanation* (New York: Random House, 1968).

Dennett, Daniel, *Brainstorms* (Montgomery, Vermont: Bradford, 1978).

Concerning Difficulties with Functionalism

Block, Ned, "Troubles with Functionalism," in *Minnesota Studies in the Philosophy of Science,* vol. IX ed. C. W. Savage (Minneapolis: University of Minnesota Press, 1978). Reprinted in *Readings in Philosophy of Psychology,* ed. N. Block (Cambridge, MA: Harvard University Press, 1980).

Churchland, Paul and Patricia, "Functionalism, Qualia, and Intentionality," *Philosophical Topics,* vol. 12, no. 1 (1981). Reprinted in *Mind, Brain, and Function,* eds. J. Biro and R. Shahan (Norman, OK: University of Oklahoma Press, 1982).

Churchland, Paul, "Eliminative Materialism and the Propositional Attitudes," *Journal of Philosophy,* vol. LXXVIII, no. 2 (1981).

Shoemaker, Sidney, "The Inverted Spectrum," *Journal of Philosophy,* vol. LXXIX, no. 7 (1982).

Enc, Berent, "In Defense of the Identity Theory," *Journal of Philosophy,* vol. LXXX, no. 5 (1983).

Chapter 3 Personal Identity and the Immortality of the Soul

Personal Identity

Look around you. You will undoubtedly identify a variety of different kinds of objects. I am certain that many of these objects are fairly familiar to you from previous encounters. I am sure you can identify and re-identify them. Yet all these objects continuously change. They change because they are in space and time and all object in space and time change. You too are subject to continuous change, whether or not you actually are aware of such changes on a regular basis. In order to highlight this point fetch a photograph of yours taken, let's say, ten years earlier. Now position yourself in front of a mirror. Look at the photograph and then at your reflection in the mirror. I am sure you will notice how different your reflection looks in the mirror compared to the manner you appear in the photograph from ten years earlier. Your current physical appearance is quite different than the way you looked ten years ago.

You have changed physically. But you have also changed in other respects. For instance, your beliefs, desires, aspirations, plans, hopes, emotions, and even some personality traits have changed as you grew up and matured. Now think about the following question: What makes you the same person as you were ten, fifteen, or twenty years earlier? Or to put the same question somewhat differently: Is there any feature, trait, or property that is (a) unique to you and you only; and (b) remained constant throughout all the myriad of other changes that you have undergone? This is in a nutshell the problem of *personal identity*.

The problem of personal identity is a special case of a more general problem. The more general problem is the problem of *identity through* (changes in) *time*. In this chapter, however, we will discuss only the problem of personal identity.

As you were reading these words you naturally might have had some ideas about how to solve this problem. For instance, you might have thought that the experiences that you have had throughout the years are unique to you and are therefore that is what remains constant. But while this idea is a good starting point, ultimately it will not solve the problem. First, notice that your experiences themselves change. Second, there is not one experience that remains constant as you go through life. Third, to call an experience '*mine*' already presupposes that there is an '**I**'; i.e., a *self*, that remains constant through time. Hence, two quite different experiences that happened at different timed and places are *my* experiences because we assume that there is a *self* that grounds our identity through time; this is why these two quite different experiences belong to the *same self*. What is that same self?

Several proposals have been suggested by various thinkers. One very influential such proposal is to entertain the idea that each of us has a *unique soul* that remains constant throughout time. Since the soul is not a physical sort of a thing, it is not in space and maybe not even in time, it is not subject to change like every other object in space and time. The soul-hypothesis has been influential because it was used to serve many other purposes as well. For instance, many people believed in the past and many still believe in survival after the death of the body. One way that such survival can be explained is by holding that we are an amalgam of both a soul and a body. And since the former, unlike the later, is indestructible, it survives the annihilation of the body.

But, alas, there are some serious problems with positing a soul. First, it was never made clear what sort of a thing is a soul. Second, the following question arises: How can something that is not in space and perhaps not even in time be connected, linked, or fused, with our body that is in both space and time? In the absence of clear answers to this and other questions, the soul-hypothesis is deemed by many to be an unsatisfactory solution to the problem of our identity through time.

A second proposal is Locke's view, which is represented as one of the selections in this chapter. Locke thought that the one thing that remains constant throughout time and therefore can ground our identity is the **continuity of the stream of our conscious memories**. Notice how similar Locke's view is to what I thought you entertained earlier; namely, that our self is grounded upon our experiences.

Locke's view, however, faces two serious objections, one of which I have already hinted at in connection with your own idea about grounding the self upon our experiences. The first objection has to do with cases of severe amnesia or even coma. Suppose a person goes into a coma for six months and then wakes up. Clearly, during the period this person was in coma, his stream of memories is broken. Nevertheless we consider the person who emerged from the coma as (in a real sense) the very same person as the one that fell into the coma six months earlier. So **continuity of the stream of our conscious memories cannot be a necessary condition** for identity through time.

The second objection against Locke's idea, and any other variant of it, is even more problematical. In order to see this objection we need to distinguish between two different concepts of memory. The first concept of memory goes something like this. If a person A is said to remembers at time t an event e that occurred in the past, say at time t* that is before t, then A had to be present in the event e at t*. Call this *veridical memory*. Notice that veridical memory presupposes that the person who does the remembering at t is **one and the same person** who was present at the event remembered at a prior time t*.

The second concept of memory, call it **notional memory**, is when a person has the *experience of remembering* some past event e, yet the person was never present when e occurred. In the case of notional memory the mind puts together elements that are already present and, for some reason, dumps the resulting construction into the memory component. In short, notional memory is purely a fabrication of the mind and, therefore, the person was never present in any event that corresponds to the fabricated construct. Therefore, the person who **notionally remembers** need not have been present in any event resembling the one constructed, even if such an event actually occurred.

Now, armed with the distinction between veridical and notional memory, the objection against Locke's account of personal identity should be clear. First, veridical memory cannot be the *basis* of personal identity, since veridical memory *presupposes* personal identity. Second, since notional memory is fabricated by the mind of the person, it cannot be the basis of personal identity because such "memories" are invented and therefore do not require that the person who construct the memory is the same person throughout time. It is quite possible that person A constructs a notional memory of an event in which a different person B actually was present. But we do not wish to claim that A and B are the same person. Therefore, Locke's account of personal identity based on memory will not work.

It seems like the question of personal identity is not as easy to solve as one might initially suppose. It is for this reason, among others, that Hume and others have concluded that the search for a continuing and unchanging self to ground personal identity is an illusion. Hume actually maintained that the concept of the *self* itself is a fabricated notion and there really is no such a thing as a self. I will let you figure out Hume's argument on behalf of this radical and skeptical conclusion.

Identity and Diversity
John Locke

1. Wherein Identity consists

ANOTHER occasion the mind often takes of comparing, is the very being of things, when, considering ANYTHING AS EXISTING AT ANY DETERMINED TIME AND PLACE, we compare it with ITSELF EXISTING AT ANOTHER TIME, and thereon form the ideas of IDENTITY and DIVERSITY. When we see anything to be in any place in any instant of time, we are sure (be it what it will) that it is that very thing, and not another which at that same time exists in another place, how like and undistinguishable soever it may be in all other respects: and in this consists IDENTITY, when the ideas it is attributed to vary not at all from what they were that moment wherein we consider their former existence, and to which we compare the present. For we never finding, nor conceiving it possible, that two things of the same kind should exist in the same place at the same time, we rightly conclude, that, whatever exists anywhere at any time, excludes all of the same kind, and is there itself alone. When therefore we demand whether anything be the SAME or no, it refers always to something that existed such a time in such a place, which it was certain, at that instant, was the same with itself, and no other. From whence it follows, that one thing cannot have two beginnings of existence, nor two things one beginning; it being impossible for two things of the same kind to be or exist in the same instant, in the very same place; or one and the same thing in different places. That, therefore, that had one beginning, is the same thing; and that which had a different beginning in time and place from that, is not the same, but diverse. That which has made the difficulty about this relation has been the little care and attention used in having precise notions of the things to which it is attributed.

2. Identity of Substances

We have the ideas but of three sorts of substances: 1. GOD. 2. FINITE INTELLIGENCES. 3. BODIES.

First, GOD is without beginning, eternal, unalterable, and everywhere, and therefore concerning his identity there can be no doubt.

Secondly, FINITE SPIRITS having had each its determinated time and place of beginning to exist, the relation to that time and place will always determine to each of them its identity, as long as it exists.

Thirdly, The same will hold of every PARTICLE OF MATTER, to which no addition or subtraction of matter being made, it is the same. For, though these three sorts of substances, as we term them, do not exclude one another out of the same place, yet we cannot conceive but that they must necessarily each of them exclude any of the same kind out of the same place: or else the notions and names of identity and diversity would be in vain, and there could be no such distinctions of substances, or anything else one from another. For example: could two bodies be in the same place at the same time; then those two parcels of matter must be one and the same, take them great or little; nay, all bodies must be one and the same. For, by the same reason that two particles of matter may be in one place, all bodies may be in one place: which, when it can be supposed, takes away the distinction of identity and diversity of one and more, and renders it ridiculous. But it being a contradiction that two or more should be one, identity and diversity are relations and ways of comparing well founded, and of use to the understanding.

3. Identity of modes and relations

All other things being but modes or relations ultimately terminated in substances, the identity and diversity of each particular existence of them too will be by the same way determined: only as to things whose existence is in succession, such as are the actions of finite beings, v. g. MOTION and THOUGHT, both which consist in a continued train of succession, concerning THEIR diversity there can be no question: because each perishing the moment it begins, they cannot exist in different times, or in different places, as permanent beings can at different times exist in distant places; and therefore no motion or thought, considered as at different times, can be the same, each part thereof having a different beginning of existence.

4. Principium Individuationis

From what has been said, it is easy to discover what is so much inquired after, the PRINCIPIUM INDIVIDUATIONIS; and that, it is plain, is existence itself; which determines a being of any sort to a particular time and place, incommunicable to two beings of the same kind. This, though it seems easier to conceive in simple substances or modes; yet, when reflected on, is not more difficult in compound ones, if care be taken to what it is applied: v.g. let us suppose an atom, i.e. a continued body under one immutable superficies, existing in a determined time and place; it is evident, that, considered in any instant of its existence, it is in that instant the same with itself. For, being at that instant what it is, and nothing else, it is the same, and so must continue as long as its existence is continued; for so long it will be the same, and no other. In like manner, if two or more atoms be joined together into the same mass, every one of those atoms will be the same, by the foregoing rule: and whilst they exist united together, the mass, consisting of the same atoms, must be the same mass, or the same body, let the parts be ever so differently jumbled. But if one of these atoms be taken away, or one new one added, it is no longer the same mass or the same body. In the state of living creatures, their identity depends not on a mass of the same particles, but on something else. For in them the variation of great parcels of matter alters not the identity: an oak growing from a plant to a great tree, and then lopped, is still the same oak; and a colt grown up to a horse, sometimes fat, sometimes lean, is all the while the same horse: though, in both these cases, there may be a manifest change of the parts; so that truly they are not either of them the same masses of matter, though they be truly one of them the same oak, and the other the same horse. The reason whereof is, that, in these two cases—a MASS OF MATTER and a LIVING BODY—identity is not applied to the same thing.

5. Identity of Vegetables

We must therefore consider wherein an oak differs from a mass of matter, and that seems to me to be in this, that the one is only the cohesion of particles of matter any how united, the other such a disposition of them as constitutes the parts of an oak; and such an organization of those parts as is fit to receive and distribute nourishment, so as to continue and frame the wood, bark, and leaves, &c., of an oak, in which consists the vegetable life. That being then one plant which has such an organization of parts in one coherent body, partaking of one common life, it continues to be the same plant as long as it partakes of the same life, though that life be communicated to new particles of matter vitally united to the living plant, in a like continued organization conformable to that sort of plants. For this organization, being at any one instant in any one collection of matter, is in that particular concrete distinguished from all other, and IS that individual life, which existing constantly from that moment both forwards and backwards, in the same continuity of insensibly succeeding parts united to the living body of the plant, it has that identity which makes the same plant, and all the parts of it, parts of the same plant, during all the time that they exist united in that continued organization, which is fit to convey that common life to all the parts so united.

6. Identity of Animals

The case is not so much different in BRUTES but that any one may hence see what makes an animal and continues it the same. Something we have like this in machines, and may serve to illustrate it. For example, what is a watch? It is plain it is nothing but a fit organization or construction of parts to a certain end, which, when a sufficient force is added to it, it is capable to attain. If we would suppose this machine one continued body, all whose organized parts were repaired, increased, or diminished by a constant addition or separation of insensible parts, with one common life, we should have something very much like the body of an animal; with this difference, That, in an animal the fitness of the organization, and the motion wherein life consists, begin together, the motion coming from within; but in machines the force coming sensibly from without, is often away when the organ is in order, and well fitted to receive it.

7. The Identity of Man

This also shows wherein the identity of the same MAN consists; viz. in nothing but a participation of the same continued life, by constantly fleeting particles of matter, in succession vitally united to the same organized body. He that shall place the identity of man in anything else, but, like that of other animals, in one fitly organized body, taken in any one instant, and from thence continued, under one organization of life, in several successively fleeting particles of matter united to it, will find it hard to make an embryo, one of years, mad and sober, the SAME man, by any supposition, that will not make it possible for Seth, Ismael, Socrates, Pilate, St. Austin, and Caesar Borgia, to be the same man. For if the identity of SOUL ALONE makes the same MAN; and there be nothing in the nature of matter why the same individual spirit may not be united to different bodies, it will be possible that those men, living in distant ages, and of different tempers, may have been the same man: which way of speaking must be from a very strange use of the word man, applied to an idea out of which body and shape are excluded. And that way of speaking would agree yet worse with the notions of those philosophers who allow of transmigration, and are of opinion that the souls of men may, for their miscarriages, be detruded into the bodies of beasts, as fit habitations, with organs suited to the satisfaction of their brutal inclinations. But yet I think nobody, could he be sure that the SOUL of Heliogabalus were in one of his hogs, would yet say that hog were a MAN or Heliogabalus.

8. Idea of Identity suited to the Idea it is applied to

It is not therefore unity of substance that comprehends all sorts of identity, or will determine it in every case; but to conceive and judge of it aright, we must consider what idea the word it is applied to stands for: it being one thing to be the same SUBSTANCE, another the same MAN, and a third the same PERSON, if PERSON, MAN, and SUB-STANCE, are three names standing for three different ideas;—for such as is the idea belonging to that name, such must be the identity; which, if it had been a little more carefully attended to, would possibly have prevented a great deal of that confusion which often occurs about this matter, with no small seeming difficulties, especially concerning PERSONAL identity, which therefore we shall in the next place a little consider.

9. Same man

An animal is a living organized body; and consequently the same animal, as we have observed, is the same continued LIFE communicated to different particles of matter, as they happen successively to be united to that organized living body. And whatever is talked of other definitions, ingenious observation puts it past doubt, that the idea in our minds, of which the sound man in our mouths is the sign, is nothing else but of an animal of such a certain form. Since I think I may be confident, that, whoever should see a creature of his own shape or make, though it had no more reason all its life than a cat or a parrot, would call him still a MAN; or whoever should hear a cat or a parrot discourse, reason, and philosophize, would call or think it nothing but a CAT or a PARROT; and say, the one was a dull irrational man, and the other a very intelligent rational parrot.

10. Same man

For I presume it is not the idea of a thinking or rational being alone that makes the IDEA OF A MAN in most people's sense: but of a body, so and so shaped, joined to it; and if that be the idea of a man, the same successive body not shifted all at once, must, as well as the same immaterial spirit, go to the making of the same man.

11. Personal Identity

This being premised, to find wherein personal identity consists, we must consider what PERSON stands for;—which, I think, is a thinking intelligent being, that has reason and reflection, and can consider itself as itself, the same thinking thing, in different times and places; which it does only by that consciousness which is inseparable from thinking, and, as it seems to me, essential to it: it being impossible for any one to perceive without PERCEIVING that he does perceive. When we see, hear, smell, taste, feel, meditate, or will anything, we know that we do so. Thus it is always as to our present sensations and perceptions: and by this every one is to himself that which he calls SELF:—it not being considered, in this case, whether the same self be continued in the same or divers substances. For, since consciousness always accompanies thinking, and it is that which makes every one to be what he calls self, and thereby distinguishes himself from all other thinking things, in this alone consists personal identity, i.e. the sameness of a rational being: and as far as this consciousness can be extended backwards to any past action or thought, so far reaches the identity of that person; it is the same self now it was then; and it is by the same self with this present one that now reflects on it, that that action was done.

12. Consciousness makes personal Identity

But it is further inquired, whether it be the same identical substance. This few would think they had reason to doubt of, if these perceptions, with their consciousness, always remained present in the mind, whereby the same thinking thing would be always consciously present, and, as would be thought, evidently the same to itself. But that which seems to make the difficulty is this, that this consciousness being interrupted always by forgetfulness, there being no moment of our lives wherein we have the whole train of all our past actions before our eyes in one view, but even the best memories losing the sight of one part whilst they are viewing another; and we sometimes, and that the greatest part of our lives, not reflecting on our past selves, being intent on our present thoughts, and in sound sleep having no thoughts at all, or at least none with that consciousness which remarks our waking thoughts,—I say, in all these cases, our consciousness being interrupted, and we losing the sight of our past selves, doubts are raised whether we are the same thinking thing, i.e. the same SUBSTANCE or no. Which, however reasonable or unreasonable, concerns not PERSONAL identity at all. The question being what makes the same person; and not whether it be the same identical substance, which always thinks in the same person, which, in this case, matters not at all: different substances, by the same consciousness (where they do partake in it) being united into one person, as well as different bodies by the same life are united into one animal, whose identity is preserved in that change of substances by the unity of one continued life. For, it being the same consciousness that makes a man be himself to himself, personal identity depends on that only, whether it be annexed solely to one individual substance, or can be continued in a succession of several substances. For as far as any intelligent being CAN repeat the idea of any past action with the same consciousness it had of it at first, and with the same consciousness it has of any present action; so far it is the same personal self. For it is by the consciousness it has of its present thoughts and actions, that it is SELF TO ITSELF now, and so will be the same self, as far as the same consciousness can extend to actions past or to come; and would be by distance of time, or change of substance, no more two persons, than a man be two men by wearing other clothes to-day than he did yesterday, with a long or a short sleep between: the same consciousness uniting those distant actions into the same person, whatever substances contributed to their production.

13. Personal Identity in Change of Substance

That this is so, we have some kind of evidence in our very bodies, all whose particles, whilst vitally united to this same thinking conscious self, so that WE FEEL when they are touched, and are affected by, and conscious of good or harm that happens to them, are a part of ourselves; i.e. of our thinking conscious self. Thus, the limbs of his body are to every one a part of himself; he sympathizes and is concerned for them. Cut off a hand, and thereby separate it from that consciousness he had of its heat, cold, and other affections, and it is then no longer a part of that which is himself, any more than the remotest part of matter. Thus, we see the SUBSTANCE whereof personal self consisted at one time may be varied at another, without the change of personal identity; there being no question about the same person, though the limbs which but now were a part of it, be cut off.

14. Personality in Change of Substance

But the question is, Whether if the same substance which thinks be changed, it can be the same person; or, remaining the same, it can be different persons?

And to this I answer: First, This can be no question at all to those who place thought in a purely material animal constitution, void of an immaterial substance. For, whether their supposition be true or no, it is plain they conceive personal identity preserved in something else than identity of substance; as animal identity is preserved in identity of life, and not of substance. And therefore those who place thinking in an immaterial substance only, before they can come to deal with these men, must show why personal identity cannot be preserved in the change of immaterial substances, or variety of particular immaterial substances, as well as animal identity is preserved in the change of material substances, or variety of particular bodies: unless they will say, it is one immaterial spirit that makes the same life in brutes, as it is one immaterial spirit that makes the same person in men; which the Cartesians at least will not admit, for fear of making brutes thinking things too.

15. Whether in Change of thinking Substances there can be one Person

But next, as to the first part of the question, Whether, if the same thinking substance (supposing immaterial substances only to think) be changed, it can be the same person? I answer, that cannot be resolved but by those who know there can what kind of substances they are that do think; and whether the consciousness of past actions can be transferred from one thinking substance to another. I grant were the same consciousness the same individual action it could not: but it being a present representation of a past action, why it may not be possible, that that may be represented to the mind to have been which really never was, will remain to be shown. And therefore how far the consciousness of past actions is annexed to any individual agent, so that another cannot possibly have it, will be hard for us to determine, till we know what kind of action it is that cannot be done without a reflex act of perception accompanying it, and how performed by thinking substances, who cannot think without being conscious of it. But that which we call the same consciousness, not being the same individual act, why one intellectual substance may not have represented to it, as done by itself, what IT never did, and was perhaps done by some other agent—why, I say, such a representation may not possibly be without reality of matter of fact, as well as several representations in dreams are, which yet whilst dreaming we take for true—will be difficult to conclude from the nature of things. And that it never is so, will by us, till we have clearer views of the nature of thinking substances, be best resolved into the goodness of God; who, as far as the happiness or misery of any of his sensible creatures is concerned in it, will not, by a fatal error of theirs, transfer from one to another that consciousness which draws reward or punishment with it. How far this may be an argument against those who would place thinking in a system of fleeting animal spirits, I leave to be considered. But yet, to return to the question before us, it must be allowed, that, if the same consciousness (which, as has been shown, is quite a different thing from the same numerical figure or motion in body) can be transferred from one thinking substance to another, it will be possible that two thinking substances may make but one person. For the same consciousness being preserved, whether in the same or different substances, the personal identity is preserved.

16. Whether, the same immaterial Substance remaining, there can be two Persons

As to the second part of the question, Whether the same immaterial substance remaining, there may be two distinct persons; which question seems to me to be built on this,— Whether the same immaterial being, being conscious of the action of its past duration, may be wholly stripped of all the consciousness of its past existence, and lose it beyond the power of ever retrieving it again: and so as it were beginning a new account from a new period, have a consciousness that CANNOT reach beyond this new state. All those who hold pre-existence are evidently of this mind; since they allow the soul to have no remaining consciousness of what it did in that pre-existent state, either wholly separate from body, or informing any other body; and if they should not, it is plain experience would be against them. So that personal identity, reaching no further than consciousness reaches, a pre-existent spirit not having continued so many ages in a state of silence, must needs make different persons. Suppose a Christian Platonist or a Pythagorean should, upon God's having ended all his works of creation the seventh day, think his soul hath existed ever since; and should imagine it has revolved in several human bodies; as I once met with one, who was persuaded his had been the SOUL of Socrates (how reasonably I will not dispute; this I know, that in the post he filled, which was no inconsiderable one, he passed for a very rational man, and the press has shown that he wanted not parts or learning;)—would any one say, that he, being not conscious of any of Socrates's actions or thoughts, could be the same PERSON with Socrates? Let any one reflect upon him-self, and conclude that he has in himself an immaterial spirit, which is that which thinks in him, and, in the constant change of his body keeps him the same: and is that which he calls HIMSELF: let his also suppose it to be the same soul that was in Nestor or Ther-sites, at the siege of Troy, (for souls being, as far as we know anything of them, in their nature indifferent to any parcel of matter, the supposition has no apparent absurdity in it,) which it may have been, as well as it is now the soul of any other man: but he now having no consciousness of any of the actions either of Nestor or Thersites, does or can he conceive himself the same person with either of them? Can he be concerned in either of their actions? attribute them to himself, or think them his own more than the actions of any other men that ever existed? So that this consciousness, not reaching to any of the actions of either of those men, he is no more one SELF with either of them than of the soul of immaterial spirit that now informs him had been created, and began to exist, when it began to inform his present body; though it were never so true, that the same SPIRIT that informed Nestor's or Thersites' body were numerically the same that now informs his. For this would no more make him the same person with Nestor, than if some of the particles of smaller that were once a part of Nestor were now a part of this man the same immaterial substance, without the same consciousness, no more making the same person, by being united to any body, than the same particle of matter, without conscious-ness, united to any body, makes the same person. But let him once find himself conscious of any of the actions of Nestor, he then finds himself the same person with Nestor.

17. The body, as well as the soul, goes to the making of a Man

And thus may we be able, without any difficulty, to conceive the same person at the res-urrection, though in a body not exactly in make or parts the same which he had here,—the same consciousness going along with the soul that inhabits it. But yet the soul alone, in the change of bodies, would scarce to any one but to him that makes the soul the man, be enough to make the same man. For should the soul of a prince, carrying with it the consciousness of the prince's past life, enter and inform the body of a cobbler, as soon as deserted by his own soul, every one sees he would be the same PERSON with the prince, accountable only for the prince's actions: but who would say it was the same MAN? The body too goes to the making the man, and would, I guess, to everybody determine the man in this case, wherein the soul, with all its princely thoughts about it, would not make another man: but he would be the same cobbler to every one besides himself. I know that, in the ordinary way of speaking, the same person, and the same man, stand for one and the same thing. And indeed every one will always have a liberty to speak as he pleases, and to apply what articulate sounds to what ideas he thinks fit, and change them as often as he pleases. But yet, when we will inquire what makes the same SPIRIT,

MAN, or PERSON, we must fix the ideas of spirit, man, or person in our minds; and having resolved with ourselves what we mean by them, it will not be hard to determine, in either of them, or the like, when it is the same, and when not.

18. Consciousness alone unites actions into the same Person

But though the same immaterial substance or soul does not alone, wherever it be, and in whatsoever state, make the same MAN; yet it is plain, consciousness, as far as ever it can be extended—should it be to ages past—unites existences and actions very remote in time into the same PERSON, as well as it does the existences and actions of the immediately preceding moment: so that whatever has the consciousness of present and past actions, is the same person to whom they both belong. Had I the same consciousness that I saw the ark and Noah's flood, as that I saw an overflowing of the Thames last winter, or as that I write now, I could no more doubt that I who write this now, that saw the Thames overflowed last winter, and that viewed the flood at the general deluge, was the same SELF,—place that self in what SUBSTANCE you please—than that I who write this am the same MYSELF now whilst I write (whether I consist of all the same substance material or immaterial, or no) that I was yesterday. For as to this point of being the same self, it matters not whether this present self be made up of the same or other substances—I being as much concerned, and as justly accountable for any action that was done a thousand years since, appropriated to me now by this self-consciousness, as I am for what I did the last moment.

19. Self depends on Consciousness, not on Substance

SELF is that conscious thinking thing,—whatever substance made up of, (whether spiritual or material, simple or compounded, it matters not)—which is sensible or conscious of pleasure and pain, capable of happiness or misery, and so is concerned for itself, as far as that consciousness extends. Thus every one finds that, whilst comprehended under that consciousness, the little finger is as much a part of himself as what is most so. Upon separation of this little finger, should this consciousness go along with the little finger, and leave the rest of the body, it is evident the little finger would be the person, the same person; and self then would have nothing to do with the rest of the body. As in this case it is the consciousness that goes along with the substance, when one part is separate from another, which makes the same person, and constitutes this inseparable self: so it is in reference to substances remote in time. That with which the consciousness of this present thinking thing CAN join itself, makes the same person, and is one self with it, and with nothing else; and so attributes to itself, and owns all the actions of that thing, as its own, as far as that consciousness reaches, and no further; as every one who reflects will perceive.

20. Persons, not Substances, the Objects of Reward and Punishment

In this personal identity is founded all the right and justice of reward and punishment; happiness and misery being that for which every one is concerned for HIMSELF, and not mattering what becomes of any SUBSTANCE, not joined to, or affected with that consciousness. For, as it is evident in the instance I gave but now, if the consciousness went along with the little finger when it was cut off, that would be the same self which was concerned for the whole body yesterday, as making part of itself, whose actions then it cannot but admit as its own now. Though, if the same body should still live, and immediately from the separation of the little finger have its own peculiar consciousness, whereof the little finger knew nothing, it would not at all be concerned for it, as a part of itself, or could own any of its actions, or have any of them imputed to him.

21. Which shows wherein Personal identity consists

This may show us wherein personal identity consists: not in the identity of substance, but, as I have said, in the identity of consciousness, wherein if Socrates and the present mayor of Queenborough agree, they are the same person: if the same Socrates waking and sleeping do not partake of the same consciousness, Socrates waking and sleeping is not the same person. And to punish Socrates waking for what sleeping Socrates thought, and waking Socrates was never conscious of, would be no more of right, than to punish one twin for what his brother-twin did, whereof he knew nothing, because their outsides were so like, that they could not be distinguished; for such twins have been seen.

22. Absolute oblivion separates what is thus forgotten from the person, but not from the man

But yet possibly it will still be objected,—Suppose I wholly lose the memory of some parts of my life, beyond a possibility of retrieving them, so that perhaps I shall never be conscious of them again; yet am I not the same person that did those actions, had those thoughts that I once was conscious of, though I have now forgot them? To which I answer, that we must here take notice what the word I is applied to; which, in this case, is the MAN only. And the same man being presumed to be the same person, I is easily here supposed to stand also for the same person. But if it be possible for the same man to have distinct incommunicable consciousness at different times, it is past doubt the same man would at different times make different persons; which, we see, is the sense of mankind in the solemnest declaration of their opinions, human laws not punishing the mad man for the sober man's actions, nor the sober man for what the mad man did,—thereby making them two persons: which is somewhat explained by our way of speaking in English when we say such an one is 'not himself,' or is 'beside himself'; in which phrases it is insinuated, as if those who now, or at least first used them, thought that self was changed; the selfsame person was no longer in that man.

23. Difference between Identity of Man and of Person

But yet it is hard to conceive that Socrates, the same individual man, should be two persons. To help us a little in this, we must consider what is meant by Socrates, or the same individual MAN.

First, it must be either the same individual, immaterial, thinking substance; in short, the same numerical soul, and nothing else.

Secondly, or the same animal, without any regard to an immaterial soul.

Thirdly, or the same immaterial spirit united to the same animal.

Now, take which of these suppositions you please, it is impossible to make personal identity to consist in anything but consciousness; or reach any further than that does.

For, by the first of them, it must be allowed possible that a man born of different women, and in distant times, may be the same man. A way of speaking which, whoever admits, must allow it possible for the same man to be two distinct persons, as any two that have lived in different ages without the knowledge of one another's thoughts.

By the second and third, Socrates, in this life and after it, cannot be the same man any way, but by the same consciousness; and so making human identity to consist in the same thing wherein we place personal identity, there will be difficulty to allow the same man to be the same person. But then they who place human identity in consciousness only, and not in something else, must consider how they will make the infant Socrates the same man with Socrates after the resurrection. But whatsoever to some men makes a man, and consequently the same individual man, wherein perhaps few are agreed, personal identity can by us be placed in nothing but consciousness, (which is that alone which makes what we call SELF,) without involving us in great absurdities.

24. Not the substance with which the consciousness may be united

But is not a man drunk and sober the same person? why else is he punished for the fact he commits when drunk, though he be never afterwards conscious of it? Just as much the same person as a man that walks, and does other things in his sleep, is the same person, and is answerable for any mischief he shall do in it. Human laws punish both, with a justice suitable to THEIR way of knowledge;—because, in these cases, they cannot distinguish certainly what is real, what counterfeit: and so the ignorance in drunkenness or sleep is not admitted as a plea. But in the Great Day, wherein the secrets of all hearts shall be laid open, it may be reasonable to think, no one shall be made to answer for what he knows nothing of; but shall receive his doom, his conscience accusing or excusing him.

25. Consciousness alone unites remote existences into one Person

Nothing but consciousness can unite remote existences into the same person: the identity of substance will not do it; for whatever substance there is, however framed, without consciousness there is no person: and a carcass may be a person, as well as any sort of substance be so, without consciousness.

Could we suppose two distinct incommunicable consciousnesses acting the same body, the one constantly by day, the other by night; and, on the other side, the same consciousness, acting by intervals, two distinct bodies: I ask, in the first case, whether the day and the night—man would not be two as distinct persons as Socrates and Plato? And whether, in the second case, there would not be one person in two distinct bodies, as much as one man is the same in two distinct clothings? Nor is it at all material to say, that this same, and this distinct consciousness, in the cases above mentioned, is owing to the same and distinct immaterial substances, bringing it with them to those bodies; which, whether true or no, alters not the case: since it is evident the personal identity would equally be determined by the consciousness, whether that consciousness were annexed to some individual immaterial substance or no. For, granting that the thinking substance in man must be necessarily supposed immaterial, it is evident that immaterial thinking thing may sometimes part with its past consciousness, and be restored to it again: as appears in the forgetfulness men often have of their past actions; and the mind many times recovers the memory of a past consciousness, which it had lost for twenty years together. Make these intervals of memory and forgetfulness to take their turns regularly by day and night, and you have two persons with the same immaterial spirit, as much as in the former instance two persons with the same body. So that self is not determined by identity or diversity of substance, which it cannot be sure of, but only by identity of consciousness.

26. Not the substance with which the consciousness may be united

Indeed it may conceive the substance whereof it is now made up to have existed formerly, united in the same conscious being: but, consciousness removed, that substance is no more itself, or makes no more a part of it, than any other substance; as is evident in the instance we have already given of a limb cut off, of whose heat, or cold, or other affections, having no longer any consciousness, it is no more of a man's self than any other matter of the universe. In like manner it will be in reference to any immaterial substance, which is void of that consciousness whereby I am myself to myself: so that I cannot upon recollection join with that present consciousness whereby I am now myself, it is, in that part of its existence, no more MYSELF than any other immaterial being. For, whatsoever any substance has thought or done, which I cannot recollect, and by my consciousness make my own thought and action, it will no more belong to me, whether a part of me thought or did it, than if it had been thought or done by any other immaterial being anywhere existing.

27. Consciousness unites substances, material or spiritual, with the same personality

I agree, the more probable opinion is, that this consciousness is annexed to, and the affection of, one individual immaterial substance.

But let men, according to their diverse hypotheses, resolve of that as they please. This every intelligent being, sensible of happiness or misery, must grant—that there is something that is HIMSELF, that he is concerned for, and would have happy; that this self has existed in a continued duration more than one instant, and therefore it is possible may exist, as it has done, months and years to come, without any certain bounds to be set to its duration; and may be the same self, by the same consciousness continued on for the future. And thus, by this consciousness he finds himself to be the same self which did such and such an action some years since, by which he comes to be happy or miserable now. In all which account of self, the same numerical SUBSTANCE is not considered a making the same self; but the same continued CONSCIOUSNESS, in which several substances may have been united, and again separated from it, which, whilst they continued in a vital union with that wherein this consciousness then resided, made a part of that same self. Thus any part of our bodies, vitally united to that which is conscious in us, makes a part of ourselves: but upon separation from the vital union by which that consciousness is communicated, that which a moment since was part of ourselves, is now no more so than a part of another man's self is a part of me: and it is not impossible but in a little time may become a real part of another person. And so we have the same numerical substance become a part of two different persons; and the same person preserved under the change of various substances. Could we suppose any spirit wholly stripped of all its memory of consciousness of past actions, as we find our minds always are of a great part of ours, and sometimes of them all; the union or separation of such a spiritual substance would make no variation of personal identity, any more than that of any particle of matter does. Any substance vitally united to the present thinking being is a part of that very same self which now is; anything united to it by a consciousness of former actions, makes also a part of the same self, which is the same both then and now.

28. Person a forensic Term

PERSON, as I take it, is the name for this self. Wherever a man finds what he calls himself, there, I think, another may say is the same person. It is a forensic term, appropriating actions and their merit; and so belongs only to intelligent agents, capable of a law, and happiness, and misery. This personality extends itself beyond present existence to what is past, only by consciousness,—whereby it becomes concerned and accountable; owns and imputes to itself past actions, just upon the same ground and for the same reason as it does the present. All which is founded in a concern for happiness, the unavoidable concomitant of consciousness; that which is conscious of pleasure and pain, desiring that that self that is conscious should be happy. And therefore whatever past actions it cannot reconcile or APPROPRIATE to that present self by consciousness, it can be no more concerned in than if they had never been done: and to receive pleasure or pain, i.e. reward or punishment, on the account of any such action, is all one as to be made happy or miserable in its first being, without any demerit at all. For, supposing a MAN punished now for what he had done in another life, whereof he could be made to have no consciousness at all, what difference is there between that punishment and being CREATED miserable? And therefore, conformable to this, the apostle tells us, that, at the great day, when every one shall 'receive according to his doings, the secrets of all hearts shall be laid open.' The sentence shall be justified by the consciousness all persons shall have, that THEY THEMSELVES, in what bodies soever they appear, or what substances soever that consciousness adheres to, are the SAME that committed those actions, and deserve that punishment for them.

29. Suppositions that look strange are pardonable in our ignorance

I am apt enough to think I have, in treating of this subject, made some suppositions that will look strange to some readers, and possibly they are so in themselves. But yet, I think they are such as are pardonable, in this ignorance we are in of the nature of that thinking thing that is in us, and which we look on as OURSELVES. Did we know what it was; or how it was tied to a certain system of fleeting animal spirits; or whether it could or could not perform its operations of thinking and memory out of a body organized as ours is; and whether it has pleased God that no one such spirit shall ever be united to any but one such body, upon the right constitution of whose organs its memory should depend; we might see the absurdity of some of those suppositions I have made. But taking, as we ordinarily now do (in the dark concerning these matters,) the soul of a man for an immaterial substance, independent from matter, and indifferent alike to it all; there can, from the nature of things, be no absurdity at all to suppose that the same SOUL may at different times be united to different BODIES, and with them make up for that time one MAN: as well as we suppose a part of a sheep's body yesterday should be a part of a man's body to-morrow, and in that union make a vital part of Meliboeus himself, as well as it did of his ram.

30. The Difficulty from ill Use of Names

To conclude: Whatever substance begins to exist, it must, during its existence, necessarily be the same: whatever compositions of substances begin to exist, during the union of those substances, the concrete must be the same: whatsoever mode begins to exist, during its existence it is the same: and so if the composition be of distinct substances and different modes, the same rule holds. Whereby it will appear, that the difficulty or obscurity that has been about this matter rather rises from the names ill-used, than from any obscurity in things themselves. For whatever makes the specific idea to which the name is applied, if that idea be steadily kept to, the distinction of anything into the same and divers will easily be conceived, and there can arise no doubt about it.

31. Continuance of that which we have made to be our complex idea of man makes the same man

For, supposing a rational spirit be the idea of a MAN, it is easy to know what is the same man, viz. the same spirit—whether separate or in a body—will be the SAME MAN. Supposing a rational spirit vitally united to a body of a certain conformation of parts to make a man; whilst that rational spirit, with that vital conformation of parts, though continued in a fleeting successive body, remains, it will be the SAME MAN. But if to any one the idea of a man be but the vital union of parts in a certain shape; as long as that vital union and shape remain in a concrete, no otherwise the same but by a continued succession of fleeting particles, it will be the SAME MAN. For, whatever be the composition whereof the complex idea is made, whenever existence makes it one particular thing under any denomination, THE SAME EXISTENCE CONTINUED preserves it the SAME individual under the same denomination.

Of Personal Identity

David Hume

There are some philosophers who imagine we are every moment intimately conscious of what we call our SELF; that we feel its existence and its continuance in existence; and are certain, beyond the evidence of a demonstration, both o its perfect identity and simplicity. The strongest sensation, the most violent passion, say they, instead of distracting us from this view, only fix it the more intensely, and make us consider their influence on self either by their pain or pleasure. To attempt a farther proof of this were to weaken its evidence; since no proof can be derived from any fact, of which we are so intimately conscious; nor is there any thing, of which we can be certain, if we doubt of this.

Unluckily all these positive assertions are contrary to that very experience, which is pleaded for them, nor have we any idea of self, after the manner it is here explained. For from what impression coued this idea be derived? This question it is impossible to answer without a manifest contradiction and absurdity; and yet it is a question, which must necessarily be answered, if we would have the idea of self pass for clear and intelligible, It must be some one impression, that gives rise to every real idea. But self or person is not any one impression, but that to which our several impressions and ideas are supposed to have a reference. If any impression gives rise to the idea of self, that impression must continue invariably the same, through the whole course of our lives; since self is supposed to exist after that manner. But there is no impression constant and invariable. Pain and pleasure, grief and joy, passions and sensations succeed each other, and never all exist at the same time. It cannot, therefore, be from any of these impressions, or from any other, that the idea of self is derived; and consequently there is no such idea.

But farther, what must become of all our particular perceptions upon this hypothesis? All these are different, and distinguishable, and separable from each other, and may be separately considered, and may exist separately, and have no Deed of tiny thing to support their existence. After what manner, therefore, do they belong to self; and how are they connected with it? For my part, when I enter most intimately into what I call myself, I always stumble on some particular perception or other, of heat or cold, light or shade, love or hatred, pain or pleasure. I never can catch myself at any time without a perception, and never can observe any thing but the perception. When my perceptions are removed for any time, as by sound sleep; so long am I insensible of myself, and may truly be said not to exist. And were all my perceptions removed by death, and coued I neither think, nor feel, nor see, nor love, nor hate after the dissolution of my body, I should be entirely annihilated, nor do I conceive what is farther requisite to make me a perfect non-entity. If any one, upon serious and unprejudiced reflection thinks he has a different notion of himself, I must confess I call reason no longer with him. All I can allow him is, that he may be in the right as well as I, and that we are essentially different in this particular. He may, perhaps, perceive something simple and continued, which he calls himself; though I am certain there is no such principle in me.

But setting aside some metaphysicians of this kind, I may venture to affirm of the rest of mankind, that they are nothing but a bundle or collection of different perceptions, which succeed each other with an inconceivable rapidity, and are in a perpetual flux and movement. Our eyes cannot turn in their sockets without varying our perceptions. Our thought is still more variable than our sight; and all our other senses and faculties contribute to this change; nor is there any single power of the soul, which remains unalterably the same, perhaps for one moment. The mind is a kind of theatre, where several perceptions successively make their appearance; pass, re-pass, glide away, and mingle in an infinite variety of postures and situations. There is properly no simplicity in it at one time, nor identity in different; whatever natural propension we may have to imagine that simplicity and identity. The comparison of the theatre must not mislead us. They are the successive perceptions only, that constitute the mind; nor have we the most distant notion of the place, where these scenes are represented, or of the materials, of which it is composed.

What then gives us so great a propension to ascribe an identity to these successive perceptions, and to suppose ourselves possest of an invariable and uninterrupted existence through the whole course of our lives? In order to answer this question, we must distinguish betwixt personal identity, as it regards our thought or imagination, and as it regards our passions or the concern we take in ourselves. The first is our present subject; and to explain it perfectly we must take the matter pretty deep, and account for that identity, which we attribute to plants and animals; there being a great analogy betwixt it, and the identity of a self or person.

We have a distinct idea of an object, that remains invariable and uninterrupted through a supposed variation of time; and this idea we call that of identity or sameness. We have also a distinct idea of several different objects existing in succession, and connected together by a close relation; and this to an accurate view affords as perfect a notion of diversity, as if there was no manner of relation among the objects. But though these two ideas of identity, and a succession of related objects be in themselves perfectly distinct, and even contrary, yet it is certain, that in our common way of thinking they are generally confounded with each other. That action of the imagination, by which we consider the uninterrupted and invariable object, and that by which we reflect on the succession of related objects, are almost the same to the feeling, nor is there much more effort of thought required in the latter case than in the former. The relation facilitates the transition of the mind from one object to another, and renders its passage as smooth as if it contemplated one continued object. This resemblance is the cause of the confusion and mistake, and makes us substitute the notion of identity, instead of that of related objects. However at one instant we may consider the related succession as variable or interrupted, we are sure the next to ascribe to it a perfect identity, and regard it as enviable and uninterrupted. Our propensity to this mistake is so great from the resemblance above-mentioned, that we fall into it before we are aware; and though we incessantly correct ourselves by reflection, and return to a more accurate method of thinking, yet we cannot long sustain our philosophy, or take off this biass from the imagination. Our last resource is to yield to it, and boldly assert that these different related objects are in effect the same, however interrupted and variable. In order to justify to ourselves this absurdity, we often feign some new and unintelligible principle, that connects the objects together, and prevents their interruption or variation. Thus we feign the continued existence of the perceptions of our senses, to remove the interruption: and run into the notion of a soul, and self, and substance, to disguise the variation. But we may farther observe, that where we do not give rise to such a fiction, our propension to confound identity with relation is so great, that we are apt to imagine [FN 10] something unknown and mysterious, connecting the parts, beside their relation; and this I take to be the case with regard to the identity we ascribe to plants and vegetables. And even when this does not take place, we still feel a propensity to confound these ideas, though we a-re not able fully to satisfy ourselves in that particular, nor find any thing invariable and uninterrupted to justify our notion of identity.

We now proceed to explain the nature of personal identity, which has become so great a question ill philosophy, especially of late years in England, where all the abstruser sciences are studied with a peculiar ardour and application. And here it is evident, the same method of reasoning must be continued which has so successfully explained the identity of plants, and animals, and ships, and houses, and of all the compounded and changeable productions either of art or nature. The identity, which we ascribe to the mind of man, is only a fictitious one, and of a like kind with that which we ascribe to vegetables and animal bodies. It cannot, therefore, have a different origin, but must proceed from a like operation of the imagination upon like objects.

But lest this argument should not convince the reader; though in my opinion perfectly decisive; let him weigh the following reasoning, which is still closer and more immediate. It is evident, that the identity, which we attribute to the human mind, however perfect we may imagine it to be, is not able to run the several different perceptions into one, and make them lose their characters of distinction and difference, which are essential to them. It is still true, that every distinct perception, which enters into the composition of the mind, is a distinct existence, and is different, and distinguishable, and separable from every other perception, either contemporary or successive. But, as, notwithstanding this distinction and separability, we suppose the whole train of perceptions to be united by identity, a question naturally arises concerning this relation of identity; whether it be something that really binds our several perceptions together, or only associates their ideas in the imagination. That is, in other words, whether in pronouncing concerning the identity of a person, we observe some real bond among his perceptions, or only feel one among the ideas we form of them. This question we might easily decide, if we would recollect what has been already proud at large, that the understanding never observes any real connexion among objects, and that even the union of cause and effect, when strictly examined, resolves itself into a customary association of ideas. For from thence it evidently follows, that identity is nothing really belonging to these different perceptions, and uniting them together; but is merely a quality, which we attribute to them, because of the union of their ideas in the imagination, when we reflect upon them. Now the only qualities, which can give ideas an union in the imagination, are these three relations above-mentioned. There are the uniting principles in the ideal world, and without them every distinct object is separable by the mind, and may be separately considered, and appears not to have any more connexion with any other object, than if disjoined by the greatest difference and remoteness. It is, therefore, on some of these three relations of resemblance, contiguity and causation, that identity depends; and as the very essence of these relations consists in their producing an easy transition of ideas; it follows, that our notions of personal identity, proceed entirely from the smooth and uninterrupted progress of the thought along a train of connected ideas, according to the principles above-explained.

The only question, therefore, which remains, is, by what relations this uninterrupted progress of our thought is produced, when we consider the successive existence of a mind or thinking person. And here it is evident we must confine ourselves to resemblance and causation, and must drop contiguity, which has little or no influence in the present case.

To begin with resemblance; suppose we coued see clearly into the breast of another, and observe that succession of perceptions, which constitutes his mind or thinking principle, and suppose that he always preserves the memory of a considerable part of past perceptions; it is evident that nothing coued more contribute to the bestowing a relation on this succession amidst all its variations. For what is the memory but a faculty, by which we raise up the images of past perceptions? And as an image necessarily resembles its object, must not. The frequent placing of these resembling perceptions in the chain of thought, convey the imagination more easily from one link to another, and make the whole seem like the continuance of one object? In this particular, then, the memory not only discovers the identity, but also contributes to its production, by producing the relation of resemblance among the perceptions. The case is the same whether we consider ourselves or others.

As to causation; we may observe, that the true idea of the human mind, is to consider it as a system of different perceptions or different existences, which are linked together by the relation of cause and effect, and mutually produce, destroy, influence, and modify each other. Our impressions give rise to their correspondent ideas; said these ideas in their turn produce other impressions. One thought chaces another, and draws after it a third, by which it is expelled in its turn. In this respect, I cannot compare the soul more properly to any thing than to a republic or commonwealth, in which the several members are united by the reciprocal ties of government and subordination, and give rise to other persons, who propagate the same republic in the incessant changes of its parts. And as the same individual republic may not only change its members, but also its laws and constitutions; in like manner the same person may vary his character and disposition, as well as his impressions and ideas, without losing his identity. Whatever changes he endures, his several parts are still connected by the relation of causation. And in this view our identity with regard to the passions serves to corroborate that with regard to the imagination, by the making our distant perceptions influence each other, and by giving us a present concern for our past or future pains or pleasures.

As a memory alone acquaints us with the continuance and extent of this succession of perceptions, it is to be considered, upon that account chiefly, as the source of personal identity. Had we no memory, we never should have any notion of causation, nor consequently of that chain of causes and effects, which constitute our self or person. But having once acquired this notion of causation from the memory, we can extend the same chain of causes, and consequently the identity of car persons beyond our memory, and can comprehend times, and circumstances, and actions, which we have entirely forgot, but suppose in general to have existed. For how few of our past actions are there, of which we have any memory? Who can tell me, for instance, what were his thoughts and actions on the 1st of January 1715, the 11th of March 1719, and the 3rd of August 1733? Or will he affirm, because he has entirely forgot the incidents of these days, that the present self is not the same person with the self of that time; and by that means overturn all the most established notions of personal identity? In this view, therefore, memory does not so much produce as discover personal identity, by shewing us the relation of cause and effect among our different perceptions. It will be incumbent on those, who affirm that memory produces entirely our personal identity, to give a reason why we cm thus extend our identity beyond our memory.

The whole of this doctrine leads us to a conclusion, which is of great importance in the present affair, viz. that all the nice and subtile questions concerning personal identity can never possibly be decided, and are to be regarded rather as gramatical than as philosophical difficulties. Identity depends on the relations of ideas; and these relations produce identity, by means of that easy transition they occasion. But as the relations, and the easiness of the transition may diminish by insensible degrees, we have no just standard, by which we can decide any dispute concerning the time, when they acquire or lose a title to the name of identity. All the disputes concerning the identity of connected objects are merely verbal, except so fax as the relation of parts gives rise to some fiction or imaginary principle of union, as we have already observed.

What I have said concerning the first origin and uncertainty of our notion of identity, as applied to the human mind, may be extended with little or no variation to that of simplicity. An object, whose different co-existent parts are bound together by a close relation, operates upon the imagination after much the same manner as one perfectly simple and indivisible and requires not a much greater stretch of thought in order to its conception. From this similarity of operation we attribute a simplicity to it, and feign a principle of union as the support of this simplicity, and the center of all the different parts and qualities of the object.

Thus we have finished our examination of the several systems of philosophy, both of the intellectual and natural world; and in our miscellaneous way of reasoning have been led into several topics; which will either illustrate and confirm some preceding part of this discourse, or prepare the way for our following opinions. It is now time to return to a more close examination of our subject, and to proceed in the accurate anatomy of human nature, having fully explained the nature of our judgment and understandings.

Immortality

Do we survive death? This question haunted human beings since we existed on this earth. Before we can even approach this question, we need to be somewhat clearer about what it is that we are looking for. I will offer here a couple of distinctions that are relevant to this subject.

Survival vs. Immortality: It is possible that human beings survive the death of the body, but it does not mean that there is anything that survives forever: i.e., it is possible that survival is true, but immortality is false. For while some part of us may survive death, let's say for a few hundred or thousand years, but then that which survives is annihilated. Hence, there is no immortality, which means survival for an infinite amount of time. So when afterlife is discussed, it is important to be clear whether we are talking about survival or immortality.

Individual vs. Impersonal Survival: Many people who believe that there is some form of afterlife mean that the very same person who lived in this body survives after the body is gone. Hence, such a belief assumes *individual* survival. We survive after death as unique individuals and we remain unique individuals throughout the whole survival period. Of course, this raises the question what is it that makes us unique individuals and this question leads us back to the question of personal identity.

But there is also a line of thought whereby human persons survive after the death of the body, but once the body is gone, that which survives fuses into a *universal* or *absolute* mind without any trace of their individuality. Hence, this view of survival is impersonal. To some impersonal survival may not be very gratifying, for what good is it to survive not as a unique individual, but rather as an indistinguishable part of some universal mind. Still it is worthwhile to consider impersonal survival, if for no other reason than to reflect upon what exactly is involved in human yearning for surviving after death.

The Immortal Soul

Plato

When Socrates had finished, Cebes made his reply. The rest of your statement, Socrates, he said, seems excellent to me, but what you said about the soul leaves the average person with grave misgivings that when it is released from the body it may no longer exist anywhere, but may be dispersed and destroyed on the very day that the man himself dies, as soon as it is freed from the body, that as it emerges it may be dissipated like breath or smoke, and vanish away, so that nothing is left of it anywhere. Of course if it still existed as an independent unity, released from all the evils which you have just described, there would be a strong and glorious hope, Socrates, that what you say is true. But I fancy that it requires no little faith and assurance to believe that the soul exists after death and retains some active force and intelligence.

Quite true, Cebes, said Socrates. But what are we to do about it? Is it your wish that we should go on speculating about the subject, to see whether this view is likely to be true or not?

For my part, said Cebes, I should be very glad to hear what you think about it.

At any rate, said Socrates, I hardly think that anyone who heard us now—even a comic poet—would say that I am wasting time and discoursing on subjects which do not concern me. So if that is how you feel, we had better continue our inquiry. Let us approach it from this point of view. Do the souls of the departed exist in another world or not?

There is an old legend, which we still remember, to the effect that they *do* exist there, after leaving here, and that they return again to this world and come into being from the dead. If this is so—that the living come into being again from the dead—does it not follow that our souls exist in the other world? They could not come into being again if they did not exist, and it will be sufficient proof that my contention is true if it really becomes apparent that the living come from the dead, and from nowhere else. But if this is not so, we shall need some other argument.

Quite so, said Cebes.

If you want to understand the question more readily, said Socrates, consider it with reference not only to human beings but to all animals and plants. Let us see whether in general everything that admits of generation is generated in this way and no other— opposites from opposites, wherever there is an opposite—as for instance beauty is opposite to ugliness and right to wrong, and there are countless other examples. Let us consider whether it is a necessary law that everything which has an opposite is generated from that opposite and from no other source. For example, when a thing becomes bigger, it must, I suppose, have been smaller first before it became bigger?

Yes.

And similarly if it becomes smaller, it must be bigger first, and become smaller afterward?

That is so, said Cebes.

And the weaker comes from the stronger, and the faster from the slower?

Certainly.

One more instance. If a thing becomes worse, is it not from being better? And if more just, from being more unjust?

Of course.

Are we satisfied, then, said Socrates, that everything is generated in this way—opposites from opposites?

Perfectly.

Here is another question. Do not these examples present another feature, that between each pair of opposites there are two processes of generation, one from the first to the second, and another from the second to the first? Between a larger and a smaller object are there are the processes of increase and decrease, and do we not describe them in this way as increasing and decreasing?

Yes, said Cebes.

Is it not the same with separating and combining, cooling and heating, and all the rest of them? Even if we sometimes do not use the actual terms, must it not in fact hold good universally that they come one from the other, and that there is a process of generation from each to the other?

Certainly, said Cebes.

Well then, said Socrates, is there an opposite to living, as sleeping is opposite to waking?

Certainly.

What?

Being dead.

So if they are opposites, they come from one another, and have their two processes of generation between the two of them?

Of course.

Very well, then, said Socrates, I will state one pair of opposites which I mentioned just now—the opposites themselves and the processes between them—and you shall state the other. My opposites are sleeping and waking, and I say that waking comes from sleeping and sleeping from waking, and that the processes between them are going to sleep and waking up. Does that satisfy you, he asked, or not?

Perfectly.

Now you tell me in the same way, he went on, about life and death. Do you not admit that death is the opposite of life?

I do.

And that they come from one another?

Yes.

Then what comes from the living?

The dead.

And what, asked Socrates, comes from the dead?

I must admit, he said, that it is the living.

So it is from the dead, Cebes, that living things and people come?

Evidently.

Then our souls do exist in the next world.

So it seems.

And one of the two processes in this case is really quite certain—dying is certain enough, isn't it?

Yes, it is, said Cebes.

What shall we do, then? Shall we omit the complementary process, and leave a defect here in the law of nature? Or must we supply an opposite process to that of dying?

Surely we must supply it, he said.

And what is it?

Coming to life again.

Then if there is such a thing as coming to life again, said Socrates, it must be a process from death to life?

Quite so.

So we agree upon this too—that the living have come from the dead no less than the dead from the living. But I think we decided that if this was so, it was a sufficient proof that the souls of the dead must exist in some place from which they are reborn.

It seems to me, Socrates, he said, that this follows necessarily from our agreement.

I think there is another way too, Cebes, in which you can see that we were not wrong in our agreement. If there were not a constant correspondence in the process of generation between the two sets of opposites, going round in a sort of cycle, if generation were a straight path to the opposite extreme without any return to the starting point or any deflection, do you realize that in the end everything would have the same quality and reach the same state, and change would cease altogether?

What do you mean?

Nothing difficult to understand, replied Socrates. For example, if 'falling asleep' existed, and 'waking up' did not balance it by making something come out of sleep, you must realize that in the end everything would make Endymion look foolish. He would be nowhere, because the whole world would be in the same state—asleep. And if everything were combined and nothing separated, we should soon have Anaxagoras' 'all things together.' In just the same way, my dear Cebes, if everything that has some share of life were to die, and if after death the dead remained in that form and did not come to life again, would it not be quite inevitable that in the end everything should be dead and nothing alive? If living things came from other living things, and the living things died, what possible means could prevent their number from being exhausted by death?

None that I can see, Socrates, said Cebes. What you say seems to be perfectly true.

Yes. Cebes, he said, if anything is true, I believe that this is, and we were not mistaken in our agreement upon it. Coming to life again is a fact, and it is a fact that the living come from the dead, and a fact that the souls of the dead exist.

Besides, Socrates, rejoined Cebes, there is that theory which you have often described to us—that what we call learning is really just recollection. If that is true, then surely what we recollect now we must have learned at some time before, which is impossible unless our souls existed somewhere before they entered this human shape. So in that way too it seems likely that the soul is immortal.

How did the proofs of that theory go, Cebes? broke in Simmias, Remind me, because at the moment I can't quite remember.

One very good argument, said Cebes, is that when people are asked questions, if the question is put in the right way they can give a perfectly correct answer, which they could not possibly do unless they had some knowledge and a proper grasp of the subject. And then if you confront people with a diagram or anything like that, the way in which they react is an unmistakable proof that the theory is correct.

And if you don't find that convincing, Simmias, said Socrates, see whether this appeals to you. I suppose that you find it hard to understand how what we call learning can be recollection?

Not at all, said Simmias. All that I want is to be helped to do what we are talking about—to recollect. I can practically remember enough to satisfy me already, from Cebes' approach to the subject, but I should be nonetheless glad to hear how you meant to approach it.

I look at it in this way, said Socrates. We are agreed, I suppose, that if a person is to be reminded of anything, he must first know it at some time or other?

Quite so.

Are we also agreed in calling it recollection when knowledge comes in a particular way? I will explain what I mean. Suppose that a person on seeing or hearing or otherwise noticing one thing not only becomes conscious of that thing but also thinks of a something-thing else which is an object of a different sort of knowledge. Are we not justified in saying that he was reminded of the object which he thought of?

What do you mean?

Let me give you an example. A human being and a musical instrument, I suppose you will agree, are different objects of knowledge.

Yes, certainly.

Well, you know what happens to lovers when they see a musical instrument or a piece of clothing or any other private property of the person whom they love. When they recognize the thing, their minds conjure up a picture of its owner. That is recollection. In the same way the sight of Simmias often reminds one of Cebes, and of course there are thousands of other examples.

Yes, of course there are, said Simmias.

So by recollection we mean the sort of experience which I have just described, especially when it happens with reference to things which we had not seen for such a long time that we had forgotten them.

Quite so.

Well, then, is it possible for a person who sees a picture of a horse or a musical instrument to be reminded of a person, or for someone who sees a picture of Simmias to be reminded of Cebes?

Perfectly.

And is it possible for someone who sees a portrait of Simmias to be reminded of Simmias himself?

Yes, it is.

Does it not follow from all this that recollection may be caused either by similar or by dissimilar objects?

Yes, it does.

When you are reminded by similarity, surely you must also be conscious whether the similarity is perfect or only partial.

Yes, you must.

Here is a further step, said Socrates. We admit, I suppose, that there is such a thing as equality—not the equality of stick to stick and stone to stone, and so on, but something beyond all that and distinct from it—absolute equality. Are we to admit this or not?

Yes indeed, said Simmias, most emphatically.

And do we know what it is?

Certainly.

Where did we get our knowledge? Was it not from the particular examples that we mentioned just now? Was it not from seeing equal sticks or stones or other equal objects that we got the notion of equality, although it is something quite distinct from them?

Look at it in this way. Is it not true that equal stones and sticks sometimes, without changing in themselves, appear equal to one person and unequal to another?

Certainly.

Well, now, have you ever thought that things which were absolutely equal were unequal, or that equality was inequality?

No, never, Socrates.

Then these equal things are not the same as absolute equality.

Not in the least, as I see it, Socrates.

And yet it is these equal things that have suggested and conveyed to you your knowledge of absolute equality, although they are distinct from it?

Perfectly true.

Whether it is similar to them or dissimilar?

Certainly.

It makes no difference, said Socrates. So long as the sight of one thing suggests another to you, it must be a cause of recollection, whether the two things are alike or not.

Quite so.

Well, now, he said, what do we find in the case of the equal sticks and other things of which we were speaking just now? Do they seem to us to be equal in the-sense of absolute equality, or do they fall short of it in so far as they only approximate to equality? Or don't they fall short at all?

They do, said Simmias, a long way.

Suppose that when you see something you say to yourself, This thing which I can see has a tendency to be like something else, but it falls short and cannot be really like it, only a poor imitation. Don't you agree with me that anyone who receives that impression must in fact have previous knowledge of that thing which he says that the other resembles, but inadequately?

Certainly he must.

Very well, then, is that our position with regard to equal things and absolute equality?

Exactly.

Then we must have had some previous knowledge of equality before the time when we first saw equal things and realized that they were striving after equality, but fell short of it.

That is so.

And at the same time we are agreed also upon this point, that we have not and could not have acquired this notion of equality except by sight or touch or one of the other senses. I am treating them as being all the same.

They are the same, Socrates, for the purpose of our argument.

So it must be through the senses that we obtained the notion that all sensible equals are striving after absolute equality but falling short of it. Is that correct?

Yes, it is.

So before we began to see and hear and use our other senses we must somewhere have acquired the knowledge that there is such a thing as absolute equality. Otherwise we could never have realized, by using it as a standard for comparison, that all equal objects of sense are desirous of being like it, but are only imperfect copies.

That is the logical conclusion, Socrates.

Did we not begin to see and hear and possess our other senses from the moment of birth?

Certainly.

But we admitted that we must have obtained our knowledge of equality before we obtained them.

Yes.

So we must have obtained it before birth.

So it seems.

Then if we obtained it before our birth, and possessed it when we were born, we had knowledge, both before and at the moment of birth, not only of equality and relative magnitudes, but of all absolute standards. Our present argument applies no more to equality than it does to absolute beauty, goodness, uprightness, holiness, and, as I maintain, all those characteristics which we designate in our discussions by the term 'absolute.' So we must have obtained knowledge of all these characteristics before our birth.

That is so.

And unless we invariably forget it after obtaining it we must always be born *knowing* and continue to *know* all through our lives, because 'to know' means simply to retain the knowledge which one has acquired, and not to lose it. Is not what we call 'forgetting' simply the loss of knowledge, Simmias?

Most certainly, Socrates.

And if it is true that we acquired our knowledge before our birth, and lost it at the moment of birth, but afterward, by the exercise of our senses upon sensible objects, recover the knowledge which we had once before, I suppose that what we call learning will be the recovery of our own knowledge, and surely we should be right in calling this recollection.

Quite so.

Yes, because we saw that it is possible for the perception of an object by sight or hearing or any of the other senses to suggest to the percipient, through association, whether there is any similarity or not, another object which he has forgotten. So, as I maintain, there are two alternatives. Either we are all born with knowledge of these standards, and retain it throughout our lives, or else, when we speak of people learning, they are simply recollecting what they knew before. In other words, learning is recollection.

Yes, that must be so, Socrates.

Which do you choose, then, Simmias? That we are born with knowledge, or that we recollect after we are born the things of which we possessed knowledge before we were born?

I don't know which to choose on the spur of the moment, Socrates.

Well, here is another choice for you to make. What do you think about this? Can a person who knows a subject thoroughly explain what he knows?

Most certainly he can.

Do you think that everyone can explain these questions about which we have just been talking?

I should like to think so, said Simmias, but I am very much afraid that by this time tomorrow there will be no one on this earth who can do it properly.

So you don't think, Simmias, that everyone has knowledge about them?

Far from it.

Then they just recollect what they once learned.

That must be the right answer.

When do our souls acquire this knowledge? It cannot be after the beginning of our mortal life.

No, of course not.

Then it must be before.

Yes.

Then our souls had a previous existence, Simmias, before they took on this human shape. They were independent of our bodies, and they were possessed of intelligence.

Unless perhaps it is at the moment of birth that we acquire knowledge of these things, Socrates. There is still that time available.

No doubt, my dear fellow, but just tell me, what other time is there to lose it in? We have just agreed that we do not possess it when we are born. Do we lose it at the same moment that we acquire it? Or can you suggest any other time?

No, of course not, Socrates. I didn't realize what nonsense I was talking.

Well, how do we stand now, Simmias? If all these absolute realities, such as beauty and goodness, which we are always talking about, really exist, if it is to them, as we rediscover our own former knowledge of them, that we refer, as copies to their patterns, all the objects of our physical perception—if these realities exist, does it not follow that our souls must exist too even before our birth, whereas if they do not exist, our discussion would seem to be a waste of time? Is this the position, that it is logically just as certain that our souls exist before our birth as it is that these realities exist, and that if the one is impossible, so is the other?

It is perfectly obvious to me, Socrates, said Simmias, that the same logical necessity applies to both. It suits me very well that your argument should rely upon the point that our soul's existence before our birth stands or falls with the existence of your grade of reality. I cannot imagine anything more self-evident than the fact that absolute beauty and goodness and all the rest that you mentioned just now exist in the fullest possible sense. In my opinion the proof is quite satisfactory.

What about Cebes? said Socrates. We must convince Cebes too.

To the best of my belief he is satisfied, replied Simmias. It is true that he is the most obstinate person in the world at resisting an argument, but I should think that he needs nothing more to convince him that our souls existed before our birth. As for their exist- ing after we are dead as well, even I don't feel that that has been proved, Socrates. Cebes' objection still holds—the common fear that a man's soul may be disintegrated at the very moment of his death, and that this may be the end of its existence. Supposing that it *is* born and constituted from some source or other, and exists before it enters a human body. After it has entered one, is there any reason why, at the moment of release, it should not come to an end and be destroyed itself?

Quite right, Simmias, said Cebes. It seems that we have got the proof of one half of what we wanted—that the soul existed before birth—but now we need also to prove that it will exist after death no less than before birth, if our proof is to be complete.

As a matter of fact, my dear Simmias and Cebes, said Socrates, it is proved already, if you will combine this last argument with the one about which we agreed before, that every living thing comes from the dead. If the soul exists before birth, and if when it pro- ceeds toward life and is born it must be born from death or the dead state, surely it must also exist after death, if it must be born again. So the point which you mention has been proved already. But in spite of this I believe that you and Simmias would like to spin out the discussion still more. You are afraid, as children are, that when the soul emerges from the body the wind may really puff it away and scatter it, especially when a person does not die on a calm day but with a gale blowing.

Cebes laughed. Suppose that we are afraid, Socrates, he said, and try to convince us. Or rather don't suppose that it is we that are afraid. Probably even in us there is a little boy who has these childish terrors. Try to persuade him not to be afraid of death as though it were a bogy.

What you should do, said Socrates, is to say a magic spell over him every day until you have charmed his fears away.

But, Socrates, said Simmias, where shall we find a magician who understands these spells now that you . . . are leaving us?

Greece is a large country, Cebes, he replied, which must have good men in it, and there are many foreign races too. You must ransack all of them in your search for this magician, without sparing money or trouble, because you could not spend your money more opportunely on any other object. And you must search also by your own united efforts, because it is probable that you would not easily find anyone better fitted for the task.

We will see to that, said Cebes. But let us return to the point where we left off, if you have no objection.

Of course not. Why should I?

Thank you, said Cebes.

We ought, I think, said Socrates, to ask ourselves this. What sort of thing is it that would naturally suffer the fate of being dispersed? For what sort of thing should we fear this fate, and for what should we not? When we have answered this, we should next consider to which class the soul belongs, and then we shall know whether to feel confidence or fear about the fate of our souls.

Quite true.

Would you not expect a composite object or a natural compound to be liable to break up where it was put together? And ought not anything which is really incomposite to be the one thing of all others which is not affected in this way?

That seems to be the case, said Cebes.

Is it not extremely probable that what is always constant and invariable is incomposite, and what is inconstant and variable is composite?

That is how it seems to me.

Then let us return to the same examples which we were discussing before. Does that absolute reality which we define in our discussions remain always constant and invariable, or not? Does absolute equality or beauty or any other independent entity which really exists ever admit change of any kind? Or does each one of these uniform and independent entities remain always constant and invariable, never admitting any alteration in any respect or in any sense?

They must be constant and invariable, Socrates, said Cebes.

Well, what about the concrete instances of beauty—such as men, horses, clothes, and so on—or of equality, or any other members of a class corresponding to an absolute entity? Are they constant, or are they, on the contrary, scarcely ever in the same relation in any sense either to themselves or to one another?

With them, Socrates, it is just the opposite; they are never free from variation.

And these concrete objects you can touch and see and perceive by your other senses, but those constant entities you cannot possibly apprehend except by thinking; they are invisible to our sight.

That is perfectly true, said Cebes.

So you think that we should assume two classes of things, one visible and the other invisible?

Yes, we should.

The invisible being invariable, and the visible never being the same?

Yes, we should assume that too.

Well, now, said Socrates, are we not part body, part soul?

Certainly.

Then to which class do we say that the body would have the closer resemblance and relation?

Quite obviously to the visible.

And the soul, is it visible or invisible?

Invisible to men, at any rate, Socrates, he said.

But surely we have been speaking of things visible or invisible to our human nature. Do you think that we had some other nature in view?

No, human nature.

What do we say about the soul, then? Is it visible or invisible?

Not visible.

Invisible, then?

Yes.

So soul is more like the invisible, and body more like the visible?

That follows inevitably, Socrates.

Did we not say some time ago that when the soul uses the instrumentality of the body for any inquiry, whether through sight or hearing or any other sense—because using the body implies using the senses—it is drawn away by the body into the realm of the variable, and loses its way and becomes confused and dizzy, as though it were fuddled, through contact with things of a similar nature?

Certainly.

But when it investigates by itself, it passes into the realm of the pure and everlasting and immortal and changeless, and being of a kindred nature, when it is once independent and free from interference, consorts with it always and strays no longer, but remains, in that realm of the absolute, constant and invariable; through contact with beings of a similar nature. And this condition of the soul we call wisdom.

An excellent description, and perfectly true, Socrates.

Very well, then, in the light of all that we have said, both now and before, to which class do you think that the soul bears the closer resemblance and relation?

I think, Socrates, said Cebes, that even the dullest person would agree, from this line of reasoning, that the soul is in every possible way more like the invariable than the variable.

And the body?

To the other.

Look at it in this way too. When soul and body are both in the same place, nature teaches the one to serve and be subject, the other to rule and govern. In this relation which do you think resembles the divine and which the mortal part? Don't you think that it is the nature of the divine to rule and direct, and that of the mortal to be subject and serve?

I do.

Then which does the soul resemble?

Obviously, Socrates, soul resembles the divine, and body the mortal.

Now, Cebes, he said, see whether this is our conclusion from all that we have said. The soul is most like that which is divine, immortal, intelligible, uniform, indissoluble, and ever self-consistent and invariable, whereas body is most like that which is human, mortal, multiform, unintelligible, dissoluble, and never self-consistent. Can we adduce any conflicting argument, my dear Cebes, to show that this is not so?

No, we cannot.

Very well, then, in that case is it not natural for body to disintegrate rapidly, but for soul to be quite or very nearly indissoluble?

Certainly.

Of course you know that when a person dies, although it is nature for the visible and physical part of him, which lies here in the visible world and which we call his corpse, to decay and fall to pieces and be dissipated, none of this happens to it immediately. It remains as it was for quite a long time, even if death takes place when the body is well nourished and in the warm season. Indeed, when the body is dried and embalmed, as in Egypt, it remains almost intact for an incredible time, and even if the rest of the body decays, some parts of it—the bones and sinews and anything else like them—are practically everlasting. That is so, is it not?

Yes.

But the soul, the invisible part, which goes away to a place that is, like itself, glorious, pure, and invisible—the true Hades or unseen world—into the presence of the good and wise God, where, if God so wills, my soul must shortly go—will it, if its very nature is such as I have described, be dispersed and destroyed at the moment of its release from the body, as is the popular view? Far from it, my dear Simmias and Cebes. The truth is much more like this. If at its release the soul is pure and carries with it no contamination of the body, because it has never willingly associated with it in life, but has shunned it and kept itself separate as its regular practice—in other words, if it has pursued philosophy in the right way and really practiced how to face death easily—this is what 'practicing death' means, isn't it?

Most decidedly.

Very well, if this is its condition, then it departs to that place which is, like itself, invisible, divine, immortal, and wise, where, on its arrival, happiness awaits it, and release from uncertainty and folly, from fears and uncontrolled desires, and all other human evils, and where, as they say of the initiates in the Mysteries, it really spends the rest of time with God. Shall we adopt this view, Cebes, or some other?

This one, by all means, said Cebes.

That seems likely enough, Socrates.

Yes, it does, Cebes. Of course these are not the souls of the good,

Immortality

John Stuart Mill

The indications of immortality may be considered in two divisions: those which are independent of any theory respecting the Creator and his intentions, and those which depend upon an antecedent belief on that subject.

Of the former class of arguments speculative men have in different ages put forward a considerable variety, of which those in the *Phædon* of Plato are an example; but they are for the most part such as have no adherents, and need not be seriously refuted, now. They are generally founded upon preconceived theories as to the nature of the thinking principle in man, considered as distinct and separable from the body, and on other preconceived theories respecting death. As, for example, that death, or dissolution, is always a separation of parts; and the soul being without parts, being simple and indivisible, is not susceptible of this separation. Curiously enough, one of the interlocutors in the *Phædon* anticipates the answer by which an objector of the present day would meet this argument: namely, that thought and consciousness, though mentally distinguishable from the body, may not be a substance separable from it, but a result of it, standing in a relation to it (the illustration is Plato's) like that of a tune to the musical instrument on which it is played; and that the arguments used to prove that the soul does not die with the body, would equally prove that the tune does not die with the instrument, but survives its destruction and continues to exist apart.[*] In fact, those moderns who dispute the evidences of the immortality of the soul, do not, in general, believe the soul to be a substance *per se,* but regard it as the name of a bundle of attributes, the attributes of feeling, thinking, reasoning, believing, willing, &c., and these attributes they regard as a consequence of the bodily organization, which therefore, they argue, it is as unreasonable to suppose surviving when that organization is dispersed, as to suppose the colour or odour of a rose surviving when the rose itself has perished. Those, therefore, who would deduce the immortality of the soul from its own nature have first to prove that the attributes in question are not attributes of the body but of a separate substance. Now what is the verdict of science on this point? It is not perfectly conclusive either way. In the first place, it does not prove, experimentally, that any mode of organization has the power of producing feeling or thought. To make that proof good it would be necessary that we should be able to produce an organism, and try whether it would feel; which we cannot do; organisms cannot by any human means be produced, they can only be developed out of a previous organism. On the other hand, the evidence is well nigh complete that all thought and feeling has some action of the bodily organism for its immediate antecedent or accompaniment; that the specific variations and especially the different degrees of complication of the nervous and cerebral organization, correspond to differences in the development of the mental faculties; and though we have no evidence, except negative, that the mental consciousness ceases for ever when the functions of the brain are at an end, we do know that diseases of the brain disturb the mental functions and that decay or weakness of the brain enfeebles them. We have therefore sufficient evidence that cerebral action is, if not the cause, at least, in our present state of existence, a condition *sine quâ non* of mental operations; and that assuming the mind to be a distinct substance, its separation from the body would not be, as some have vainly flattered themselves, a liberation from trammels and restoration to freedom, but would simply put a stop to its functions and remand it to unconsciousness, unless and until some other set of conditions supervenes, capable of recalling it into activity, but of the existence of which experience does not give us the smallest indication.

At the same time it is of importance to remark that these considerations only amount to defect of evidence; they afford no positive argument against immortality. We must beware of giving *à priori* validity to the conclusions of an *à posteriori* philosophy. The root of all *à priori* thinking is the tendency to transfer to outward things a strong association between the corresponding ideas in our own minds; and the thinkers who most sincerely attempt to limit their beliefs by experience, and honestly believe that they do so, are not always sufficiently on their guard against this mistake. There are thinkers who regard it as a truth of reason that miracles are impossible; and in like manner there are others who because the phenomena of life and consciousness are associated in their minds by undeviating experience with the action of material organs, think it an absurdity *per se* to imagine it possible that those phenomena can exist under any other conditions. But they should remember that the uniform coexistence of one fact with another does not make the one fact a part of the other, or the same with it. The relation of thought to a material brain is no metaphysical necessity; but simply a constant coexistence within the limits of observation. And when analysed to the bottom on the principles of the Associative Psychology, the brain, just as much as the mental functions is, like matter itself, merely a set of human sensations either actual or inferred as possible, namely those which the anatomist has when he opens the skull, and the impressions which we suppose we should receive of molecular or some other movements when the cerebral action was going on, if there were no bony envelope and our senses or our instruments were sufficiently delicate. Experience furnishes us with no example of any series of states of consciousness, without this group of contingent sensations attached to it; but it is as easy to imagine such a series of states without, as with, this accompaniment, and we know of no reason in the nature of things against the possibility of its being thus disjoined. We may suppose that the same thoughts, emotions, volitions and even sensations which we have here, may persist or recommence somewhere else under other conditions, just as we may suppose that other thoughts and sensations may exist under other conditions in other parts of the universe. And in entertaining this supposition we need not be embarrassed by any metaphysical difficulties about a thinking substance. Substance is but a general name for the perdurability of attributes: wherever there is a series of thoughts connected together by memories, that constitutes a thinking substance. This absolute distinction in thought and separability in representation of our states of consciousness from the set of conditions with which they are united only by constancy of concomitance, is equivalent in a practical point of view to the old distinction of the two substances, Matter and Mind.

There is, therefore, in science, no evidence against the immortality of the soul but that negative evidence, which consists in the absence of evidence in its favour. And even the negative evidence is not so strong as negative evidence often is. In the case of witchcraft, for instance, the fact that there is no proof which will stand examination of its having ever existed, is as conclusive as the most positive evidence of its non-existence would be; for it exists, if it does exist, on this earth, where if it had existed the evidence of fact would certainly have been available to prove it. But it is not so as to the soul's existence after death. That it does not remain on earth and go about visibly or interfere in the events of life, is proved by the same weight of evidence which disproves witchcraft. But that it does not exist elsewhere, there is absolutely no proof. A very faint, if any, presumption, is all that is afforded by its disappearance from the surface of this planet.

Some may think that there is an additional and very strong presumption against the immortality of the thinking and conscious principle, from the analysis of all the other objects of Nature, All things in Nature perish, the most beautiful and perfect being, as philosophers and poets alike complain, the most perishable. A flower of the most exquisite form and colouring grows up from a root, comes to perfection in weeks or months, and lasts only a few hours or days, Why should it be otherwise with man? Why indeed. But why, also, should it *not* be otherwise? Feeling and thought are not merely different from what we call inanimate matter, but are at the opposite pole of existence, and analogical inference has little or no validity from the one to the other. Feeling and thought are much more real than anything else; they are the only things which we directly know to be real, all things else being merely the unknown conditions on which these, in our present state of existence or in some other, depend. All matter apart from the feelings of sentient beings has but an hypothetical and unsubstantial existence: it is a mere assumption to account for our sensations; itself we do not perceive, we are not conscious of it, but only of the sensations which we are said to receive from it: in reality it is a mere name for our expectation of sensations, or for our belief that we can have certain sensations when certain other sensations give indication of them. Because these contingent possibilities of sensation sooner or later come to an end and give place to others, is it implied in this, that the series of our feelings must itself be broken off? This would not be to reason from one kind of substantive reality to another, but to draw from something which has no reality except in reference to something else, conclusions applicable to that which is the only substantive reality. Mind, (or whatever name we give to what is implied in consciousness of a continued series of feelings) is in a philosophical point of view the only reality of which we have any evidence; and no analogy can be recognized or comparison made between it and other realities because there are no other known realities to compare it with. That is quite consistent with its being perishable; but the question whether it is so or not is *res integra,* untouched by any of the results of human knowledge and experience. The case is one of those very rare cases in which there is really a total absence of evidence on either side, and in which the absence of evidence for the affirmative does not, as in so many cases it does, create a strong presumption in favour of the negative.

The belief, however, in human immortality, in the minds of mankind generally, is probably not grounded on any scientific arguments either physical or metaphysical, but on foundations with most minds much stronger, namely on one hand the disagreeableness of giving up existence, (to those at least to whom it has hitherto been pleasant) and on the other the general traditions of mankind. The natural tendency of belief to follow these two inducements, our own wishes and the general assent of other people, has been in this instance reinforced by the utmost exertion of the power of public and private teaching; rulers and instructors having at all times, with the view of giving greater effect to their mandates whether from selfish or from public motives, encouraged to the utmost of their power the belief that there is a life after death, in which pleasures and sufferings far greater than on earth, depend on our doing or leaving undone while alive, what we are commanded to do in the name of the unseen powers. As causes of belief these various circumstances are most powerful. As rational grounds of it they carry no weight at all.

That what is called the consoling nature of an opinion, that is, the pleasure we should have in believing it to be true, can be a ground for believing it, is a doctrine irrational in itself and which would sanction half the mischievous illusions recorded in history or which mislead individual life. It is sometimes, in the case now under consideration, wrapt up in a quasi-scientific language. We are told that the desire of immortality is one of our instincts, and that there is no instinct which has not corresponding to it a real object fitted to satisfy it. Where there is hunger there is somewhere food, where there is sexual feeling there is somewhere sex, where there is love there is somewhere something to be loved, and so forth: in like manner since there is the instinctive desire of eternal life, eternal life there must be. The answer to this is patent on the very surface of the subject. It is unnecessary to go into any recondite considerations concerning instincts, or to discuss whether the desire in question is an instinct or not. Granting that wherever there is an instinct there exists something such as that instinct demands, can it be affirmed that this something exists in boundless quantity, or sufficient to satisfy the infinite craving of human desires? What is called the desire of eternal life is simply the desire of life; and does there not exist that which this desire calls for? Is there not life? And is not the instinct, if it be an instinct, gratified by the possession and preservation of life? To suppose that the desire of life guarantees to us personally the reality of life through all eternity, is like supposing that the desire of food assures us that we shall always have as much as we can eat through our whole lives and as much longer as we can conceive our lives to be protracted to.

The argument from tradition or the general belief of the human race, if we accept it as a guide to our own belief, must be accepted entire: if so we are bound to believe that the souls of human beings not only survive after death but show themselves as ghosts to the living; for we find no people who have had the one belief without the other. Indeed it is probable that the former belief originated in the latter, and that primitive men would never have supposed that the soul did not die with the body if they had not fancied that it visited them after death. Nothing could be more natural than such a fancy; it is, in appearance, completely realized in dreams, which in Homer and in all ages like Homer's, are supposed to be real apparitions. To dreams we have to add not merely waking hallucinations but the delusions, however baseless, of sight and hearing, or rather the misinterpretations of those senses, sight or hearing supplying mere hints from which imagination paints a complete picture and invests it with reality. These delusions are not to be judged of by a modern standard: in early times the line between imagination and perception was by no means clearly defined; there was little or none of the knowledge we now possess of the actual course of nature, which makes us distrust or disbelieve any appearance which is at variance with known laws. In the ignorance of men as to what were the limits of nature and what was or was not compatible with it, no one thing seemed, as far as physical considerations went, to be much more improbable than another. In rejecting, therefore, as we do, and as we have the best reason to do, the tales and legends of the actual appearance of disembodied spirits, we take from under the general belief of mankind in a life after death, what in all probability was its chief ground and support, and deprive it of even the very little value which the opinion of rude ages can ever have as evidence of truth. If it be said that this belief has maintained itself in ages which have ceased to be rude and which reject the superstitions with which it once was accompanied, the same may be said of many other opinions of rude ages, and especially on the most important and interesting subjects, because it is on those subjects that the reigning opinion, whatever it may be, is the most sedulously inculcated upon all who are born into the world. This particular opinion, moreover, if it has on the whole kept its ground, has done so with a constantly increasing number of dissentients, and those especially among cultivated minds. Finally, those cultivated minds which adhere to the belief ground it, we may reasonably suppose, not on the belief of others, but on arguments and evidences; and those arguments and evidences, therefore, are what it concerns us to estimate and judge.

The preceding are a sufficient sample of the arguments for a future life which do not suppose an antecedent belief in the existence, or any theory respecting the attributes of the Godhead. It remains to consider what arguments are supplied by such lights, or such grounds of conjecture, as natural theology affords, on those great questions.

We have seen that these lights are but faint; that of the existence of a Creator they afford no more than a preponderance of probability; of his benevolence a considerably less preponderance; that there is, however, some reason to think that he cares for the pleasures of his creatures, but by no means that this is his sole care, or that other purposes do not often take precedence of it. His intelligence must be adequate to the contrivances apparent in the universe, but need not be more than adequate to them, and his power is not only not proved to be infinite, but the only real evidences in natural theology tend to show that it is limited, contrivance being a mode of overcoming difficulties, and always supposing difficulties to be overcome.

We have now to consider what inference can legitimately be drawn from these premises, in favour of a future life. It seems to me, apart from express revelation, none at all.

The common arguments are, the goodness of God; the improbability that he would ordain the annihilation of his noblest and richest work, after the greater part of its few years of life had been spent in the acquisition of faculties which time is not allowed him to turn to fruit; and the special improbability that he would have implanted in us an instinctive desire of eternal life, and doomed that desire to complete disappointment.

These might be arguments in a world the constitution of which made it possible without contradiction to hold it for the work of a Being at once omnipotent and benevolent. But they are not arguments in a world like that in which we live. The benevolence of the divine Being may be perfect, but his power being subject to unknown limitations, we know not that he could have given us what we so confidently assert that he must have given; *could* (that is) without sacrificing something more important. Even his benevolence, however justly inferred, is by no means indicated as the interpretation of his whole purpose, and since we cannot tell how far other purposes may have interfered with the exercise of his benevolence, we know not that he *would,* even if he could have granted us eternal life. With regard to the supposed improbability of his having given the wish without its gratification, the same answer may be made; the scheme which either limitation of power, or conflict of purposes, compelled him to adopt, may have *required* that we should have the wish although it were not destined to be gratified. One thing, however, is quite certain in respect to God's government of the world; that he either could not, or would not, grant to us every thing we wish. We wish for life, and he has granted some life: that we wish (or some of us wish) for a boundless extent of life and that it is not granted, is no exception to the ordinary modes of his government. Many a man would like to be a Crœsus or an Augustus Cæsar, but has his wishes gratified only to the moderate extent of a pound a week or the Secretaryship of his Trades Union. There is, therefore, no assurance whatever of a life after death, on grounds of natural religion. But to any one who feels it conducive either to his satisfaction or to his usefulness to hope for a future state as a possibility, there is no hindrance to his indulging that hope. Appearances point to the existence of a Being who has great power over us—all the power implied in the creation of the Kosmos, or of its organized beings at least—and of whose goodness we have evidence though not of its being his predominant attribute: and as we do not know the limits either of his power or of his goodness, there is room to hope that both the one and the other may extend to granting us this gift provided that it would really be beneficial to us. The same ground which permits the hope warrants us in expecting that if there be a future life it will be at least as good as the present, and will not be wanting in the best feature of the present life, improvability by our own efforts. Nothing can be more opposed to every estimate we can form of probability, than the common idea of the future life as a state of rewards and punishments in any other sense than that the consequences of our actions upon our own character and susceptibilities will follow us in the future as they have done in the past and present. Whatever be the probabilities *of* a future life, all the probabilities *in case of* a future life are that such as we have been made or have made ourselves before the change, such we shall enter into the life hereafter; and that the fact of death will make no sudden break in our spiritual life, nor influence our character any otherwise than as any important change in our mode of existence may always be expected to modify it. Our thinking principle has its laws which in this life are invariable, and any analogies drawn from this life must assume that the same laws will continue, To imagine that a miracle will be wrought at death by the act of God making perfect every one whom it is his will to include among his elect, might be justified by an express revelation duly authenticated, but is utterly opposed to every presumption that can be deduced from the light of Nature.

Chapter 4 Free Will and Determinism: Is There Free Will?

The proposition that ***human agents (suitably qualified) have free-will and that at least some of the time they exercise their free will in their actions*** is an indispensible assumption to our self-conception, to our relations with others, and is woven into most of our social practices and institutions.

We view ***ourselves*** as beings that make decisions, deliberate, choose projects and goals for ourselves, and often act voluntarily and freely. Our ***relationships*** and ***interactions*** with others (e.g., friends, relatives, family, colleagues, etc.,) are often predicated on the assumption that both parties are free agents. The concept of ***moral*** (and legal) ***responsibility*** requires that human agents act freely. Thus, without free-will the concept of moral-responsibility can hardly make any sense. The idea of ***merit*** or ***desert*** presupposes that accomplishments are achieved through the exercise of free choices of agents. The ***political institution of voting*** (democracy) and the various ***legal institutions***, to name just two social institutions, all depend upon the assumption that we can, and often do, act freely. For all of the above reasons, we are reasonably certain that the following proposition is true:

A. Human agents have free-will.

Our conception of the world includes the belief that ***everything that happens in the world is determined by a cause***. The idea of ***causal-determination*** has been a very fruitful research paradigm in the progress of science. But causal-determination is a guiding principle in our own life as well. We look for a causal explanation whenever something goes wrong with the functions of our body (medicine) and we often explore causal explanations whenever we try to understand the behavior of others or even ourselves (psychology). We are able to formulate the principle of **causal-determination** more precisely as follows:

B. *Every event is fully determined by causal-laws and initial-conditions.*

A few clarifications are in order regarding B:

  i. First, the term *initial conditions* refers to a set of conditions in which an object is situated at a given time.
  ii. Second, the term *causal-laws* refers to the physical laws which govern all entities in the physical universe.
  iii. Third, *causal-explanation* is assumed to take the form of an inference which features as premises a set of relevant laws together with a specification of initial conditions from which a description of the event to be explained is deduced.
  iv. Fourth, the form of causal-explanation outlined in (iii) entails that no random events can ever occur. This assumption may (and again it may not) be falsified

by the Theory of Quantum Mechanics in which it *appears* that random events occur. This is not a problem for the principle of causal determination (i.e., B) because the principle of causal determination can be suitably modified in order to accommodate quantum randomness. This modification will not help us with the problem of free-will since even if free-will exists, it cannot be identified with randomness.

I hope you already sensed that there is an *apparent tension* between propositions A and B. If every event is fully determined (in the sense specified in B), then so are *all* our actions, since actions are a subclass of events. But if all our actions are fully determined, then no actions are the result of free-will, for to act freely is (so it seems) precisely not to be causally determined.

The intuition behind the claim that A and B (i.e., free-will and determinism) are inconsistent is best articulated by the *Libertarian Theory of Free-Will*, which captures one of the most important intuitions we have about the nature of free-will:

Libertarian Free-Will: Agent **A** does act **X** freely *only if* agent **A** *could have done* otherwise: i.e., agent **A** could have done **not-X** (or an alternative course of action that is not X).

Now, clearly, if every event is causally determined, then so are all of our actions. And if agent A actually did X, then agent A was causally determined to do X. But if Agent A was causally determined to do X, then agent A *could not have done anything other than* X. This violates the only-if clause of the Libertarian Free-Will. Therefore, according to Libertarian Free-Will, free will and determinism are *incompatible*.

The above conclusion is at the heart of the so-called *Incompatibilist* position regarding free-will and determinism. The incompatibilist's position is that free-will and determinism are inconsistent: only one or the other can be true. The opposite position is *Compatibislism*, which maintains that free will and determinism are compatible. While there are many versions of Compatibilism, I will here state a generic version.

Compatibilism:

a. Determinism is true;
b. Free-Will exists;
c. There is a distinction between **Internal** vs. **External** causes regarding actions;
d. An agent A performs act X freely if (and only if) act X was produced by a cause *internal* to the agent.

You might already wonder as to how exactly does the compatibilist distinguishes between internal vs. external causes. Well, we can *begin* by simply specifying that anything internal to our skin is an internal cause, whereas anything external to our skin is an external cause.

Let me emphasize that the distinction I have proposed above is just a starting point. Compatibilists offer much more sophisticated ways of making this distinction. However, I should say that those who oppose compatibilism deny that any of these alternative ways succeeds to reconcile clauses (a) and (b) in the compatibilists statement above. I will leave it up to you to decide whether the initial distinction between internal vs. external causes I have proposed works and whether other alternatives will be better. Think about clear counterexamples to the proposal I have made and use them to refine and alter the manner the distinction is stated. It is a wonderful exercise in philosophical skills.

However, it is important to note that compatibilism offers an important insight about free will, whether or not it is ultimately successful in unproblematically drawing a distinction between internal and external causes. This insight is that, contrary to the libertarian concept of free will, in many contexts our concept of free will has to do with the fact that some internal process caused an agent's behavior. So it is quite possible that we have (at least) two different concepts of free will: the libertarian conception of free will and the agent causation conception and both operate simultaneously in our daily life as we somehow able to apply them properly to the right cases.

Of the System of Man's free agency
Paul & d'Holback

Those who have pretended that the *soul* is distinguished from the body, is immaterial, draws its ideas from its own peculiar source, acts by its own energies without the aid of any exterior object; by a consequence of their own system, have enfranchised it from those physical laws, according to which all beings of which we have a knowledge are obliged to act. They have believed that the foul is mistress of its own conduct, is able to regulate its own peculiar operations; has the faculty to determine its will by its own natural energy; in a word, they have pretended man is a *free agent*.

It has been already sufficiently proved, that the soul is nothing more than the body, considered relatively to some of its functions, more concealed than others: it has been shewn, that this soul, even when it shall be supposed immaterial, is continually modified conjointly with the body; is submitted to all its motion; that without this it would remain inert and dead: that, consequently, it is subjected to the influence of those material, to the operation those physical causes, which give impulse to the body; of which the mode of existence, whether habitual or transitory, depends upon the material elements by which it is surrounded; that form its texture; that constitute its temperament; that enter into it by the means of the aliments; that penetrate it by their subtility; the faculties which are called intellectual, and those qualities which are styled moral, have been explained in a manner purely physical; entirely natural: in the last place, it has been demonstrated, that all the ideas, all the systems, all the affections, all the opinions, whether true or false, which man forms to himself, are to be attributed to his physical powers; are to be ascribed to his material senses. Thus man is a being purely physical; in whatever manner he is considered, he is connected to universal Nature: submitted to the necessary, to the immutable laws that she imposes on all the beings she contains, according to their peculiar essences; conformable to the respective properties with which, without consulting them, she endows each particular species. Man's life is a line that Nature commands him to describe upon the surface of the earth: without his ever being able to swerve from it even for an instant. He is born without his own consent; his organizations does in no wise depend upon himself; his ideas come to him involuntarily; his habits are in the power of those who cause him to contract them; he is unceasingly modified by causes, whether visible or concealed, over which he has no controul; give the hue to his way of thinking, and determine his manner of acting. He is good or bad—happy or miserable—wise or foolish—reasonable or irrational, without his will going for anything in these various states. Nevertheless, in despite of the shackles by which he is bound, it is pretended he is a free agent, or that independent of the causes by which he is moved, he determines his own will; regulates his own condition.

However slender the foundation of this opinion, of which every thing ought to point out to him the error; it is current at this day for an incontestible truth, and believed enlightened; it is the basis or religion, which has been incapable of imagining how man could either merit reward or deserve punishment if he was not a free agent. Society has been believed interested in this system, because an idea has gone abroad, that if all the actions of man were to be contemplated as necessary, the right of punishing those who injure their associates would no longer exist. At length human vanity accommodated itself to an hypothesis which, unquestionable, appears to distinguish man from all other physical beings, by assigning to him the special privilege of a total independence of all other causes; but of which a very little reflection would have shewn him the absurdity or even the impossibility.

As a part, subordinate to the great whole, man is obliged to experience its influence. To be a free agent it were needful that each individual was of greater strength than the entire of Nature; or, that he was out of this Nature: who, always in action herself, obliges all the beings she embraces, to act, and to concur to her general motion; or, as it has been said elsewhere, to conserve her active existence, by the motion that all beings produce in consequence of their particular energies, which result from their being submitted to fixed, eternal, and immutable laws. In order that man might be a free agent, it were needful that all beings should lose their essences; it is equally necessary that he himself should no longer enjoy physical sensibility; that he should neither know good nor evil; pleasure nor pain; but if this was the case, from that moment he would no longer be in a state to conserve himself, or render his existence happy; all beings would become indifferent to him; he would no longer have any choice; he would cease to know what he ought to love; what it was right he should fear; he would not have any acquaintance with that which he should seek after; or with that which it is requisite he should avoid. In short, man would be an unnatural being; totally incapable of acting in the manner we behold. It is the actual essence of man to tend to his well-being; to be desirous to conserve his existence; if all the motion of his machine springs as a necessary consequence from this primitive impulse; if pain warns him of that which he ought to avoid; if pleasure announces to him that which he should desire; if it is in his essence to love that which either excites delight, or, that from which he expects agreeable sensations; to hate that which makes him either fear contrary impressions; or, that which afflicts him with uneasiness; it must necessarily be, that he will be attracted by that which he deems advantageous; that his will shall be determined by those objects which he judges useful; that he will be repelled by those beings which he believes prejudicial, either to his habitual, or to his transitory mode of existence; by that which he considers disadvantageous. It is only by the aid of experience, that man acquires the faculty of understanding what he ought to love; of knowing what he ought to fear. Are his organs sound? his experience will be true: are they unsound? it will be false: in the first instance he will have reason, prudence, foresight; he will frequently foresee very remote effects; he will know, that what he sometimes contemplates as a good, may possibly become an evil, by its necessary or probable consequences: that what must be to him a transient evil, may by its result procure him a solid and durable good. It is thus experience enables him to foresee that the amputation of a limb will cause him painful sensation, he consequently is obliged to fear this operation, and he endeavours to avoid the pain; but if experience has also shewn him, that the transitory pain this amputation will cause him may be the means of saving his life; the preservation, of his existence being of necessity dear to him, he is obliged to submit himself to the momentary pain with a view to procuring a permanent good, by which it will be overbalanced.

The will, as we have elsewhere said, is a modification of the brain, by which it is disposed to action or prepared to give play to the organs. This will is necessarily determined by the qualities, good or bad, agreeable or painful, of the object or the motive that acts upon his senses; or of which the idea remains with him, and is resuscitated by his memory. In consequence, he acts necessarily; his action is the result of the impulse he receives either from the motive, from the object, or from the idea, which has modified his brain, or disposed his will. When he does not act according to this impulse, it is because there comes some new cause, some new motive, some new idea, which modifies his brain in a different manner, gives him a new impulse, determines his will in another way; by which the action of the former impulse is suspended: thus, the sight of an agreeable object, or its idea, determines his will to set him in action to procure it; but if a new object or a new idea more powerfully attracts him, it gives a new direction to his will, annihilates the effect of the former, and prevents the action by which it was to be procured. This is the mode in which reflection, experience, reason, necessarily arrests or suspends the action of man's will; without this, he would, of necessity, have followed the anterior impulse which carried him towards a then desirable object. In all this he always acts according to necessary laws, from which he has no means of emancipating himself.

If, when tormented with violent thirst, he figures to himself an idea, or really perceives a fountain, whose limpid streams might cool his feverish habit, is he sufficient master of himself to desire or not to desire the object competent to satisfy so lively a want? It will no doubt be conceded, that it is impossible he should not be desirous to satisfy it; but it will be said,—If at this moment it is announced to him, the water he so ardently desires is poisoned, he will, notwithstanding his vehement thirst, abstain from drinking it; and it has, therefore, been falsely concluded that he is a free agent. The fact, however, is, that the motive in either case is exactly the same: his own conservation. The same necessity that determined him to drink, before he knew the water was deleterious, upon this new discovery, equally determines him not to drink; the desire of conserving himself, either annihilates or suspends the former impulse; the second motive becomes stronger than the preceding; that is, the fear of death, or the desire of preserving himself, necessarily prevails over the painful sensation caused by his eagerness to drink. But, (it will be said) if the thirst is very parching, an inconsiderate man, without regarding the danger, will risque swallowing the water. Nothing is gained by this remark: in this case, the anterior impulse only regains the ascendency; he is persuaded, that life may possibly be longer preserved, or that he shall derive a greater good by drinking the poisoned water, than by enduring the torment, which, to his mind, threatens instant dissolution: thus, the first becomes the strongest, and necessarily urges him on to action. Nevertheless, in either case, whether he partakes of the water, or whether he does not, the two actions will be equally necessary; they will be the effect of that motive which finds itself most puissant; which consequently acts in a most coercive manner upon his will.

This example will serve to explain the whole phaenomena of the human will. This will, or rather the brain, finds itself in the same situation as a bowl, which although it has received an impulse that drives it forward in a straight line, is deranged in its course, whenever a force, superior to the first, obliges it to change its direction. The man who drinks the poisoned water, appears a madman; but the actions of fools are as necessary as those of the most prudent individuals. The motives that determine the voluptuary, that actuate the debauchee to risk their health, are as powerful, their actions are as necessary, as those which decide the wise man to manage his. But, it will be insisted, the debauchee may be prevailed on to change his conduct; this does not imply that he is a free agent; but, that motives may be found sufficiently powerful to annihilate the effect of those that previously acted upon him; then these new motives determine his will to the new mode of conduct he may adopt, as necessarily as the former did to the old mode.

Man is said to *deliberate* when the action of the will is suspended; this happens when two opposite motives act alternately upon him. To deliberate, is to hate and to love in succession; it is to be alternately attracted and repelled; it is to be moved sometimes by one motive, sometimes by another. Man only deliberates when he does not distinctly understand the quality of the objects from which he receives impulse, or when experience has not sufficiently apprised him of the effects, more or less remote, which his actions will produce. He would take the air, but the weather is uncertain; he deliberates in consequence; he weighs the various motives that urge his will to go out or to stay at home; he is at length determined by that motive which is most probable; this removes his indecision, which necessarily settles his will either to remain within or to go abroad:

this motive is always either the immediate or ultimate advantage he finds or thinks he finds in the action to which he is persuaded.

Man's will frequently fluctuates between two objects, of which either the presence or the ideas move him alternately: he waits until he has contemplated the objects or the ideas they have left in his brain; which solicit him to different actions; he then compares these objects or ideas: but even in the time of deliberation, during the comparison, pending these alternatives of love and hatred, which succeed each other sometimes with the utmost rapidity, he is not a free agent for a single instant; the good or the evil which he believes he finds successively in the objects, are the necessary motives of these momentary wills; of the rapid motion of desire or fear that he experiences as long as his uncertainty continues. From this it will be obvious, that deliberation is necessary; that uncertainty is necessary; that whatever part he takes, in consequence of this deliberation, it will always necessarily be that which he has judged, whether well or ill, is most probable to turn to his advantage.

When the soul is assailed by two motives that act alternately upon it, or modify it successively, it deliberates; the brain is in a sort of equilibrium, accompanied with perpetual oscillations, sometimes towards one object, sometimes towards the other, until the most forcible carries the point, and thereby extricates it, from this state of suspense, in which consists the indecision of his will. But when the brain is simultaneously assailed by causes equally strong, that move it in opposite directions; agreeable to the general law of all bodies, when they are struck equally by contrary powers, it stops, it is in *nisu*; it is neither capable to will nor to act; it waits until one of the two causes has obtained sufficient force to overpower the other, to determine its will, to attract it in such a manner that it may prevail over the efforts of the other cause.

This mechanism, so simple, so natural, suffices to demonstrate, why uncertainty is painful; why suspense is always a violent state for man. The brain, an organ so delicate, so mobile, experiences such rapid modifications, that it is fatigued; or when it is urged in contrary directions, by causes equally powerful, it suffers a kind of compression, that prevents the activity which is suitable to the preservation of the whole, which is necessary to procure what is advantageous to its existence. This mechanism will also explain the irregularity, the indecision, the inconstancy of man; and account for that conduct, which frequently appears an inexplicable mystery, which indeed it is, under the received systems. In consulting experience, it will be found that the soul is submitted to precisely the same physical laws as the material body. If the will of each individual, during a given time, was only moved by a single cause or passion, nothing would be more easy than to foresee his actions; but his heart is frequently assailed by contrary powers, by adverse motives, which either act on him simultaneously or in succession; then his brain, attracted in opposite directions, is either fatigued, or else tormented by a state of compression, which deprives it of activity. Sometimes it is in a state of incommodious inaction; sometimes it is the sport of the alternate shocks it undergoes. Such, no doubt, is the state in which man finds himself, when a lively passion solicits him to the commission of crime, whilst fear points out to him the danger by which it is attended: such, also, is the condition of him whom remorse, by the continued labour of his distracted soul, prevents from enjoying the objects he has criminally obtained.

If the powers or causes, whether exterior or interior, acting on the mind of man, tend towards opposite points, his soul, is well as all other bodies, will take a mean direction between the two; in consequence of the violence with which his soul is urged, his condition becomes sometimes so painful that his existence is troublesome: he has no longer a tendency to his own peculiar conservation; he seeks after death, as a sanctuary against himself—as the only remedy to his despair: it is thus we behold men, miserable and discontented, voluntarily destroy themselves, whenever life becomes insupportable. Man is competent to cherish his existence, no longer than life holds out charms to him; when he is wrought upon by painful sensations, or drawn by contrary impulsions, his natural tendency is deranged, he is under the necessity to follow a new route; this conducts him to his end, which it even displays to him as the most desirable good. In this manner may be explained, the conduct of those melancholy beings, whose vicious temperaments, whose tortured consciences, whose chagrin, whose *ennui,* sometimes determine them to renounce life.

The various powers, frequently very complicated, that act either successively or simultaneously upon the brain of man, which modify him so diversely in the different periods of his existence, are the true causes of that obscurity in morals, of that difficulty which is found, when it is desired to unravel the concealed springs of his enigmatical conduct. The heart of man is a labyrinth, only because it very rarely happens that we possess the necessary gift of judging it; from whence it will appear, that his circumstances, his indecision, his conduct, whether ridiculous, or unexpected, are the necessary consequences of the changes operated in him; are nothing but the effect of motives that successively determine his will; which are dependent on the frequent variations experienced by his machine. According to these variations, the same motives have not, always, the same influence over his will, the same objects no longer enjoy the faculty of pleasing him; his temperament has changed, either for the moment, or for ever. It follows as a consequence, that his taste, his desires, his passions, will change; there can be no kind of uniformity in his conduct, nor any certitude in the effects to be expected.

Choice by no means proves the free-agency of man; he only deliberates when he does not yet know which to choose of the many objects that move him, he is then in an embarrassment, which does not terminate, until his will as decided by the greater advantage he believes be shall find in the object he chooses, or the action he undertakes. From whence it may he seen that choice is necessary, because he would not determine for an object, or for an action, if he did not believe that he should find in it some direct advantage. That man should have free-agency, it were needful that he should be able to will or choose without motive; or, that he could prevent motives coercing his will. Action always being the effect of his will once determined, as his will cannot be determined but by a motive, which is not in his own power, it follows that he is never the master of the determination of his own peculiar will; that consequently he never acts as a free agent. It has been believed that man was a free agent, because he had a will with the power of choosing; but attention has not been paid to the fact, that even his will is moved by causes independent of himself, is owing to that which is inherent in his own organization, or which belongs to the nature of the beings acting on him. Indeed, man passes a great portion of his life without even willing. His will attends the motive by which it is determined. If he was to render an exact account of every thing he does in the course of each day, from rising in the morning to lying down at night, he would find, that not one of his actions have been in the least voluntary; that they have been mechanical, habitual, determined by causes he was not able to foresee, to which he was either obliged to, yield, or with which he was allured to acquiesce; he would discover, that all the motives of his labours, of his amusements, of his discourses, of his thoughts, have been necessary; that they have evidently either seduced him or drawn him along. Is he the master of willing, not to withdraw his hand from the fire when he fears it will be burnt? Or has he the power to take away from fire the property which makes him fear it? Is he the master of not choosing a dish of meat which he knows to be agreeable, or analogous to his palate; of not preferring it to that which he knows to be disagreeable or dangerous? It is always according to his sensations, to his own peculiar experience, or to his suppositions, that he judges of things either well or ill; but whatever way be his judgment, it depends necessarily on his mode of feeling, whether habitual or accidental, and the qualities he finds in the causes that move him, which exist in despite of himself...........

It has been believed man was a free agent, because it has been imagined that his soul could at will recall ideas, which sometimes suffice to check his most unruly desires. Thus, the idea of a remote evil frequently prevents him from enjoying a present and actual good: thus, remembrance, which is an almost insensible, a slight modification of his brain, annihilates, at each instant, the real objects that act upon his will. But he is not master of recalling to himself his ideas at pleasure; their association is independent of him; they are arranged in his brain, in despite of him, without his own knowledge, where they have made an impression more or less profound; his memory itself depends upon his organization; its fidelity depends upon the habitual or momentary state in which he finds himself; when his will is vigorously determined to some object or idea that excites a very lively passion in him, those objects or ideas that would be able to arrest his action no longer present themselves to his mind; in those moments his eyes are shut to the dangers that menace him, of which the idea ought to make him forbear; he marches forward headlong towards the object by whose image he is hurried on; reflection cannot operate upon him in any way; he sees nothing but the object of his desires; the salutary ideas which might be able to arrest his progress disappear, or else display themselves either too faintly or too late to prevent his acting. Such is the case with all those who, blinded by some strong passion, are not in a condition to recal to themselves those motives, of which the idea alone, in cooler moments, would be sufficient to deter them from proceeding; the disorder in which they are, prevents their judging soundly; render them incapable of foreseeing the consequence of their actions; precludes them from applying to their experience; from making use of their reason; natural operations, which suppose a justness in the manner of associating their ideas; but to which their brain is then not more competent, in consequence of the momentary delirium it suffers, than their hand is to write whilst they are taking violent exercise.

Man's mode of thinking is necessarily determined by his manner of being; it must, therefore, depend on his natural organization, and the modification his system receives independently of his will. From this we are obliged to conclude, that his thoughts, his reflections, his manner of viewing things, of feeling, of judging, of combining ideas, is neither voluntary nor free. In a word, that his soul is neither mistress of the motion excited in it, nor of representing to itself, when wanted, those images or ideas that are capable of counterbalancing the impulse it receives. This is the reason why man, when in a passion, ceases to reason; at that moment reason is as impossible to be heard, as it is during an extacy, or in a fit of drunkenness. The wicked are never more than men who are either drunk or mad: if they reason, it is not until tranquillity is reestablished in their machine; then, and not till then, the tardy ideas that present themselves to their mind, enable them to see the consequence of their actions, and give birth to ideas, that bring on them that trouble, which is designated *shame, regret, remorse.*

The errors of philosophers on the free-agency of man, have arisen from their regarding his will as the *primum mobile,* the original motive of his actions; for want of recurring back, they have not perceived the multiplied, the complicated causes, which, independently of him, give motion to the will itself, or which dispose and modify his brain, whilst he himself is purely passive in the motion he receives. Is he the master of desiring or not desiring an object that appears desirable to him? Without doubt it will be answered, No: but he is the master of resisting his desire, if he reflects on the consequences. But, I ask, is he capable of reflecting on these consequences when his soul is hurried along by a very lively passion, which entirely depends upon his natural organization, and the causes by which he is modified? Is it in his power to add to these consequences all the weight necessary to counterbalance his desire? Is he the master of preventing the qualities which render an object desirable from residing in it? I shall be told, he ought to have learned to resist his passions; to contract a habit of putting a curb on his desires. I agree to it without any difficulty: but in reply, I again ask, Is his nature susceptible of this modification?

Does his boiling blood, his unruly imagination, the igneous fluid that circulates in his veins, permit him to make, enable him to apply true experience in the moment when it is wanted? And, even when his temperament has capacitated him, has his education, the examples set before him, the ideas with which he has been inspired in early life, been suitable to make him contract this habit of repressing his desires? Have not all these things rather contributed to induce him to seek with avidity, to make him actually desire those objects which you say he ought to resist..............

In short, the actions of man are never free; they are always the necessary consequence of his temperament, of the received ideas, of the notions, either true or false, which he has formed to himself of happiness: of his opinions, strengthened by example, forfeited by education, consolidated by daily experience. So many crimes are witnessed on the earth, only because every thing conspires to render man vicious, to make him criminal; very frequently, the superstitions he has adopted, his government, his education, the examples set before him, irresistibly drive him on to evil: under these circumstances morality preaches virtue to him in vain. In those societies where vice is esteemed, where crime is crowned, where venality is constantly recompenced, where the most dreadful disorders are punished, only in those who are too weak to enjoy the privilege of committing them with impunity; the practice of virtue is considered nothing more than a painful sacrifice of fancied happiness. Such societies chastise, in the lower orders, those excesses which they respect in the higher ranks; and frequently have the injustice to condemn those in penalty of death, whom public prejudices, maintained by constant example, have rendered criminal.

Man, then, is not a free agent in any one instant of his life; he is necessarily guided in each step by those advantages, whether real or fictitious, that he attaches to the objects by which his passions are roused: these passions themselves are necessary in a being who, unceasingly tends towards his own happiness; their energy is necessary, since that depends on his temperament; his temperament is necessary, because it depends on the physical elements which enter into his composition; the modification of this temperament is necessary, as it is the infallible result, the inevitable consequence of the impulse he receives from the incessant action of moral and physical beings.............

It is said that free-agency is the absence of those obstacles competent to oppose themselves to the actions of man, or to the exercise of his faculties: it is pretended that he is a free agent, whenever, making use of these faculties, he produces the effect he has proposed to himself. In reply to this reasoning, it is sufficient to consider that it in no wise depends upon himself to place or remove the obstacles that either determine or resist him; the motive that causes his action is no more in his own power than the obstacle that impedes him, whether this obstacle or motive be within his own machine or exterior of his person: he is not master of the thought presented to his mind which determines his will; this thought is excited by some cause independent of himself.

To be undeceived on the system of his free-agency, man has simply to recur to the motive by which his will is determined, he will always find this motive is out of his own controul. It is said, that in consequence of an idea to which the mind gives birth, man acts freely if he encounters no obstacle. But the question is, what gives birth to this idea in his brain? has he the power either to prevent it from presenting itself, or from renewing itself in his brain? Does not this idea depend either upon objects that strike him exteriorly and in despite of himself, or upon causes that without his knowledge act within himself and modify his brain? Can he prevent his eyes, cast without design upon any object whatever, from giving him an idea of this object, from moving his brain? He is not more master of the obstacles; they are the necessary effects of either interior or exterior causes, which always act according to their given properties. A man insults a coward, who is necessarily irritated against his insulter, but his will cannot vanquish the obstacle that cowardice places to the object of his desire, which is, to resent the insult; because his natural conformation, which does not depend upon himself, prevents his having courage. In this case the coward is insulted in despite of himself, and against his will is obliged patiently to brook the insult he has received.

The partizans of the system of free-agency appear ever to have confounded constraint with necessity. Man believes he acts as a free agent, every time he does not see any thing that places obstacles to his actions; he does not perceive that the motive which causes him to will is always necessary, is ever independent of himself. A prisoner loaded with chains is compelled to remain in prison, but he is not a free agent, he is not able to resist the desire to emancipate himself; his chains prevent him from acting, but they do not prevent him from willing; he would save himself if they would loose his fetters, but he would not save himself as a free agent, fear or the idea of punishment would be sufficient motives for his action.

Man may therefore cease to be restrained, without, for that reason, becoming a free agent: in whatever manner he acts, he will act necessarily; according to motives by which he shall be determined. He may be compared to a heavy body, that finds itself arrested in its descent by any obstacle whatever: take away this obstacle, it will gravitate or continue to fall; but who shall say this dense body is free to fall or not? Is not its descent the necessary effect of its own specific gravity? The virtuous Socrates submitted to the laws of his country, although they were unjust; notwithstanding the doors of his gaol were left open to him he would not save himself; but in this he did not act as a free agent; the invisible chains of opinion, the secret love of decorum, the inward respect for the laws, even when they were iniquitous, the fear of tarnishing his glory, kept him in his prison: they were motives sufficiently powerful, with this enthusiast for virtue, to induce him to wait death with tranquillity; it was not in his power to save himself, because he could find no potential motive to bring him to depart, even for an instant, from those principles to which his mind was accustomed.

Man, says he, frequently acts against his inclination, from whence he has falsely concluded he is a free agent; when he appears to act contrary to his inclination, he is determined to it by some motive sufficiently efficacious to vanquish this inclination. A sick man, with a view to his cure, arrives at conquering his repugnance to the most disgusting remedies: the fear of pain, the dread of death, then become necessary and intelligent motives; consequently, this sick man cannot be said, with truth, by any means, to act freely.

When it is said, that man is not a free agent, it is not pretended to compare him to a body moved by a simple impulsive cause: he contains within himself causes inherent to his existence; he is moved by an interior organ, which has its own peculiar laws; which is itself necessarily determined, in consequence of ideas formed from perceptions, resulting from sensations, which it receives from exterior objects. As the mechanism of these sensations, of these perceptions, and the manner they engrave ideas on the brain of man, are not known to him, because he is unable to unravel all these motions; because he cannot perceive the chain of operations in his soul, or the motive-principle that acts within him, he supposes himself a free agent; which, literally translated, signifies that he moves himself by himself; that he determines himself without cause; when he rather ought to say, he is ignorant how or for why he acts in the manner he does. It is true the soul enjoys an activity peculiar to itself, but it is equally certain that this activity would never be displayed if some motive or some cause did not put it in a condition to exercise itself, at least it will not be pretended that the soul is able either to love or to hate without being moved, without knowing the objects, without having some idea of their qualities. Gunpowder has unquestionably a particular activity, but this activity will never display itself, unless fire be applied to it; this, however, immediately sets in motion.

It is the great complication of motion in man, it is the variety of his action, it is the multiplicity of causes that move him, whether simultaneously or in continual succession, that persuades him he is a free agent: if all his motions were simple, if the causes that move him did not confound themselves with each other, if they were distinct, if his machine was less complicated, he would perceive that all his actions were necessary, because he would be enabled to recur instantly to the cause that made him act. A man who should be always obliged to go towards the west would always go on that side, but he would feel extremely well, that in so going he was not a free agent: if he had another sense, as his actions or his motion augmented by a sixth would be still more varied, much more complicated, he would believe himself still more a free agent than he does with his five senses.

It is, then, for want of recurring to the causes that move him, for want of being able to analyse, from not being competent to decompose the complicated motion of his machine, that man believes himself a free agent; it is only upon his own ignorance that he founds the profound yet deceitful notion he has of his free-agency, that he builds those opinions which he brings forward as a striking proof of his pretended freedom of action. If, for a short time, each man was willing to examine his own peculiar actions, to search out their true motives, to discover their concatenation, he would remain convinced that the sentiment he has of his natural free-agency is a chimera that must speedily be destroyed by experience..................

In despite of the gratuitous ideas which man has formed to himself on his pretended free-agency; in defiance of the illusions of this suppose intimate sense, which, contrary to his experience, persuades him that he is master of his will,—all his institutions are really founded upon necessity: on this, as on a variety of other occasions, practice throws aside speculation. Indeed, if it was not believed that certain motives embraced the power requisite to determine the will of man, to arrest the progress of his passions, to direct them towards an end, to modify him; of what use would be the faculty of speech? What benefit could arise from education itself? What does education achieve, save give the first impulse to the human will, make man contract habits, oblige him to persist in them, furnish him with motives, whether true or false, to act after a given manner? When the father either menaces his son with punishment, or promises him a reward, is he not convinced these things will act upon his will? What does legislation attempt, except it be to present to the citizens of a state those motives which are supposed necessary to determine them to perform some actions that are considered worthy; to abstain from committing others that are looked upon as unworthy? What is the object of morals, if it be not to shew man that his interest exacts he should suppress the momentary ebullition of his passions, with a view to promote a more certain happiness, a more lasting well-being, than can possibly result from the gratification of his transitory desires? Does not the religion of all countries suppose the human race, together with the entire of Nature, submitted to the irresistible will of a necessary being, who regulates their condition after the eternal laws of immutable wisdom? Is not God the absolute master of their destiny? Is it not this divine being who chooses and rejects? The anathemas fulminated by religion, the promises it holds forth, are they not founded upon the idea of the effects they will necessarily produce upon mankind? Is not man brought into existence without his own knowledge? Is he not obliged to play a part against his will? Does not either his happiness or his misery depend on the part he plays?

Alternate Possibilities and Moral Responsibility

Harry G. Frankfurt

A DOMINANT role in nearly all recent inquiries into the free-will problem has been played by a principle which I shall call "the principle of alternate possibilities." This principle states that a person is morally responsible for what he has done only if he could have done otherwise. Its exact meaning is a subject of controversy, particularly concerning whether someone who accepts it is thereby committed to believing that moral responsibility and determinism are incompatible. Practically no one, however, seems inclined to deny or even to question that the principle of alternate possibilities (construed in some way or other) is true. It has generally seemed so overwhelmingly plausible that some philosophers have even characterized it as an *a priori* truth. People whose accounts of free will or of moral responsibility are radically at odds evidently find in it a firm and convenient common ground upon which they can profitably take their opposing stands.

But the principle of alternate possibilities is false. A person may well be morally responsible for what he has done even though he could not have done otherwise. The principle's plausibility is an illusion, which can be made to vanish by bringing the relevant moral phenomena into sharper focus.

I

In seeking illustrations of the principle of alternate possibilities, it is most natural to think of situations in which the same circumstances both bring it about that a person does something and make it impossible for him to avoid doing it. These include, for example, situations in which a person is coerced into doing something, or in which he is impelled to act by a hypnotic suggestion, or in which some inner compulsion drives him to do what he does. In situations of these kinds there are circumstances that make it impossible for the person to do otherwise, and these very circumstances also serve to bring it about that he does whatever it is that he does.

However, there may be circumstances that constitute sufficient conditions for a certain action to be performed by someone and that therefore make it impossible for the person to do otherwise, but that do not actually impel the person to act or in any way produce his action. A person may do something in circumstances that leave him no alternative to doing it, without these circumstances actually moving him or leading him to do it—without them playing any role, indeed, in bringing it about that he does what he does.

An examination of situations characterized by circumstances of this sort casts doubt, I believe, on the relevance to questions of moral responsibility of the fact that a person

Source: *The Journal of Philosophy*, Vol. 66, No. 23 (Dec. 4, 1969), pp. 829–839.

who has done something could not have done otherwise. I propose to develop some examples of this kind in the context of a discussion of coercion and to suggest that our moral intuitions concerning these examples tend to disconfirm the principle of alternate possibilities. Then I will discuss the principle in more general terms, explain what I think is wrong with it, and describe briefly and without argument how it might appropriately be revised.

II

It is generally agreed that a person who has been coerced to do something did not do it freely and is not morally responsible for having done it. Now the doctrine that coercion and moral responsibility are mutually exclusive may appear to be no more than a somewhat particularized version of the principle of alternate possibilities. It is natural enough to say of a person who has been coerced to do something that he could not have done otherwise. And it may easily seem that being coerced deprives a person of freedom and of moral responsibility simply because it is a special case of being unable to do otherwise. The principle of alternate possibilities may in this way derive some credibility from its association with the very plausible proposition that moral responsibility is excluded by coercion.

It is not right, however, that it should do so. The fact that a person was coerced to act as he did may entail both that he could not have done otherwise and that he bears no moral responsibility for his action. But his lack of moral responsibility is not entailed by his having been unable to do otherwise. The doctrine that coercion excludes moral responsibility is not correctly understood, in other words, as a particularized version of the principle of alternate possibilities.

Let us suppose that someone is threatened convincingly with a penalty he finds unacceptable and that he then does what is required of him by the issuer of the threat. We can imagine details that would make it reasonable for us to think that the person was coerced to perform the action in question, that he could not have done otherwise, and that he bears no moral responsibility for having done what he did. But just what is it about situations of this kind that warrants the judgment that the threatened person is not morally responsible for his act?

This question may be approached by considering situations of the following kind. Jones decides for reasons of his own to do something, then someone threatens him with a very harsh penalty (so harsh that any reasonable person would submit to the threat) unless he does precisely that, and Jones does it. Will we hold Jones morally responsible for what he has done? I think this will depend on the roles we think were played, in leading him to act, by his original decision and by the threat.

One possibility is that Jones[1] is not a reasonable man: he is, rather, a man who does what he has once decided to do no matter what happens next and no matter what the cost. In that case, the threat actually exerted no effective force upon him. He acted without any regard to it, very much as if he were not aware that it had been made. If this is indeed the way it was, the situation did not involve coercion at all. The threat did not lead Jones[1] to do what he did. Nor was it in fact sufficient to have prevented him from doing otherwise: if his earlier decision had been to do something else, the threat would not have deterred him in the slightest. It seems evident that in these circumstances the fact that Jones1 was threatened in no way reduces the moral responsibility he would otherwise bear for his act. This example, however, is not a counterexample either to the doctrine that coercion excuses or to the principle of alternate possibilities. For we have supposed that Jones1 is a man upon whom the threat had no coercive effect and, hence, that it did not actually deprive him of alternatives to doing what he did.

Another possibility is that Jones[2] was stampeded by the threat. Given that threat, he would have performed that action regardless of what decision he had already made. The threat upset him so profoundly, moreover, that he completely forgot his own earlier decision and did what was demanded of him entirely because he was terrified of the penalty with which he was threatened. In this case, it is not relevant to his having performed the action that he had already decided on his own to perform it. When the chips were down he thought of nothing but the threat, and fear alone led him to act. The fact that at an earlier time Jones[2] had decided for his own reasons to act in just that way may be relevant to an evaluation of his character; he may bear full moral responsibility for having made *that* decision. But he can hardly be said to be morally responsible for his action. For he performed the action simply as a result of the coercion to which he was subjected. His earlier decision played no role in bringing it about that he did what he did, and it would therefore be gratuitous to assign it a role in the moral evaluation of his action.

Now consider a third possibility. Jones[3] was neither stampeded by the threat nor indifferent to it. The threat impressed him, as it would impress any reasonable man, and he would have submitted to it wholeheartedly if he had not already made a decision that coincided with the one demanded of him. In fact, however, he performed the action in question on the basis of the decision he had made before the threat was issued. When he acted, he was not actually motivated by the threat but solely by the considerations that had originally commended the action to him. It was not the threat that led him to act, though it would have done so if he had not already provided himself with a sufficient motive for performing the action in question.

No doubt it will be very difficult for anyone to know, in a case like this one, exactly what happened. Did Jones[3] perform the action because of the threat, or were his reasons for acting simply those which had already persuaded him to do so? Or did he act on the basis of two motives, each of which was sufficient for his action? It is not impossible, however, that the situation should be clearer than situations of this kind usually are. And suppose it is apparent to us that Jones[3] acted on the basis of his own decision and not because of the threat. Then I think we would be justified in regarding his moral responsibility for what he did as unaffected by the threat even though, since he would in any case have submitted to the threat, he could not have avoided doing what he did. It would be entirely reasonable for us to make the same judgment concerning his moral responsibility that we would have made if we had not known of the threat. For the threat did not in fact influence his performance of the action. He did what he did just as if the threat had not been made at all.

III

The case of Jones[3] may appear at first glance to combine coercion and moral responsibility, and thus to provide a counterexample to the doctrine that coercion excuses. It is not really so certain that it does so, however, because it is unclear whether the example constitutes a genuine instance of coercion. Can we say of Jones[3] that he was coerced to do something, when he had already decided on his own to do it and when he did it entirely on the basis of that decision? Or would it be more correct to say that Jones[3] was not coerced to do what he did, even though he himself recognized that there was an irresistible force at work in virtue of which he had to do it? My own linguistic intuitions lead me toward the second alternative, but they are somewhat equivocal. Perhaps we can say either of these things, or perhaps we must add a qualifying explanation to whichever of them we say.

This murkiness, however, does not interfere with our drawing an important moral from an examination of the example. Suppose we decide to say that Jones[3] was *not* coerced. Our basis for saying this will clearly be that it is incorrect to regard a man as being coerced to do something unless he does it *because of* the coercive force exerted against him. The fact that an irresistible threat is made will not, then, entail that the person who receives it is coerced to do what he does. It will also be necessary that the threat is what actually accounts for his doing it. On the other hand, suppose we decide to say that Jones³ *was* coerced. Then we will be bound to admit that being coerced does not exclude being morally responsible. And we will also surely be led to the view that coercion affects the judgment of a person's moral responsibility only when the person acts as he does because he is coerced to do so—i.e., when the fact that he is coerced is what accounts for his action.

Whichever we decide to say, then, we will recognize that the doctrine that coercion excludes moral responsibility is not a particularized version of the principle of alternate possibilities. Situations in which a person who does something cannot do otherwise because he is subject to coercive power are either not instances of coercion at all, or they are situations in which the person may still be morally responsible for what he does if it is not because of the coercion that he does it. When we excuse a person who has been coerced, we do not excuse him because he was unable to do otherwise. Even though a person is subject to a coercive force that precludes his performing any action but one, he may nonetheless bear full moral responsibility for performing that action.

IV

To the extent that the principle of alternate possibilities derives its plausibility from association with the doctrine that coercion excludes moral responsibility, a clear understanding of the latter diminishes the appeal of the former. Indeed the case of Jones³ may appear to do more than illuminate the relationship between the two doctrines. It may well seem to provide a decisive counterexample to the principle of alternate possibilities and thus to show that this principle is false. For the irresistibility of the threat to which Jones³ is subjected might well be taken to mean that he cannot but perform the action he performs. And yet the threat, since Jones³ performs the action without regard to it, does not reduce his moral responsibility for what he does.

The following objection will doubtless be raised against the suggestion that the case of Jones³ is a counterexample to the principle of alternate possibilities. There is perhaps a sense in which Jones³ cannot do otherwise than perform the action he performs, since he is a reasonable man and the threat he encounters is sufficient to move any reasonable man. But it is not this sense that is germane to the principle of alternate possibilities. His knowledge that he stands to suffer an intolerably harsh penalty does not mean that Jones³, strictly speaking, *cannot* perform any action but the one he does perform. After all it is still open to him, and this is crucial, to defy the threat if he wishes to do so and to accept the penalty his action would bring down upon him. In the sense in which the principle of alternate possibilities employs the concept of "could have done otherwise," Jones³'s inability to resist the threat does not mean that he cannot do otherwise than perform the action he performs. Hence the case of Jones³ does not constitute an instance contrary to the principle.

I do not propose to consider in what sense the concept of "could have done otherwise" figures in the principle of alternate possibilities, nor will I attempt to measure the force of the objection I have just described.[1] For I believe that whatever force this objection may be thought to have can be deflected by altering the example in the following way.[2] Suppose someone—Black, let us say—wants Jones⁴ to perform a certain action.

---

[1] The two main concepts employed in the principle of alternate possibilities are "morally responsible" and "could have done otherwise." To discuss the principle without analyzing either of these concepts may well seem like an attempt at piracy. The reader should take notice that my Jolly Roger is now unfurled.

[2] After thinking up the example that I am about to develop I learned that Robert Nozick, in lectures given several years ago, had formulated an example of the same general type and had proposed it as a counterexample to the principle of alternate possibilities.

Black is prepared to go to considerable lengths to get his way, but he prefers to avoid showing his hand unnecessarily. So he waits until Jones[4] is about to make up his mind what to do, and he does nothing unless it is clear to him (Black is an excellent judge of such things) that Jones[4] is going to decide to do something *other* than what he wants him to do. If it does become clear that Jones[4] is going to decide to do something else, Black takes effective steps to ensure that Jones[4] decides to do, and that he does do, what he wants him to do.[3] Whatever Jones[4]'s initial preferences and inclinations, then, Black will have his way.

What steps will Black take, if he believes he must take steps, in order to ensure that Jones[4] decides and acts as he wishes? Anyone with a theory concerning what "could have done otherwise" means may answer this question for himself by describing whatever measures he would regard as sufficient to guarantee that, in the relevant sense, Jones[4] cannot do otherwise. Let Black pronounce a terrible threat, and in this way both force Jones[4] to perform the desired action and prevent him from performing a forbidden one. Let Black give Jones[4] a potion, or put him under hypnosis, and in some such way as these generate in Jones[4] an irresistible inner compulsion to perform the act Black wants performed and to avoid others. Or let Black manipulate the minute processes of Jones[4]'s brain and nervous system in some more direct way, so that causal forces running in and out of his synapses and along the poor man's nerves determine that he chooses to act and that he does act in the one way and not in any other. Given any conditions under which it will be maintained that Jones[4] cannot do otherwise, in other words, let Black bring it about that those conditions prevail. The structure of the example is flexible enough, I think, to find a way around any charge of irrelevance by accommodating the doctrine on which the charge is based.[4]

Now suppose that Black never has to show his hand because Jones[4], for reasons of his own, decides to perform and does perform the very action Black wants him to perform. In that case, it seems clear, Jones[4] will bear precisely the same moral responsibility for what he does as he would have borne if Black had not been ready to take steps to ensure that he do it. It would be quite unreasonable to excuse Jones[4] for his action, or to with-hold the praise to which it would normally entitle him, on the basis of the fact that he could not have done otherwise. This fact played no role at all in leading him to act as he did. He would have acted the same even if it had not been a fact. Indeed, everything happened just as it would have happened without Black's presence in the situation and without his readiness to intrude into it.

In this example there are sufficient conditions for Jones[4]'s performing the action in question. What action he performs is not up to him. Of course it is in a way up to him whether he acts on his own or as a result of Black's intervention. That depends upon

---

[3] The assumption that Black can predict what Jones4 will decide to do does not beg the question of determinism. We can imagine that Jones[4] has often confronted the alternatives—*A* and *B*—that he now confronts, and that his face has invariably twitched when he was about to decide to do *A* and never when he was about to decide to do *B*. Knowing this, and observing the twitch, Black would have a basis for prediction. This does, to be sure, suppose that there is some sort of causal relation between Jones4's state at the time of the twitch and his subsequent states. But any plausible view of decision or of action will allow that reaching a decision and performing an action both involve earlier and later phases, with causal relations between them, and such that the earlier phases are not themselves part of the decision or of the action. The example does not require that these earlier phases be deterministically related to still earlier events.

[4] The example is also flexible enough to allow for the elimination of Black altogether. Anyone who thinks that the effectiveness of the example is undermined by its reliance on a human manipulator, who imposes his will on Jones₄, can substitute for Black a machine programmed to do what Black does. If this is still not good enough, forget both Black and the machine and suppose that their role is played by natural forces involving no will or design at all.

what action he himself is inclined to perform. But whether he finally acts on his own or as a result of Black's intervention, he performs the same action. He has no alternative but to do what Black wants him to do. If he does it on his own, however, his moral responsibility for doing it is not affected by the fact that Black was lurking in the background with sinister intent, since this intent never comes into play.

V

The fact that a person could not have avoided doing something is a sufficient condition of his having done it. But, as some of my examples show, this fact may play no role whatever in the explanation of why he did it. It may not figure at all among the circumstances that actually brought it about that he did what he did, so that his action is to be accounted for on another basis entirely. Even though the person was unable to do otherwise, that is to say, it may not be the case that he acted as he did *because* he could not have done otherwise. Now if someone had no alternative to performing a certain action but did not perform it because he was unable to do otherwise, then he would have performed exactly the same action even if he *could* have done otherwise. The circumstances that made it impossible for him to do otherwise could have been subtracted from the situation without affecting what happened or why it happened in any way. Whatever it was that actually led the person to do what he did, or that made him do it, would have led him to do it or made him do it even if it had been possible for him to do something else instead.

Thus it would have made no difference, so far as concerns his action or how he came to perform it, if the circumstances that made it impossible for him to avoid performing it had not prevailed. The fact that he could not have done otherwise clearly provides no basis for supposing that he *might* have done otherwise if he had been able to do so. When a fact is in this way irrelevant to the problem of accounting for a person's action it seems quite gratuitous to assign it any weight in the assessment of his moral responsibility. Why should the fact be considered in reaching a moral judgment concerning the person when it does not help in any way to understand either what made him act as he did or what, in other circumstances, he might have done?

This, then, is why the principle of alternate possibilities is mistaken. It asserts that a person bears no moral responsibility—that is, he is to be excused—for having performed an action if there were circumstances that made it impossible for him to avoid performing it. But there may be circumstances that make it impossible for a person to avoid performing some action without those circumstances in any way bringing it about that he performs that action. It would surely be no good for the person to refer to circumstances of this sort in an effort to absolve himself of moral responsibility for performing the action in question. For those circumstances, by hypothesis, actually had nothing to do with his having done what he did. He would have done precisely the same thing, and he would have been led or made in precisely the same way to do it, even if they had not prevailed.

We often do, to be sure, excuse people for what they have done when they tell us (and we believe them) that they could not have done otherwise. But this is because we assume that what they tell us serves to explain why they did what they did. We take it for granted that they are not being disingenuous, as a person would be who cited as an excuse the fact that he could not have avoided doing what he did but who knew full well that it was not at all because of this that he did it.

What I have said may suggest that the principle of alternate possibilities should be revised so as to assert that a person is not morally responsible for what he has done if he did it because he could not have done otherwise. It may be noted that this revision of the principle does not seriously affect the arguments of those who have relied on the original principle in their efforts to maintain that moral responsibility and determinism are incompatible. For if it was causally determined that a person perform a certain action, then it will be true that the person performed it because of those causal determinants. And if the fact that it was causally determined that a person perform a certain action means that the person could not have done otherwise, as philosophers who argue for the incompatibility thesis characteristically suppose, then the fact that it was causally determined that a person perform a certain action will mean that the person performed it because he could not have done otherwise. The revised principle of alternate possibilities will entail, on this assumption concerning the meaning of 'could have done otherwise', that a person is not morally responsible for what he has done if it was causally determined that he do it. I do not believe, however, that this revision of the principle is acceptable.

Suppose a person tells us that he did what he did because he was unable to do otherwise; or suppose he makes the similar statement that he did what he did because he had to do it. We do often accept statements like these (if we believe them) as valid excuses, and such statements may well seem at first glance to invoke the revised principle of alternate possibilities. But I think that when we accept such statements as valid excuses it is because we assume that we are being told more than the statements strictly and literally convey. We understand the person who offers the excuse to mean that he did what he did *only because* he was unable to do otherwise, or *only because* he had to do it. And we understand him to mean, more particularly, that when he did what he did it was not because that was what he really wanted to do. The principle of alternate possibilities should thus be replaced, in my opinion, by the following principle: a person is not morally responsible for what he has done if he did it only because he could not have done otherwise. This principle does not appear to conflict with the view that moral responsibility is compatible with determinism.

The following may all be true: there were circumstances that made it impossible for a person to avoid doing something; these circumstances actually played a role in bringing it about that he did it, so that it is correct to say that he did it because he could not have done otherwise; the person really wanted to do what he did; he did it because it was what he really wanted to do, so that it is not correct to say that he did what he did only because he could not have done otherwise. Under these conditions, the person may well be morally responsible for what he has done. On the other hand, he will not be morally responsible for what he has done if he did it only because he could not have done otherwise, even if what he did was something he really wanted to do.

HARRY G. FRANKFURT
The Rockefeller University

BOOK REVIEWS

Selected Letters of Friedrich Nietzsche. Edited and translated by CHRISTOPHER MIDDLE-TON. Chicago: University Press. xvii, 370 p. $10.

Nietzsche is one of the small company of important philosophers who were also great writers. But not even his most ardent admirers need claim that he was a great letter writer. There are fascinating passages in many of his letters, and there is evidence in his correspondence of the power of his literary style, his wisdom, and his wit, but the place to find these most fully and at their best is in the works he himself designed for publication.

Though Christopher Middleton, professor of Germanic languages and literatures at the University of Texas, apparently recognizes this, he makes what seem to me somewhat excessive claims for the book under review. In his Introduction to the 206 letters he selected for translation, approximately one-tenth of the total number available, the editor expresses the hope that these "letters would reveal the man behind the immoralist, behind the visionary, behind the terrorist of metaphysical revolt." Middleton himself states the principal difficulty in realizing this hope: Nietzsche, he writes, "was a reticent man, in his conversation as in his letters." Though Nietzsche "seldom takes us down the darker galleries of his labyrinth . . . nevertheless I believe that the selection (here provided) presents a ground plan of the labyrinth."

Freedom of the Will and the Concept of a Person

Harry G. Frankfurt

WHAT philosophers have lately come to accept as analysis of the concept of a person is not actually analysis of *that* concept at all. Strawson, whose usage represents the current standard, identifies the concept of a person as "the concept of a type of entity such that *both* predicates ascribing states of consciousness *and* predicates ascribing corporeal characteristics . . . are equally applicable to a single individual of that single type."[1] But there are many entities besides persons that have both mental and physical properties. As it happens—though it seems extraordinary that this should be so—there is no common English word for the type of entity Strawson has in mind, a type that includes not only human beings but animals of various lesser species as well. Still, this hardly justifies the misappropriation of a valuable philosophical term.

Whether the members of some animal species are persons is surely not to be settled merely by determining whether it is correct to apply to them, in addition to predicates ascribing corporeal characteristics, predicates that ascribe states of consciousness. It does violence to our language to endorse the application of the term 'person' to those numerous creatures which do have both psychological and material properties but which are manifestly not persons in any normal sense of the word. This misuse of language is doubtless innocent of any theoretical error. But although the offense is "merely verbal," it does significant harm. For it gratuitously diminishes our philosophical vocabulary, and it increases the likelihood that we will overlook the important area of inquiry with which the term 'person' is most naturally associated. It might have been expected that no problem would be of more central and persistent concern to philosophers than that of understanding what we ourselves essentially are. Yet this problem is so generally neglected that it has been possible to make off with its very name almost without being noticed and, evidently, without evoking any widespread feeling of loss.

There is a sense in which the word 'person' is merely the singular form of 'people' and in which both terms connote no more than membership in a certain biological species. In those senses of the word which are of greater philosophical interest, however, the criteria for being a person do not serve primarily to distinguish the members of our own species from the members of other species. Rather, they are designed to capture those attributes which are the subject of our most humane concern with ourselves and the source of what we regard as most important and most problematical in our lives. Now these attributes would be of equal significance to us even if they were not in fact peculiar and common to

---

[1] P. F. Strawson, *Individuals* (London: Methuen, 1959), pp. 101–102. Ayer's usage of 'person' is similar: "it is characteristic of persons in this sense that besides having various physical properties . . . they are also credited with various forms of consciousness" [A. J. Ayer, *The Concept of a Person* (New York: St. Martin's, 1963), p. 82]. What concerns Strawson and Ayer is the problem of understanding the relation between mind and body, rather than the quite different problem of understanding what it is to be a creature that not only has a mind and a body but is also a person.

the members of our own species. What interests us most in the human condition would not interest us less if it were also a feature of the condition of other creatures as well.

Our concept of ourselves as persons is not to be understood, therefore, as a concept of attributes that are necessarily species-specific. It is conceptually possible that members of novel or even of familiar nonhuman species should be persons; and it is also conceptually possible that some members of the human species are not persons. We do in fact assume, on the other hand, that no member of another species is a person. Accordingly, there is a presumption that what is essential to persons is a set of characteristics that we generally suppose—whether rightly or wrongly—to be uniquely human.

It is my view that one essential difference between persons and other creatures is to be found in the structure of a person's will. Human beings are not alone in having desires and motives, or in making choices. They share these things with the members of certain other species, some of whom even appear to engage in deliberation and to make decisions based upon prior thought. It seems to be peculiarly characteristic of humans, however, that they are able to form what I shall call "second-order desires" or "desires of the second order."

Besides wanting and choosing and being moved *to do* this or that, men may also want to have (or not to have) certain desires and motives. They are capable of wanting to be different, in their preferences and purposes, from what they are. Many animals appear to have the capacity for what I shall call "first-order desires" or "desires of the first order," which are simply desires to do or not to do one thing or another. No animal other than man, however, appears to have the capacity for reflective self-evaluation that is manifested in the formation of second-order desires.[2]

I

The concept designated by the verb 'to want' is extraordinarily elusive. A statement of the form "*A* wants to *X*"—taken by itself, apart from a context that serves to amplify or to specify its meaning—conveys remarkably little information. Such a statement may be consistent, for example, with each of the following statements: (a) the prospect of doing *X* elicits no sensation or introspectible emotional response in *A*; (b) *A* is unaware that he wants to *X*; (c) *A* believes that he does not want to *X*; (d) *A* wants to refrain from *X*-ing; (e) *A* wants to *Y* and believes that it is impossible for him both to *Y* and to *X*; (f) *A* does not "really" want to *X*; (g) *A* would rather die than *X*; and so on. It is therefore hardly sufficient to formulate the distinction between first-order and second-order desires, as I have done, by suggesting merely that someone has a first-order desire when he wants to do or not to do such-and-such, and that he has a second-order desire when he wants to have or not to have a certain desire of the first order.

As I shall understand them, statements of the form "*A* wants to *X*" cover a rather broad range of possibilities.[3] They may be true even when statements like (a) through (g)

---

[2] For the sake of simplicity, I shall deal only with what someone wants or desires, neglecting related phenomena such as choices and decisions. I propose to use the verbs 'to want' and 'to desire' interchangeably, although they are by no means perfect synonyms. My motive in forsaking the established nuances of these words arises from the fact that the verb 'to want', which suits my purposes better so far as its meaning is concerned, does not lend itself so readily to the formation of nouns as does the verb 'to desire'. It is perhaps acceptable, albeit graceless, to speak in the plural of someone's "wants." But to speak in the singular of someone's "want" would be an abomination.

[3] What I say in this paragraph applies not only to cases in which 'to *X*' refers to a possible action or inaction. It also applies to cases in which 'to *X*' refers to a first-order desire and in which the statement that '*A* wants to *X*' is therefore a shortened version of a statement—"*A* wants to want to *X*"—that identifies a desire of the second order.

are true: when *A* is unaware of any feelings concerning *X*-ing, when he is unaware that he wants to *X,* when he deceives himself about what he wants and believes falsely that he does not want to *X,* when he also has other desires that conflict with his desire to *X,* or when he is ambivalent. The desires in question may be conscious or unconscious, they need not be univocal, and *A* may be mistaken about them. There is a further source of uncertainty with regard to statements that identify someone's desires, however, and here it is important for my purposes to be less permissive.

Consider first those statements of the form "*A* wants to *X*" which identify first-order desires—that is, statements in which the term 'to *X*' refers to an action. A statement of this kind does not, by itself, indicate the relative strength of *A*'s desire to *X*. It does not make it clear whether this desire is at all likely to play a decisive role in what *A* actually does or tries to do. For it may correctly be said that *A* wants to *X* even when his desire to *X* is only one among his desires and when it is far from being paramount among them. Thus, it may be true that *A* wants to *X* when he strongly prefers to do something else instead; and it may be true that he wants to *X* despite the fact that, when he acts, it is not the desire to X that motivates him to do what he does. On the other hand, someone who states that *A* wants to *X* may mean to convey that it is this desire that is motivating or moving *A* to do what he is actually doing or that *A* will in fact be moved by this desire (unless he changes his mind) when he acts.

It is only when it is used in the second of these ways that, given the special usage of 'will' that I propose to adopt, the statement identifies *A*'s will. To identify an agent's will is either to identify the desire (or desires) by which he is motivated in some action he performs or to identify the desire (or desires) by which he will or would be motivated when or if he acts. An agent's will, then, is identical with one or more of his first-order desires. But the notion of the will, as I am employing it, is not coextensive with the notion of first-order desires. It is not the notion of something that merely inclines an agent in some degree to act in a certain way. Rather, it is the notion of an *effective* desire—one that moves (or will or would move) a person all the way to action. Thus the notion of the will is not coextensive with the notion of what an agent intends to do. For even though someone may have a settled intention to do *X,* he may nonetheless do something else instead of doing *X* because, despite his intention, his desire to do *X* proves to be weaker or less effective than some conflicting desire.

Now consider those statements of the form "*A* wants to *X*" which identify second-order desires—that is, statements in which the term 'to *X*' refers to a desire of the first order. There are also two kinds of situation in which it may be true that *A* wants to want to *X*. In the first place, it might be true of *A* that he wants to have a desire to *X* despite the fact that he has a univocal desire, altogether free of conflict and ambivalence, to refrain from *X*-ing. Someone might want to have a certain desire, in other words, but univocally want that desire to be unsatisfied.

Suppose that a physician engaged in psychotherapy with narcotics addicts believes that his ability to help his patients would be enhanced if he understood better what it is like for them to desire the drug to which they are addicted. Suppose that he is led in this way to want to have a desire for the drug. If it is a genuine desire that he wants, then what he wants is not merely to feel the sensations that addicts characteristically feel when they are gripped by their desires for the drug. What the physician wants, insofar as he wants to have a desire, is to be inclined or moved to some extent to take the drug.

It is entirely possible, however, that, although he wants to be moved by a desire to take the drug, he does not want this desire to be effective. He may not want it to move him all the way to action. He need not be interested in finding out what it is like to take the drug. And insofar as he now wants only to *want* to take it, and not to *take* it, there is nothing in what he now wants that would be satisfied by the drug itself. He may now have, in fact, an altogether univocal desire *not* to take the drug; and he may prudently arrange to make it impossible for him to satisfy the desire he would have if his desire to want the drug should in time be satisfied.

It would thus be incorrect to infer, from the fact that the physician now wants to desire to take the drug, that he already does desire to take it. His second-order desire to be moved to take the drug does not entail that he has a first-order desire to take it. If the drug were now to be administered to him, this might satisfy no desire that is implicit in his desire to want to take it. While he wants to want to take the drug, he may have *no* desire to take it; it may be that *all* he wants is to taste the desire for it. That is, his desire to have a certain desire that he does not have may not be a desire that his will should be at all different than it is.

Someone who wants only in this truncated way to want to X stands at the margin of preciosity, and the fact that he wants to want to X is not pertinent to the identification of his will. There is, however, a second kind of situation that may be described by 'A wants to want to X'; and when the statement is used to describe a situation of this second kind, then it does pertain to what A wants his will to be. In such cases the statement means that A wants the desire to X to be the desire that moves him effectively to act. It is not merely that he wants the desire to X to be among the desires by which, to one degree or another, he is moved or inclined to act. He wants this desire to be effective—that is, to provide the motive in what he actually does. Now when the statement that A wants to want to X is used in this way, it does entail that A already has a desire to X. It could not be true both that A wants the desire to X to move him into action and that he does not want to X. It is only if he does want to X that he can coherently want the desire to X not merely to be one of his desires but, more decisively, to be his will.[4]

Suppose a man wants to be motivated in what he does by the desire to concentrate on his work. It is necessarily true, if this supposition is correct, that he already wants to concentrate on his work. This desire is now among his desires. But the question of whether or not his second-order desire is fulfilled does not turn merely on whether the desire he wants is one of his desires. It turns on whether this desire is, as he wants it to be, his effective desire or will. If, when the chips are down, it is his desire to concentrate on his work that moves him to do what he does, then what he wants at that time is indeed (in the relevant sense) what he wants to want. If it is some other desire that actually moves him when he acts, on the other hand, then what he wants at that time is not (in the relevant sense) what he wants to want. This will be so despite the fact that the desire to concentrate on his work continues to be among his desires.

II

Someone has a desire of the second order either when he wants simply to have a certain desire or when he wants a certain desire to be his will. In situations of the latter kind, I shall call his second-order desires "second-order volitions" or "volitions of the second order." Now it is having second-order volitions, and not having second-order desires generally, that I regard as essential to being a person. It is logically possible, however

---

[4] It is not so clear that the entailment relation described here holds in certain kinds of cases, which I think may fairly be regarded as nonstandard, where the essential difference between the standard and the non-standard cases lies in the kind of description by which the first-order desire in question is identified. Thus, suppose that A admires B so fulsomely that, even though he does not know what B wants to do, he wants to be effectively moved by whatever desire effectively moves B; without knowing what B's will is, in other words, A wants his own will to be the same. It certainly does not follow that A already has, among his desires, a desire like the one that constitutes B's will. I shall not pursue here the questions of whether there are genuine counterexamples to the claim made in the text or of how, if there are, that claim should be altered.

unlikely, that there should be an agent with second-order desires but with no volitions of the second order. Such a creature, in my view, would not be a person. I shall use the term 'wanton' to refer to agents who have first-order desires but who are not persons because, whether or not they have desires of the second order, they have no second-order volitions.[5]

The essential characteristic of a wanton is that he does not care about his will. His desires move him to do certain things, without its being true of him either that he wants to be moved by those desires or that he prefers to be moved by other desires. The class of wantons includes all nonhuman animals that have desires and all very young children. Perhaps it also includes some adult human beings as well. In any case, adult humans may be more or less wanton; they may act wantonly, in response to first-order desires concerning which they have no volitions of the second order, more or less frequently.

The fact that a wanton has no second-order volitions does not mean that each of his first-order desires is translated heedlessly and at once into action. He may have no opportunity to act in accordance with some of his desires. Moreover, the translation of his desires into action may be delayed or precluded either by conflicting desires of the first order or by the intervention of deliberation. For a wanton may possess and employ rational faculties of a high order. Nothing in the concept of a wanton implies that he cannot reason or that he cannot deliberate concerning how to do what he wants to do. What distinguishes the rational wanton from other rational agents is that he is not concerned with the desirability of his desires themselves. He ignores the question of what his will is to be. Not only does he pursue whatever course of action he is most strongly inclined to pursue, but he does not care which of his inclinations is the strongest.

Thus a rational creature, who reflects upon the suitability to his desires of one course of action or another, may nonetheless be a wanton. In maintaining that the essence of being a person lies not in reason but in will, I am far from suggesting that a creature without reason may be a person. For it is only in virtue of his rational capacities that a person is capable of becoming critically aware of his own will and of forming volitions of the second order. The structure of a person's will presupposes, accordingly, that he is a rational being.

The distinction between a person and a wanton may be illustrated by the difference between two narcotics addicts. Let us suppose that the physiological condition accounting for the addiction is the same in both men, and that both succumb inevitably to their periodic desires for the drug to which they are addicted. One of the addicts hates his addiction and always struggles desperately, although to no avail, against its thrust. He tries everything that he thinks might enable him to overcome his desires for the drug. But these desires are too powerful for him to withstand, and invariably, in the end, they conquer him. He is an unwilling addict, helplessly violated by his own desires.

The unwilling addict has conflicting first-order desires: he wants to take the drug, and he also wants to refrain from taking it. In addition to these first-order desires, however, he has a volition of the second order. He is not a neutral with regard to the conflict between his desire to take the drug and his desire to refrain from taking it. It is the latter desire, and not the former, that he wants to constitute his will; it is the latter desire, rather than the former, that he wants to be effective and to provide the purpose that he will seek to realize in what he actually does.

---

[5] Creatures with second-order desires but no second-order volitions differ significantly from brute animals, and, for some purposes, it would be desirable to regard them as persons. My usage, which withholds the designation 'person' from them, is thus somewhat arbitrary. I adopt it largely because it facilitates the formulation of some of the points I wish to make. Hereafter, whenever I consider statements of the form "*A* wants to want to *X*," I shall have in mind statements identifying second-order volitions and not statements identifying second-order desires that are not second-order volitions.

The other addict is a wanton. His actions reflect the economy of his first-order desires, without his being concerned whether the desires that move him to act are desires by which he wants to be moved to act. If he encounters problems in obtaining the drug or in administering it to himself, his responses to his urges to take it may involve deliberation. But it never occurs to him to consider whether he wants the relations among his desires to result in his having the will he has. The wanton addict may be an animal, and thus incapable of being concerned about his will. In any event he is, in respect of his wanton lack of concern, no different from an animal.

The second of these addicts may suffer a first-order conflict similar to the first-order conflict suffered by the first. Whether he is human or not, the wanton may (perhaps due to conditioning) both want to take the drug and want to refrain from taking it. Unlike the unwilling addict, however, he does not prefer that one of his conflicting desires should be paramount over the other; he does not prefer that one first-order desire rather than the other should constitute his will. It would be misleading to say that he is neutral as to the conflict between his desires, since this would suggest that he regards them as equally acceptable. Since he has no identity apart from his first-order desires, it is true neither that he prefers one to the other nor that he prefers not to take sides.

It makes a difference to the unwilling addict, who is a person, which of his conflicting first-order desires wins out. Both desires are his, to be sure; and whether he finally takes the drug or finally succeeds in refraining from taking it, he acts to satisfy what is in a literal sense his own desire. In either case he does something he himself wants to do, and he does it not because of some external influence whose aim happens to coincide with his own but because of his desire to do it. The unwilling addict identifies himself, however, through the formation of a second-order volition, with one rather than with the other of his conflicting first-order desires. He makes one of them more truly his own and, in so doing, he withdraws himself from the other. It is in virtue of this identification and withdrawal, accomplished through the formation of a second-order volition, that the unwilling addict may meaningfully make the analytically puzzling statements that the force moving him to take the drug is a force other than his own, and that it is not of his own free will but rather against his will that this force moves him to take it.

The wanton addict cannot or does not care which of his conflicting first-order desires wins out. His lack of concern is not due to his inability to find a convincing basis for preference. It is due either to his lack of the capacity for reflection or to his mindless indifference to the enterprise of evaluating his own desires and motives.[6] There is only one issue in the struggle to which his first-order conflict may lead: whether the one or the other of his conflicting desires is the stronger. Since he is moved by both desires, he will not be altogether satisfied by what he does no matter which of them is effective. But it makes no difference *to him* whether his craving or his aversion gets the upper hand. He has no stake in the conflict between them and so, unlike the unwilling addict, he can neither win nor lose the struggle in which he is engaged. When a *person* acts, the desire by which he is moved is either the will he wants or a will he wants to be without. When a *wanton* acts, it is neither.

---

[6] In speaking of the evaluation of his own desires and motives as being characteristic of a person, I do not mean to suggest that a person's second-order volitions necessarily manifest a *moral* stance on his part toward his first-order desires. It may not be from the point of view of morality that the person evaluates his first-order desires. Moreover, a person may be capricious and irresponsible in forming his second-order volitions and give no serious consideration to what is at stake. Second-order volitions express evaluations only in the sense that they are preferences. There is no essential restriction on the kind of basis, if any, upon which they are formed.

III

There is a very close relationship between the capacity for forming second-order volitions and another capacity that is essential to persons—one that has often been considered a distinguishing mark of the human condition. It is only because a person has volitions of the second order that he is capable both of enjoying and of lacking freedom of the will. The concept of a person is not only, then, the concept of a type of entity that has both first-order desires and volitions of the second order. It can also be construed as the concept of a type of entity for whom the freedom of its will may be a problem. This concept excludes all wantons, both infrahuman and human, since they fail to satisfy an essential condition for the enjoyment of freedom of the will. And it excludes those suprahuman beings, if any, whose wills are necessarily free.

Just what kind of freedom is the freedom of the will? This question calls for an identification of the special area of human experience to which the concept of freedom of the will, as distinct from the concepts of other sorts of freedom, is particularly germane. In dealing with it, my aim will be primarily to locate the problem with which a person is most immediately concerned when he is concerned with the freedom of his will.

According to one familiar philosophical tradition, being free is fundamentally a matter of doing what one wants to do. Now the notion of an agent who does what he wants to do is by no means an altogether clear one: both the doing and the wanting, and the appropriate relation between them as well, require elucidation. But although its focus needs to be sharpened and its formulation refined, I believe that this notion does capture at least part of what is implicit in the idea of an agent who *acts* freely. It misses entirely, however, the peculiar content of the quite different' idea of an agent whose *will* is free.

We do not suppose that animals enjoy freedom of the will, although we recognize that an animal may be free to run in whatever direction it wants. Thus, having the freedom to do what one wants to do is not a sufficient condition of having a free will. It is not a necessary condition either. For to deprive someone of his freedom of action is not necessarily to undermine the freedom of his will. When an agent is aware that there are certain things he is not free to do, this doubtless affects his desires and limits the range of choices he can make. But suppose that someone, without being aware of it, has in fact lost or been deprived of his freedom of action. Even though he is no longer free to do what he wants to do, his will may remain as free as it was before. Despite the fact that he is not free to translate his desires into actions or to act according to the determinations of his will, he may still form those desires and make those determinations as freely as if his freedom of action had not been impaired.

When we ask whether a person's will is free we are not asking whether he is in a position to translate his first-order desires into actions. That is the question of whether he is free to do as he pleases. The question of the freedom of his will does not concern the relation between what he does and what he wants to do. Rather, it concerns his desires themselves. But what question about them is it?

It seems to me both natural and useful to construe the question of whether a person's will is free in close analogy to the question of whether an agent enjoys freedom of action. Now freedom of action is (roughly, at least) the freedom to do what one wants to do. Analogously, then, the statement that a person enjoys freedom of the will means (also roughly) that he is free to want what he wants to want. More precisely, it means that he is free to will what he wants to will, or to have the will he wants. Just as the question about the freedom of an agent's action has to do with whether it is the action he wants to perform, so the question about the freedom of his will has to do with whether it is the will he wants to have.

It is in securing the conformity of his will to his second-order volitions, then, that a person exercises freedom of the will. And it is in the discrepancy between his will and his second-order volitions, or in his awareness that their coincidence is not his own doing but only a happy chance, that a person who does not have this freedom feels its lack. The unwilling addict's will is not free. This is shown by the fact that it is not the will he wants. It is also true, though in a different way, that the will of the wanton addict is not free. The wanton addict neither has the will he wants nor has a will that differs from the will he wants. Since he has no volitions of the second order, the freedom of his will cannot be a problem for him. He lacks it, so to speak, by default.

People are generally far more complicated than my sketchy account of the structure of a person's will may suggest. There is as much opportunity for ambivalence, conflict, and self-deception with regard to desires of the second order, for example, as there is with regard to first-order desires. If there is an unresolved conflict among someone's second-order desires, then he is in danger of having no second-order volition; for unless this conflict is resolved, he has no preference concerning which of his first-order desires is to be his will. This condition, if it is so severe that it prevents him from identifying himself in a sufficiently decisive way with *any* of his conflicting first-order desires, destroys him as a person. For it either tends to paralyze his will and to keep him from acting at all, or it tends to remove him from his will so that his will operates without his participation. In both cases he becomes, like the unwilling addict though in a different way, a helpless bystander to the forces that move him.

Another complexity is that a person may have, especially if his second-order desires are in conflict, desires and volitions of a higher order than the second. There is no theoretical limit to the length of the series of desires of higher and higher orders; nothing except common sense and, perhaps, a saving fatigue prevents an individual from obsessively refusing to identify himself with any of his desires until he forms a desire of the next higher order. The tendency to generate such a series of acts of forming desires, which would be a case of humanization run wild, also leads toward the destruction of a person.

It is possible, however, to terminate such a series of acts without cutting it off arbitrarily. When a person identifies himself *decisively* with one of his first-order desires, this commitment "resounds" throughout the potentially endless array of higher orders. Consider a person who, without reservation or conflict, wants to be motivated by the desire to concentrate on his work. The fact that his second-order volition to be moved by this desire is a decisive one means that there is no room for questions concerning the pertinence of desires or volitions of higher orders. Suppose the person is asked whether he wants to want to want to concentrate on his work. He can properly insist that this question concerning a third-order desire does not arise. It would be a mistake to claim that, because he has not considered whether he wants the second-order volition he has formed, he is indifferent to the question of whether it is with this volition or with some other that he wants his will to accord. The decisiveness of the commitment he has made means that he has decided that no further question about his second-order volition, at any higher order, remains to be asked. It is relatively unimportant whether we explain this by saying that this commitment implicitly generates an endless series of confirming desires of higher orders, or by saying that the commitment is tantamount to a dissolution of the pointedness of all questions concerning higher orders of desire.

Examples such as the one concerning the unwilling addict may suggest that volitions of the second order, or of higher orders, must be formed deliberately and that a person characteristically struggles to ensure that they are satisfied. But the conformity of a person's will to his higher-order volitions may be far more thoughtless and spontaneous than this. Some people are naturally moved by kindness when they want to be kind, and by nastiness when they want to be nasty, without any explicit forethought and without any need for energetic self-control. Others are moved by nastiness when they want to be kind and by kindness when they intend to be nasty, equally without forethought and without active resistance to these violations of their higher-order desires. The enjoyment of freedom comes easily to some. Others must struggle to achieve it.

IV

My theory concerning the freedom of the will accounts easily for our disinclination to allow that this freedom is enjoyed by the members of any species inferior to our own. It also satisfies another condition that must be met by any such theory, by making it apparent why the freedom of the will should be regarded as desirable. The enjoyment of a free will means the satisfaction of certain desires—desires of the second or of higher orders—whereas its absence means their frustration. The satisfactions at stake are those which accrue to a person of whom it may be said that his will is his own. The corresponding frustrations are those suffered by a person of whom it may be said that he is estranged from himself, or that he finds himself a helpless or a passive bystander to the forces that move him.

A person who is free to do what he wants to do may yet not be in a position to have the will he wants. Suppose, however, that he enjoys both freedom of action and freedom of the will. Then he is not only free to do what he wants to do; he is also free to want what he wants to want. It seems to me that he has, in that case, all the freedom it is possible to desire or to conceive. There are other good things in life, and he may not possess some of them. But there is nothing in the way of freedom that he lacks.

It is far from clear that certain other theories of the freedom of the will meet these elementary but essential conditions: that it be understandable why we desire this freedom and why we refuse to ascribe it to animals. Consider, for example, Roderick Chisholm's quaint version of the doctrine that human freedom entails an absence of causal determination.[7] Whenever a person performs a free action, according to Chisholm, it's a miracle. The motion of a person's hand, when the person moves it, is the outcome of a series of physical causes; but some event in this series, "and presumably one of those that took place within the brain, was caused by the agent and not by any other events" (18). A free agent has, therefore, "a prerogative which some would attribute only to God: each of us, when we act, is a prime mover unmoved" (23).

This account fails to provide any basis for doubting that animals of subhuman species enjoy the freedom it defines. Chisholm says nothing that makes it seem less likely that a rabbit performs a miracle when it moves its leg than that a man does so when he moves his hand. But why, in any case, should anyone *care* whether he can interrupt the natural order of causes in the way Chisholm describes? Chisholm offers no reason for believing that there is a discernible difference between the experience of a man who miraculously initiates a series of causes when he moves his hand and a man who moves his hand without any such breach of the normal causal sequence. There appears to be no concrete basis for preferring to be involved in the one state of affairs rather than in the other.[8]

It is generally supposed that, in addition to satisfying the two conditions I have mentioned, a satisfactory theory of the freedom of the will necessarily provides an analysis of

---

[7] "Freedom and Action," in K. Lehrer, ed., *Freedom and Determinism* (New York: Random House, 1966), pp. 11–44.

[8] I am not suggesting that the alleged difference between these two states of affairs is unverifiable. On the contrary, physiologists might well be able to show that Chisholm's conditions for a free action are not satisfied, by establishing that there is no relevant brain event for which a sufficient physical cause cannot be found.

one of the conditions of moral responsibility. The most common recent approach to the problem of understanding the freedom of the will has been, indeed, to inquire what is entailed by the assumption that someone is morally responsible for what he has done. In my view, however, the relation between moral responsibility and the freedom of the will has been very widely misunderstood. It is not true that a person is morally responsible for what he has done only if his will was free when he did it. He may be morally responsible for having done it even though his will was not free at all.

A person's will is free only if he is free to have the will he wants. This means that, with regard to any of his first-order desires, he is free either to make that desire his will or to make some other first-order desire his will instead. Whatever his will, then, the will of the person whose will is free could have been otherwise; he could have done otherwise than to constitute his will as he did. It is a vexed question just how 'he could have done otherwise' is to be understood in contexts such as this one. But although this question is important to the theory of freedom, it has no bearing on the theory of moral responsibility. For the assumption that a person is morally responsible for what he has done does not entail that the person was in a position to have whatever will he wanted.

This assumption *does* entail that the person did what he did freely, or that he did it of his own free will. It is a mistake, however, to believe that someone acts freely only when he is free to do whatever he wants or that he acts of his own free will only if his will is free. Suppose that a person has done what he wanted to do, that he did it because he wanted to do it, and that the will by which he was moved when he did it was his will because it was the will he wanted. Then he did it freely and of his own free will. Even supposing that he could have done otherwise, he would not have done otherwise; and even supposing that he could have had a different will, he would not have wanted his will to differ from what it was. Moreover, since the will that moved him when he acted was his will because he wanted it to be, he cannot claim that his will was forced upon him or that he was a passive bystander to its constitution. Under these conditions, it is quite irrelevant to the evaluation of his moral responsibility to inquire whether the alternatives that he opted against were actually available to him.[9]

In illustration, consider a third kind of addict. Suppose that his addiction has the same physiological basis and the same irresistible thrust as the addictions of the unwilling and wanton addicts, but that he is altogether delighted with his condition. He is a willing addict, who would not have things any other way. If the grip of his addiction should somehow weaken, he would do whatever he could to reinstate it; if his desire for the drug should begin to fade, he would take steps to renew its intensity.

The willing addict's will is not free, for his desire to take the drug will be effective regardless of whether or not he wants this desire to constitute his will. But when he takes the drug, he takes it freely and of his own free will. I am inclined to understand his situation as involving the overdetermination of his first-order desire to take the drug. This desire is his effective desire because he is physiologically addicted. But it is his effective desire also because he wants it to be. His will is outside his control, but, by his second-order desire that his desire for the drug should be effective, he has made this will his own. Given that it is therefore not only because of his addiction that his desire for the drug is effective, he may be morally responsible for taking the drug.

My conception of the freedom of the will appears to be neutral with regard to the problem of determinism. It seems conceivable that it should be causally determined that a person is free to want what he wants to want. If this is conceivable, then it might be

---

[9] For another discussion of the considerations that cast doubt on the principle that a person is morally responsible for what he has done only if he could have done otherwise, see my "Alternate Possibilities and Moral Responsibility," this JOURNAL, LXVI, 28 (Dec. 4, 1969): 829–839.

causally determined that a person enjoys a free will. There is no more than an innocuous appearance of paradox in the proposition that it is determined, ineluctably and by forces beyond their control, that certain people have free wills and that others do not. There is no incoherence in the proposition that some agency other than a person's own is responsible (even *morally* responsible) for the fact that he enjoys or fails to enjoy freedom of the will. It is possible that a person should be morally responsible for what he does of his own free will and that some other person should also be morally responsible for his having done it.[10]

On the other hand, it seems conceivable that it should come about by chance that a person is free to have the will he wants. If this is conceivable, then it might be a matter of chance that certain people enjoy freedom of the will and that certain others do not. Perhaps it is also conceivable, as a number of philosophers believe, for states of affairs to come about in a way other than by chance or as the outcome of a sequence of natural causes. If it is indeed conceivable for the relevant states of affairs to come about in some third way, then it is also possible that a person should in that third way come to enjoy the freedom of the will.

HARRY G. FRANKFURT
The Rockefeller University

---

[10] There is a difference between being *fully* responsible and being *solely* responsible. Suppose that the willing addict has been made an addict by the deliberate and calculated work of another. Then it may be that both the addict and this other person are fully responsible for the addict's taking the drug, while neither of them is solely responsible for it. That there is a distinction between full moral responsibility and sole moral responsibility is apparent in the following example. A certain light can be turned on or off by flicking either of two switches, and each of these switches is simultaneously flicked to the "on" position by a different person, neither of whom is aware of the other. Neither person is solely responsible for the light's going on, nor do they share the responsibility in the sense that each is partially responsible; rather, each of them is fully responsible.

Chapter 1 General Introduction

In everyday life as well as in many of the sciences knowledge *claims* are made on a regular basis. But to make a claim to know is obviously not the same as actually knowing. This important distinction is in play every time we withdraw a claim to knowledge. We all have had the opportunity to think that we knew something only to discover that we were wrong. Intellectual integrity requires that we then withdraw our claim to knowledge. So it is important that we distinguish between *knowledge claims* and *knowledge*.

The branch of philosophy specializing in the study of the concept of **knowledge** is called *Epistemology* (the origin of the term is from the Greek *episteme*, which means *to know*). What is the subject matter of Epistemology or the Theory of Knowledge? The three most fundamental questions that Epistemology addresses are:

A. What is knowledge?
B. Do we have any knowledge?
C. If we do have knowledge, how do we get it?

Before we proceed to explore each of these questions, it is important to emphasize that in everyday life we use the phrase 'know' in a variety of different ways. Some typical uses of 'to know' are the following:

i. John knows *that Mary went to Boston*;
ii. John knows *Mary*; (or John knows who *Mary* is)
iii. Mary knows *how to ride a bicycle*;
iv. Mary knows *what chocolate ice-cream really tastes like*.

Each of the italicized phrases in (i)-(iv) can be viewed as the object of the relevant kind of knowledge. As you can see, there are four different kinds of objects of knowledge in (i)-(iv). In (i), for instance, the object of knowledge is a **proposition**; i.e., the proposition *that Mary went to Boston*. And so (i) can be seen as stating that John knows this proposition (i.e., the proposition expressed in English by the words 'Mary went to Boston'). The word 'that' indicates that it is a proposition that is the object of John's knowledge. This type of knowledge is called in philosophy **propositional knowledge** and it will be the primary subject of our study in the theory of knowledge. It is important to emphasize that one of the primary properties of propositions is that they are true or false (or in professional philosophical lingo: **propositions are truth-bearers**).

In (ii), on the other hand, the object of knowledge is a person; i.e., Mary. And while knowing a person may involve knowing many true propositions about her (i.e., having true **propositional knowledge** about her), knowing a person cannot be the same as knowing a conjunction of true propositions about her. Thus, while I know many true propositions about Socrates, I cannot be said to know Socrates.

Similarly, while knowing *how* to ride a bicycle may involve knowing certain true propositions (having **propositional knowledge**), knowing *how* to ride a bicycle is not the same as having propositional knowledge. One must actually ride a bicycle (and occasionally fall down) before one masters the art of riding a bicycle.

The same goes for knowing *what* chocolate ice-cream tastes like. It does not matter how many true propositions one might know about chocolate ice-cream, such knowledge alone cannot substitute for actually experiencing *what chocolate ice-cream tastes like*. Only by tasting it can one acquire the knowledge of *what chocolate ice-cream tastes like*. As noted above, our primary interest in theory of knowledge will be with **propositional knowledge**: i.e., with examples of knowledge that have the form of (i) above.

A Matter of Definition: What is Knowledge?

The first question we need to ask about propositional knowledge is this: under what conditions a person genuinely knows a proposition? i.e., under what conditions claims of knowledge such as (i) above are in fact true? One might think of these questions as seeking a definition of the concept 'to know', in the propositional sense described above.

There are several answers to this question. The traditional definition (or theory) about what it is to know a proposition goes all the way back to Plato (See chapter 3 of this Part). In order to simplify things and allow us the freedom of being as general as we need to be, let us replace names of persons with the letter 'X' and propositions with the letter 'P'. Our question can be rephrased as follows:

What are the *necessary* and *sufficient* conditions under which claims such as 'X knows that P' are true?

The Traditional Definition of Knowledge:

X knows that P *if and only if*

a. X believes that P;
b. P is true;
c. X is justified in believing that P.

This definition is called the *true, justified, belief* (or TJB) definition, or account, or theory of knowledge. The intuition behind the TJB account is this.

First, one cannot genuinely know a proposition P unless P is true. Why? Because one of the conditions under which you retract a knowledge claim is precisely when you are shown that the proposition you claimed to know is false. So condition (b) above makes sense for propositional knowledge. Second, clearly in order to know a proposition, you must believe it. Thus, condition (a) is clearly correct.

And, third, true belief is clearly not sufficient for propositional knowledge. For suppose that you are lucky enough to *correctly* guess that Smarty wins tomorrow's horse race. Surely, you do not wish to claim that you know that Smarty wins tomorrow's race; after all, you are willing to admit that it is a lucky guess. And the reason you cannot be said to have knowledge in such cases is precisely because your belief was not *properly justified*; i.e., you did not base your belief on suitable evidence. So condition (c) of TJB is properly motivated.

TJB makes two important assumptions:

Assumption 1: TJB assumes that conditions (a), (b), and (c) are individually *necessary* and jointly *sufficient* for a claim to propositional knowledge to be true.
Assumption 2: TJB also assumes that *belief* and *truth* are not identical concepts.

It is easy to recast **Assumption 2** as follows. Take anyone's beliefs at a given time and collect them into a set. Call this set B and call the set of all true propositions T. TJB assumes that for any set B, the sets B and T are not identical, although they *may* overlap. Hence, there will be some beliefs in B that are not in T (i.e., are not true); and there are going to be some members of T that are not in B (i.e., some true propositions are not believed). The Diagram below depicts this case clearly.

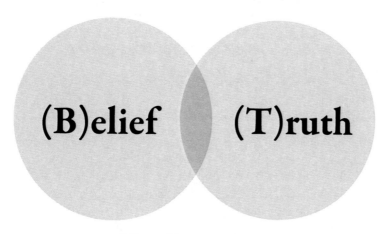

Van Diagram 1
(The shaded area of B and T is their intersection that contains the beliefs that are true)

Consider any belief **b** and ask yourself the following question: "What assurance do I have that **b** is in the overlap between my set of beliefs B and the set of truths T?" Examining the content of the belief itself does not seem to provide the requisite assurance that **b** is indeed true (although see how Foundationalism claims precisely that content may do just that). And now ask yourself the following question: "How do I know that **any** of my beliefs are in the intersection between my set of beliefs B and the set of truths T?" It is possible (even if you think it is unlikely) that the totality of all your beliefs B is disjoint from the set of truths T. Van Diagram 2 below depicts this situation:

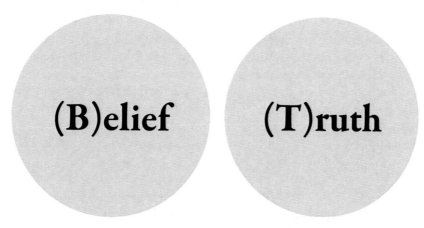

Van Diagram 2
(The two circles (**B**)elief and (**T**)ruth are disjoint; i.e., no beliefs are true)

It is because beliefs can, and often do, diverge from truth that we need condition (c). The concept of *justification* or *evidence* or *proof* is required in order to bridge the gap between belief and truth. TJB maintains that given a belief in P and given that P is true, in order for a claim to be knowledge, the knower must also properly bridge the gap between belief and truth by obtaining the right sort of evidence to support their belief in P.

Assumption 1 of TJB maintains that if all the conditions (a)-(c) are satisfied, then a ***claim*** to knowledge is indeed knowledge. However, one of the most persistent philosophical problems that have plagued TJB is whether or not the three conditions (a)-(c) can ever be satisfied regarding any of our beliefs. In other words, how do we know that our situation is not as depicted in Van-Diagram-2? And this problem leads to question B stated above. This problem is called the problem of *Radical Skepticism about the External World* or *Radical Skepticism*.

Radical Skepticism about the External World

The radical skeptic maintains that it is not possible ever to bridge the gap between belief and truth. In other words, the radical skeptic maintains that it is not possible ever to be certain that the set of all of our beliefs B is not completely disjoint from the set of all truths T (as depicted in Van Diagram 2). The radical skeptic challenges the proponent of TJB to demonstrate how he can rule out the possibility depicted in Van Diagram 2, given **Assumption 2**.

The proponent of TJB may respond as follows. Condition (c) requires that a belief must be justified by some evidence in order for it to count as knowledge. Consider again the case of some belief **b** about the external world. According to TJB, in order for the belief **b** to qualify as knowledge it must be justified by appeal to suitable evidence.

Suppose that some observation, call it **e**, is offered as evidence for belief **b**. The trouble is that observation **e** itself qualifies as evidence only if it induces in us a *belief* that the world is as observation **e** informs us. Call this second belief, namely the belief acquired based on observation **e**, belief **b***.

The radical skeptic now offers the following objection. Observation **e** cannot guarantee that our original belief **b** is true (i.e., bridge the gap between belief and truth in the case of belief **b**) *unless belief **b*** is itself knowledge* and, therefore, true. But the skeptic asks: "How do we know that?"

In order to answer the skeptic, the proponent of TJB must bridge the gap between belief and truth with respect to the new belief **b***. In other words, he must show that the new belief b* itself qualifies as knowledge. How would he do that?

Well, the proponent of TJB may attempt to justify **b*** by appeal to some new observation **e***. The trouble is that the radical skeptic will undoubtedly repeat the very same pattern of objections as we have seen regarding the original belief **b**. Namely, the radical skeptic will point out that **e*** offers adequate support for **b*** only if it gives rise to another true belief b**. But how do we know that **b**** is true?

At this point the radical skeptic strategy becomes quite apparent. For every pair of belief and observation <b, c>, the radical skeptic points out that e supports b so as to bridge the gap between b and the truth only if we are assured that the belief that things are as our observation (i.e., e) reports is true. And in order to insure that this is so, we need to justify yet another belief and this process repeats itself.

There are now two possibilities:

Either this process of justification ends at some point or it continues indefinitely

If the process of justification continues indefinitely, then we are never able to be sure that any of our beliefs qualify as knowledge. The process stops not because we found a legitimate way of closing the gap between belief and truth for some belief. If the process stops, it stops because we give up, in which case the radical skeptic prevails, or because we are dead.

If the process of justification ends with some beliefs, then we must show that the beliefs which end it are guaranteed to be true and, therefore, qualify as knowledge. But what sort of beliefs can give us a guarantee of truth without appeal to some independent evidence? The problem facing the proponent of TJB is to find some special sort of beliefs which can stop the indefinite regress forced by the radical skeptic and at the same time this special set of beliefs must satisfy **Assumptions A** and **B** in order to qualify as knowledge.

It turns out that this task is dauntingly difficult. We will now explore some of the most common moves which the proponents of TJB attempted to adopt in order to answer the radical skeptic's challenge. And so we are entering the sphere of the third question posed in the beginning of the present chapter.

The Problem of Justification

As noted in the previous section, the only hope for TJB is to find a way to stop the indefinite process of justification with some special brand of beliefs: let us call these beliefs by the name 'privileged-beliefs'.

I must emphasize that simply introducing a label for a putative (i.e., alleged) set of beliefs is not in itself sufficient to conclude that there are beliefs so labeled. We do not even know at this point what properties these *privileged beliefs* are supposed to have in virtue of which they can stop the indefinite process of justification, let alone be convinced that beliefs with such properties actually exist. The strategy proposed above is simply a reasonable hypothesis that charts a way for the proponents of TJB to respond to the skeptic's challenge.

There are two approaches traditionally adopted by philosophers to try to make sense of these putative *privileged* beliefs:

A. **The Self-Justifying Approach**: There must be a set of beliefs that are *self-justifying*: i.e., there must be at least *some* privileged beliefs that have the following two properties:

(S1) Privileged beliefs are justified;
(S2) The justification of privileged beliefs does not depend upon anything else (including other beliefs, observations, etc.) other than what is already included in their **content** (i.e., in what the proposition believed *means*).

B. **The Reliable Mechanism Approach**: We posses certain *perceptual mechanisms or modalities* that are **reliable**, *given specific ideal conditions*. For instance, given ideal conditions, our *visual perception is reliable* (otherwise, so the argument might go, we could not have survived). Thus, the privileged beliefs we can trust to be true are precisely those beliefs that are produced by reliable perceptual mechanisms under ideal conditions.

In the present book we will not discuss the reliable mechanism approach. I mention it only so that you are aware that it exists. I should note that the reliable mechanism approach faces considerable difficulties on its own. I will however discuss the self-justifying approach.

Throughout the history of the theory of knowledge or epistemology there have been two dominant approaches: **Empiricism** and **Rationalism**. The disagreement between Empiricists and Rationalists involves the question of how do we acquire beliefs that constitute knowledge. There are several ways in which we can characterize the differences between empiricism and rationalism. I will introduce two intimately related ways.

The Empiricist approach can be stated in a nutshell as follows:

Empiricism: All knowledge is acquired by means of sense experience

The basic claim of Empiricism, then, is that the **only** source of knowledge about the world is our senses. You might wonder at this point what job empiricists give to **reason**. Roughly, the answer is that the role of reason is to take the material delivered by the senses and perform certain operations on it. It is at this point that you must read the selections by Locke and Hume to see how this idea is supposed to work in some detail.

The Rationalist position, by contrast, can be stated in a nutshell as the negation of Empiricism:

> **Rationalism: Not all knowledge is acquired from sense experience. Therefore, there must be a source of knowledge other than, or in addition to, sense experience.**

"And what according to rationalism is this *other* source of knowledge?" you might ask. The answer is: **Reason**.

The fundamental disagreement between Empiricists and Rationalists is about the role of Reason in the acquisition of knowledge. Empiricists limit the role of reason in the process of the acquisition of knowledge to a secondary role of assembling prior material already obtained through our senses. Empiricists insist, however, that the truth or falsity of the resulting beliefs does not depend upon the assemblage but upon the authenticity of the original material delivered by the senses.

The Rationalists, by contrast, argue that the empiricist approach fails to explain how knowledge is possible. For by delegating to reason the diminished role of merely assembling prior material delivered by the senses, the empiricists deprive the mind from resources that are necessary in order to account for the possibility of knowledge.

Here it is useful to imagine the manufacturing process called the *assembly-line*. The assembly-line consists of mechanized instruments which follow a certain sequence of tasks that put together (or assemble) parts that are delivered on the assembly line. The empiricists maintain that reason is analogous to the mechanized instruments which merely put together parts already obtained previously through the senses. The rationalists deny this model.[1]

The disagreement between Empiricism and Rationalism can be viewed from a related, but somewhat different, angle. I will now re-introduce to you two technical terms and define each.[2] Remember, merely defining a term is not tantamount to showing that there are any items that satisfy this definition.

Epistemologists distinguish between two kinds of knowledge:

A-Priori Knowledge = df Any knowledge that is or can be acquired *prior* to and/
  or *independently* of any sense experience.
Examples of *a-priori* knowledge are: mathematical propositions such as 2 + 3 = 5;
  linguistic propositions such as "all bachelors are unmarried" or "every *effect* has

---

[1]https://en.wikipedia.org/wiki/Assembly_line
[2]You encountered the definitions of these terms when we discussed the three proofs for the existence of God in Part I.

a cause". A sign that a proposition is *a-priori* is that its denial either is or leads to a contradiction.

   A-Posteriori Knowledge = df. Knowledge that is based solely on sense experience.

   Examples of *a-posteriori* knowledge are: There are five coins in my pocket; John is a bachelor; every *event* has a cause.

While Rationalists insist that there exist some knowledge that is *a-priori*, Empiricists deny that *a-priori* knowledge exists. Why do Rationalists claim that some knowledge is *a-priori*? The motivation of rationalists to endorse *a-priori* knowledge is related to their position that reason is a substantive source of some knowledge. So what is the connection between the rationalists' thesis that reason is a substantive source of some knowledge and *a-priori* truths? Note that according to rationalism reason is a source of *some* knowledge. Note also that *a-prior* knowledge is defined as knowledge obtained *prior* to and/or *independently* from any sense experience. So putting these two together you already can guess that rationalists will maintain that *a-priori* knowledge can be obtained only by the aid of reason.

   How can we obtain *a-priori* knowledge based on reason alone? Consider the proposition "all bachelors are unmarried" which was given above as an example of *a-priori* knowledge. Clearly, the concept of a *bachelor* includes the concepts of *unmarried* and *male*. So if one grasps by the aid of reason these three concepts, then one can easily conclude based upon reason alone that everything that is a bachelor must be unmarried, *even if one never met face to face any actual flesh and blood bachelors*. Thus, encountering bachelors is not necessary in order to know that every bachelor is unmarried.

Foundationalism

We are now well equipped to return to our original problem: i.e., how does a proponent of TJB respond to the skeptic's challenge and show that the situation depicted in Diagram 2 is ruled out?

   If you remember, above we defined two different ways of defining the set of *privileged beliefs*. According to the first approach, which we labeled the *Self-Justifying Approach*, privileged beliefs are justified and their justification does not require anything other than what is already included in the content of the belief itself.

   Any approach in the theory of knowledge which holds that there are self-justifying beliefs, in the sense defined, is called **Foundationalism**. The idea of Foundationalism is intuitively perspicuous (i.e., easy to understand). Foundationalism can be described with three simple clauses:

Foundationalism:

   a. Self-justifying beliefs are true;
   b. Self justifying beliefs are knowledge because they satisfy the three conditions stated by TJB: i.e., self-justifying beliefs are believed; they are true; and they are justified;
   c. Any belief that is justified based upon self-justifying beliefs is also true and, therefore, constitutes knowledge.

   Thus, Foundationalism attempts to meet the challenge posed by radical skepticism by proposing that since there are self-justifying beliefs, which are known to be true, the situation depicted in Diagram 2, where our set of beliefs is disjoint from the set of truths, is ruled out. Therefore, knowledge is possible and the skeptic's challenge is met.

Foundationalism finds its adherents among both Rationalists and Empiricists. For Rationalists the set of self-justifying beliefs is the set of *a-priori* truths. Since the truth of *a-priori* propositions is guaranteed, Rationalists take them as the foundation of knowledge.

For empiricists the set of self-justifying beliefs is a set of special beliefs that are closely tied to sense-experience. These special beliefs are reports of what a perceiver experiences in a perceptual episode. For instance, the belief that *there is a red patch in my visual field* will be an example of a self-justifying belief from an empiricist point of view.

It is very important for you to realize that the statement that *there is a red patch in my visual field* or alternatively that *I see a red patch* is true whether or not there is in fact a red object within my visual field. For it is certainly true that I experience in my visual field a red patch *regardless of whether this experience is caused by a red object*. Empiricists contend that such statements are always true and, therefore, they are self-justifying. Hence, they constitute indisputable knowledge. Therefore, clause (a) of Foundationalism is satisfied.

Empiricists contend that based upon such self-justifying beliefs we can erect the rest of our edifice of knowledge so as to overcome the skeptics doubts about the possibility of knowledge about the external world.

It is important to note that Foundationalism, of both Rationalist and Empiricist variety, has been criticized extensively within the epistemological literature. But the substance of such criticism goes beyond the present introductory book.

In the following chapters you will have the opportunity to read some of the original literature on the subject of the theory of knowledge. I hope you enjoy the readings.

Chapter 2 The True, Justified, Belief Definition of Knowledge

In the present chapter you will read some of the original essays that defend in some form or another the true, justified, belief (TJB – see Chapter 1) approach to knowledge. It is worth noting that other approaches to knowledge have been proposed that aim to avoid some of the most serious difficulties that plague the traditional approach. Two such approaches that deserve mention hereare: *Coherence Theory of Knowledge* and the *Pragmatist Theory of Knowledge*. Unfortunately we will not be able to cover these alternatives in the present book.

Plato Theatetus

Plato

THEAETETUS: At any rate, Socrates, after such an exhortation I should be ashamed of not trying to do my best. Now he who knows perceives what he knows, and, as far as I can see at present, knowledge is perception.

SOCRATES: Bravely said, boy; that is the way in which you should express your opinion. And now, let us examine together this conception of yours, and see whether it is a true birth or a mere wind-egg:—You say that knowledge is perception?

THEAETETUS: Yes.

SOCRATES: Well, you have delivered yourself of a very important doctrine about knowledge; it is indeed the opinion of Protagoras, who has another way of expressing it. Man, he says, is the measure of all things, of the existence of things that are, and of the non-existence of things that are not:—You have read him?

THEAETETUS: O yes, again and again.

SOCRATES: Does he not say that things are to you such as they appear to you, and to me such as they appear to me, and that you and I are men?

THEAETETUS: Yes, he says so.

SOCRATES: A wise man is not likely to talk nonsense. Let us try to understand him: the same wind is blowing, and yet one of us may be cold and the other not, or one may be slightly and the other very cold?

THEAETETUS: Quite true.

SOCRATES: Now is the wind, regarded not in relation to us but absolutely, cold or not; or are we to say, with Protagoras, that the wind is cold to him who is cold, and not to him who is not?

THEAETETUS: I suppose the last.

SOCRATES: Then it must appear so to each of them?

THEAETETUS: Yes.

SOCRATES: And 'appears to him' means the same as 'he perceives.'

THEAETETUS: True.

SOCRATES: Then appearing and perceiving coincide in the case of hot and cold, and in similar instances; for things appear, or may be supposed to be, to each one such as he perceives them?

THEAETETUS: Yes.

SOCRATES: Then perception is always of existence, and being the same as knowledge is unerring?

THEAETETUS: Clearly.

SOCRATES: In the name of the Graces, what an almighty wise man Protagoras must have been! He spoke these things in a parable to the common herd, like you and me, but told the truth, 'his Truth,' (In allusion to a book of Protagoras' which bore this title.) in secret to his own disciples.

THEAETETUS: What do you mean, Socrates?

SOCRATES: I am about to speak of a high argument, in which all things are said to be relative; you cannot rightly call anything by any name, such as great or small, heavy or light, for the great will be small and the heavy light—there is no single thing or quality, but out of motion and change and admixture all things are becoming relatively to one another, which 'becoming' is by us incorrectly called being, but is really becoming, for nothing ever is, but all things are becoming. Summon all philosophers—Protagoras, Heracleitus, Empedocles, and the rest of them, one after another, and with the exception of Parmenides they will agree with you in this. Summon the great masters of either kind of poetry—Epicharmus, the prince of Comedy, and Homer of Tragedy; when the latter sings of 'Ocean whence sprang the gods, and mother Tethys,'

does he not mean that all things are the offspring, of flux and motion?

THEAETETUS: I think so.

SOCRATES: And who could take up arms against such a great army having Homer for its general, and not appear ridiculous? (Compare Cratylus.)

THEAETETUS: Who indeed, Socrates?

SOCRATES: Yes, Theaetetus; and there are plenty of other proofs which will show that motion is the source of what is called being and becoming, and inactivity of not-being and destruction; for fire and warmth, which are supposed to be the parent and guardian of all other things, are born of movement and of friction, which is a kind of motion;—is not this the origin of fire?

THEAETETUS: It is.

SOCRATES: And the race of animals is generated in the same way?

THEAETETUS: Certainly.

SOCRATES: And is not the bodily habit spoiled by rest and idleness, but preserved for a long time by motion and exercise?

THEAETETUS: True.

SOCRATES: And what of the mental habit? Is not the soul informed, and improved, and preserved by study and attention, which are motions; but when at rest, which in the soul only means want of attention and study, is uninformed, and speedily forgets whatever she has learned?

THEAETETUS: True.

SOCRATES: Then motion is a good, and rest an evil, to the soul as well as to the body?

THEAETETUS: Clearly.

SOCRATES: I may add, that breathless calm, stillness and the like waste and impair, while wind and storm preserve; and the palmary argument of all, which I strongly urge, is the golden chain in Homer, by which he means the sun, thereby indicating that so long as the sun and the heavens go round in their orbits, all things human and divine are and are preserved, but if they were chained up and their motions ceased, then all things would be destroyed, and, as the saying is, turned upside down.

THEAETETUS: I believe, Socrates, that you have truly explained his meaning.

SOCRATES: Then now apply his doctrine to perception, my good friend, and first of all to vision; that which you call white colour is not in your eyes, and is not a distinct thing which exists out of them. And you must not assign any place to it: for if it had position it would be, and be at rest, and there would be no process of becoming.

THEAETETUS: Then what is colour?

SOCRATES: Let us carry the principle which has just been affirmed, that nothing is self-existent, and then we shall see that white, black, and every other colour, arises out of the eye meeting the appropriate motion, and that what we call a colour is in each case neither the active nor the passive element, but something which passes between them, and is peculiar to each percipient; are you quite certain that the several colours appear to a dog or to any animal whatever as they appear to you?

THEAETETUS: Far from it.

SOCRATES: Or that anything appears the same to you as to another man? Are you so profoundly convinced of this? Rather would it not be true that it never appears exactly the same to you, because you are never exactly the same?

THEAETETUS: The latter.

SOCRATES: And if that with which I compare myself in size, or which I apprehend by touch, were great or white or hot, it could not become different by mere contact with another unless it actually changed; nor again, if the comparing or apprehending subject were great or white or hot, could this, when unchanged from within, become changed by any approximation or affection of any other thing. The fact is that in our ordinary way of speaking we allow ourselves to be driven into most ridiculous and wonderful contradictions, as Protagoras and all who take his line of argument would remark.

THEAETETUS: How? and of what sort do you mean?

SOCRATES: A little instance will sufficiently explain my meaning: Here are six dice, which are more by a half when compared with four, and fewer by a half than twelve—they are more and also fewer. How can you or any one maintain the contrary?

THEAETETUS: Very true.

SOCRATES: Well, then, suppose that Protagoras or some one asks whether anything can become greater or more if not by increasing, how would you answer him, Theaetetus?

THEAETETUS: I should say 'No,' Socrates, if I were to speak my mind in reference to this last question, and if I were not afraid of contradicting my former answer.

SOCRATES: Capital! excellent! spoken like an oracle, my boy! And if you reply 'Yes,' there will be a case for Euripides; for our tongue will be unconvinced, but not our mind. (In allusion to the well-known line of Euripides, Hippol.: e gloss omomoch e de thren anomotos.)

THEAETETUS: Very true.

SOCRATES: The thoroughbred Sophists, who know all that can be known about the mind, and argue only out of the superfluity of their wits, would have had a regular sparring-match over this, and would have knocked their arguments together finely. But you and I, who have no professional aims, only desire to see what is the mutual relation of these principles,—whether they are consistent with each or not.

THEAETETUS: Yes, that would be my desire.

SOCRATES: And mine too. But since this is our feeling, and there is plenty of time, why should we not calmly and patiently review our own thoughts, and thoroughly examine and see what these appearances in us really are? If I am not mistaken, they will be described by us as follows:—first, that nothing can become greater or less, either in number or magnitude, while remaining equal to itself— you would agree?

THEAETETUS: Yes.

SOCRATES: Secondly, that without addition or subtraction there is no increase or diminution of anything, but only equality.

THEAETETUS: Quite true.

SOCRATES: Thirdly, that what was not before cannot be afterwards, without becoming and having become.

THEAETETUS: Yes, truly.

SOCRATES: These three axioms, if I am not mistaken, are fighting with one another in our minds in the case of the dice, or, again, in such a case as this—if I were to say that I, who am of a certain height and taller than you, may within a year, without gaining or losing in height, be not so tall—not that I should have lost, but that you would have increased. In such a case, I am afterwards what I once was not, and yet I have not become; for I could not have become without becoming, neither could I have become less without losing somewhat of my height; and I could give you ten thousand examples of similar contradictions, if we admit them at all. I believe that you follow me, Theaetetus; for I suspect that you have thought of these questions before now.

THEAETETUS: Yes, Socrates, and I am amazed when I think of them; by the Gods I am! and I want to know what on earth they mean; and there are times when my head quite swims with the contemplation of them.

SOCRATES: I see, my dear Theaetetus, that Theodorus had a true insight into your nature when he said that you were a philosopher, for wonder is the feeling of a philosopher, and philosophy begins in wonder. He was not a bad genealogist who said that Iris (the messenger of heaven) is the child of Thaumas (wonder). But do you begin to see what is the explanation of this perplexity on the hypothesis which we attribute to Protagoras?

THEAETETUS: Not as yet.

SOCRATES: Then you will be obliged to me if I help you to unearth the hidden 'truth' of a famous man or school.

THEAETETUS: To be sure, I shall be very much obliged.

SOCRATES: Take a look round, then, and see that none of the uninitiated are listening. Now by the uninitiated I mean the people who believe in nothing but what they can grasp in their hands, and who will not allow that action or generation or anything invisible can have real existence.

THEAETETUS: Yes, indeed, Socrates, they are very hard and impenetrable mortals.

SOCRATES: Yes, my boy, outer barbarians. Far more ingenious are the brethren whose mysteries I am about to reveal to you. Their first principle is, that all is motion, and upon this all the affections of which we were just now speaking are supposed to depend: there is nothing but motion, which has two forms, one active and the other passive, both in endless number; and out of the union and friction of them there is generated a progeny endless in number, having two forms, sense and the object of sense, which are ever breaking forth and coming to the birth at the same moment. The senses are variously named hearing, seeing, smelling; there is the sense of heat, cold, pleasure, pain, desire, fear, and many more which have names, as well as innumerable others which are without them; each has its kindred object,—each variety of colour has a corresponding variety of sight, and so with sound and hearing, and with the rest of the senses and the objects akin to them. Do you see, Theaetetus, the bearings of this tale on the preceding argument?

THEAETETUS: Indeed I do not.

SOCRATES: Then attend, and I will try to finish the story. The purport is that all these things are in motion, as I was saying, and that this motion is of two kinds, a slower and a quicker; and the slower elements have their motions in the same place and with reference to things near them, and so they beget; but what is begotten is swifter, for it is carried to fro, and moves from place to place. Apply this to sense:—When the eye and the appropriate object meet together and give birth to whiteness and the sensation connatural with it, which could not have been given by either of them going elsewhere, then, while the sight is flowing from the eye, whiteness proceeds from the object which combines in producing the colour;

and so the eye is fulfilled with sight, and really sees, and becomes, not sight, but a seeing eye; and the object which combined to form the colour is fulfilled with whiteness, and becomes not whiteness but a white thing, whether wood or stone or whatever the object may be which happens to be coloured white. And this is true of all sensible objects, hard, warm, and the like, which are similarly to be regarded, as I was saying before, not as having any absolute existence, but as being all of them of whatever kind generated by motion in their intercourse with one another; for of the agent and patient, as existing in separation, no trustworthy conception, as they say, can be formed, for the agent has no existence until united with the patient, and the patient has no existence until united with the agent; and that which by uniting with something becomes an agent, by meeting with some other thing is converted into a patient. And from all these considerations, as I said at first, there arises a general reflection, that there is no one self-existent thing, but everything is becoming and in relation; and being must be altogether abolished, although from habit and ignorance we are compelled even in this discussion to retain the use of the term. But great philosophers tell us that we are not to allow either the word 'something,' or 'belonging to something,' or 'to me,' or 'this,' or 'that,' or any other detaining name to be used, in the language of nature all things are being created and destroyed, coming into being and passing into new forms; nor can any name fix or detain them; he who attempts to fix them is easily refuted. And this should be the way of speaking, not only of particulars but of aggregates; such aggregates as are expressed in the word 'man,' or 'stone,' or any name of an animal or of a class. O Theaetetus, are not these speculations sweet as honey? And do you not like the taste of them in the mouth?

THEAETETUS: I do not know what to say, Socrates; for, indeed, I cannot make out whether you are giving your own opinion or only wanting to draw me out.

SOCRATES: You forget, my friend, that I neither know, nor profess to know, anything of these matters; you are the person who is in labour, I am the barren midwife; and this is why I soothe you, and offer you one good thing after another, that you may taste them. And I hope that I may at last help to bring your own opinion into the light of day: when this has been accomplished, then we will determine whether what you have brought forth is only a wind-egg or a real and genuine birth. Therefore, keep up your spirits, and answer like a man what you think.

THEAETETUS: Ask me.

SOCRATES: Then once more: Is it your opinion that nothing is but what becomes?—the good and the noble, as well as all the other things which we were just now mentioning?

THEAETETUS: When I hear you discoursing in this style, I think that there is a great deal in what you say, and I am very ready to assent.

SOCRATES: Let us not leave the argument unfinished, then; for there still remains to be considered an objection which may be raised about dreams and diseases, in particular about madness, and the various illusions of hearing and sight, or of other senses. For you know that in all these cases the esse-percipi theory appears to be unmistakably refuted, since in dreams and illusions we certainly have false perceptions; and far from saying that everything is which appears, we should rather say that nothing is which appears.

THEAETETUS: Very true, Socrates.

SOCRATES: But then, my boy, how can any one contend that knowledge is perception, or that to every man what appears is?

THEAETETUS: I am afraid to say, Socrates, that I have nothing to answer, because you rebuked me just now for making this excuse; but I certainly cannot undertake to argue that madmen or dreamers think truly, when they imagine, some of them that they are gods, and others that they can fly, and are flying in their sleep.

SOCRATES: Do you see another question which can be raised about these phenomena, notably about dreaming and waking?

THEAETETUS: What question?

SOCRATES: A question which I think that you must often have heard persons ask:—How can you determine whether at this moment we are sleeping, and all our thoughts are a dream; or whether we are awake, and talking to one another in the waking state?

THEAETETUS: Indeed, Socrates, I do not know how to prove the one any more than the other, for in both cases the facts precisely correspond;—and there is no difficulty in supposing that during all this discussion we have been talking to one another in a dream; and when in a dream we seem to be narrating dreams, the resemblance of the two states is quite astonishing.

SOCRATES: You see, then, that a doubt about the reality of sense is easily raised, since there may even be a doubt whether we are awake or in a dream. And as our time is equally divided between sleeping and waking, in either sphere of existence the soul contends that the thoughts which are present to our minds at the time are true; and during one half of our lives we affirm the truth of the one, and, during the other half, of the other; and are equally confident of both.

THEAETETUS: Most true.

SOCRATES: And may not the same be said of madness and other disorders? the difference is only that the times are not equal.

THEAETETUS: Certainly.

SOCRATES: And is truth or falsehood to be determined by duration of time?

THEAETETUS: That would be in many ways ridiculous.

SOCRATES: But can you certainly determine by any other means which of these opinions is true?

THEAETETUS: I do not think that I can.

SOCRATES: Listen, then, to a statement of the other side of the argument, which is made by the champions of appearance. They would say, as I imagine—Can that which is wholly other than something, have the same quality as that from which it differs? and observe, Theaetetus, that the word 'other' means not 'partially,' but 'wholly other.'

THEAETETUS: Certainly, putting the question as you do, that which is wholly other cannot either potentially or in any other way be the same.

SOCRATES: And must therefore be admitted to be unlike?

THEAETETUS: True.

SOCRATES: If, then, anything happens to become like or unlike itself or another, when it becomes like we call it the same—when unlike, other?

THEAETETUS: Certainly.

SOCRATES: Were we not saying that there are agents many and infinite, and patients many and infinite?

THEAETETUS: Yes.

SOCRATES: And also that different combinations will produce results which are not the same, but different?

THEAETETUS: Certainly.

SOCRATES: Let us take you and me, or anything as an example:—There is Socrates in health, and Socrates sick—Are they like or unlike?

THEAETETUS: You mean to compare Socrates in health as a whole, and Socrates in sickness as a whole?

SOCRATES: Exactly; that is my meaning.

THEAETETUS: I answer, they are unlike.

SOCRATES: And if unlike, they are other?

THEAETETUS: Certainly.

SOCRATES: And would you not say the same of Socrates sleeping and waking, or in any of the states which we were mentioning?

THEAETETUS: I should.

SOCRATES: All agents have a different patient in Socrates, accordingly as he is well or ill.

THEAETETUS: Of course.

SOCRATES: And I who am the patient, and that which is the agent, will produce something different in each of the two cases?

THEAETETUS: Certainly.

SOCRATES: The wine which I drink when I am in health, appears sweet and pleasant to me?

THEAETETUS: True.

SOCRATES: For, as has been already acknowledged, the patient and agent meet together and produce sweetness and a perception of sweetness, which are in simultaneous motion, and the perception which comes from the patient makes the tongue percipient, and the quality of sweetness which arises out of and is moving about the wine, makes the wine both to be and to appear sweet to the healthy tongue.

THEAETETUS: Certainly; that has been already acknowledged.

SOCRATES: But when I am sick, the wine really acts upon another and a different person?

THEAETETUS: Yes.

SOCRATES: The combination of the draught of wine, and the Socrates who is sick, produces quite another result; which is the sensation of bitterness in the tongue, and the motion and creation of bitterness in and about the wine, which becomes not bitterness but something bitter; as I myself become not perception but percipient?

THEAETETUS: True.

SOCRATES: There is no other object of which I shall ever have the same perception, for another object would give another perception, and would make the percipient other and different; nor can that object which affects me, meeting another subject, produce the same, or become similar, for that too would produce another result from another subject, and become different.

THEAETETUS: True.

SOCRATES: Neither can I by myself, have this sensation, nor the object by itself, this quality.

THEAETETUS: Certainly not.

SOCRATES: When I perceive I must become percipient of something—there can be no such thing as perceiving and perceiving nothing; the object, whether it become sweet, bitter, or of any other quality, must have relation to a percipient; nothing can become sweet which is sweet to no one.

THEAETETUS: Certainly not.

SOCRATES: Then the inference is, that we (the agent and patient) are or become in relation to one another; there is a law which binds us one to the other, but not to any other existence, nor each of us to himself; and therefore we can only be bound to one another; so that whether a person says that a thing is or becomes, he must say that it is or becomes to or of or in relation to something else; but he must not say or allow any one else to say that anything is or becomes absolutely:—such is our conclusion.

THEAETETUS: Very true, Socrates.

SOCRATES: Then, if that which acts upon me has relation to me and to no other, I and no other am the percipient of it?

THEAETETUS: Of course.

SOCRATES: Then my perception is true to me, being inseparable from my own being; and, as Protagoras says, to myself I am judge of what is and what is not to me.

THEAETETUS: I suppose so.

SOCRATES: How then, if I never err, and if my mind never trips in the conception of being or becoming, can I fail of knowing that which I perceive?

THEAETETUS: You cannot.

SOCRATES: Then you were quite right in affirming that knowledge is only perception; and the meaning turns out to be the same, whether with Homer and Heracleitus, and all that company, you say that all is motion and flux, or with the great sage Protagoras, that man is the measure of all things; or with Theaetetus, that, given these premises, perception is knowledge. Am I not right, Theaetetus, and is not this your new-born child, of which I have delivered you? What say you?

THEAETETUS: I cannot but agree, Socrates.

SOCRATES: Then this is the child, however he may turn out, which you and I have with difficulty brought into the world. And now that he is born, we must run round the hearth with him, and see whether he is worth rearing, or is only a wind-egg and a sham. Is he to be reared in any case, and not exposed? or will you bear to see him rejected, and not get into a passion if I take away your first-born?

THEODORUS: Theaetetus will not be angry, for he is very good-natured. But tell me, Socrates, in heaven's name, is this, after all, not the truth?

SOCRATES: You, Theodorus, are a lover of theories, and now you innocently fancy that I am a bag full of them, and can easily pull one out which will overthrow its predecessor. But you do not see that in reality none of these theories come from me; they all come from him who talks with me. I only know just enough to extract them from the wisdom of another, and to receive them in a spirit of fairness. And now I shall say nothing myself, but shall endeavour to elicit something from our young friend.

THEODORUS: Do as you say, Socrates; you are quite right.

SOCRATES: Shall I tell you, Theodorus, what amazes me in your acquaintance Protagoras?

THEODORUS: What is it?

SOCRATES: I am charmed with his doctrine, that what appears is to each one, but I wonder that he did not begin his book on Truth with a declaration that a pig or a dog-faced baboon, or some other yet stranger monster which has sensation, is the measure of all things; then he might have shown a magnificent contempt for our opinion of him by informing us at the outset that while we were reverencing him like a God for his wisdom he was no better than a tadpole, not to speak of his fellow-men—would not this have produced an overpowering effect? For if truth is only sensation, and no man can discern another's feelings better than he, or has any superior right to determine whether his opinion is true or false, but each, as we have several times repeated, is to himself the sole judge, and everything that he judges is true and right, why, my friend, should Protagoras be preferred to the place of wisdom and instruction, and deserve to be well paid, and we poor ignoramuses have to go to him, if each one is the measure of his own wisdom? Must he not be talking 'ad captandum' in all this? I say nothing of the ridiculous predicament in which my own midwifery and the whole art of dialectic is placed; for the attempt to supervise or refute the notions or opinions of others would be a tedious and enormous piece of folly, if to each man his own are right; and this must be the case if Protagoras' Truth is the real truth, and the philosopher is not merely amusing himself by giving oracles out of the shrine of his book.

THEODORUS: He was a friend of mine, Socrates, as you were saying, and therefore I cannot have him refuted by my lips, nor can I oppose you when I agree with you; please, then, to take Theaetetus again; he seemed to answer very nicely.

SOCRATES: If you were to go into a Lacedaemonian palestra, Theodorus, would you have a right to look on at the naked wrestlers, some of them making a poor figure, if you did not strip and give them an opportunity of judging of your own person?

THEODORUS: Why not, Socrates, if they would allow me, as I think you will, in consideration of my age and stiffness; let some more supple youth try a fall with you, and do not drag me into the gymnasium.

SOCRATES: Your will is my will, Theodorus, as the proverbial philosophers say, and therefore I will return to the sage THEAETETUS: Tell me, Theaetetus, in reference to what I was saying, are you not lost in wonder, like myself, when you find that all of a sudden you are raised to the level of the wisest of men, or indeed of the gods?—for you would assume the measure of Protagoras to apply to the gods as well as men?

THEAETETUS: Certainly I should, and I confess to you that I am lost in wonder. At first hearing, I was quite satisfied with the doctrine, that whatever appears is to each one, but now the face of things has changed.

SOCRATES: Why, my dear boy, you are young, and therefore your ear is quickly caught and your mind influenced by popular arguments. Protagoras, or some one speaking on his behalf, will doubtless say in reply,—Good people, young and old, you meet and harangue, and bring in the gods, whose existence or non-existence I banish from writing and speech, or you talk about the reason of man being degraded to the level of the brutes, which is a telling argument with the multitude, but not one word of proof or demonstration do you offer. All is probability with you, and yet surely you and Theodorus had better reflect whether you are disposed to admit of probability and figures of speech in matters of such importance. He or any other mathematician who argued from probabilities and likelihoods in geometry, would not be worth an ace.

THEAETETUS: But neither you nor we, Socrates, would be satisfied with such arguments.

SOCRATES: Then you and Theodorus mean to say that we must look at the matter in some other way?

THEAETETUS: Yes, in quite another way.

SOCRATES: And the way will be to ask whether perception is or is not the same as knowledge; for this was the real point of our argument, and with a view to this we raised (did we not?) those many strange questions.

THEAETETUS: Certainly.

SOCRATES: Shall we say that we know every thing which we see and hear? for example, shall we say that not having learned, we do not hear the language of foreigners when they speak to us? or shall we say that we not only hear, but know what they are saying? Or again, if we see letters which we do not understand, shall we say that we do not see them? or shall we aver that, seeing them, we must know them?

THEAETETUS: We shall say, Socrates, that we know what we actually see and hear of them—that is to say, we see and know the figure and colour of the letters, and we hear and know the elevation or depression of the sound of them; but we do not perceive by sight and hearing, or know, that which grammarians and interpreters teach about them.

SOCRATES: Capital, Theaetetus; and about this there shall be no dispute, because I want you to grow; but there is another difficulty coming, which you will also have to repulse.

THEAETETUS: What is it?

SOCRATES: Some one will say, Can a man who has ever known anything, and still has and preserves a memory of that which he knows, not know that which he remembers at the time when he remembers? I have, I fear, a tedious way of putting a simple question, which is only, whether a man who has learned, and remembers, can fail to know?

THEAETETUS: Impossible, Socrates; the supposition is monstrous.

SOCRATES: Am I talking nonsense, then? Think: is not seeing perceiving, and is not sight perception?

THEAETETUS: True.

SOCRATES: And if our recent definition holds, every man knows that which he has seen?

THEAETETUS: Yes.

SOCRATES: And you would admit that there is such a thing as memory?

THEAETETUS: Yes.

SOCRATES: And is memory of something or of nothing?

THEAETETUS: Of something, surely.

SOCRATES: Of things learned and perceived, that is?

THEAETETUS: Certainly.

SOCRATES: Often a man remembers that which he has seen?

THEAETETUS: True.

SOCRATES: And if he closed his eyes, would he forget?

THEAETETUS: Who, Socrates, would dare to say so?

SOCRATES: But we must say so, if the previous argument is to be maintained.

THEAETETUS: What do you mean? I am not quite sure that I understand you, though I have a strong suspicion that you are right.

SOCRATES: As thus: he who sees knows, as we say, that which he sees; for perception and sight and knowledge are admitted to be the same.

THEAETETUS: Certainly.

SOCRATES: But he who saw, and has knowledge of that which he saw, remembers, when he closes his eyes, that which he no longer sees.

THEAETETUS: True.

SOCRATES: And seeing is knowing, and therefore not-seeing is not-knowing?

THEAETETUS: Very true.

SOCRATES: Then the inference is, that a man may have attained the knowledge of something, which he may remember and yet not know, because he does not see; and this has been affirmed by us to be a monstrous supposition.

THEAETETUS: Most true.

SOCRATES: Thus, then, the assertion that knowledge and perception are one, involves a manifest impossibility?

THEAETETUS: Yes.

SOCRATES: Then they must be distinguished?

THEAETETUS: I suppose that they must.

Plato Theaetetus—Epistemology

Plato

THEAETETUS: Indeed, Socrates, I do not know what we are to say.

SOCRATES: Are not his reproaches just, and does not the argument truly show that we are wrong in seeking for false opinion until we know what knowledge is; that must be first ascertained; then, the nature of false opinion?

THEAETETUS: I cannot but agree with you, Socrates, so far as we have yet gone.

SOCRATES: Then, once more, what shall we say that knowledge is?—for we are not going to lose heart as yet.

THEAETETUS: Certainly, I shall not lose heart, if you do not.

SOCRATES: What definition will be most consistent with our former views?

THEAETETUS: I cannot think of any but our old one, Socrates.

SOCRATES: What was it?

THEAETETUS: Knowledge was said by us to be true opinion; and true opinion is surely unerring, and the results which follow from it are all noble and good.

SOCRATES: He who led the way into the river, Theaetetus, said 'The experiment will show;' and perhaps if we go forward in the search, we may stumble upon the thing which we are looking for; but if we stay where we are, nothing will come to light.

THEAETETUS: Very true; let us go forward and try.

SOCRATES: The trail soon comes to an end, for a whole profession is against us.

THEAETETUS: How is that, and what profession do you mean?

SOCRATES: The profession of the great wise ones who are called orators and lawyers; for these persuade men by their art and make them think whatever they like, but they do not teach them. Do you imagine that there are any teachers in the world so clever as to be able to convince others of the truth about acts of robbery or violence, of which they were not eye-witnesses, while a little water is flowing in the clepsydra?

THEAETETUS: Certainly not, they can only persuade them.

SOCRATES: And would you not say that persuading them is making them have an opinion?

THEAETETUS: To be sure.

SOCRATES: When, therefore, judges are justly persuaded about matters which you can know only by seeing them, and not in any other way, and when thus judging of them from report they attain a true opinion about them, they judge without knowledge, and yet are rightly persuaded, if they have judged well.

THEAETETUS: Certainly.

SOCRATES: And yet, O my friend, if true opinion in law courts and knowledge are the same, the perfect judge could not have judged rightly without knowledge; and therefore I must infer that they are not the same.

THEAETETUS: That is a distinction, Socrates, which I have heard made by some one else, but I had forgotten it. He said that true opinion, combined with reason, was knowledge, but that the opinion which had no reason was out of the sphere of knowledge; and that things of which there is no rational account are not knowable—such was the singular expression which he used—and that things which have a reason or explanation are knowable.

SOCRATES: Excellent; but then, how did he distinguish between things which are and are not 'knowable'? I wish that you would repeat to me what he said, and then I shall know whether you and I have heard the same tale.

THEAETETUS: I do not know whether I can recall it; but if another person would tell me, I think that I could follow him.

SOCRATES: Let me give you, then, a dream in return for a dream:—Methought that I too had a dream, and I heard in my dream that the primeval letters or elements out of which you and I and all other things are compounded, have no reason or explanation; you can only name them, but no predicate can be either affirmed or denied of them, for in the one case existence, in the other non-existence is already implied, neither of which must be added, if you mean to speak of this or that thing by itself alone. It should not be called itself, or that, or each, or alone, or this, or the like; for these go about everywhere and are applied to all things, but are distinct from them; whereas, if the first elements could be described, and had a definition of their own, they would be spoken of apart from all else. But none of these primeval elements can be defined; they can only be named, for they have nothing but a name, and the things which are compounded of them, as they are complex, are expressed by a combination of names, for the combination of names is the essence of a definition. Thus, then, the elements or letters are only objects of perception, and cannot be defined or known; but the syllables or combinations of them are known and expressed, and are apprehended by true opinion. When, therefore, any one forms the true opinion of anything without rational explanation, you may say that his mind is truly exercised, but has no knowledge; for he who cannot give and receive a reason for a thing, has no knowledge of that thing; but when he adds rational explanation, then, he is perfected in knowledge and may be all that I have been denying of him. Was that the form in which the dream appeared to you?

THEAETETUS: Precisely.

SOCRATES: And you allow and maintain that true opinion, combined with definition or rational explanation, is knowledge?

THEAETETUS: Exactly.

SOCRATES: Then may we assume, Theaetetus, that to-day, and in this casual manner, we have found a truth which in former times many wise men have grown old and have not found?

THEAETETUS: At any rate, Socrates, I am satisfied with the present statement.

SOCRATES: Which is probably correct—for how can there be knowledge apart from definition and true opinion? And yet there is one point in what has been said which does not quite satisfy me.

THEAETETUS: What was it?

SOCRATES: What might seem to be the most ingenious notion of all:—That the elements or letters are unknown, but the combination or syllables known.

THEAETETUS: And was that wrong?

SOCRATES: We shall soon know; for we have as hostages the instances which the author of the argument himself used.

THEAETETUS: What hostages?

SOCRATES: The letters, which are the clements; and the syllables, which are the combinations;—he reasoned, did he not, from the letters of the alphabet?

THEAETETUS: Yes; he did.

SOCRATES: Let us take them and put them to the test, or rather, test ourselves:— What was the way in which we learned letters? and, first of all, are we right in saying that syllables have a definition, but that letters have no definition?

THEAETETUS: I think so.

SOCRATES: I think so too; for, suppose that some one asks you to spell the first syllable of my name:—Theaetetus, he says, what is SO?

THEAETETUS: I should reply S and O.

SOCRATES: That is the definition which you would give of the syllable?

THEAETETUS: I should.

SOCRATES: I wish that you would give me a similar definition of the S.

THEAETETUS: But how can any one, Socrates, tell the elements of an element? I can only reply, that S is a consonant, a mere noise, as of the tongue hissing; B, and most other letters, again, are neither vowel-sounds nor noises. Thus letters may be most truly said to be undefined; for even the most distinct of them, which are the seven vowels, have a sound only, but no definition at all.

SOCRATES: Then, I suppose, my friend, that we have been so far right in our idea about knowledge?

THEAETETUS: Yes; I think that we have.

SOCRATES: Well, but have we been right in maintaining that the syllables can be known, but not the letters?

THEAETETUS: I think so.

SOCRATES: And do we mean by a syllable two letters, or if there are more, all of them, or a single idea which arises out of the combination of them?

THEAETETUS: I should say that we mean all the letters.

SOCRATES: Take the case of the two letters S and O, which form the first syllable of my own name; must not he who knows the syllable, know both of them?

THEAETETUS: Certainly.

SOCRATES: He knows, that is, the S and O?

THEAETETUS: Yes.

SOCRATES: But can he be ignorant of either singly and yet know both together?

THEAETETUS: Such a supposition, Socrates, is monstrous and unmeaning.

SOCRATES: But if he cannot know both without knowing each, then if he is ever to know the syllable, he must know the letters first; and thus the fine theory has again taken wings and departed.

THEAETETUS: Yes, with wonderful celerity.

SOCRATES: Yes, we did not keep watch properly. Perhaps we ought to have maintained that a syllable is not the letters, but rather one single idea framed out of them, having a separate form distinct from them.

THEAETETUS: Very true; and a more likely notion than the other.

SOCRATES: Take care; let us not be cowards and betray a great and imposing theory.

THEAETETUS: No, indeed.

SOCRATES: Let us assume then, as we now say, that the syllable is a simple form arising out of the several combinations of harmonious elements—of letters or of any other elements.

THEAETETUS: Very good.

SOCRATES: And it must have no parts.

THEAETETUS: Why?

SOCRATES: Because that which has parts must be a whole of all the parts. Or would you say that a whole, although formed out of the parts, is a single notion different from all the parts?

THEAETETUS: I should.

SOCRATES: And would you say that all and the whole are the same, or different?

THEAETETUS: I am not certain; but, as you like me to answer at once, I shall hazard the reply, that they are different.

SOCRATES: I approve of your readiness, Theaetetus, but I must take time to think whether I equally approve of your answer.

THEAETETUS: Yes; the answer is the point.

SOCRATES: According to this new view, the whole is supposed to differ from all?

THEAETETUS: Yes.

SOCRATES: Well, but is there any difference between all (in the plural) and the all (in the singular)? Take the case of number:—When we say one, two, three, four, five, six; or when we say twice three, or three times two, or four and two, or three and two and one, are we speaking of the same or of different numbers?

THEAETETUS: Of the same.

SOCRATES: That is of six?

THEAETETUS: Yes.

SOCRATES: And in each form of expression we spoke of all the six?

THEAETETUS: True.

SOCRATES: Again, in speaking of all (in the plural) is there not one thing which we express?

THEAETETUS: Of course there is.

SOCRATES: And that is six?

THEAETETUS: Yes.

SOCRATES: Then in predicating the word 'all' of things measured by number, we predicate at the same time a singular and a plural?

THEAETETUS: Clearly we do.

SOCRATES: Again, the number of the acre and the acre are the same; are they not?

THEAETETUS: Yes.

SOCRATES: And the number of the stadium in like manner is the stadium?

THEAETETUS: Yes.

SOCRATES: And the army is the number of the army; and in all similar cases, the entire number of anything is the entire thing?

THEAETETUS: True.

SOCRATES: And the number of each is the parts of each?

THEAETETUS: Exactly.

SOCRATES: Then as many things as have parts are made up of parts?

THEAETETUS: Clearly.

SOCRATES: But all the parts are admitted to be the all, if the entire number is the all?

THEAETETUS: True.

SOCRATES: Then the whole is not made up of parts, for it would be the all, if consisting of all the parts?

THEAETETUS: That is the inference.

SOCRATES: But is a part a part of anything but the whole?

THEAETETUS: Yes, of the all.

SOCRATES: You make a valiant defence, Theaetetus. And yet is not the all that of which nothing is wanting?

THEAETETUS: Certainly.

SOCRATES: And is not a whole likewise that from which nothing is absent? but that from which anything is absent is neither a whole nor all;—if wanting in anything, both equally lose their entirety of nature.

THEAETETUS: I now think that there is no difference between a whole and all.

SOCRATES: But were we not saying that when a thing has parts, all the parts will be a whole and all?

THEAETETUS: Certainly.

SOCRATES: Then, as I was saying before, must not the alternative be that either the syllable is not the letters, and then the letters are not parts of the syllable, or that the syllable will be the same with the letters, and will therefore be equally known with them?

THEAETETUS: You are right.

SOCRATES: And, in order to avoid this, we suppose it to be different from them?

THEAETETUS: Yes.

SOCRATES: But if letters are not parts of syllables, can you tell me of any other parts of syllables, which are not letters?

THEAETETUS: No, indeed, Socrates; for if I admit the existence of parts in a syllable, it would be ridiculous in me to give up letters and seek for other parts.

SOCRATES: Quite true, Theaetetus, and therefore, according to our present view, a syllable must surely be some indivisible form?

THEAETETUS: True.

SOCRATES: But do you remember, my friend, that only a little while ago we admitted and approved the statement, that of the first elements out of which all other things are compounded there could be no definition, because each of them when taken by itself is uncompounded; nor can one rightly attribute to them the words 'being' or 'this,' because they are alien and inappropriate words, and for this reason the letters or elements were indefinable and unknown?

THEAETETUS: I remember.

SOCRATES: And is not this also the reason why they are simple and indivisible? I can see no other.

THEAETETUS: No other reason can be given.

SOCRATES: Then is not the syllable in the same case as the elements or letters, if it has no parts and is one form?

THEAETETUS: To be sure.

SOCRATES: If, then, a syllable is a whole, and has many parts or letters, the letters as well as the syllable must be intelligible and expressible, since all the parts are acknowledged to be the same as the whole?

THEAETETUS: True.

SOCRATES: But if it be one and indivisible, then the syllables and the letters are alike undefined and unknown, and for the same reason?

THEAETETUS: I cannot deny that.

SOCRATES: We cannot, therefore, agree in the opinion of him who says that the syllable can be known and expressed, but not the letters.

THEAETETUS: Certainly not; if we may trust the argument.

SOCRATES: Well, but will you not be equally inclined to disagree with him, when you remember your own experience in learning to read?

THEAETETUS: What experience?

SOCRATES: Why, that in learning you were kept trying to distinguish the separate letters both by the eye and by the ear, in order that, when you heard them spoken or saw them written, you might not be confused by their position.

THEAETETUS: Very true.

SOCRATES: And is the education of the harp-player complete unless he can tell what string answers to a particular note; the notes, as every one would allow, are the elements or letters of music?

THEAETETUS: Exactly.

SOCRATES: Then, if we argue from the letters and syllables which we know to other simples and compounds, we shall say that the letters or simple elements as a class are much more certainly known than the syllables, and much more indispensable to a perfect knowledge of any subject; and if some one says that the syllable is known and the letter unknown, we shall consider that either intentionally or unintentionally he is talking nonsense?

THEAETETUS: Exactly.

SOCRATES: And there might be given other proofs of this belief, if I am not mistaken. But do not let us in looking for them lose sight of the question before us, which is the meaning of the statement, that right opinion with rational definition or explanation is the most perfect form of knowledge.

THEAETETUS: We must not.

SOCRATES: Well, and what is the meaning of the term 'explanation'? I think that we have a choice of three meanings.

THEAETETUS: What are they?

SOCRATES: In the first place, the meaning may be, manifesting one's thought by the voice with verbs and nouns, imaging an opinion in the stream which flows from the lips, as in a mirror or water. Does not explanation appear to be of this nature?

THEAETETUS: Certainly; he who so manifests his thought, is said to explain himself.

SOCRATES: And every one who is not born deaf or dumb is able sooner or later to manifest what he thinks of anything; and if so, all those who have a right opinion about anything will also have right explanation; nor will right opinion be anywhere found to exist apart from knowledge.

THEAETETUS: True.

SOCRATES: Let us not, therefore, hastily charge him who gave this account of knowledge with uttering an unmeaning word; for perhaps he only intended to say, that when a person was asked what was the nature of anything, he should be able to answer his questioner by giving the elements of the thing.

THEAETETUS: As for example, Socrates. . . ?

SOCRATES: As, for example, when Hesiod says that a waggon is made up of a hundred planks. Now, neither you nor I could describe all of them individually; but if any one asked what is a waggon, we should be content to answer, that a waggon consists of wheels, axle, body, rims, yoke.

THEAETETUS: Certainly.

SOCRATES: And our opponent will probably laugh at us, just as he would if we professed to be grammarians and to give a grammatical account of the name of Theaetetus, and yet could only tell the syllables and not the letters of your name—that would be true opinion, and not knowledge; for knowledge, as has been already remarked, is not attained until, combined with true opinion, there is an enumeration of the elements out of which anything is composed.

THEAETETUS: Yes.

SOCRATES: In the same general way, we might also have true opinion about a waggon; but he who can describe its essence by an enumeration of the hundred planks, adds rational explanation to true opinion, and instead of opinion has art and knowledge of the nature of a waggon, in that he attains to the whole through the elements.

THEAETETUS: And do you not agree in that view, Socrates?

SOCRATES: If you do, my friend; but I want to know first, whether you admit the resolution of all things into their elements to be a rational explanation of them, and the consideration of them in syllables or larger combinations of them to be irrational—is this your view?

THEAETETUS: Precisely.

SOCRATES: Well, and do you conceive that a man has knowledge of any element who at one time affirms and at another time denies that element of something, or thinks that the same thing is composed of different elements at different times?

THEAETETUS: Assuredly not.

SOCRATES: And do you not remember that in your case and in that of others this often occurred in the process of learning to read?

THEAETETUS: You mean that I mistook the letters and misspelt the syllables?

SOCRATES: Yes.

THEAETETUS: To be sure; I perfectly remember, and I am very far from supposing that they who are in this condition have knowledge.

SOCRATES: When a person at the time of learning writes the name of Theaetetus, and thinks that he ought to write and does write Th and e; but, again, meaning to write the name of Theododorus, thinks that he ought to write and does write T and e—can we suppose that he knows the first syllables of your two names?

THEAETETUS: We have already admitted that such a one has not yet attained knowledge.

SOCRATES: And in like manner be may enumerate without knowing them the second and third and fourth syllables of your name?

THEAETETUS: He may.

SOCRATES: And in that case, when he knows the order of the letters and can write them out correctly, he has right opinion?

THEAETETUS: Clearly.

SOCRATES: But although we admit that he has right opinion, he will still be without knowledge?

THEAETETUS: Yes.

SOCRATES: And yet he will have explanation, as well as right opinion, for he knew the order of the letters when he wrote; and this we admit to be explanation.

THEAETETUS: True.

SOCRATES: Then, my friend, there is such a thing as right opinion united with definition or explanation, which does not as yet attain to the exactness of knowledge.

THEAETETUS: It would seem so.

SOCRATES: And what we fancied to be a perfect definition of knowledge is a dream only. But perhaps we had better not say so as yet, for were there not three explanations of knowledge, one of which must, as we said, be adopted by him who maintains knowledge to be true opinion combined with rational explanation? And very likely there may be found some one who will not prefer this but the third.

THEAETETUS: You are quite right; there is still one remaining. The first was the image or expression of the mind in speech; the second, which has just been mentioned, is a way of reaching the whole by an enumeration of the elements. But what is the third definition?

SOCRATES: There is, further, the popular notion of telling the mark or sign of difference which distinguishes the thing in question from all others.

THEAETETUS: Can you give me any example of such a definition?

SOCRATES: As, for example, in the case of the sun, I think that you would be contented with the statement that the sun is the brightest of the heavenly bodies which revolve about the earth.

THEAETETUS: Certainly.

SOCRATES: Understand why:—the reason is, as I was just now saying, that if you get at the difference and distinguishing characteristic of each thing, then, as many persons affirm, you will get at the definition or explanation of it; but while you lay hold only of the common and not of the characteristic notion, you will only have the definition of those things to which this common quality belongs.

THEAETETUS: I understand you, and your account of definition is in my judgment correct.

SOCRATES: But he, who having right opinion about anything, can find out the difference which distinguishes it from other things will know that of which before he had only an opinion.

THEAETETUS: Yes; that is what we are maintaining.

SOCRATES: Nevertheless, Theaetetus, on a nearer view, I find myself quite disappointed; the picture, which at a distance was not so bad, has now become altogether unintelligible.

THEAETETUS: What do you mean?

SOCRATES: I will endeavour to explain: I will suppose myself to have true opinion of you, and if to this I add your definition, then I have knowledge, but if not, opinion only.

THEAETETUS: Yes.

SOCRATES: The definition was assumed to be the interpretation of your difference.

THEAETETUS: True.

SOCRATES: But when I had only opinion, I had no conception of your distinguishing characteristics.

THEAETETUS: I suppose not.

SOCRATES: Then I must have conceived of some general or common nature which no more belonged to you than to another.

THEAETETUS: True.

SOCRATES: Tell me, now—How in that case could I have formed a judgment of you any more than of any one else? Suppose that I imagine Theaetetus to be a man who has nose, eyes, and mouth, and every other member complete; how would that enable me to distinguish Theaetetus from Theodorus, or from some outer barbarian?

THEAETETUS: How could it?

SOCRATES: Or if I had further conceived of you, not only as having nose and eyes, but as having a snub nose and prominent eyes, should I have any more notion of you than of myself and others who resemble me?

THEAETETUS: Certainly not.

SOCRATES: Surely I can have no conception of Theaetetus until your snub-nosedness has left an impression on my mind different from the snub-nosedness of all others whom I have ever seen, and until your other peculiarities have a like distinctness; and so when I meet you to-morrow the right opinion will be re-called?

THEAETETUS: Most true.

SOCRATES: Then right opinion implies the perception of differences?

THEAETETUS: Clearly.

SOCRATES: What, then, shall we say of adding reason or explanation to right opinion? If the meaning is, that we should form an opinion of the way in which something differs from another thing, the proposal is ridiculous.

THEAETETUS: How so?

SOCRATES: We are supposed to acquire a right opinion of the differences which distinguish one thing from another when we have already a right opinion of them, and so we go round and round:—the revolution of the scytal, or pestle, or any other rotatory machine, in the same circles, is as nothing compared with such a requirement; and we may be truly described as the blind directing the blind; for to add those things which we already have, in order that we may learn what we already think, is like a soul utterly benighted.

THEAETETUS: Tell me; what were you going to say just now, when you asked the question?

SOCRATES: If, my boy, the argument, in speaking of adding the definition, had used the word to 'know,' and not merely 'have an opinion' of the difference, this which is the most promising of all the definitions of knowledge would have come to a pretty end, for to know is surely to acquire knowledge.

THEAETETUS: True.

SOCRATES: And so, when the question is asked, What is knowledge? this fair argument will answer 'Right opinion with knowledge,'—knowledge, that is, of difference, for this, as the said argument maintains, is adding the definition.

THEAETETUS: That seems to be true.

SOCRATES: But how utterly foolish, when we are asking what is knowledge, that the reply should only be, right opinion with knowledge of difference or of anything! And so, Theaetetus, knowledge is neither sensation nor true opinion, nor yet definition and explanation accompanying and added to true opinion?

THEAETETUS: I suppose not.

SOCRATES: And are you still in labour and travail, my dear friend, or have you brought all that you have to say about knowledge to the birth?

THEAETETUS: I am sure, Socrates, that you have elicited from me a good deal more than ever was in me.

SOCRATES: And does not my art show that you have brought forth wind, and that the offspring of your brain are not worth bringing up?

THEAETETUS: Very true.

SOCRATES: But if, Theaetetus, you should ever conceive afresh, you will be all the better for the present investigation, and if not, you will be soberer and humbler and gentler to other men, and will be too modest to fancy that you know what you do not know. These are the limits of my art; I can no further go, nor do I know aught of the things which great and famous men know or have known in this or former ages. The office of a midwife I, like my mother, have received from God; she delivered women, I deliver men; but they must be young and noble and fair.

And now I have to go to the porch of the King Archon, where I am to meet Meletus and his indictment. To-morrow morning, Theodorus, I shall hope to see you again at this place.

Knowing as having the right to be sure

A. J. Ayer

The answers which we have found for the questions we have so far been discussing have not yet put us in a position to give a complete account of what it is to know that something is the case. The first requirement is that what is known should be true, but this is not sufficient; not even if we add to it the further condition that one must be completely sure of what one knows. For it is possible to be completely sure of something which is in fact true, but yet not to know it. The circumstances may be such that one is not entitled to be sure. For instance, a superstitious person who had inadvertently walked under a ladder might be convinced as a result that he was about to suffer some misfortune; and he might in fact be right. But it would not be correct to say that he knew that this was going to be so. He arrived at his belief by a process of reasoning which would not be generally reliable; so, although his prediction came true, it was not a case of knowledge. Again, if someone were fully persuaded of a mathematical proposition by a proof which could be shown to be invalid, he would not, without further evidence, be said to know the proposition, even though it was true. But while it is not hard to find examples of true and fully confident beliefs which in some ways fail to meet the standards required for knowledge, it is not at all easy to determine exactly what these standards are.

One way of trying to discover them would be to consider what would count as satisfactory answers to the question How do you know? Thus people may be credited with knowing truths of mathematics or logic if they are able to give a valid proof of them, or even if, without themselves being able to set out such a proof, they have obtained this information from someone who can. Claims to know empirical statements may be upheld by a reference to perception, or to memory, or to testimony, or to historical records, or to scientific laws. But such backing is not always strong enough for knowledge. Whether it is so or not depends upon the circumstances of the particular case. If I were asked how I knew that a physical object of a certain sort was in such and such a place, it would, in general, be a sufficient answer for me to say that I could see it; but if my eyesight were bad and the light were dim, this answer might not be sufficient. Even though I was right, it might still be said that I did not really know that the object was there. If I have a poor memory and the event which I claim to remember is remote, my memory of it may still not amount to knowledge, even though in this instance it does not fail me. If a witness is unreliable, his unsupported evidence may not enable us to know that what he says is true, even in a case where we completely trust him and he is not in fact deceiving us. In a given instance it is possible to decide whether the backing is strong enough to justify a claim to knowledge. But to say in general how strong it has to be would require our drawing up a list of the conditions under which perception, or memory, or testimony, or other forms of evidence are reliable. And this would be a very complicated matter, if indeed it could be done at all.

Moreover, we cannot assume that, even in particular instances, an answer to the question How do you know? will always be forthcoming. There may very well be cases in which one knows that something is so without its being possible to say how one knows it.

I am not so much thinking now of claims to know facts of immediate experience, statements like 'I know that I feel pain', which raise problems of their own into which we shall enter later on.[1] In cases of this sort it may be argued that the question how one knows does not arise. But even when it clearly does arise, it may not find an answer. Suppose that someone were consistently successful in predicting events of a certain kind, events, let us say, which are not ordinarily thought to be predictable, like the results of a lottery. If his run of successes were sufficiently impressive, we might very well come to say that he knew which number would win, even though he did not reach this conclusion by any rational method, or indeed by any method at all. We might say that he knew it by intuition, but this would be to assert no more than that he did know it but that we could not say how. In the same way, if someone were consistently successful in reading the minds of others without having any of the usual sort of evidence, we might say that he knew these things telepathically. But in default of any further explanation this would come down to saying merely that he did know them, but not by an ordinary means. Words like 'intuition' and 'telepathy' are brought in just to disguise the fact that no explanation has been found.

But if we allow this sort of knowledge to be even theoretically possible, what becomes of the distinction between knowledge and true belief? How does our man who knows what the results of the lottery will be differ from one who only makes a series of lucky guesses? The answer is that, so far as the man himself is concerned, there need not be any difference. His procedure and his state of mind, when he is said to know what will happen, may be exactly the same as when it is said that he is only guessing. The difference is that to say that he knows is to concede to him the right to be sure, while to say that he is only guessing is to withhold it. Whether we make this concession will depend upon the view which we take of his performance. Normally we do not say that people know things unless they have followed one of the accredited routes to knowledge. If someone reaches a true conclusion without appearing to have any adequate basis for it, we are likely to say that he does not really know it. But if he were repeatedly successful in a given domain, we might very well come to say that he knew the facts in question, even though we could not explain how he knew them. We should grant him the right to be sure, simply on the basis of his success. This is, indeed, a point on which people's views might be expected to differ. Not everyone would regard a successful run of predictions, however long sustained, as being by itself a sufficient backing for a claim to knowledge. And here there can be no question of proving that this attitude is mistaken. Where there are recognized criteria for deciding when one has the right to be sure, anyone who insists that their being satisfied is still not enough for knowledge may be accused, for what the charge is worth, of misusing the verb 'to know'. But it is possible to find, or at any rate to devise, examples which are not covered in this respect by any established rule of usage. Whether they are to count as instances of knowledge is then a question which we are left free to decide.

It does not, however, matter very greatly which decision we take. The main problem is to state and assess the grounds on which these claims to knowledge are made, to settle, as it were, the candidate's marks. It is a relatively unimportant question what titles we then bestow upon them. So long as we agree about the marking, it is of no great consequence where we draw the line between pass and failure, of between the different levels of distinction. If we choose to set a very high standard, we may find ourselves committed to saying that some of what ordinarily passes for knowledge ought rather to be described as probable opinion. And some critics will then take us to task for flouting ordinary usage. But the question is purely one of terminology. It is to be decided, if at all, on grounds of practical convenience.

---

[1] *Vide* ch. 2, section iv.

One must not confuse this case, where the markings are agreed upon, and what is in dispute is only the bestowal of honours, with the case where it is the markings themselves that are put in question. For this second case is philosophically important, in a way in which the other is not. The sceptic who asserts that we do not know all that we think we know, or even perhaps that we do not strictly know anything at all, is not suggesting that we are mistaken when we conclude that the recognized criteria for knowing have been satisfied. Nor is he primarily concerned with getting us to revise our usage of the verb 'to know', any more than one who challenges our standards of value is trying to make us revise our usage of the word 'good'. The disagreement is about the application of the word, rather than its meaning. What the sceptic contends is that our markings are too high; that the grounds on which we are normally ready to concede the right to be sure are worth less than we think; he may even go so far as to say that they are not worth anything at all. The attack is directed, not against the way in which we apply our standards of proof, but against these standards themselves. It has, as we shall see, to be taken seriously because of the arguments by which it is supported.

I conclude then that the necessary and sufficient conditions for knowing that something is the case are first that what one is said to know be true, secondly that one be sure of it, and thirdly that one should have the right to be sure. This right may be earned in various ways; but even if one could give a complete description of them it would be a mistake to try to build it into the definition of knowledge, just as it would be a mistake to try to incorporate our actual standards of goodness into a definition of good. And this being so, it turns out that the questions which philosophers raise about the possibility of knowledge are not all to be settled by discovering what knowledge is. For many of them reappear as questions about the legitimacy of the title to be sure. They need to be severally examined; and this is the main concern of what is called the theory of knowledge.

Chapter 3 Gettier's Challenge to the Tradiional Approach

On of the most serious challenges to the traditional definition of knowledge is presented by Gettier in a very short essay titled "Is Justified True Belief Knowledge?" This essay is reproduced below. The importance of Gettier's argument cannot be overstated. I will here summarize briefly how Gettier's argument against the traditional definition works.

Gettier shows that there are cases where the three conditions of the TJB view are satisfied, but contrary to the traditional definition, we do not feel that in such cases there is knowledge. In short, Gettier produces cases which show that the three conditions of knowledge proposed by the traditional approach are not jointly *sufficient* for knowledge. How can that be?

Gettier's example exploit a certain weakness of the traditional definition that is related in certain ways to the radical skeptic's challenge, but are not exactly the same point. Consider any proposition P about the external world. Let us call the state of affairs that *makes* this proposition true P's *truth-maker*. Let us ignore for the moment the ambiguity of the notion of a state of affairs making a proposition true. Now, Gettier shows that we can construct certain cases such that P is true and X (some agent) is justified in believing P, but since X's justification is unrelated to the truth maker of P, X fails to know P.

Note that the traditional definition of knowledge does not place any restrictions on the nature of the justification for believing a proposition. In particular, the traditional definition does not require that the justification obtained must be related in a certain way to the circumstances in the world that make the proposition in question true. Gettier's essay exploits this neglect and shows that the traditional definition is therefore inadequate.

Is Justified True Belief Knowledge?

Edmund L. Gettier

VARIOUS attempts have been made in recent years to state necessary and sufficient conditions for someone's knowing a given proposition. The attempts have often been such that they can be stated in a form similar to the following:[1]

    a. S knows that P *IFF*
        i. P is true,
        ii. S believes that P, and
        iii. S is justified in believing that P.

For example, Chisholm has held that the following gives the necessary and sufficient conditions for knowledge:[2]

    b. S knows that P *IFF*
        i. S accepts P,
        ii. S has adequate evidence for P, and
        iii. P is true.

Ayer has stated the necessary and sufficient conditions for knowledge as follows:[3]

    c. S knows that P *IFF*
        i. P is true,
        ii. S is sure that P is true, and
        iii. S has the right to be sure that P is true.

I shall argue that (a) is false in that the conditions stated therein do not constitute a *sufficient* condition for the truth of the proposition that S knows that P. The same argument will show that (b) and (c) fail if 'has adequate evidence for' or 'has the right to be sure that' is substituted for 'is justified in believing that' throughout.

I shall begin by noting two points. First, in that sense of 'justified' in which S's being justified in believing P is a necessary condition of S's knowing that P, it is possible for a person to be justified in believing a proposition that is in fact false. Secondly, for any proposition P, if S is justified in believing P, and P entails Q, and S deduces Q from P and accepts Q as a result of this deduction, then S is justified in believing Q. Keeping these two points in mind, I shall now present two cases in which the conditions stated in (a) are true for some proposition, though it is at the same time false that the person in question knows that proposition.

Case I:

Suppose that Smith and Jones have applied for a certain job. And suppose that Smith has strong evidence for the following conjunctive proposition:

    d. Jones is the man who will get the job, and Jones has ten coins in his pocket.

---

[1] Plato seems to be considering some such definition at *Theaetetus* 201, and perhaps accepting one at *Meno* 98.
[2] Roderick M. Chisholm, *Perceiving: a Philosophical Study,* Cornell University Press (Ithaca, New York, 1957), p. 16.
[3] A. J. Ayer, *The Problem of Knowledge,* Macmillan (London, 1956), p. 34.

Smith's evidence for (d) might be that the president of the company assured him that Jones would in the end be selected, and that he, Smith, had counted the coins in Jones's pocket ten minutes ago. Proposition (d) entails:

e. The man who will get the job has ten coins in his pocket.

Let us suppose that Smith sees the entailment from (d) to (e), and accepts (e) on the grounds of (d), for which he has strong evidence. In this case, Smith is clearly justified in believing that (e) is true.

But imagine, further, that unknown to Smith, he himself, not Jones, will get the job. And, also, unknown to Smith, he himself has ten coins in his pocket. Proposition (e) is then true, though proposition (d), from which Smith inferred (e), is false. In our example, then, all of the following are true: (*i*) (e) is true, (*ii*) Smith believes that (e) is true, and (*iii*) Smith is justified in believing that (e) is true. But it is equally clear that Smith does not *know* that (e) is true; for (e) is true in virtue of the number of coins in Smith's pocket, while Smith does not know how many coins are in Smith's pocket, and bases his belief in (e) on a count of the coins in Jones's pocket, whom he falsely believes to be the man who will get the job.

Case II:
Let us suppose that Smith has strong evidence for the following proposition:

f. Jones owns a Ford.

Smith's evidence might be that Jones has at all times in the past within Smith's memory owned a car, and always a Ford, and that Jones has just offered Smith a ride while driving a Ford. Let us imagine, now, that Smith has another friend, Brown, of whose whereabouts he is totally ignorant. Smith selects three place-names quite at random, and constructs the following three propositions:

g. Either Jones owns a Ford, or Brown is in Boston;
h. Either Jones owns a Ford, or Brown is in Barcelona;
i. Either Jones owns a Ford, or Brown is in Brest-Litovsk.

Each of these propositions is entailed by (f). Imagine that Smith realizes the entailment of each of these propositions he has constructed by (f), and proceeds to accept (g), (h), and (i) on the basis of (f). Smith has correctly inferred (g), (h), and (i) from a proposition for which he has strong evidence. Smith is therefore completely justified in believing each of these three propositions. Smith, of course, has no idea where Brown is.

But imagine now that two further conditions hold. First, Jones does *not* own a Ford, but is at present driving a rented car. And secondly, by the sheerest coincidence, and entirely unknown to Smith, the place mentioned in proposition (h) happens really to be the place where Brown is. If these two conditions hold then Smith does *not* know that (h) is true, even though (*i*) (h) *is* true, (*ii*) Smith does believe that (h) is true, and (*iii*) Smith is justified in believing that (h) is true.

These two examples show that definition (a) does not state a *sufficient* condition for someone's knowing a given proposition. The same cases, with appropriate changes, will suffice to show that neither definition (b) nor definition (c) do so either.
Wayne State University

Chapter 4 Empericist Foundation of Knowledge

In the present chapter you will have the opportunity to familiarize yourself with some of the first empiricists who actually tried to develop the empiricist project of knowledge as outlined in Chapter 1 of the present Part. I have included in this chapter excerpts from Locke and Hume. I hope you read them carefully and learn from some of the best empiricist philosophers. As you read these authors it is worth occasionally return to the section on empiricism in the first chapter of Part IV. Enjoy!

Hume Excerpts from An Inquiry Concerning Human Understanding

David Hume

Section II
Of the Origin of Ideas

11. Every one will readily allow, that there is a considerable difference between the perceptions of the mind, when a man feels the pain of excessive heat, or the pleasure of moderate warmth, and when he afterwards recalls to his memory this sensation, or anticipates it by his imagination. These faculties may mimic or copy the perceptions of the senses; but they never can entirely reach the force and vivacity of the original sentiment. The utmost we say of them, even when they operate with greatest vigour, is, that they represent their object in so lively a manner, that we could almost say we feel or see it: But, except the mind be disordered by disease or madness, they never can arrive at such a pitch of vivacity, as to render these perceptions altogether undistinguishable. All the colours of poetry, however splendid, can never paint natural objects in such a manner as to make the description be taken for a real landskip. The most lively thought is still inferior to the dullest sensation.

We may observe a like distinction to run through all the other perceptions of the mind. A man in a fit of anger, is actuated in a very different manner from one who only thinks of that emotion. If you tell me, that any person is in love, I easily understand your meaning, and form a just conception of his situation; but never can mistake that conception for the real disorders and agitations of the passion. When we reflect on our past sentiments and affections, our thought is a faithful mirror, and copies its objects truly; but the colours which it employs are faint and dull, in comparison of those in which our original perceptions were clothed. It requires no nice discernment or metaphysical head to mark the distinction between them.

12. Here therefore we may divide all the perceptions of the mind into two classes or species, which are distinguished by their different degrees of force and vivacity. The less forcible and lively are commonly denominated Thoughts or Ideas. The other species want a name in our language, and in most others; I suppose, because it was not requisite for any, but philosophical purposes, to rank them under a general term or appellation. Let us, therefore, use a little freedom, and call them Impressions; employing that word in a sense somewhat different from the usual. By the term impression, then, I mean all our more lively perceptions, when we hear, or see, or feel, or love, or hate, or desire, or will. And impressions are distinguished from ideas, which are the less lively perceptions, of which we are conscious, when we reflect on any of those sensations or movements above mentioned.

13. Nothing, at first view, may seem more unbounded than the thought of man, which not only escapes all human power and authority, but is not even restrained within the limits of nature and reality. To form monsters, and join incongruous shapes and

appearances, costs the imagination no more trouble than to conceive the most natural and familiar objects. And while the body is confined to one planet, along which it creeps with pain and difficulty; the thought can in an instant transport us into the most distant regions of the universe; or even beyond the universe, into the unbounded chaos, where nature is supposed to lie in total confusion. What never was seen, or heard of, may yet be conceived; nor is any thing beyond the power of thought, except what implies an absolute contradiction.

But though our thought seems to possess this unbounded liberty, we shall find, upon a nearer examination, that it is really confined within very narrow limits, and that all this creative power of the mind amounts to no more than the faculty of compounding, transposing, augmenting, or diminishing the materials afforded us by the senses and experience. When we think of a golden mountain, we only join two consistent ideas, gold, and mountain, with which we were formerly acquainted. A virtuous horse we can conceive; because, from our own feeling, we can conceive virtue; and this we may unite to the figure and shape of a horse, which is an animal familiar to us. In short, all the materials of thinking are derived either from our outward or inward sentiment: the mixture and composition of these belongs alone to the mind and will. Or, to express myself in philosophical language, all our ideas or more feeble perceptions are copies of our impressions or more lively ones.

14. To prove this, the two following arguments will, I hope, be sufficient. First, when we analyze our thoughts or ideas, however compounded or sublime, we always find that they resolve themselves into such simple ideas as were copied from a precedent feeling or sentiment. Even those ideas, which, at first view, seem the most wide of this origin, are found, upon a nearer scrutiny, to be derived from it. The idea of God, as meaning an infinitely intelligent, wise, and good Being, arises from reflecting on the operations of our own mind, and augmenting, without limit, those qualities of goodness and wisdom. We may prosecute this enquiry to what length we please; where we shall always find, that every idea which we examine is copied from a similar impression. Those who would assert that this position is not universally true nor without exception, have only one, and that an easy method of refuting it; by producing that idea, which, in their opinion, is not derived from this source. It will then be incumbent on us, if we would maintain our doctrine, to produce the impression, or lively perception, which corresponds to it.

15. Secondly. If it happen, from a defect of the organ, that a man is not susceptible of any species of sensation, we always find that he is as little susceptible of the correspondent ideas. A blind man can form no notion of colours; a deaf man of sounds. Restore either of them that sense in which he is deficient; by opening this new inlet for his sensations, you also open an inlet for the ideas; and he finds no difficulty in conceiving these objects. The case is the same, if the object, proper for exciting any sensation, has never been applied to the organ. A Laplander or Negro has no notion of the relish of wine. And though there are few or no instances of a like deficiency in the mind, where a person has never felt or is wholly incapable of a sentiment or passion that belongs to his species; yet we find the same observation to take place in a less degree. A man of mild manners can form no idea of inveterate revenge or cruelty; nor can a selfish heart easily conceive the heights of friendship and generosity. It is readily allowed, that other beings may possess many senses of which we can have no conception; because the ideas of them have never been introduced to us in the only manner by which an idea can have access to the mind, to wit, by the actual feeling and sensation.

16. There is, however, one contradictory phenomenon, which may prove that it is not absolutely impossible for ideas to arise, independent of their correspondent impressions. I believe it will readily be allowed, that the several distinct ideas of colour, which enter by the eye, or those of sound, which are conveyed by the ear, are really different from each other; though, at the same time, resembling. Now if this be true of different

colours, it must be no less so of the different shades of the same colour; and each shade produces a distinct idea, independent of the rest. For if this should be denied, it is possible, by the continual gradation of shades, to run a colour insensibly into what is most remote from it; and if you will not allow any of the means to be different, you cannot, without absurdity, deny the extremes to be the same. Suppose, therefore, a person to have enjoyed his sight for thirty years, and to have become perfectly acquainted with colours of all kinds except one particular shade of blue, for instance, which it never has been his fortune to meet with. Let all the different shades of that colour, except that single one, be placed before him, descending gradually from the deepest to the lightest; it is plain that he will perceive a blank, where that shade is wanting, and will be sensible that there is a greater distance in that place between the contiguous colours than in any other. Now I ask, whether it be possible for him, from his own imagination, to supply this deficiency, and raise up to himself the idea of that particular shade, though it had never been conveyed to him by his senses? I believe there are few but will be of opinion that he can: and this may serve as a proof that the simple ideas are not always, in every instance, derived from the correspondent impressions; though this instance is so singular, that it is scarcely worth our observing, and does not merit that for it alone we should alter our general maxim.

17. Here, therefore, is a proposition, which not only seems, in itself, simple and intelligible; but, if a proper use were made of it, might render every dispute equally intelligible, and banish all that jargon, which has so long taken possession of metaphysical reasonings, and drawn disgrace upon them. All ideas, especially abstract ones, are naturally faint and obscure: the mind has but a slender hold of them: they are apt to be confounded with other resembling ideas; and when we have often employed any term, though without a distinct meaning, we are apt to imagine it has a determinate idea annexed to it. On the contrary, all impressions, that is, all sensations, either outward or inward, are strong and vivid: the limits between them are more exactly determined: nor is it easy to fall into any error or mistake with regard to them. When we entertain, therefore, any suspicion that a philosophical term is employed without any meaning or idea (as is but too frequent), we need but enquire, from what impression is that supposed idea derived? And if it be impossible to assign any, this will serve to confirm our suspicion. By bringing ideas into so clear a light we may reasonably hope to remove all dispute, which may arise, concerning their nature and reality.1

Section III
Of the Association of Ideas

18. It is evident that there is a principle of connexion between the different thoughts or ideas of the mind, and that, in their appearance to the memory or imagination, they introduce each other with a certain degree of method and regularity. In our more serious thinking or discourse this is so observable that any particular thought, which breaks in upon the regular tract or chain of ideas, is immediately remarked and rejected. And even in our wildest and most wandering reveries, nay in our very dreams, we shall find, if we reflect, that the imagination ran not altogether at adventures, but that there was still a connexion upheld among the different ideas, which succeeded each other. Were the loosest and freest conversation to be transcribed, there would immediately be observed something which connected it in all its transitions. Or where this is wanting, the person who broke the thread of discourse might still inform you, that there had secretly revolved in his mind a succession of thought, which had gradually led him from the subject of conversation. Among different languages, even where we cannot suspect the least connexion or communication, it is found, that the words, expressive of ideas, the most

compounded, do yet nearly correspond to each other: a certain proof that the simple ideas, comprehended in the compound ones, were bound together by some universal principle, which had an equal influence on all mankind.

19. Though it be too obvious to escape observation, that different ideas are connected together; I do not find that any philosopher has attempted to enumerate or class all the principles of association; a subject, however, that seems worthy of curiosity. To me, there appear to be only three principles of connexion among ideas, namely, Resemblance, Contiguity in time or place, and Cause or Effect.

That these principles serve to connect ideas will not, I believe, be much doubted. A picture naturally leads our thoughts to the original2: the mention of one apartment in a building naturally introduces an enquiry or discourse concerning the others3: and if we think of a wound, we can scarcely forbear reflecting on the pain which follows it4. But that this enumeration is complete, and that there are no other principles of association except these, may be difficult to prove to the satisfaction of the reader, or even to a man's own satisfaction. All we can do, in such cases, is to run over several instances, and examine carefully the principle which binds the different thoughts to each other, never stopping till we render the principle as general as possible5. The more instances we examine, and the more care we employ, the more assurance shall we acquire, that the enumeration, which we form from the whole, is complete and entire.

Section IV
Sceptical Doubts Concerning the Operations of the Understanding
Part I

20. All the objects of human reason or enquiry may naturally be divided into two kinds, to wit, Relations of Ideas, and Matters of Fact. Of the first kind are the sciences of Geometry, Algebra, and Arithmetic; and in short, every affirmation which is either intuitively or demonstratively certain. That the square of the hypothenuse is equal to the square of the two sides, is a proposition which expresses a relation between these figures. That three times five is equal to the half of thirty, expresses a relation between these numbers. Propositions of this kind are discoverable by the mere operation of thought, without dependence on what is anywhere existent in the universe. Though there never were a circle or triangle in nature, the truths demonstrated by Euclid would for ever retain their certainty and evidence.

21. Matters of fact, which are the second objects of human reason, are not ascertained in the same manner; nor is our evidence of their truth, however great, of a like nature with the foregoing. The contrary of every matter of fact is still possible; because it can never imply a contradiction, and is conceived by the mind with the same facility and distinctness, as if ever so conformable to reality. That the sun will not rise to-morrow is no less intelligible a proposition, and implies no more contradiction than the affirmation, that it will rise. We should in vain, therefore, attempt to demonstrate its falsehood. Were it demonstratively false, it would imply a contradiction, and could never be distinctly conceived by the mind.

It may, therefore, be a subject worthy of curiosity, to enquire what is the nature of that evidence which assures us of any real existence and matter of fact, beyond the present testimony of our senses, or the records of our memory. This part of philosophy, it is observable, has been little cultivated, either by the ancients or moderns; and therefore our doubts and errors, in the prosecution of so important an enquiry, may be the more excusable; while we march through such difficult paths without any guide or direction.

They may even prove useful, by exciting curiosity, and destroying that implicit faith and security, which is the bane of all reasoning and free enquiry. The discovery of defects in the common philosophy, if any such there be, will not, I presume, be a discouragement, but rather an incitement, as is usual, to attempt something more full and satisfactory than has yet been proposed to the public.

22. All reasonings concerning matter of fact seem to be founded on the relation of Cause and Effect. By means of that relation alone we can go beyond the evidence of our memory and senses. If you were to ask a man, why he believes any matter of fact, which is absent; for instance, that his friend is in the country, or in France; he would give you a reason; and this reason would be some other fact; as a letter received from him, or the knowledge of his former resolutions and promises. A man finding a watch or any other machine in a desert island, would conclude that there had once been men in that island. All our reasonings concerning fact are of the same nature. And here it is constantly supposed that there is a connexion between the present fact and that which is inferred from it. Were there nothing to bind them together, the inference would be entirely precarious. The hearing of an articulate voice and rational discourse in the dark assures us of the presence of some person: Why? because these are the effects of the human make and fabric, and closely connected with it. If we anatomize all the other reasonings of this nature, we shall find that they are founded on the relation of cause and effect, and that this relation is either near or remote, direct or collateral. Heat and light are collateral effects of fire, and the one effect may justly be inferred from the other.

23. If we would satisfy ourselves, therefore, concerning the nature of that evidence, which assures us of matters of fact, we must enquire how we arrive at the knowledge of cause and effect.

I shall venture to affirm, as a general proposition, which admits of no exception, that the knowledge of this relation is not, in any instance, attained by reasonings a priori; but arises entirely from experience, when we find that any particular objects are constantly conjoined with each other. Let an object be presented to a man of ever so strong natural reason and abilities; if that object be entirely new to him, he will not be able, by the most accurate examination of its sensible qualities, to discover any of its causes or effects. Adam, though his rational faculties be supposed, at the very first, entirely perfect, could not have inferred from the fluidity and transparency of water that it would suffocate him, or from the light and warmth of fire that it would consume him. No object ever discovers, by the qualities which appear to the senses, either the causes which produced it, or the effects which will arise from it; nor can our reason, unassisted by experience, ever draw any inference concerning real existence and matter of fact.

24. This proposition, that causes and effects are discoverable, not by reason but by experience, will readily be admitted with regard to such objects, as we remember to have once been altogether unknown to us; since we must be conscious of the utter inability, which we then lay under, of foretelling what would arise from them. Present two smooth pieces of marble to a man who has no tincture of natural philosophy; he will never discover that they will adhere together in such a manner as to require great force to separate them in a direct line, while they make so small a resistance to a lateral pressure. Such events, as bear little analogy to the common course of nature, are also readily confessed to be known only by experience; nor does any man imagine that the explosion of gunpowder, or the attraction of a loadstone, could ever be discovered by arguments a priori. In like manner, when an effect is supposed to depend upon an intricate machinery or secret structure of parts, we make no difficulty in attributing all our knowledge of it to experience. Who will assert that he can give the ultimate reason, why milk or bread is proper nourishment for a man, not for a lion or a tiger?

But the same truth may not appear, at first sight, to have the same evidence with regard to events, which have become familiar to us from our first appearance in the world, which bear a close analogy to the whole course of nature, and which are supposed to depend on the simple qualities of objects, without any secret structure of parts. We are apt to imagine that we could discover these effects by the mere operation of our reason, without experience. We fancy, that were we brought on a sudden into this world, we could at first have inferred that one Billiard-ball would communicate motion to another upon impulse; and that we needed not to have waited for the event, in order to pronounce with certainty concerning it. Such is the influence of custom, that, where it is strongest, it not only covers our natural ignorance, but even conceals itself, and seems not to take place, merely because it is found in the highest degree.

25. But to convince us that all the laws of nature, and all the operations of bodies without exception, are known only by experience, the following reflections may, perhaps, suffice. Were any object presented to us, and were we required to pronounce concerning the effect, which will result from it, without consulting past observation; after what manner, I beseech you, must the mind proceed in this operation? It must invent or imagine some event, which it ascribes to the object as its effect; and it is plain that this invention must be entirely arbitrary. The mind can never possibly find the effect in the supposed cause, by the most accurate scrutiny and examination. For the effect is totally different from the cause, and consequently can never be discovered in it. Motion in the second Billiard-ball is a quite distinct event from motion in the first; nor is there anything in the one to suggest the smallest hint of the other. A stone or piece of metal raised into the air, and left without any support, immediately falls: but to consider the matter a priori, is there anything we discover in this situation which can beget the idea of a downward, rather than an upward, or any other motion, in the stone or metal? And as the first imagination or invention of a particular effect, in all natural operations, is arbitrary, where we consult not experience; so must we also esteem the supposed tie or connexion between the cause and effect, which binds them together, and renders it impossible that any other effect could result from the operation of that cause. When I see, for instance, a Billiard-ball moving in a straight line towards another; even suppose motion in the second ball should by accident be suggested to me, as the result of their contact or impulse; may I not conceive, that a hundred different events might as well follow from that cause? May not both these balls remain at absolute rest? May not the first ball return in a straight line, or leap off from the second in any line or direction? All these suppositions are consistent and conceivable. Why then should we give the preference to one, which is no more consistent or conceivable than the rest? All our reasonings a priori will never be able to show us any foundation for this preference.

In a word, then, every effect is a distinct event from its cause. It could not, therefore, be discovered in the cause, and the first invention or conception of it, a priori, must be entirely arbitrary. And even after it is suggested, the conjunction of it with the cause must appear equally arbitrary; since there are always many other effects, which, to reason, must seem fully as consistent and natural. In vain, therefore, should we pretend to determine any single event, or infer any cause or effect, without the assistance of observation and experience.

26. Hence we may discover the reason why no philosopher, who is rational and modest, has ever pretended to assign the ultimate cause of any natural operation, or to show distinctly the action of that power, which produces any single effect in the universe. It is confessed, that the utmost effort of human reason is to reduce the principles, productive of natural phenomena, to a greater simplicity, and to resolve the many particular effects into a few general causes, by means of reasonings from analogy, experience, and observation. But as to the causes of these general causes, we should in vain attempt their discovery; nor shall we ever be able to satisfy ourselves, by any particular explication of them. These ultimate springs and principles are totally shut up from human curiosity and enquiry. Elasticity, gravity, cohesion of parts, communication of motion by impulse; these

are probably the ultimate causes and principles which we shall ever discover in nature; and we may esteem ourselves sufficiently happy, if, by accurate enquiry and reasoning, we can trace up the particular phenomena to, or near to, these general principles. The most perfect philosophy of the natural kind only staves off our ignorance a little longer: as perhaps the most perfect philosophy of the moral or metaphysical kind serves only to discover larger portions of it. Thus the observation of human blindness and weakness is the result of all philosophy, and meets us at every turn, in spite of our endeavours to elude or avoid it.

27. Nor is geometry, when taken into the assistance of natural philosophy, ever able to remedy this defect, or lead us into the knowledge of ultimate causes, by all that accuracy of reasoning for which it is so justly celebrated. Every part of mixed mathematics proceeds upon the supposition that certain laws are established by nature in her operations; and abstract reasonings are employed, either to assist experience in the discovery of these laws, or to determine their influence in particular instances, where it depends upon any precise degree of distance and quantity. Thus, it is a law of motion, discovered by experience, that the moment or force of any body in motion is in the compound ratio or proportion of its solid contents and its velocity; and consequently, that a small force may remove the greatest obstacle or raise the greatest weight, if, by any contrivance or machinery, we can increase the velocity of that force, so as to make it an overmatch for its antagonist. Geometry assists us in the application of this law, by giving us the just dimensions of all the parts and figures which can enter into any species of machine; but still the discovery of the law itself is owing merely to experience, and all the abstract reasonings in the world could never lead us one step towards the knowledge of it. When we reason a priori, and consider merely any object or cause, as it appears to the mind, independent of all observation, it never could suggest to us the notion of any distinct object, such as its effect; much less, show us the inseparable and inviolable connexion between them. A man must be very sagacious who could discover by reasoning that crystal is the effect of heat, and ice of cold, without being previously acquainted with the operation of these qualities.

Part II

28. But we have not yet attained any tolerable satisfaction with regard to the question first proposed. Each solution still gives rise to a new question as difficult as the foregoing, and leads us on to farther enquiries. When it is asked, What is the nature of all our reasonings concerning matter of fact? the proper answer seems to be, that they are founded on the relation of cause and effect. When again it is asked, What is the foundation of all our reasonings and conclusions concerning that relation? it may be replied in one word, Experience. But if we still carry on our sifting humour, and ask, What is the foundation of all conclusions from experience? this implies a new question, which may be of more difficult solution and explication. Philosophers, that give themselves airs of superior wisdom and sufficiency, have a hard task when they encounter persons of inquisitive dispositions, who push them from every corner to which they retreat, and who are sure at last to bring them to some dangerous dilemma. The best expedient to prevent this confusion, is to be modest in our pretensions; and even to discover the difficulty ourselves before it is objected to us. By this means, we may make a kind of merit of our very ignorance.